Praise for *The Industrialisation of Care: co...*
*impact of IAPT*

CW00540264

This excellent and incisive book exposes the many misleading ...
our national IAPT programme is based. Not only are its outcomes poor and its
neoliberal 'back-to-work' agenda contrary to what people both need and want;
IAPT is also a demoralising service in which to work. Its co-option of therapy
as an economic tool both depoliticises and medicalises the psychosocial roots
of the pains of modern life and should deeply concern us all. These writers
are fearless in exposing the faults in the system and suggesting avenues for
necessary and vital reform.
*Dr James Davies, Reader in Social Anthropology & Mental Health, University
of Roehampton*

This book just has to be read by anyone concerned with 'mental health' – from
the generality of psychotherapists and counsellors to politicians to cultural
commentators. Students and trainees need to read it to know what world they
are entering. With erudition and passion, and also with statistics, we are shown
clearly that, as far as the psychological therapies are concerned, 'something' is
definitely not better than 'nothing'. Indeed, the chapters lay bare the destructive
impact on therapy and counselling in the public and voluntary sectors of
IAPT's hoovering up of all available increased funding for psychological
therapies. IAPT is disclosed as a second-class service for people deemed to be
second class, reflecting Britain's intensifying social and economic stratification.
*Professor Andrew Samuels, former Chair, UK Council for Psychotherapy*

In the words of Austrian philosopher and person-centred therapist Peter F
Schmid, 'Psychotherapy is political or it is not psychotherapy.' This book, edited
by Rosemary Rizq and Catherine Jackson, is one of the major contributions
to a political analysis of the state of psychotherapy today and how it arrived
here. Of course, the primary focus is the government's Improving Access
to Psychological Therapies programme but the questions go far beyond.
Neoliberalism, the product of the capitalist political system that currently
dominates modern nation states, is at the very heart of what all psychological
therapists must engage with in a critical way in order to save anything of the
psychotherapy project of the last 150 years. This book should be on every
reading list for every training course in psychotherapy.
*David Murphy, Associate Professor and Course Director for the MA in Person-
Centred Experiential Counselling and Psychotherapy, University of Nottingham*

# THE INDUSTRIALISATION OF CARE

## COUNSELLING, PSYCHOTHERAPY AND THE IMPACT OF IAPT

EDITED BY
## CATHERINE JACKSON
## AND ROSEMARY RIZQ

First published 2019

PCCS Books Ltd
Wyastone Business Park
Wyastone Leys
Monmouth
NP25 3SR
United Kingdom
contact@pccs-books.co.uk
www.pccs-books.co.uk

**The Industrialisation of Care: counselling, psychotherapy and the impact of IAPT**

British Library Cataloguing in Publication data: a catalogue record for this book is
available from the British Library.

ISBN  978 1 910919 45 3

Cover design by Jason Anscomb
Typeset in-house by PCCS Books using Minion Pro and Myriad Pro
Printed in the UK by Short Run Press, Exeter

# CONTENTS

## PART 3: THE STATE OF THE WORKPLACE

# Foreword

## Nikolas Rose

If only there could be a technical, a technological, solution to the burden of mental distress, mental disorder and mental illness on individuals, families, economies and societies. If only mental distress was like a disease, a specific pathology, and we could find a specific treatment that would rapidly restore the individual to a fully functioning, responsible subject, sustaining her or himself through paid employment. And if only that could all be shown to provide a rational and evidence-based way of managing the messy problems posed by those who have previously been exempted from the obligations of contemporary subjectivity by virtue of their disturbed mental states.

Perhaps that was the dream that lay behind the invention of Improving Access to Psychological Therapies (IAPT) and why it has proved so attractive to our governors: its justification on economic grounds, its claim to be based in scientific evidence, to be targeted at the causes of the disorder, its outcomes achievable in a few weeks and measurable and amenable to the objective judgement of audit.

This, indeed is what Richard Layard and David Clark seemed to promise when they campaigned, successfully, for the implementation of IAPT:[1] the

---

1. All quotes and glosses of phrases are from Layard & Clark, 2014. I will not dwell on the use of the phrase 'the evil of mental illness' – perhaps the authors are merely 'channelling' the phrase used by Beveridge, though of course one would want to point out that most mental health problems are not 'illnesses' and, however debilitating they can be, to refer to them as 'evils' is, to put it mildly, insulting, and, indeed, likely to exacerbate all the problems encountered by those who experience such difficulties.

'evil of mental illness' – as they termed it – was a sixth great giant to be slain, in addition to Beveridge's Want, Idleness, Ignorance, Squalor and Disease, and if we were to tackle it, we would have a better – yes, even a happier – society. The scandal, for so it seemed to them, was that we did indeed have ways of addressing this problem: therapies that people want, that are not expensive, that have good success rates measured by clinical trials: thus the 'evil of mental illness' must be tackled and could be tackled in a way that would 'not cost us an arm and a leg. Dealing with it is... a "no brainer"'.

From the outset, then, IAPT embodied what Rosemary Rizq refers to in her introduction as 'the myth of consumer sovereignty; the myth of transparency, and the myth of the medical cure'. Central to this programme was its economic rationale – if those with mental illness do not work, national economic output is lower, not to mention the costs of absenteeism, disability benefits and 'presenteeism' – for, even when people with these conditions do work, their work is less effective because 'their mind is a mess'. And they are more likely to suffer from physical illnesses, use expensive healthcare facilities and take up much costly doctors' time. So, obviously, if one gets those people back to working effectively, national economic output would increase, costs of benefits would reduce, physical health would improve along with mental health – the programme would more than pay for itself! In fact, unemployment is itself a psychological condition, as much as an economic one, and so a suitable case for psychological evaluation and treatment. But there is yet another advantage, for work itself is therapeutic – it integrates people into society, it combats isolation, teaches all sorts of social skills and, crucially, provides those previously mired in dependency with the dignity of a wage. A programme of this sort is indeed a 'no brainer'.

We do not have to question the motives of those who proposed this approach, or even those who put it into effect, in order to characterise the inevitable effects of this strategy. While there is a long history to the belief that work is itself an antidote to mental ill health, the context in which IAPT took shape embodied some of the central premises of the welfare strategies that have appeared across Europe and in many other regions since the 1980s. These pre-existed the 'financial crisis' of 2008, but they have undoubtedly been exacerbated by the policies of austerity that made the poorest pay for the high-risk, high-return gambles of those who inhabited the corrupting world of hedge funds, credit default swaps, collateralised debt obligations and all the other shady dodges designed to make profit without creating value. Thus, the more or less explicit aim of this strategy at the start was to gain the political benefit of reducing the unemployment figures by transforming into active 'job seekers' and then returning back into the workplace as many as possible of those who had been placed on incapacity benefit on account of their mental ill health. This would simultaneously improve budgetary economy and enhance moral economy, through the civilising and disciplining consequences of employment.

Paradoxically, the belief in maximising virtue through entry into wage labour and the constraints on future conduct imposed by the need to secure one's employment career were being extolled at the very moment when that image of secure work was already becoming a thing of the past, with its belief in a universal and timeless pattern of life – the move from the disciplines of the family through those of schooling to those of a job for life, followed by a brief retirement and then death. This pattern, which underpinned the welfare strategies that took shape over the 20th century, the forms of industrial employment that they were predicated upon, the family forms that they valorised and sought to promote, the moral order of probity and prudentialism that they sought to protect and not undermine by social security – all these and more now largely exist as images in our rear-view mirror, already coloured in the sepia tones of nostalgia, their own inequities and injustices rapidly fading from memory.

Nonetheless, the practice of IAPT has become integral to the work of jobcentres, and hence inextricably linked to repeated assessment of capabilities to work devised with physical disabilities in mind and administered by poorly trained operatives employed by commercial organisations paid by 'results.' As Diana Rose has pointed out, it is impossible to read the advice on completing the Work Capability Assessment questionnaire given by the mental health charity Rethink without recognising how humiliating this process is for those who are forced to undergo it (Rose, 2018).[2] The 'therapies' IAPT practitioners administer are undertaken in a disciplinary context where missing an appointment with the IAPT practitioner can result in a reduction in benefits. They are constrained by manuals that prescribe exactly the course of the interventions, and managed by targets where the throughput of subjects is the key criterion and entry into work counts as a health outcome. Psychological therapy is conceived along the lines of a course of pharmaceutical treatment, with its effects being 'dose dependent' – that is to say, the benefits depend on the number of 'doses', or 'treatment

---

2. See Mental Health and Money Advice. *How do I fill in the health questionnaire?* [Online.] www.mentalhealthandmoneyadvice.org/en/advice-topics/welfare-benefits/will-i-need-a-work-capability-assessment-to-claim-benefits/how-do-i-fill-in-the-health-questionnaire (accessed 15 February 2019).

episodes', up to the completion of the prescribed course. No wonder that, as elsewhere in our audit culture, data are manipulated to seem to demonstrate the efficacy of these interventions.

But, even in its own terms, IAPT has proved expensive, its effects on social security budgets minimal, its results disappointing in terms of those returned to enduring employment, and the consequences of the recurrent humiliation experienced by so many at the hands of those charged with enacting this strategy have increased, not reduced, human misery.

Should one then reject the whole idea out of hand? Perhaps not. Proponents of IAPT were far from alone in stressing the role that paid employment can have in restoring dignity and self-sufficiency to individuals who are excluded, isolated and stigmatised by their dependence on benefits. One thinks, perhaps, of the research carried out by Loren Mosher on the prejudice and discrimination that still today prevents many with a history of mental distress and psychiatric treatment from obtaining the employment opportunities that match their skills and capacities, and prevents many in employment from disclosing their status as mental health services users.[3] But those who thought like Mosher did not regard the unemployment of mental health service users as a consequence of the psychological deficits of the person on benefits; rather, it was seen as a structural problem of widespread, institutional discrimination. Mosher's strategy of 'moral treatment' – of empathy, of 'being with' the other person, of developing a shared understanding of the social and biographical events that contributed to a person's current plight – was precisely the reverse of the moral premise that seems to underlie IAPT: that what is necessary is attitude and behaviour change in the unemployed person in order to reactivate the psychological motivation for work.

And, while IAPT has largely failed to restore to full citizenship those isolated and excluded on grounds of their mental ill health, we have not yet seen the assertive demand for an alternative strategy, expanding the bandwidth of ways of being a citizen, recognising and attuning policies and strategies to the changing realities of work, exploring alternatives such as a guaranteed basic income, or recognising that there are other ways of contributing to society than wage labour. That would certainly require a radical change in the ways in which support is offered, eliminating the deplorable 'for-profit' organisations that have sprung up to leech on those in

---

3. This research was described in a compelling talk given by Loren Mosher at the Institute of Psychiatry shortly before his death in 2004. For details of Mosher's approach, see Mosher, Hendrix & Fort (2004).

receipt of disability benefits, with their procedures that would be pitiful if they were not so damaging and their targets that incentivise the worst practice.

And what of 'therapy' itself? There is no doubt that the particular form of psychological therapy that has come to characterise IAPT is mechanistic at best, risible at worst. But there is also no doubt that psychiatric medication, though often helpful in symptom reduction in the short term, is largely ineffective and often damaging in the long term. We do not need a massive programme of short-term, cognitively oriented psychological therapy, for all the reasons set out in the contributions to this book. But we do need a massive programme to fund and support a myriad small projects at local level[4] that can not only increase access to multiple forms of supportive facilities – not just talking therapy but self-help groups, drop-in centres, short-term crisis houses, peer support and so forth – and also tackle the social and environmental processes that throw so many of us into mental distress, isolate and exclude, and inhibit the path to full and equal citizenship of those who are differently abled.

**Nikolas Rose**
**January 2019**

Nikolas Rose is Professor of Sociology in the Department of Global Health and Social Medicine at King's College London. His many books include (most recently) *Our Psychiatric Future: the politics of mental health* (Polity, 2018) and *Governing the Soul: the shaping of the private self* (Free Association Books, 1999). His work has covered many fields, including the sociology of the biomedicine, the history of the human sciences, the genealogy of subjectivity, law and criminology, and changing forms of political power.

4. We could start by recognising and resourcing the mutual support groups – formal and informal – that service users have been organising for themselves for decades. We could also build on the alternative strategies of 'thriving' that one finds in Thrive NYC, Thrive LDN and a growing number of urban thrive programmes that, with wholly inadequate financial support, are beginning to do just this.

## References

Layard R, Clark DM (2014). *Thrive: the power of evidence-based psychological therapies.* London: Penguin Books.

Mosher LR, Hendrix V, Fort DC (2004). *Soteria: through madness to deliverance.* Bloomington, IN: Xlibris Corporation.

Rose D (2018). A hidden activism and its changing contemporary forms: mental health service users/survivors mobilising. *Journal of Social and Political Psychology* 6(2): 728–744.

# Introduction
# The modern myths of IAPT

## Rosemary Rizq

Proud of his success,
the foolish Icarus forsook his guide,
and, bold in vanity, began to soar,
rising upon his wings to touch the skies;
but as he neared the scorching sun, its heat
softened the fragrant wax that held his plumes;
and heat increasing melted the soft wax –
with no more feathers to sustain his flight.
his voice was smothered in the dark blue sea,
now called Icarian from the dead boy's name.

Ovid, *Metamorphoses*

We commonly understand myths to be persuasive stories – fictions that are capable of arousing strong feelings and profoundly influencing our beliefs and actions. Ovid's beautiful tale of Icarus (1986), from which the above quote is taken, is one of many Greek myths that, like the legend of King Arthur and the moral fables of Aesop, have been told and retold over the centuries to entertain, teach and guide us. But myth is not always to be understood as some kind of primordial or sacred truth. Very often we use the term to refer to an outdated or obsolete worldview, something to be taken at least with a pinch of salt, if not as an outright lie. Alternatively, we may view myth simply as a kind of fantastic tale, a story fit for children rather than for adults. Yet

Midgley (2004) suggests that myths are far more than simply fiction. They are closer to foundational accounts of the world, offering a perspective on reality that provides meaning and direction to a community. While some have argued that myth-making is characteristic of the 'pre-scientific' or primitive mindset (Cassirer, 1946), others (eg. Armstrong, 2006) suggest that humans are myth-making creatures and that no society, including ours, is able to function without its own particular myths and ways of myth-making (Vattimo, 1992).

Even so, the idea that myths might have a role to play in the UK government's Improving Access to Psychological Therapies (IAPT) programme might be expected to raise a postmodern eyebrow or two. Yanow (1992) argues, however, that myths remain prevalent within the arena of public policy and that organisational myths are central to the work of institutions. In the context of work, myths can be thought of as tacit but widely held beliefs, ideas and ideological positions that are in turn sustained by institutional discourses, practices and ways of thinking that are deployed in order to support specific political, ideological and societal goals. Indeed, Meyer and Rowan (1977) have argued that institutionalised myths sponsor many of the formal structures, organisational processes and work practices that are familiar to us today.

It is not surprising that mental health institutions and services should be sites of myth. From early notions of evil spirits, witchcraft and divine retribution, through to the Enlightenment's 'fear of unreason' and Victorian assumptions about hysteria, myths about mental illness have resulted in centuries of stigma and marginalisation that form a dark backdrop to historic problems in the organisation, funding and availability of mental health services, both in the UK and internationally. The introduction of the IAPT programme within the NHS in England in 2008 has been the most recent in a line of government policies designed to herald a new era in the treatment of mental health problems. Aimed at reversing what was acknowledged to be years of chronic underfunding, poor organisation and ineffective treatments, IAPT claimed to make empirically supported psychological treatments much more widely available.

Focusing on 'short, forward-looking treatments that enable people to challenge their negative thinking' (Layard et al, 2006: 1), the programme was developed and implemented not only as a means of organising delivery of and access to 'evidence-based' talking therapies, but also as a way of improving social inclusion and economic productivity. It is currently set to expand exponentially under the government's *Next Steps on the NHS Five Year*

*Forward View for Mental Health* (NHS England, 2017). Despite claims for the 'mass public benefit' of IAPT (Clark, 2018), it continues to attract considerable criticism on empirical (eg. Guy et al, 2012; Williams, 2015) as well as political grounds (eg. Marzillier & Hall, 2009; Rizq, 2012, 2013; Scanlon, 2015; Scanlon & Adlam, 2013). Indeed, given Fotaki's (2010) illuminating thoughts about the omnipotent, imaginary basis of many government policies, we might do well to hesitate before we endorse IAPT's hugely ambitious aims and reach. Certainly, its rapid rise and expansion within the ranks of public sector mental health services may have less to do with rational decision-making and more with how the programme has come to encompass and enact a number of highly potent contemporary myths that today remain deeply embedded within its discourse, policies and practices.

Before outlining the nature of these myths, let us pause for a moment to consider how best to recognise a myth when we come across it, for myths have particular characteristics, as Yanow (1992) notes. First, they are frequently available in narrative or discursive form, deploying what appear to be common-sense statements that are nonetheless 'immune to factual attack' (Cuthbertson, 1975: 157). Yet myths are not necessarily conveyed in overtly coercive language or persuasive rhetoric. On the contrary, as Barthes (1972) points out, myths are frequently deemed 'innocent' speech, offering up a natural, taken-for-granted justification for the intentions of the organisation –something that 'goes without saying'.

Second, and relatedly, while myths present themselves as universal, they are in fact social constructions, produced and developed in response to a particular time, context and culture. They reflect historical, ideological and political realities, hidden in depoliticised speech, where apparently anonymous statements of fact conceal the fabricated, constructed and contingent aspects of an organisation. Myths therefore operate in a manner akin to what Lakoff and Johnson (1980) have called 'dead metaphors' – ways of thinking that have become so conventional, so embedded in normative habits and traditions of thought and speech that we fail to notice their figurative status. This is one reason for their persistence and intractability within an organisation.

Third, and as a consequence of the above, myths are genuinely believed by those who subscribe to them. A myth may be powerfully cathected by an organisation that treats it as a sacred narrative whose truth and validity cannot be questioned. Unlike an ideology that is subject to rational inquiry or a fallacy whose faulty reasoning can be critiqued, the 'truth' of a myth cannot be ascertained and, indeed, is rarely investigated. Any attempt to examine or deconstruct the myth reveals a lack of belief in it, which may be regarded as a form of betrayal within the organisation.

Finally, myths mask organisational dilemmas that emerge from irreconcilable value systems within the organisation. Where there are conflicting ideas or values, policy myths are constituted to obscure the conflict, sponsoring the belief that it has either disappeared or been resolved. In line with this idea, Yanow (1992) suggests that a myth is a narrative 'created and believed by a group of people that diverts attention away from a puzzling part of their reality' (p. 401). In other words, organisational myths frequently act to obscure or occlude something troubling within the organisation, maintaining a powerful 'pull' despite contradictory evidence, inconvenient facts or alternative narratives. In this way, I suggest that myths not only permit organisations to communicate knowledge, validate beliefs and legitimate behaviours without having explicitly to justify the basis on which they are doing so; they also permit organisations to authorise and maintain their policies and practices in the teeth of inconsistent evidence. In this way, they may act tacitly to sustain the prevailing social, political and economic order.

To set the scene for the discussion that follows, let us now take a brief look at how a mental health policy invented by an economist has come so profoundly to re-shape the landscape of NHS psychological therapies provision across England. Based on Layard and colleagues' (2006) economic case for improved access to evidence-based psychological therapies, IAPT promised savings to the Department for Work and Pensions by returning those with depression and anxiety to work and reducing their dependence on welfare payments, tax benefits and healthcare resources. The initial investment in 2008 of £173 million was increased to £400 million in 2011, when the programme reached over 400,000 people. By 2018, 900,000 people a year were accessing IAPT services, with expansion set to continue. The government's *Next Steps on the Five Year Forward View for Mental Health* (2017) has pledged to invest £1.3 billion in mental health services by 2020/21, anticipating that at least 1.5 million people with depression and anxiety will be able to access IAPT by then. IAPT services for children and young people and those with long-term physical health conditions, medically unexplained symptoms and psychosis are included in the overall expansion programme, and there are plans to increase provision through the use of digital, online and mobile applications.

The success of the IAPT programme with commissioners and managers of mental health services is not only due to the provision of what it claims are scientifically-validated, evidence-based psychological therapies; it is also due to a tightly regulated and highly standardised culture in which the collection of huge amounts of data through session-by-session outcome monitoring is deemed essential to service evaluation and thus to continued political support. 'Routine outcome monitoring' is said to support the development of a 'positive and shared approach to the goals of therapy' (IAPT, 2018), with data 'anonymized and published' in order to promote transparency and enhanced performance. But it is the rapid proliferation of IAPT's bureaucratic assemblages and structures, penetrating fast and deep into the psychotherapeutic field, that has undoubtedly had the most significant impact. Many of the contributors to this book offer vivid descriptions and analyses of the way in which the birth and rapid expansion of IAPT within the family of psychotherapeutic practice and research has shifted the development of the profession as a whole, skewing, shrinking and overwhelming the smaller, more varied traditions of psychotherapeutic practice and research that have been patiently nurtured in the UK over time. Yet the very scale and reach of the IAPT programme, together with the rapidity of the changes it has wrought in the field of the psychological therapies, should alert us to its likely basis in a fantasmatic hope: the hope that equal access to 'evidence-based' therapy for all will sponsor social inclusion and improved economic prosperity in a time of extended global austerity. I want to suggest that the very ambitiousness of this plan is underpinned by three tacit but compelling myths that not only constitute the foundation of the entire IAPT programme but also propel its continued rise and rapid expansion within the public sector: the myth of consumer sovereignty; the myth of transparency, and the myth of the medical cure.

In the following discussion, I will briefly outline how the myth of the sovereign consumer holds that the needs of psychologically-distressed patients are best served by market-style reforms within the public sector; how the myth of transparency is embedded in the assumption that collecting increasing amounts of information will lead to a corresponding increase in knowledge and understanding, and how the myth of the medical cure is rooted in the belief that the practice of therapy can be understood and evaluated in the same way as a prescribed drug. I suggest that, while these dominant contemporary myths are powerfully presented, articulated and legitimated within the documentation, policies, discourses and practices of IAPT services, they simultaneously act to obscure the very real difficulties that exist in trying to understand the complex aetiology of psychological distress and its intersection with social, cultural, economic and political factors. As contributors to this book will show, these myths also act to instate a level of homogeneity, surveillance, compliance and conformity on a field whose values traditionally embrace privacy, ambiguity, the intuitive and the mysterious (Cayne & Loewenthal, 2008).

## The myth of the sovereign consumer

The myth of consumer sovereignty within healthcare is perhaps one of the most pervasive and powerful circulating within the public sector generally and within the IAPT programme in particular. The narrative of the patient as 'consumer' of healthcare services has become very familiar to us, yet hegemonic acceptance of what is often taken to be an inclusive and empowering term should not blind us to the difficulties of transposing the discourse of the marketplace into the healthcare sector.

At the end of the 1970s, there was a shift from a collectivist, Liberal welfare form of government based on Keynesian economics to Margaret Thatcher's Conservative government, based on market-style reforms. There is no doubt that this paved the way for the emergence of neoliberal ideologies whose economic discourse has since given consumerism considerable heft. Neoliberalism, according to Harvey (2007), holds that 'human wellbeing can best be advanced by the maximisation of entrepreneurial freedoms within an institutional framework characterized by private property rights, individual liberty, unencumbered markets, and free trade. The role of the state is to create and preserve an institutional framework appropriate to these practices' (p22). It is a political philosophy emphasising the significance of contractual relations within the marketplace, where 'the social good will be maximised by maximising the reach and frequency of market transactions, and it seeks to bring all human action into the domain of the market' (Harvey 2007: 3). Many of our contributors make it clear that the IAPT programme is psychological heir to the contemporary neoliberal regime, being deeply and problematically embedded within the consumer model that has increasingly gripped public sector services since the 1980s.

Philip Thomas's chapter, 'Neoliberalism: what it is and why it matters', provides us with a compelling overview of the wider cultural shifts that are linked to the political ideology of neoliberalism and its impact on mental healthcare. Pointing to the rise of 'positive psychology', cognitive behavioural therapy and other interventions aimed at improving happiness and 'wellbeing' that have rapidly gained credence within mental health policies, he argues that neoliberalism distorts and erodes our fundamental human values of compassion, solidarity and connectedness. He takes a hard-hitting look at political and psychological philosophies that impose individualised and interiorised explanations of misery, hopelessness and despair and fail to recognise the social and political determinants of poverty and inequality underpinning much mental distress. Indeed, unemployment, the main target of IAPT's efforts, is currently in danger of being re-cast as a psychological problem deemed subject to psychological intervention. Thomas takes issue with how such 'malignant individualism' is threatening to replace the ethic of care, concern and compassion that historically has been at the heart of therapy and mental health practice.

Penelope Campling's chapter, 'The Industrialisation and Marketisation of Healthcare', examines how competitive industrial processes deemed necessary to efficient working practices have impacted on the early hopes for change within mental health services. She argues persuasively that IAPT's use of mass-production techniques, with large numbers of staff producing high-volume, easily measured output, reduces the opportunity for relational and reflective work necessary to empathic therapeutic care. Pointing to the 'techno-centric' processes endemic within IAPT services, she discusses the increasing anxiety induced by a competitive healthcare system that breeds mistrust, cynicism and a 'culture of insatiable accountability and regulation'.

The status of the sovereign consumer of healthcare services is overwhelmingly indexed by the way in which the patient as 'customer' has come to be an utterly taken-for-granted feature of the NHS and other services. The rhetoric of 'choice' is now central; indeed, since 'choice defines the democratic capitalist state' (Appleby, Harrison & Devlin, 2003), the case for its continued implementation and extension 'scarcely needs to be argued'. However, Marianna Fotaki's chapter, 'Throwing Good Money after Bad: health services without care under marketised welfare', takes issue with this taken-for-granted assumption. She argues that the introduction of market logic and profit maximisation into public healthcare services taps into unconscious dynamics and fantasies that defend against anxieties of ageing, illness and death. The 'invisible hand' of the marketplace that endorses choice and competition ignores the notion of dependency on others, replacing a welfare state based on a collective responsibility for each other's vulnerability and precarity with the notion of the rational, sovereign consumer maximising utility through choice.

Importantly, Fotaki points out how neoliberal economies make us 'infinitely sentimental about ourselves but methodically ruthless toward others', suggesting that, when individuals are turned into saleable commodities, whole groups of people come to be seen as disposable. Citing Butler's (2009) analysis of civilian casualties in the Iraq and Afghanistan wars, whose lost lives were labelled as collateral damage rather than as people to be grieved, she argues that we are currently seeing a rapid increase of various categories of undeserving 'others', such as the new poor, refugees and migrants in affluent Western societies. Ultimately, she suggests, we need to re-imagine healthcare outside the current restrictive frameworks of individualised consumerism and create social policies that reflect our common relational ties and our shared sense of precarity.

Neoliberal economies, of course, hold self-sufficiency as a moral ideal while simultaneously undermining the very conditions necessary to realise such a norm. The precaritisation of sectors of the population established via the institutionalisation of temporary labour, zero-hours contracts and the 'gig' economy, as well as the dismantling of social services and the erosion of social democracy within communities, means that those who fail to demonstrate the impossible ideal of self-sufficiency – those who are unemployed, homeless or dispossessed – are increasingly seen as dispensable to society. Indeed, welfare payments, including the currently highly-contested Universal Credit scheme, have become ever more conditional – something that is taken up in Friedli and Stearn's chapter 'Positive Affect as Coercive Strategy: conditionality, activation and the role of psychology in UK government workfare programmes'. They take a hard look at how the discourse of psychological deficit has taken root in the UK policy literature on those who find themselves in need of social security. Psycho-compulsion – the adoption of psychological explanations for unemployment and the imposition of mandatory activities designed to change beliefs, attitudes and motivations for work and improve positive affect – is now a commonplace and often humiliating aspect of many people's experiences of welfare. Friedli and Stearn argue that psychology and psychological practitioners have been recruited into increasingly coercive practices, where those in receipt of care must demonstrate 'a cheerful disposition, in combination with a thankful heart and highly developed "executive control"' – something that is now 'so widely celebrated in the policy literature that the politics of this reification are rarely questioned'. Their chapter raises worrying questions about the extent to which therapists themselves are now part and parcel of stigmatising the attitudes and behaviour of those who do not, and cannot, meet the standards set by neoliberal ideals.

By contrast, Elizabeth Cotton's chapter, 'The Industrial Relations of Mental Health', engages with the difficult topic of how therapists working in IAPT and other **mental** health services have come to feel dispensable. Drawing on a remark**able** piece of qualitative research she undertook in 2016, the 'Surviving Work Su**rvey**',[1] she draws a bleak picture of a culture of precarity within mental health **services**. She argues this is due to the downgrading and de-professionalisation **of jobs**, poor industrial relations, and a 'command and control' culture that **privil**eges financial targets and performance indicators over meaningful clini**cal ou**tcomes. More worryingly, her survey points to the growth in private em**ploym**ent agencies contracted to provide IAPT services and an increase in th**e num**ber of jobs within IAPT that no longer require a clinical training or r**egistra**tion with an accrediting professional body. Cotton is courageous in her **stand** against precarious work, taking particular issue with the increasing **preval**ence of IAPT services that offer only short-term, honorary or self-em**ploye**d contracts to their staff. She is sensitive to the ethical issues of the**rapists** being silenced within mental health services and trenchant in her su**pport** of organised, collective responses to poor pay and working conditions.

## The myth of transparency

Transparency is pe**rhaps** one of the most cherished ideals of the business world and a found**ati**onal myth of modernity. Tsoukas (1997) argues that contemporary o**rganisati**ons adopt transparency as an ideal that ensures legitimacy, respectabi**lity a**nd a guaranteed route to operating without blame. The IAPT programme **app**ears to have adopted this ideal, understood here as an axiomatic org**anisati**onal demand for openness and candour about its results. Indeed, the N**ationa**l Clinical Adviser to the IAPT programme David Clark suggests: 'The IAPT programme is a rare exception to the general absence of transparency about outcomes for mental health services,' and claims that 'well-validated self-report measures' providing symptom scores for before and after treatment are obtained for 98% of patients (Clark, 2018).

It is probably fair to say that IAPT practitioners are among the most closely monitored of any mental health practitioners in the NHS today. They are expected to train in and carry out standardised assessment and treatment protocols; to take and record multiple clinical outcome measures for each client contact; to receive frequent case management rather than clinical supervision, and to achieve ever-higher activity and clinical outcome targets. Patients, too, are subjected to weekly outcome measures and questionnaires,

---

1. https://survivingwork.org

as are managers and service leads who are similarly required to participate in a variety of quality assurance and regulatory mechanisms. They must also account in minute detail for their service activity and justify their clinical outcomes to NHS Digital, the body that collates, evaluates and disseminates the data. Indeed, these and other rationalistic, bureaucratised structures, techniques and New Public Management strategies adopted by IAPT services may be regarded as the apogee of what Power (1997) calls the 'audit culture'.

It is not altogether surprising that such workplace requirements should have had a considerable impact on therapists, counsellors and other mental health professionals. Following on from Elizabeth Cotton's chapter, we have two further chapters that examine the difficulties, ethical compromises and problems faced by therapists working within IAPT and other therapeutic services that have been influenced by the IAPT culture. Gillian Proctor and Maeta Brown's chapter, 'Industrialising Relational Therapy: ethical conflicts and threats for counsellors in IAPT', grapples with the gap they see opening up between the profoundly relational culture of professional counselling and the business-oriented organisational culture of IAPT. Drawing on detailed interviews with counsellors, Proctor and Brown discuss the way they negotiate these differing value systems and illuminate the perceived consequences to them of the organisational strain induced by the arrival of IAPT. They point to many instances where counsellors felt that meeting targets and activity levels was prioritised over relational and ethical concerns, importantly demonstrating the way in which IAPT services risk contravening the BACP *Ethical Framework* to which most of their qualified counsellors adhere.

Jude Boyles and Norma McKinnon Fathi's chapter, 'At What Cost? The impact of IAPT on third-sector psychological therapy provision', similarly examines how the widespread implementation of the IAPT model has affected therapists. They focus on those working in voluntary sector counselling and psychotherapy services whose remit is to offer psychological help to marginalised and minority communities. Based on detailed qualitative interviews with a small number of therapists, managers and clinical leads, their chapter discusses how techniques such as the repeated use of questionnaires and outcome measures are seen to have changed the values and ethos of the interviewees' services and explores the resulting impact on choice, access and services' willingness and freedom to innovate and take risks. This chapter speaks loudly to concerns that the IAPT model limits the ability meaningfully to serve marginalised communities and address complex psychological presentations. Of particular concern are the ever-shorter time frames endorsed by IAPT services and the euphemistic language of 'signposting'. Together, these all too often mean those clients most in need of help – for example, refugees, asylum-seeking migrants and those for whom English is not their first language – are sent away and may not feel able to access further help.

Transparency has become a taken-for-granted assumption within public sector services – a requirement so obvious that it no longer needs explaining. It is based on the uncritical assumption that mental health services are organisations whose performance can be seen – and hence are open to scrutiny, evaluation and, therefore, improvement. However, we might want to remember that Giddens (1997) argues that 'expert systems' such as the NHS exemplify practices that rely on experiential or tacit knowledge and, because they cannot be rendered fully transparent, cannot be fully understood by those who wish to observe them. Expert systems depend for their success and effectiveness on a significant degree of trust in the expertise and understanding of the practitioner – something that cannot be demonstrated by recourse to yet further information or statistical analysis. Indeed, one paradoxical effect of this drive for transparency is that, as Strathern (2000) suggests, the 'language of accountability takes over the language of trust' (p314). Similarly, Power (1994) points out that, 'if those engaged in everyday work are not trusted, then the locus shifts to the experts involved in policing them, and to forms of documentary evidence' (p11). But the rush to transparency ensures that transparency itself only acts to increase confusion, obfuscation and opacity. For, as the data burgeons and the statistics multiply, fewer and fewer people have time or expertise to establish the validity of the claims being made. This leads, not to increased trust in professionals, but rather to suspicion and distrust, which lead in turn to yet more calls for transparency.

One person who has the expertise to establish the validity of IAPT's claims is Scott Steen. His chapter, 'A Critical Appraisal of the Economic Model Underpinning the Improving Access to Psychological Therapies (IAPT) Programme', unpacks the economic case for IAPT on our behalf, offering a detailed breakdown of data and statistics from the latest IAPT annual report available at the time of writing. Steen is concerned with whether, or to what extent, IAPT has lived up to its promise to return people to work, thus paying for itself. His findings are comprehensive and sobering, pointing to the minimal impact of IAPT on unemployment, incapacity benefit and antidepressant prescribing, as well as to the discrepancy between actual and estimated costs associated with assessment and treatment of those referred. Crucially, he points out that IAPT's figures for treatment effectiveness fail to include the 40% of individuals entering treatment who do not complete the minimum two sessions deemed to index a 'completed' treatment episode. This omission by IAPT seriously skews its clinical results and results in a significant under-estimation of the costs associated with treatment. Overall, Steen's chapter makes a measured and evidence-based critique of IAPT's claims to cost-effectiveness, suggesting that the financial case for its implementation and expansion has not yet been made.

The demand for transparency can of course, like other bureaucratic processes, be defensive in nature. My own chapter, 'Perverting the Course of Therapy: IAPT and the fetishisation of governance', takes a psychoanalytic lens to this issue, arguing that the pressure on staff and managers to conform to ever-increasing clinical governance requirements both results from and evokes intense anxieties aroused by contact with those in psychological distress. I argue that, within mental health services such as IAPT, a 'perverse' organisational solution emerges where these anxieties are concealed and disavowed beneath a fetishised 'target culture'. I draw on an organisational case example to discuss how such a culture leads to an idealised view of the work of a mental health service that simultaneously undermines and subverts the very psychological care it is mandated by government to provide.

## The myth of the medical cure for unhappiness

It is not surprising that we look to medicine to cure unhappiness. The astonishing advances of science and technology have allowed us to find treatments for conditions that used to kill millions. We can now repair and replace the body's organs, inoculate against disease, control birth, prolong life and even create new life, among many other modern-day marvels. Small wonder that we rarely, if ever, question the validity of the medical model of psychological distress; nor that we so readily conceive of the mind as an organ best understood and treated by biomedicine. But, while biological approaches to psychological distress are endorsed by the rapidly expanding fields of neuroscience and genetics, there is an ever-closer, more worrying association between medical care and the pharmaceutical industry. Indeed, the recently published fifth edition of the *Diagnostic and Statistical Manual of Mental Disorders* (DSM-5) (American Psychiatric Association, 2013), which informs the way psychiatrists prescribe drugs, claims to have identified 15 new mental health conditions, including 'caffeine withdrawal', 'hoarding disorder' and 'premenstrual dysphoric disorder'. There seems to be no limit to the range of human unhappiness falling within the purview of biomedicine, and the potential for complicity between mental healthcare, pharmaceutical companies and political vested interests has been identified as an increasing area of concern (eg. Bracken, 2014; Moncrieff & Timimi, 2014).

While the quest for a medical cure for unhappiness has its roots in the ancient search for the philosopher's stone, in today's world 'it is a position which most people can hardly think about', as Sanders (2015) argues, 'an idea which most people can only think from' (p32). Its legitimacy is unquestioned. By contrast, many of the contributors to this book aim to help us think 'about' the medical model, arguing that feelings of sadness, unhappiness or loss do not simply emerge within the psyche of the individual akin to the way in which the symptoms of flu emerge within the body as the result of infection. Rather, such feelings are the consequence of a complex interaction between an individual's social environment – factors such as poverty, isolation and inequality playing an important role here – and how the individual makes sense of that environment. The meaning of mental illness is thus recognised as a highly complex phenomenon, something that is negotiated among individuals, groups and institutions within society and that reflects the values and power structures of the prevailing culture at any given time.

Sami Timimi's chapter, 'IAPT and the Flawed Ideology of Diagnosis', offers a critical reflection on the problems associated with both IAPT and the Children and Young People's Improving Access to Psychological Therapies (CYP-IAPT). Reviewing some of the evidence for poor mental health outcomes at both national and international levels, Timimi trenchantly points to the way that studies tend to rely on poorly validated, unreliable, yet widely used diagnostic concepts and pathways. Similarly, he argues, the IAPT programme endorses a technical, diagnostic-based and process-driven ideology that contributes to commodifying, reifying and internalising personal distress. As such, IAPT risks contributing to, rather than alleviating, significant harm to those referred to its services. Timimi is particularly concerned about the legitimacy of replacing existing CAMHS services with CYP-IAPT, arguing there is little evidence that matching treatment model to a specific diagnosis differentiates between successful and unsuccessful clinical outcomes for children. Rather, he suggests, services can improve outcomes by concentrating on developing meaningful relationships with service users that fully include them in decision-making processes.

It is probably difficult to overestimate the extent to which the medical model adopted by IAPT is threaded throughout every aspect of the programme, including its documentation. The discourse, methods and practice of biomedical science are explicitly, repeatedly and uncritically woven into its training manuals, and patients are to be conceptualised, treated and evaluated accordingly. 'All people being treated should receive an adequate dose of the treatment that is provided,' asserts the IAPT Manual (National Collaborating Centre for Mental Health, 2018), going on to insist: 'IAPT clinicians should be able to clearly communicate the evidence base… (using an analogy to the use of antibiotics to illustrate the importance of the right "dose" of therapy to feel better)' (p50).

We can see an astonishingly explicit drug metaphor here that, despite the lip service paid to the idea of 'analogy', seems completely to have lost its metaphorical status. Instead, the reference to an adequate (or 'right') 'dose' of treatment makes it clear that the active ingredient of psychological therapy is assumed to act in the same way as an antibiotic applied to fight infection. This is very far from the case. The active ingredients of therapy have little do with the particular 'brand' of therapy being offered, despite the insistence on matching specific kinds of therapy to specific kinds of mental problem, as documented in the various iterations of the National Institute for Health and Care Excellence (NICE) guidelines on the treatment of anxiety and depression. This 'guildification' of therapies within IAPT runs in direct contrast to the repeated and well-established research evidence for the equivalence effect between different psychotherapies – the 'Dodo-bird verdict' – so called because of the non-significant variation in outcome between different psychotherapies (Luborsky et al, 2002; Wampold et al, 1997; Wampold, 2015).

It is interesting that such a large body of well-established evidence was overlooked in the decision to privilege CBT in the IAPT programme. Indeed, despite the recent inclusion of some other 'IAPT-compliant' therapies, CBT remains significantly over-represented within the family of therapies on offer. Its over-valuation is perhaps best understood as an acknowledgement that CBT is a model that most straightforwardly aligns itself to the medical approach. Indeed, Rosner (2018) has recently argued convincingly that Beck's original manualised CBT protocol allowed psychotherapy in the US to 'get into the RCT game', providing proof to Congress and insurance companies of its efficacy and cost-effectiveness. The late Michael Guilfoyle's chapter, 'CBT's Integration into Societal Networks of Power', offers a formidable analysis of CBT's strategic success within institutional and political domains. Guilfoyle vividly demonstrates that the widespread acceptance of CBT within the public sector is largely due to how it recasts psychological problems in medically acceptable terms and seeks to adapt 'dysfunctional' thoughts to the prevailing political climate. He persuasively argues the case for therapists remaining 'alert to being reduced to government agents' and warns that they may need to resist the 'games of power to which CBT's technologies are so well suited'.

Andy Rogers' chapter, 'Staying Afloat: hope and despair in an age of IAPT', similarly argues that IAPT can be read as an allegory of the powerful interests operating around 'mental health'. He points out that, despite the liberating work of anti-psychiatrists and humanistic-existential therapists in the middle of the 20th century, there has been a resurgence of interest in the biomedical model, 'facilitated by a convergence of powerful influences' including Big Pharma, biological psychiatry and the cultural capital of CBT. Rogers powerfully articulates how therapists' benign intentions to help others have become subject to professional self-interest, the State's agendas around work, welfare and healthcare, and the influence of prevailing ideologies and cultural assumptions about the nature of psychological distress. Writing from his own experience as a counsellor working in further and higher education, he takes particular issue with what he calls the 'monoculture of CBT' and the consequent scaling back of many student counselling services that have either been axed or replaced with lightly trained 'wellbeing' teams. Rogers is relentless in unpicking what he sees as the profession's collusion with the evidence-based regime, arguing that for therapists, as both principled witnesses to the suffering of others and torch-bearers for empathy, connectedness and the right to self-determination, the story is becoming an 'incremental tragedy'.

## Conclusion

For Yanow (1992: 401), a myth is a narrative 'created and believed by a group of people that distracts attention away from a puzzling part of their reality'. Having examined some of the potent myths embodied within the IAPT model, perhaps it is time to conclude with a brief consideration of what these myths might conceal or disguise. What is the 'puzzling' part of reality that the IAPT model cannot get to grips with? What are the paradoxes hidden within its structures, discourses and rhetoric? What, in short, is the troubled ghost at the heart of the IAPT machine?

As a public sector mental health service offered by the NHS, IAPT rests squarely on the unique cultural status of what Kuhn (1970) calls 'normal science'; that is, a science practised by scientists who observe, theorise and experiment within traditional categories, conventional methods and familiar explanatory frameworks. The cultural hegemony of this model of scientific 'truth' and inquiry has captured psychotherapy under the net of the medical model, concealing that, for many, psychotherapy is not a medical practice at all but is rather 'the practice of truth' (Totton, 2004). It is not just that we cannot treat broken minds in the same way as we treat broken bodies. It is more that the epistemology of IAPT, wedded to the notion of a singular, empirical 'truth' or clinical outcome to be established through prescriptive, normative and standardised practice, is blind to something infinitely more complicated: the complexity and unpredictability of multiple, contingent truths established via discussion and negotiation that are the essence of therapeutic meaning-making.

It is perhaps an irony that the IAPT programme should be blind to the effects of its rhetoric, practices and ideology. Ever since the Enlightenment, knowledge has been profoundly linked with the metaphor of light; the idea that 'to see is to know' so firmly grounds our current way of being in and understanding the world that it is hard to imagine otherwise. The myth of transparency, deriving directly from this Enlightenment project, assumes all aspects of therapy to be visible, shareable and inspectable: to be reducible to information. The 'parade in the public square', as Derrida (1992) rather aptly calls it, ensures that everything – and everyone – is reduced to abstract, codified fragments of information that, in the IAPT model, can be saved, stored, collated and reported. These decontextualised pieces of information are then presumed to index or symbolise the phenomenon of interest – depression, for example, or anxiety – in a way that is deemed to be scientific, neutral, context-free and apolitical.

But information, of course, is not able to speak for itself. It requires a human perspective from which to infer and think about its meaning. Without such a perspective, the more information we are asked to provide, the easier it is to move away from the very phenomena we want to explore, and the less we are able to understand its complexity, depth and meaning. Confusingly, the greater the visibility, the greater the shadow cast by that which is invisible, by that which is not reducible to information.

Finally, the prevailing discourses and practices of consumption that have rendered us 'free to choose' (Friedman & Friedman, 1980) have simultaneously placed us under an obligation to choose. Consumption is now the principal means by which we realise ourselves as neoliberal subjects, as well as the means by which we govern ourselves (Rose, 1999). But our freedom to choose anything outside the narrow, neoliberal narrative of success privileging individual effort and personal responsibility is limited. Solidarity, emotional commitment and social and civic ties have weakened; many of those arriving at the doors of their local IAPT service have failed to achieve anything close to a version of the 'good life' endorsed by the sovereign consumer subject beloved of neoliberal rationality. They feel frightened, excluded, ashamed, depressed and anxious. And no wonder; the price of failure these days is high and no one wants to be thought of as a 'scrounger' or a 'skiver'. And so the consumerist ethos at the heart of the IAPT programme, the provision of a market for care in which we can 'choose' psychological peace of mind for ourselves and our families, is one that risks producing the very emotional distress it purports to relieve.

The modern myths of IAPT, I suggest, function as a means of obscuring these disturbing realities. Tensions and inconsistencies are smoothed over; incompatible values and principles remain concealed; the prevailing order is silently upheld. Like the wax supporting the wings of Icarus, these myths act as an invisible 'glue', holding together that which would otherwise be experienced as contradictory, irrational and ethically troubling. Indeed, it could be argued that the successful elimination of conflicting perspectives and uncomfortable truths is what has ensured the IAPT programme's continued success, expansion and upward trajectory through the corridors of power and out into public sector mental health services across the country.

We can, therefore, make no apologies in this book for seeking to focus our attention on some of the difficulties and tensions masked by the circulation and implementation of these myths within the IAPT programme, nor for drawing attention to the hidden sites of politics, power and authority folded within its bureaucratic structures and organisational processes. Our critique is driven by the realisation that, as we move into a future dominated by Brexit, post-truth, terrorism, mass migration and the ever-tightening grip of global neoliberal economic policies, there will only be more, not less, psychological distress in the population. We will need services that can meaningfully address what looks to be a rising tide of unhappiness, frustration, fear and anxiety, rather than those that seek to prioritise the needs of the state. As the IAPT programme continues its expansion and influence, we suggest the scale of its ambitions will need to be tempered by recognition of its realistic limitations. We are gratefully indebted to this book's contributors for drawing our attention to some of them.

## References

American Psychiatric Association (2013). *Diagnostic and Statistical Manual of Mental Disorders* (5th ed). Washington, DC: APA.

Appleby J, Harrison A, Devlin N (2003). *What is the Real Cost of More Patient Choice?* London: King's Fund.

Armstrong K (2006). *A Short History of Myth.* Edinburgh: Canongate Books.

Barthes R (1972). *Mythologies.* London: Paladin Press.

Bracken P (2014). Towards a hermeneutic shift in psychiatry. *World Psychiatry 13*(3): 241–243.

Cassirer E (1946). *Language and Myth.* New York, NY: Harper & Brothers.

Cayne J, Loewenthal D (2008). The between as unknown. *Philosophical Practice 3*(3): 322–332.

Clark D (2018). Realising the mass public benefit of evidence-based psychological therapy: the IAPT program. *Annual Review of Clinical Psychology 14*: 159–183.

Clark D, Canvin L, Green J, Layard R, Pilling S, Janecka M (2018). Transparency about the outcomes of mental health services (IAPT approach): an analysis of public data. *The Lancet 391*(10121): 679–686.

Cuthbertson GM (1975). *Political Myth and Epic.* Lansing, MI: Michigan State University Press.

Derrida J (1992). *Points… Interviews 1974–1994* (E Weber, ed; French Ministry of Culture, trans). Palo Alto, CA: Stanford University Press.

Fotaki M (2010). Why do public policies fail so often? Exploring health policy-making as an imaginary/symbolic construction. *Organization 17*(6): 703–720.

Friedman M, Friedman R (1980). *Free to Choose.* New York, NY: Harcourt Inc.

Giddens A (1997). *Sociology.* Oxford: Blackwells.

Guy A, Loewenthal D, Thomas R, Stephens S (2012). Scrutinising NICE: the impact of the National Institute for Health and Clinical Excellence Guidelines on the provision of counselling and psychotherapy in primary care in the UK. *Psychodynamic Practice 18*(1): 25–50.

Harvey D (2007). *A Brief History of Neoliberalism.* Oxford/New York: Oxford University Press.

Kuhn T (1970). *The Structure of Scientific Revolutions* (2nd ed). Chicago, IL: University of Chicago Press.

Lakoff G, Johnson M (1980). *Metaphors We Live By.* Chicago, IL: University of Chicago Press.

Layard R, Centre for Economic Performance's Mental Health Policy Group (2006). *The Depression Report: a new deal for depression and anxiety disorders.* London: The Centre for Economic Performance's Mental Health Policy Group, London School of Economics.

Luborsky L, Rosenthal R, Diguer L, Andrusyna T, Berman J, Levitt J, Seligman D, Krause E (2002). The Dodo bird verdict is alive and well – mostly. *Clinical Psychology: Science and Practice 9*(1): 2–12.

Marzillier J, Hall J (2009). Boldly going forward on IAPT. *Psychologist 22*(7): 564–565.

Meyer J, Rowan B (1977). Institutionalized organizations: formal structure as myth and ceremony. *American Journal of Sociology 83*(2): 340–363.

Midgley M (2004). *The Myths We Live By.* London: Routledge Classics.

Moncrieff J, Timimi S (2013). The social and cultural construction of psychiatric knowledge:

an analysis of NICE guidelines on depression and ADHD. *Anthropology & Medicine* 20(1): 59–71.

National Collaborating Centre for Mental Health (2018). *The Improving Access to Psychological Therapies Manual*. London: NHS England.

NHS England (2017). *Next Steps on the NHS Five Year Forward View for Mental Health*. London: NHS England.

Ovid (1986). Daedalus and Icarus. In: Melville AD (trans). *Metamorphoses: book VIII*. Oxford: Oxford University Press (pp171–198).

Power M (1997). *The Audit Society: rituals of verification*. Oxford: Oxford University Press.

Power M (1994). *The Audit Explosion*. London: Demos.

Rizq R (2013). States of abjection. *Organization Studies* 34(9): 1277–1297.

Rizq R (2012). The perversion of care: psychological therapies in a time of IAPT. *Psychodynamic Practice* 18(1): 7–25.

Rose N (1999). *Governing the Soul: the shaping of the private self* (2nd revised ed). London: Free Association Books.

Rosner R (2018). Manualizing psychotherapy: Aaron T Beck and the origins of 'Cognitive Therapy of Depression'. *European Journal of Psychotherapy & Counselling* 20(1): 25–47.

Sanders P (2015). *The Person-Centred Counselling Primer: a concise, accessible, comprehensive introduction*. Ross-on-Wye: PCCS Books.

Scanlon C (2015). On the perversity of an imagined psychological solution to very real social problems of unemployment (work-lessness) and social exclusion (worth-lessness): a group analytic critique. *Group Analysis* 48(1): 31–44.

Scanlon C, Adlam J (2013). Knowing your place and minding your own business: on perverse psychological solutions to the imagined problem of social exclusion. *Ethics and Social Welfare* 7(2): 170–183.

Strathern M (2000). The tyranny of transparency. *British Educational Research Journal* 26(3): 309–321.

Totton N (2016). The risk-taking practitioner: implementing freedom in clinical practice. In: Lees J (ed). *The Future of Psychological Therapy: from managed care to transformational practice*. London: Routledge (pp135–145).

Tsoukas H (1997). The tyranny of light: the temptations and paradoxes of the information society. *Futures* 29(9): 827–843.

Vattimo G (1992). *The Transparent Society*. Cambridge: Polity Press.

Wampold BE (2015). How important are the common factors in psychotherapy? An update. *World Psychiatry* 14(3): 270–277.

Wampold BE, Mondin GW, Moody M, Stich F, Benson K, Ahn HN (1997). A meta-analysis of outcome studies comparing bona fide psychotherapies: empirically 'all must have prizes'. *Psychological Bulletin 122*: 203–221.

Williams C (2015). Improving Access to Psychological Therapies and treatment outcomes: epistemological assumptions and controversies. *Journal of Psychiatric and Mental Health Nursing* 22(5): 344–351.

Yanow D (1992). Silences in public policy discourse: organizational and policy myths. *Journal of Public Administration Research and Theory 2*(4): 399–423.

# PART 1

The State We're In

# Chapter 1

# Neoliberalism: what it is and why it matters

## Philip Thomas

It seems odd that a time of austerity and great economic hardship should beget the flourishing of interest in happiness and positive psychology. In a speech at the Google Zeitgeist Conference in 2006, when still only Conservative Party leader, David Cameron argued that the main task of politicians was to increase people's happiness.[1] It was a theme that was to recur throughout his subsequent premiership. In 2008, the Kingdom of Bhutan declared the state's responsibility to promote Gross National Happiness (National Assembly of Bhutan, 2008: article 9), an act praised by the Secretary General of the United Nations.[2] Economists too have lauded the virtues of the 'science' of happiness as a measure of progress in society (Layard, 2005a). Happiness and its cognates, positive psychology and cognitive therapy, are, through the government policy in England of Increasing Access to Psychological Therapies (IAPT), changing the practice and priorities of psychotherapy in the NHS. And, all the time, austerity bites, eviscerating the welfare state and the NHS, with negative consequences for the health, wellbeing and happiness of most of us.

Although the NHS stands as the great pinnacle of post-war welfarism, shifts in economic policy linked to austerity are jeopardising its funding and challenging our understanding of the nature of care. Yet the problems facing those involved in providing psychological and emotional care and support

---

1. See http://news.bbc.co.uk/1/hi/uk_politics/5003314.stm (accessed 10 November 2017).

2. See www.un.org/press/en/2012/sgsm14204.doc.htm (accessed 12 June 2018).

for others run deeper than the issue of resources. They take us to the heart of how we see human relationships, especially our ability to feel compassion for others and to engage with their suffering. As Loewenthal (2015) observes, the state's IAPT programme may have resulted in more people receiving psychotherapy and counselling, but psychological therapies are being transformed into industrial processes delivered by technicians.

In this chapter, I will argue that our understanding of care has become distorted as part of wider cultural shifts linked to the political ideology of neoliberalism. This is eroding fundamental human values of compassion, solidarity and connectedness. I will start by outlining recent developments in psychotherapy linked to IAPT, and happiness and positive psychology in particular. These developments have taken place while income and health inequalities have increased. Inequalities are also closely linked to austerity through changes in benefit entitlements and in the nature of employment, brought about by the economic policies of neoliberalism. I will define neoliberalism and briefly describe its origins and principal features.

Marxist scholarship has provided powerful critiques of neoliberalism, but Michel Foucault's insights into the nature of power and the creation of neoliberal subjects is particularly useful in helping us to grasp its consequences for the moral nature of mental health care and psychological therapies. I will argue that positive psychology, cognitive behavioural therapy (CBT) and happiness are a set of governmental tools and practices for the creation of neoliberal subjects, and that the consequent changes in the focus of the work of therapists and mental health professionals constitute a form of malignant individualism. This imposition of individualised explanations of depression and anxiety ignores the role of adverse socio-economic contexts in the origins of human misery. In addition, I will demonstrate how neoliberalism has resulted in the emergence of strongly polarised identities, specifically the egregious distinction between 'skivers' and 'strivers'. I end by considering the moral nature of these identities and how they relate to neoliberalism.

## Happiness, positive psychology and IAPT

The use of interventions based in positive psychology, happiness and CBT in people whose misery and unhappiness originates in socio-economic and other forms of adversity raises serious moral questions. These interventions, which lie at the heart of IAPT, place the moral responsibility on the individual for the way they feel and to do something about it. This is because such interventions are driven by the assumption that depression and anxiety arise from faulty attitudes and beliefs that people hold about themselves. Beck's view of depression as a specific disorder of thinking is a prime example of this. In his seminal work on CBT, he argued that, in depression, 'the individual's cognition is *distorted and out of step with his or her context...*' (Beck, 1972: 7, emphasis added). This value judgement is difficult to justify. How can it be right for a therapist to assert that someone is wrong to feel utterly hopeless and powerless in the face of overwhelming adversity? Who has the moral authority to make such a judgement, and on what basis? To declare that the problem arises because the individual's cognitions are faulty and require correction is to blame the victim. To tell someone that feeling better is simply a matter of having the right set of positive beliefs is to shift the responsibility onto the individual, while denying the social reality of those living precarious existences. Poverty, destitution and its sequelae are seen from the perspective of individualism. This 'obscures the causes of inequality, divides communities with shared political interests, corrodes compassion for the poorest in society, and obviates any recognition of the need to challenge disadvantage' (Valentine & Harris, 2014: 87). This is a form of malignant individualism; it imposes individualised and interiorised explanations of misery, hopelessness and despair, and fails to recognise the role of social and political contexts of poverty and destitution that people are powerless to change. It is now threatening to replace the ethic of care, concern and compassion that historically has been at the heart of therapy and mental health practice.

Despite this, the enthusiasm for positive psychology, CBT and interventions aimed at making people happy is gaining impetus in contemporary health policy.[3] Public Health England has set out a framework for English public mental health leadership and workforce development (Department of Health/Public Health England, 2015; 2016) that calls for programmes based in positive psychology and happiness training. Examples include the 'Wheel of Wellbeing', which aims to train staff in a simple framework to promote positive health and wellbeing. It also includes a 'Do-It-Yourself Happiness game' (Department of Health/Public Health England 2016: 15) and DIY happiness training, which explores key concepts from positive psychology, along with 'happiness' activities that are considered to

---

3. It is important to note in passing that the theoretical origins of happiness differ from those of CBT and positive psychology, both of which can be traced back to the European Enlightenment. Recent work on happiness by economists like Richard Layard originated in the philosophy of utilitarianism and the 18th century British empiricist tradition. Nevertheless, happiness shares with CBT assumptions about the individualised and interiorised nature of the self and its relation to society (Thomas & Knight, 2018).

be beneficial for health and wellbeing. All this is intended to help participants understand the role of positive emotions in wellbeing, what contributes to happiness and wellbeing, and 'the science and findings behind wellbeing' (p16). Another course, 'Living Life to the Full', is broadly similar, but based on the principles of CBT, with sessions on 'how to fix almost anything' and '10 things you can do to feel happier straight away' (p21). These interventions are aimed at the general population, but it is their targeted use with unemployed and disabled people in Department for Work and Pensions (DWP) job centres that is a primary concern.

Pilot studies of psychological therapies in job centres have raised fears that unemployment is being redefined as a psychological problem (Gayle, 2015). These fears are amplified by proposals to prioritise IAPT for disabled unemployed people (Department for Work and Pensions/Department of Health, 2017) in order to get them back to work, and a commitment from the Royal College of Psychiatrists to use employment as a key clinical outcome for psychiatric treatment.[4]

There is a covert political agenda underlying this. The growth of interest in happiness and positive psychology in health policy coincided with the global economic crisis of 2007–2008. IAPT (Layard, 2005b; 2006) prioritised the delivery of brief, focused, cognitive behavioural therapy and other evidence-based brief psychological therapies. Its chief progenitor, Professor Lord Richard Layard argued that the cost of setting up and delivering IAPT would be offset by reduced government spending on unemployment benefits and increased revenue from taxation as the depressed and anxious were transformed into happy workers. Future priorities for IAPT include supporting people to stay in or find work.[5] The context here is one in which the proportion of benefit spending on people with mental health problems is set to rise. The Institute for Fiscal Studies found that, while the total amount spent on disability benefits had fallen, the proportion of claimants with mental health problems increased from 50% to 60% from 1999 to 2014, posing 'an increasingly central issue for future disability policy reform' (Banks, Blundell & Emmerson, 2015: 175). It is difficult to avoid the conclusion that the government is turning unemployment into an individual psychological problem to be tackled by psychological interventions.

---

4. See www.rcpsych.ac.uk/usefulresources/workandmentalhealth/clinician/workisakeyclinicaloutcome. aspx (accessed 30 January 2018).

5. See www.england.nhs.uk/mental-health/adults/iapt (accessed 30 January 2018).

## Positive psychology and happiness: origins

There is a widely held and erroneous belief that mental health practice is apolitical. This is a dangerous misconception. We can see more clearly the political forces that underpin therapy if we examine the origins of positive psychology and happiness theory. Positive psychology is closely identified with the work of the US psychologist Martin Seligman, whose early research into the phenomenon of learned helplessness (Seligman, 1975) involved a series of experiments with dogs under a variety of experimental conditions. Caged dogs who were free to escape panicked on first exposure to a severe electric shock until, by chance, they crossed an internal barrier in the cage that terminated the current. Subsequently, they rapidly learnt to cross the barrier to avoid the shock and gain freedom. However, if they were unable to escape the cage, their behaviour was quite different. Rather than attempting to escape the shocks, they passively accepted them. With repeated shocks, the animals '[took] as much shock as the experimenter [chose] to give' (Seligman, 1972: 407). After repeated exposure to this situation of powerlessness, the dogs became stressed and socially withdrawn, exhibiting signs of what in humans would be called depression.

The central tenet of positive psychology is that the primary concern of psychology is the study of strengths and virtues, not pathology and disorders. Consequently, the task of therapy is to amplify strengths rather than repair weaknesses. This shift of focus requires a change in the client-therapist relationship, from viewing the client as having a weak, passive and helpless role in therapy to ascribing to them an assertive, active, self-caring role:

> No longer do the dominant theories view the individual as a passive vessel responding to stimuli; rather, *individuals are now seen as decision makers, with choices, preferences, and the possibility of becoming masterful, efficacious,* or in malignant circumstances, helpless and hopeless. (Seligman & Csikszentmihalyi, 2000: 8, emphasis added)

The use of words like 'decision makers', 'choices' and 'preferences' smacks of consumerism, but positive psychology does not engage with 'malignant circumstances'. Instead, it ignores them, and encourages the individual to see happiness as arising from within his or her own cognitive disposition. The assumption is that, if individuals are encouraged to see themselves in a more positive light, those positive emotions will generalise into other areas in their lives. As a result, they are enabled to act and perform at a more positive level, and more effectively. This is achieved not through traditional counselling or through specific forms of therapeutic practice requiring the guidance of an expert therapist, but through:

> The cultivation of the happy life [...] a project undertaken in the intimate space of everyday life, albeit through the use of techniques gleaned from the expert discourse of positive psychology. (Binkley, 2011: 374–375)

Positive psychology shares features in common with CBT: particularly the view that it is possible to examine and reflect objectively on our thinking processes, identify faults and errors in them, and, through rational assessment and challenge, correct them (Binkley, 2011). Richard Layard, the architect of IAPT, also sees affinities between CBT and positive psychology:

> Through systematic experimentation, [CBT] has found ways to promote positive thinking and to systematically dispel the negative thoughts that affect us all. In recent years these insights have been generalised by 'positive psychology', to offer a means by which all of us, depressed or otherwise, can find meaning and increase our enjoyment of life. (Layard, 2006: 8–9)

I will return to the political consequences of this shortly.

Although the 'science' of happiness has different origins, it shares much in common with positive psychology and CBT, but its links to political philosophy are much clearer. In philosophy, the idea that happiness is an important component of the good life can be traced back to the Platonic school's concept of *eudaimonia*. In the 18th century European Enlightenment, the quest for certainty and true knowledge dominated Western philosophy (Hampson, 1968), but there were opposing views as to how this should be done. British empiricists, such as Hobbes, Locke and Hume, believed that the senses and empirical observation were the only paths to certainty. Empiricist philosophy of science emphasised the primary importance of perception, observation and data gathering, albeit recognising the essential role of reason in the form of induction and deduction. In contrast, European rationalist philosophers like Descartes, Spinoza and Leibniz proposed that reason and reflection were the source of certainty and thus true knowledge.

Jeremy Bentham, influenced by the empiricism of Lock and Hume, developed an ethical theory based in an empiricist account of human nature. He believed that political decisions should be justified by the extent to which they maximised happiness in the population. He argued that, because human beings were governed by the basic principles of pain and pleasure and these were based in natural (physiological) processes, a 'science' of happiness was feasible and could be measured objectively and manipulated mathematically through a happiness 'calculus'. From this arose the possibility of objective political decision-making based on the greatest happiness principle.

The science of happiness has had considerable influence in (utilitarian) political theories of government, which partly accounts for its prominence in recent economic and political theory[6] (Davies, 2015). The value attached to the measurement of happiness is clear in Layard's (2005) work and that of his team (Clarke et al, 2018). They see happiness as a 'new science', based in neuroscience, behaviourism and social science and built on foundations of Benthamite utilitarianism. Although its philosophical origins differ from that of CBT and positive psychology, Layard's work shares with them an interiorised and individualistic understanding of the self. And it is this feature, perhaps more than anything else, that has important political implications. In particular, there is an assumption that it is possible to measure happiness by isolating it from the social contexts in which it occurs.[7]

The utilitarian philosophy on which this 'science' of happiness is based rejects any knowledge about the world that is not based on fact, and thus accessed directly through the senses (Davies, 2015). Consequently, ethics and values, which are matters of belief, have no part to play in understanding happiness; nor is it concerned with the social and other contexts out of which our emotions arise.[8] That said, economists' interest in happiness primarily concerns its use as a measure of economic progress, not to justify psychological interventions to increase happiness in society. However, Layard's work crosses the divide between economic theory and health

6. Stiglitz (2012: especially pp182–184) describes how, in recent years, economists have recognised the limitations of Gross Domestic Product as a measure of a nation's progress. In particular he points out that it fails to recognise how individual citizens are faring. Neo-utilitarians like Layard (2005) also recognise this problem, and for this reason turn to Bentham's work on happiness as a way of measuring progress.

7. The Office for National Statistics (ONS) started measuring happiness by including four questions in its population surveys and censuses: How satisfied are you with your life nowadays? To what extent do you feel the things you do in your life are worthwhile? How happy did you feel yesterday? How anxious did you feel yesterday? See www.ons.gov.uk/peoplepopulationandcommunity/wellbeing/bulletins/measuringnational wellbeing/2015-09-23#measuring-personal-well-being-in-the-uk (accessed 24 November 2017).

8. In this regard, it is worth noting that nowhere in Layard's recent work (Clarke et al, 2018) is there any reference to Wilkinson and Pickett's (2009) work on health inequalities and their relationship to income inequality. Wilkinson and Pickett's work is, of course, grounded in empirical data (epidemiology), but it has profound implications for matters of ethics and social justice.

policy, and it is this that is particularly worrying. Atkinson (2016) notes that happiness is modern capitalism's most important sales pitch, because it turns our desire to be successful into money by attaching its products and services to our need to be happy. Neoliberalism sells us the promise of happiness, while at the same time creating conditions of misery for large numbers of people.

To summarise: psychological explanations of human emotions such as depression, sadness, hopelessness or misery assume that these states arise as a result of distorted inner mental processes.[9] Interventions based in them (CBT, positive psychology, happiness) are thus characterised by individualism, and so fail to engage with the importance of social and other contexts in our emotions, as I explore below.

## Austerity: political, economic and health contexts

Today's age of austerity originated in the global financial crisis of 2007–2008. Most commentators agree that it began in the US with the failure of the sub-prime loan markets used by low-income families.[10] This triggered a crisis in the UK and US banking industries as the value of their shares plummeted. Several collapsed, or nearly did so: Lehman Brothers in the US, HBOS in the UK, and others in Iceland and elsewhere. In October 2008, the British government was forced to rescue several major banks, including Lloyds TSB, HBOS and the Royal Bank of Scotland. At the time, the entire UK banking system was close to meltdown. Subsequently, the world economy entered a profound recession, marked by an economic crisis in the Eurozone necessitating financial bail-outs for Greece, Portugal and Ireland. One of the major consequences of this was the imposition of draconian austerity packages aimed at slashing government spending. The banking crisis of 2008 was the point at which the 'neoliberal orthodoxy that ran the world for 30 years suffered a heart attack of epic proportions' (Mathiason, 2008).

---

9. As has already been pointed out, positive psychology and happiness place the responsibility for therapy on the individual. This means the role of the therapist is much less important than in CBT. Having said that, the recent move to the provision of computerised forms of CBT is also weakening the role of the therapist. These trends are consistent with neoliberalism in a number of ways: they emphasise the importance of self-care and responsibility for the self, and the cost of such interventions is significantly lower because they are not as dependent on expensive therapists, thus contributing to reductions in state expenditure on the NHS.

10. See www.oecd-ilibrary.org/economics/economic-globalisation/the-2008-financial-crisis-a-crisis-of-globalisation_9789264111905-9-en (accessed 30 January 2018).

Austerity[11] is the outcome of a political choice. It is a government financial policy aimed at reducing the budget deficit – the shortfall between government income through taxation and expenditure on public services. This is achieved primarily through reductions in public spending and shrinking the welfare state. In 2009, David Cameron, then leader of the Conservative Party, spoke at its annual conference about the 'age of austerity',[12] and subsequent coalition and Conservative administration policies cut welfare spending, reduced central government funding to local authorities and increased VAT. A report for the Equalities and Human Rights Commission (Portes et al, 2018) found that the consequences of austerity-related reductions in benefits and increases in taxation had disproportionately negative impacts on the poor and marginalised, and especially disabled people, lone parents, women, people from BME communities and older people. Overall, the adverse economic situation resulted in higher inflation and lower pay and benefits, which contributed to widening income inequality between low and middle-income families and the wealthiest, whose share of the income regained the level it was at (8.7%) before the banking crisis (Corlett, Clarke & Tomlinson, 2017).

Compared with other countries in the global north, the UK has high levels of income inequality, whichever way you measure it. Figures from the Organisation for Economic Co-operation and Development (OECD)[13] indicate that, in 2015, the UK was ranked seventh highest in terms of income inequality, with a Gini coefficient[14] of 0.36. Over the long term, there have

---

11. Even before the financial crisis, between 1997 and 2010 the New Labour government had tightened the conditions that applied to benefit claimants on Job Seekers' Allowance (JSA) and introduced benefit 'conditionality', or sanctions, for single parents and disabled claimants who failed to meet the conditions set by Department for Work and Pensions staff. These changes were reinforced by the Coalition government in 2010, and extended to ill or disabled people on Employment and Support Allowance (ESA). Since 2012, benefits can be suspended for between four weeks to three years if, in the view of DWP officials, a claimant fails to take adequate steps to get back into employment. These can include attending a variety of courses or interventions, including those based in CBT, positive psychology and happiness. There has been a substantial increase in the number of claimants whose benefits have been stopped as a result of sanctions. According to one source, there was a 600% increase in sanctions against people with mental health problems between 2012 and 2015 (Stone, 2015).

12. See http://conservative-speeches.sayit.mysociety.org/speech/601367 (accessed 30 January 2018).

13. See www.oecd.org/social/inequality.htm (accessed 22 January 2018).

14. There are different ways of measuring a country's income inequality. The Gini coefficient assesses inequality across an entire society. A society with a coefficient of 1.0 is one in which maximum inequality exists – all the income goes to one individual, and everyone else gets nothing. A coefficient of zero indicates perfect equality, where income is shared equally between all members so everyone receives the same amount.

been significant fluctuations in levels of income inequality. After World War Two, the UK became a more equal society.[15] Since the 1980s, this has changed as inequalities rose throughout that decade, peaking in 1990. After falling slightly, income inequality continued to increase throughout the early years of the new millennium to its present level, where it has remained relatively stable (Cribb, Norris Keiller & Waters, 2018).

Income inequality is tied to austerity in a variety of ways. The most obvious is a reduction in the amount paid to individual claimants, achieved by capping benefits,[16] coupled with a reduction in the overall number of benefit claimants by tightening the criteria for eligibility. In addition, for those in employment, wages have stagnated over the last 10 years. Between 2007 and 2015, the UK was unique among countries in the global north in that our wages contracted while the economy expanded. While there may be more people in work, their pay has fallen over this period (Romei, 2017). This has arisen through changes in the nature of employment over the last 15 years, with the arrival of zero-hours contracts and the rise of the 'gig economy' – a job market characterised by short-term contracts, self-employment and greatly increased job insecurity. Over this period, rates of pay have gone down while work and quality of life for the poor have become increasingly precarious.

Under austerity, our mental health and wellbeing have deteriorated. The latest Adult Psychiatric Morbidity Survey (NHS Digital, 2016) found that, over the last 25 years, there has been a steady increase in the incidence of common mental disorders in the population. Between 2007 and 2014, reports of self-harm doubled and there was a broadly upward trend in suicide rates for both men and women. The mental health of unemployed people has been particularly badly affected. In one survey, two thirds of people receiving Employment Support Allowance (the benefit paid to people unable to work because of illness or disability) reported suicidal thoughts and nearly half said they had attempted suicide (NHS Digital, 2016). Austerity has also been linked to an annual excess of 120,000 deaths (Watkins et al, 2017). Across Europe, austerity policies have been identified as being bad for health (Brand et al, 2013). In different ways, neoliberalism is making us sick (Schrecker & Bambra, 2015).

---

15. Harvey (2005) argues that, as a result of Keynesian economics, there was a redistribution of wealth from the wealthy and powerful ruling elite to the working class. However, when growth collapsed with stagflation in the 1970s, the wealthy and ruling elite had to move swiftly in order to protect their interests from political and economic annihilation.

16. See www.gov.uk/benefit-cap (accessed 30 January 2018).

## What is neoliberalism?

If we are to understand the relationships between austerity, inequalities and health in ways that illuminate the political implications of IAPT, we must turn to political theory and neoliberalism. In doing so, we face controversy[17] and difficulties. There is a lack of agreement in how neoliberalism should be defined (Ward & England, 2007; Boas & Gans-Morse, 2009). In broad terms, most scholarly work on neoliberalism has approached it either through Marxist theory or through Foucault's work. Springer (2012) points out this is a false dichotomy: Foucault was heavily influenced by Marx's ideas, even if he had an ambiguous relationship with Marxism as a political ideology (Miller, 1993). But before considering Foucault's work, it is helpful to identify some key features of neoliberalism.

Harvey (2005: 1–2) defines neoliberalism as:

> the theory of political economic practices that proposes that human well-being can best be advanced by liberating individual entrepreneurial freedoms and skills within an institutional framework characterised by strong private property rights, free markets, and free trade.

He goes on to describe how a major consequence of neoliberal policies is a reduction in the size and role of the state. This is achieved in a number of ways. Privatisation of public utilities and services serves the dual purpose of opening up new markets to the private sector, while at the same time reducing public spending. The state withdraws from direct welfare and social provision. In addition, banks and financial markets are deregulated to facilitate competition. As an ideology, neoliberalism has become so pervasive and taken for granted that it is extremely difficult to question it. To do so is to risk ridicule and marginalisation. As Jones (2014) points out, to question the basis of economic 'progress', 'reform' or 'modernisation' is to risk being portrayed as a Luddite in the pay of powerful, shadowy vested interests, such as the unions or other left-wing organisations.[18]

Harvey draws attention to three key features of neoliberalism: the importance it attaches to individualism over collective responsibility,

---

17. Controversy because some (usually those on the political right) deny that there is such a thing as neoliberalism (eg. Talbot, 2016), while others (usually those on the political left) rage at the baleful influence it wields over our lives (eg. Springer, 2016).

18. This is ironic, given the vested interests that neoliberal policies serve – the powerful, shadowy, unaccountable multinational corporations.

its implications for social justice and democracy, and the importance it attaches to technology and expertise. I will focus here on the first, because it is directly relevant to my arguments. The notion of individual freedom lies at the heart of neoliberalism (hence 'liberal'), and the policies pursued by US president Ronald Reagan and UK premier Margaret Thatcher in the 1980s exemplify the neoliberal commitment to individual freedom over collective responsibility (the idea that through society we have a shared moral responsibility for the wellbeing of all). In order to confront the economic problems of the 1960s and '70s (so-called 'stagflation'), Thatcher slashed welfare provision and privatised public utilities and social housing. She confronted union power through the 1984–85 miners' strike, and considerably weakened the power of organised labour in the process. She also cut back the power of local government and powerful professions. At the same time, she deregulated the banks and financial markets, resulting in the 'Big Bang' of October 1986, which opened up London's financial market to large foreign banks and traders.

The importance of individualism in neoliberal ideology is captured by a famous quote from an interview Thatcher gave to *Women's Own* magazine. In it she asserted: 'There is no such thing as Society. There are individual men and women, and there are families.'[19] This symbolises the triumph of individualism over collective responsibility: individual human beings stand or fall by their own decisions and actions, for which they are personally responsible.

The importance attached to individual responsibility under neoliberalism has in recent years given rise to strongly polarised identities. If we see the origins of individual success or failure solely in terms of the outcome of an individual's choices and actions, then the consequences of these actions are thus uncoupled from the wider systemic (socio-economic and political) contexts in which the individual is situated. Those who are industrious and hard-working, and who exercise financial prudence by, for example, investing resources in self-improvement through achieving a good education and qualifications, are held up as ideal role models for us all. Their success arises from their individual efforts. Neoliberal individualism values particular types of subjects – those with an entrepreneurial sharpness; those with an eye for the main chance; the go-getters. This is reflected in the popularity of television programmes like *The Apprentice*, in which aspiring, young business people compete against each other to become Alan Sugar's

---

19. Margaret Thatcher, interviewed in *Woman's Own*, 31 October 1987. See www.margaretthatcher.org/document/106689 (accessed 3 February 2019).

apprentice, and *Dragon's Den*, in which entrepreneurs seek support from a panel of wealthy investors. In a word, the ideal neoliberal subject is a 'striver'.

In contrast, personal failure is just that – the property of an individual that has nothing to do with socio-economic or other contexts of adversity. There is a strongly held belief in some quarters that unemployment and a life on benefits is a 'lifestyle' choice (Wintour, 2010). Benefit reform has been used to combat what has been called the 'something-for-nothing' culture[20] that is popularly believed to produce 'skivers'. The popular media have caricatured skivers in TV programmes like Channel 4's *Benefits Street*, filmed in Birmingham (with a follow-up in Stockton-on-Tees), in which unemployed people are portrayed as feckless, dependent on benefits, lacking motivation to find work, and engaging in criminal activities.

If success is achieved because the individual has a positive attitude and the 'right' self-confident and positive disposition, then failure occurs because the individual has a negative attitude and the 'wrong' disposition, characterised by negative cognitive distortions and a lack of positive affect. And this is the point at which we can begin to grasp the political consequences of therapy, and why positive psychology, happiness and CBT play an important role in government attempts to manage and control the unemployed. Indeed, the movement of therapists and mental health professionals into job centres marks an important shift in the governmental role of psychologists and therapists, from working with people to maximise their productivity and efficiency to working with the unemployed in order to get them back to work (Thomas, 2016).

## Foucault and the creation of neoliberal subjects

Foucault's work on governmentality[21] enables us to explore the role of individualism in neoliberalism, how neoliberal subjects are created, and how psychological therapies fit in to this. One of the most important aspects of Foucault's work is the contribution he has made to understanding the nature of power. It is this, more than anything, that sets his political analyses apart from others. Political discourses such as Marxism or liberalism tend to see power in largely negative terms. Power conquers, subjugates, oppresses

---

20. See www.theguardian.com/politics/2013/oct/01/benefit-reforms-iain-duncan-smith-unemployed (accessed 5 July 2018).

21. Or governmental rationality.

and silences; it operates in opposition to the truth. From the 1970s on, Foucault's approach to power changed, as he recognised that power can be positive, productive and creative. Power can suppress the truth, but it also creates regimes of truth that make it possible to assert the truth of one statement against another (Bracken, Khalfa & Thomas, 2007). In this way, it plays a key role in creating and maintaining different subjectivities. Out of Foucault's analysis of the organisation of the asylums (1961/2006) and prisons (1977a) came the idea of disciplinary power. He argued that, following the Enlightenment, power came to be exercised less through the restraint and chastisement of the physical body and more through attempts to induce individuals to discipline themselves.[22] Modernity resulted in the emergence of new disciplines – psychiatry, psychology, psychoanalysis and psychotherapy – which for the state became valuable tools for the exercise of disciplinary power. Today, variants of these disciplines, particularly CBT and positive psychology, have been successfully deployed for the creation and maintenance of neoliberal subjects.

The concept of governmentality is central to Foucault's ideas about neoliberalism. Foucault used the word 'government' in a number of ways (Gordon, 1991), but here we are primarily concerned with its use to refer to what he described as 'the conduct of conduct'[23] – an activity that shapes, guides and affects the conduct of others. In this sense, governmentality operates at different sites: on private, interpersonal relationships that involve some form of control and guidance (psychotherapeutic relationships, for example), and in the exercise of political power in the relationship between social institutions and communities. The main issue here concerns governmentality as the exercise of power by the state to encourage individuals to conform to, and fulfil, its priorities, using a range of tools, mechanisms and technologies – what Foucault (1982) called 'technologies of the self'. These make it possible for subjects to become free, but only within constraints imposed by the rules, laws, discourses and

---

22. In *Discipline and Punish,* Foucault (1977a) uses Bentham's Panopticon to symbolise this shift. This is a prison that has been designed so that all the prisoners can be observed from a central position. The theory is that this imposes self-discipline on the prisoners because each prisoner has no idea if and when he is being observed by prison staff. This is one of the first instances of disciplinary power.

23. '*L'exercice du pouvoir consiste à "conduire des conduits" et à aménager la probabilité. Le pouvoir, au fond, est moins de l'ordre de l'affrontement entre deux adversaries, ou de l'engagement de l'un à l'égard de l'autre, que de l'ordre du "gouvernement"*' (Foucault, 1994). 'The exercise of power consists in "conducting conduct" and in managing the possible outcomes. It has less to do with a confrontation between two adversaries, than it has to do with the order of "government".'

scientific statements used by institutions to shape subjectivity (Foucault, 1977b). Thus, an important feature of governmentality involves a state's use of technologies such as psychology and psychotherapy on its subjects to internalise particular forms of knowledge so that we conduct ourselves in ways that conform to its neoliberal priorities.

In *The Birth of Biopolitics*, a course of lectures given at the Collège de France between 1978 and 1979, Foucault (2008) traces the origins of liberalism from ancient Greece, through Christianity to the Enlightenment, and then into the modern period, where he examines neoliberalism in three post-war countries: the US, Germany and France. One of the key insights from these lectures is the link he discerned in neoliberalism between government by the state and the government of the self. For example, he regards the recent political acceptance of unemployment as evidence of neoliberalism in action. Unemployment, he argues, can be seen as an outcome of the view of the individual as enterprise: in neoliberal societies, individuals are required to maintain themselves at maximum competitive efficiency through self-discipline and self-care so that they remain in employment. Thus, the contemporary preoccupation with CBT, positive psychology and happiness plays an important role in honing individual subjectivity into ideal, neoliberal, employable subjects.

## Neoliberalism and abject subjects

These arguments can be taken further because, as has already been noted, neoliberal subjectivities are heavily polarised (between strivers and skivers), and are tied to a set of moral assumptions about the nature of the self and how it should relate to and function in society. In recent years there have been fundamental changes in class structure, so much so that commentators have claimed that class as a social or political concept is dead (Pakulski & Waters, 1996; Beck & Beck Gersheim, 2002). There is empirical research to support this view. Savage and colleagues (2013) have shown how class structures in the UK have fragmented, with the emergence of two new groups: an 'elite' group (strivers), who are wealthy, well educated, and mainly based in the south east of England, and a precariat (skivers), whose average annual income is less than 10% of that of the elite. The precariat are unlikely to have attended university and are more likely to be found in the former industrial regions of the Midlands and North England. Occupationally, they are over-represented in the ranks of the unemployed and those working in the gig economy, as van or taxi drivers, care workers or cleaners. The term 'precariat' reflects the high levels of financial, occupational and housing uncertainty they face in their day-to-day lives.

In this light, IAPT can be seen as a set of tools to transform abject skivers into neoliberal strivers. Ideal neoliberal subjects (strivers) work hard, are successful and are motivated to do better. In the service of this ideal, positive psychology and happiness are applied to hone our strengths, wellbeing and resilience. For skivers, IAPT serves to motivate them, get them back to work, and transform them into strivers (through benefit sanctions and psycho-compulsion (see Lynne Friedli and Robert Stearn's Chapter 4 in this book) if necessary. At the same time, malignant individualism blames the personal failings of the unemployed for their ongoing plight and downplays the extent to which their misery and unhappiness are grounded in socio-economic contexts of adversity, poverty and destitution. This enables the government and politicians to avoid taking action to end income inequality through fiscal policies that would redistribute wealth (Lynch, 2017).

Gerhardt (2016) sees the polarisation between strivers and skivers as evidence that contemporary society despises our attachment needs. Neoliberalism has resulted in society becoming increasingly harsh for most people, and at the same time our emotional and relational culture has also changed. She argues that extremes of poverty and wealth lead to insensitive and authoritarian parenting, which encourages an avoidant style of emotional regulation. This results in a culture based in individualism and self-sufficiency. There is evidence that a high level of income inequality is associated with increased stress and dysfunction within family units. It is very difficult for parents to provide the sort of family environment that facilitates healthy early-infant development, both emotional and cognitive, if they are struggling to make ends meet, lack social support and face precarity in housing and at work. Wilkinson and Pickett (2009, see particularly Chapter 8, pages 103–118) report the evidence that children in low-income families are more likely to grow up amid family conflict and to experience or witness violence. As Gerhardt observes, stress linked to economic adversity can result in unresponsive or punitive parenting, which can extend to neglect and abuse (Bywaters et al, 2016).

## Conclusions

Polarisation may make it easier for the media and politicians to convince us that they have the answers to complex issues, but there is a high moral price to pay. Feminist thinkers, in particular, have drawn attention to the problems that arise with binary categories such as body–mind, sex–gender and nature–nurture.[24] Butler (1990) points out that the danger, as far as identity is concerned, is that such categories are open to negative and positive evaluations: one of the identities is valued, the other not. This is particularly relevant to the distinction between strivers and skivers. Valentine and Harris (2014) examined the moral dimensions of people's lives, based on judgements made about different social groups. They found that moral worth and value were tied to a willingness to undertake paid work: ie. to economic productivity. The subjects they interviewed saw economic failure as a personal failure unrelated to structural inequalities; poverty and disadvantage were seen as individual failings – a consequence of lack of effort, risk-taking or bad decision-making.

We see the world around us; we think, and we talk with others about what we see, unaware of the hidden assumptions we make. The crude polarisation of 'skivers' fails to recognise the complexity of people's different lives and identities: single parents, disabled, racialised groups, women, LGBTQ people, and so on, all of whom struggle to live decent lives under neoliberal austerity. It assumes that all are the same. But this assumption is betrayed by the language we use, a point made eloquently by Baroness Hollis of Heigham in a Lords debate on the Welfare Reform Bill (2011):

> Until recently, when we introduced a Bill like this, it would not have been a welfare reform Bill; it would have been a social security Bill. The gap between social security and welfare is precisely the gap between entitlement and stigma. (Hansard, 2011)

Neoliberalism has created and amplified divisions in our fractured society. Its economic policies exhort us to become happy and successful, to become more responsible for ourselves, more independent, freer, and all so that we can become less of a drain on the state and consume ever more and more. In *The Birth of Biopolitics*, Foucault (2008) points to the paradox at the heart of 18th century liberalism – that of its productive/destructive relationship with freedom:

---

24. Kristeva's (1982) notion of abjection is especially relevant here. The abject stands for that which is 'not me' and must be expelled from the body as 'Other'. Confrontation with the abject leads to horror, revulsion and loathing. Rizq (2013) notes that people with mental health problems represent the threat of the abject by confronting us with a monstrous 'Other' that defines our own normalcy. She concludes that IAPT is one of a range of new management processes that prioritises accountability and control and makes it possible for society to abject those who experience sadness, misery and distress.

> Liberalism must produce freedom, *but this very act entails the establishment of limitations, controls, forms of coercion, and obligations relying on threats* etcetera. (Foucault, 2008: 64, emphasis added)

In the 21st century, neoliberalism has mobilised a great panoply of disciplines, discourses, legal appurtenances, the media and popular opinion to ensure that those perceived as skivers are stigmatised, controlled, coerced and transmuted into strivers. Counselling and the psychotherapies are at risk of being co-opted into this project. Is it too late to resist?

## References

Atkinson P (2016). Happiness and the capture of subjectivity. *Self & Society 44*(4): 394–401.

Banks J, Blundell R, Emmerson C (2015). Disability benefit receipt and reform: reconciling trends in the United Kingdom. *Journal of Economic Perspectives 29*: 173–190.

Beck AT (1972). *The Diagnosis and Management of Depression*. Philadelphia, PA: University of Pennsylvania Press.

Beck U, Beck Gernsheim E (2002). *Individualisation*. London: Sage.

Binkley S (2011). Happiness, positive psychology and the program of neoliberal governmentality. *Subjectivity 4*: 371–394.

Boas T, Gans Morse J (2009). Neoliberalism: from new liberal philosophy to anti-liberal slogan. *Studies in Comparative International Development 44*:137–161.

Bracken P, Khalfa J, Thomas P (2007). Recent translations of Foucault on mental health. *Current Opinion in Psychiatry 20*: 605–608.

Brand H, Rosenkötter N, Clemens T, Michelsen K (2013). Austerity policies in Europe – bad for health. Editorial. *British Medical Journal 346*. doi: https://doi.org/10.1136/bmj.f3716

Butler J (1990). *Gender Trouble: feminism and the subversion of identity*. New York, NY: Routledge.

Bywaters P, Bunting L, Davidson G, Hanratty J, Mason W, McCartan C, Steils N (2016). *The Relationship Between Poverty, Child Abuse and Neglect: an evidence review*. York: Joseph Rowntree Foundation.

Clarke AE, Fléche S, Layard R, Powdthavee N, Ward G (2018). *The Origins of Happiness: the science of wellbeing over the life-course*. Princeton NJ: Princeton University Press.

Corlett A, Clarke S, Tomlinson D (2017). *The Living Standards Audit 2017*. London: Resolution Foundation.

Cribb J, Norris Keiller A, Waters T (2018). *Living standards, poverty and inequality in the UK: 2018.* London: Institute for Fiscal Studies.

Davies W (2015). *The Happiness Industry: how the government and big business sold us well-being.* London/New York: Verso.

Department of Health/Public Health England (2016). *Mental Health Promotion and Prevention Training Programmes: emerging practice examples.* London: PHE. www.yhscn.nhs.uk/media/PDFs/children/Docs%20and%20Links/Mental-health-promotion-and-prevention-training-programmes.pdf (accessed 11 February 2019).

Department of Health/Public Health England (2015). *Public Mental Health Leadership and Workforce Development Framework: confidence, competence, commitment.* London: PHE. www.gov.uk/government/uploads/system/uploads/attachment_data/file/410356/Public_Mental_Health_Leadership_and_Workforce_Development_Framework.pdf (accessed 11 February 2019).

Department for Work and Pensions/Department of Health (2017). *Improving Lives: the future of work, health and disability.* Norwich: the Stationery Office. https://assets.publishing.service.gov.uk/government/uploads/system/uploads/attachment_data/file/663399/improving-lives-the-future-of-work-health-and-disability.PDF (accessed 11 February 2019).

Foucault M (2008). *The Birth of Biopolitics: lectures at the Collège de France 1978–1979* (Senellart M, ed; Burchell G, trans). Basingstoke: Palgrave Macmillan.

Foucault M (1994). *Dits et Écrits IV.* Paris: Gallimard.

Foucault M (1982). *Technologies of the Self.* Lectures at Vermont University, October 1982. [Online.] fouccault.info. https://foucault.info/doc/documents/foucault-technologiesofself-en-html (accessed 11 February 2019).

Foucault M (1977a). *Discipline and Punish: the birth of the prison* (Sheridan A, trans). London: Allen Lane.

Foucault M (1977b). The confession of the flesh: interview. In: Gordon C (ed). *Power/Knowledge: selected interviews and other writings.* London: Harvester Wheatsheaf (pp194–228).

Foucault M (1961/2006). *History of Madness* (Murphy J, Khalfa J, trans). Routledge: London.

Friedli L, Stearn R (2015). Positive affect as coercive strategy: conditionality, activation and the role of psychology in UK government workfare programmes. *Medical Humanities* 41: 40–47.

Gayle D (2015). Mental health workers protest at move to integrate clinic with jobcentre. [Online.] *The Guardian;* 26 July. www.theguardian.com/society/2015/jun/26/mental-health-protest-clinic-jobcentre-streatham (accessed 11 February 2019).

Gerhardt S (2016). Hard times: the growth of an 'avoidant' culture. *Self & Society* 42: 55–61.

Gordon C (1991) Governmental rationality: an introduction. In: Burchell G, Cordon C, Miller P (eds). *The Foucault Effect: studies in governmentality.* Chicago, IL: University of Chicago Press (pp1–52).

Hampson N (1968). *The Enlightenment: an evaluation of its assumptions, attitudes and values.* London: Penguin.

Hansard (2011). *Welfare Reform Bill, Volume 730.* [Online.] London: UK Parliament. https://hansard.parliament.uk/Lords/2011-10-04/debates/11100456000288/WelfareReformBill (accessed 11 February 2019).

Harvey D (2005). *A Brief History of Neoliberalism.* Oxford: Oxford University Press.

Jones O (2014). *The Establishment: and how they get away with it.* London: Penguin Books.

Kristeva J (1982). *The Powers of Horror: an essay on abjection* (Roudiez L, trans). New York, NY: Columbia University Press.

Layard R (2005). *Happiness: lessons from a new science.* London: Penguin.

Layard R (2006). The case for psychological treatment centres. *British Medical Journal* 332:1030–1032.

Loewenthal D (2015). Psychotherapy and counselling: from cottage industry to factory production – can we survive, and do we want to? *Self & Society* 43(1): 52–57.

Lynch J (2017). Reframing inequality? The health inequalities turn as a dangerous frame shift. *Journal of Public Health* 39(4): 653–660.

Mathiason N (2008). Banking collapse of 2008: three weeks that changed the world. [Online.] *The Guardian;* 28 December. www.theguardian.com/business/2008/dec/28/markets-credit-crunch-banking-2008 (accessed 11 February 2019).

Miller J (1993). *The Passion of Michel Foucault.* Cambridge, MA: Harvard University Press.

National Assembly of Bhutan (2008). *The Constitution of the Kingdom of Bhutan.* Thimphu: National Council of Bhutan. http://www.nationalcouncil.bt/assets/uploads/docs/acts/2017/Constitution_of_Bhutan_2008.pdf (accessed 30 January 2018).

NHS Digital (2016. *Adult Psychiatric Morbidity Survey: survey of mental health and wellbeing, England 2014.* [Online.] Leeds: NHS Digital. http://digital.nhs.uk/catalogue/PUB21748 (accessed 11 February 2019).

Pakulski J, Waters M (1996). *The Death of Class.* London: Sage.

Portes J, Aubergine Analysis, King's College London, Reed H, Landman Economics (2018). *The Cumulative Impact of Tax and Welfare Reforms.* Manchester: Equality and Human Rights Commission. www.equalityhumanrights.com/sites/default/files/cumulative-impact-assessment-report.pdf (accessed 11 February 2019).

Rizq R (2013). States of abjection. *Organization Studies* 34: 1277–1297.

Romei V (2017). How wages fell in the UK while the economy grew. [Online.] *Financial Times;* 2 March. www.ft.com/content/83e7e87e-fe64-11e6-96f8-3700c5664d30 (accessed 11 February 2019).

Savage M, Devine F, Cunningham N, Taylor M, Yaojun L, Hjellbrekke J et al (2013). A new model of social class? Findings from the BBC's Great British Class Survey Experiment. *Sociology 4:* 219–250.

Seligman M (1975). *Helplessness: on depression, development and death.* San Francisco, CA: WH Freeman.

Seligman M (1972). Learned Helplessness. *Annual Review of Medicine 23:* 407–412.

Seligman M, Csikszentmihalyi M (2000). Positive psychology: an introduction. *American Psychologist 55:* 5–14.

Schrecker T, Bambra C (2015). *How Politics Makes Us Sick: neoliberal epidemics.* Basingstoke: Palgrave Macmillan.

Springer S (2016). Fuck neoliberalism. *ACME: An International Journal for Critical Geographies* 15(2): 285–292.

Springer S (2012). Neoliberalism as discourse: between Foucauldian political economy and Marxian poststructuralism. *Critical Discourse Studies* 9(2): 133–147.

Stiglitz J (2012). *The Price of Inequality*. London: Allen Lane.

Stone J (2015). Benefit sanctions against people with mental health problems up by 600 per cent. [Online.] *The Independent;* 12 November. www.independent.co.uk/news/uk/politics/benefit-sanctions-against-people-with-mental-health-problems-up-by-600-per-cent-a6731971.html (accessed 13 February 2019).

Talbot C (2016). *The Myth of Neoliberalism.* [Blog.] https://colinrtalbot.wordpress.com/2016/08/31/the-myth-of-neoliberalism/ (accessed 13 February 2019).

Thomas P (2016). Psycho politics, neoliberal governmentality and austerity. *Self & Society 44*(4).

Thomas P, Knight T (2019). Happiness, austerity and malignant individualism. *AHPB Magazine 2*(Winter 2018/19): 13–21. https://ahpb.org/wp/wp-content/uploads/2019/01/nl-2019-1-04_Thomas-and-Knight-paper.pdf (accessed 15 February 2019).

Valentine G, Harris C (2014). Strivers vs skivers: class prejudice and the demonisation of dependency in everyday life. *Geoforum 53*: 84–92.

Ward K, England K (2007). Introduction: reading neoliberalization. In: England K, Ward K (eds). *Neoliberalization.* Hoboken, NJ: Blackwell (pp1–22).

Watkins J, Wulaningsih W, Da Zhou C, Marshall D, Sylianteng G, Dela Rosa PG et al (2017). Effects of health and social care spending constraints on mortality in England: a time trend analysis. *BMJ Open 7*(11): e017722.

Wilkinson R, Pickett K (2009). *The Spirit Level: why equality is better for everyone.* London: Penguin Books.

Wintour P (2010). George Osborne to cut £4bn more from benefits. *The Guardian;* 9 September. www.theguardian.com/politics/2010/sep/09/george-osborne-cut-4bn-benefits-welfare (accessed 13 February 2019).

# Chapter 2

# The industrialisation and marketisation of healthcare

## Penelope Campling

Improving Access to Psychological Therapies (IAPT) is – rightly or wrongly – part of the NHS. Its funding is determined by NHS commissioners. Even where it has been subcontracted to non-NHS provider organisations, it remains part of the NHS structure. It is subject to NHS guidelines and protocols. Perhaps most importantly, there is no ring-fencing of funding, so it has to compete for resources with every other aspect of NHS provision.

Mental health has always been a Cinderella specialty, accounting for 28% of the burden of disease but receiving only 13% of the NHS budget. It is no secret that both primary care and mental health services have lost out to the acute sector over the last 25 years – a situation that has improved only very slightly since 'parity of esteem' was introduced under the 2012 Health and Social Care Act. In short, IAPT does not stand in isolation. So, an understanding of the NHS context is important to any critique.

IAPT was an initiative of the Blair/Brown New Labour government and reflects the strengths and weaknesses in thinking about the public sector and the provision of healthcare that were predominant at the time – the first decade of the 21st century. If we are to understand this context more clearly, it is important to describe the complexities inherent in providing modern healthcare, as well as the pressures on and aspirations of this particular government. I will then move on to consider how IAPT, in order to survive, has had to fight its corner in an NHS demoralised by a Conservative government determined to reduce state spending in the name of 'austerity'.

Building on the vision of a welfare state outlined in the *Beveridge Report*, the NHS was founded on optimism and for many years its achievements fed that optimism.

No system is perfect, but there is an overwhelming amount of evidence that it continues to be good value for money (House of Lords Select Committee on the Long-term Sustainability of the NHS, 2017). Even the chronic under-resourcing during the last decades of the 20th century was offset by the efficient model of provision. True, the under-spending had a detrimental effect on treatments and outcomes for some conditions, but the country's overall health status in the second part of the 20th century compared well with those of other countries (Pollock, 2004: 40–41). Life expectancy remained consistently higher than the US and European Union average and infant mortality rates were consistently lower, despite a much lower healthcare expenditure per capita than the US or the EU average, and the UK spent much less on health as a percentage of GDP, according to the Office of Health Economics (Pollock, 2004: 35).

Between 2002 and 2007, the Labour government brought spending up to the European average. This made possible large-scale increases in the workforce, improved healthcare buildings and environments, improved access to services and shorter waiting times, all during a period when demand also increased significantly. There has been justified criticism of government strategy during this period: the disruptive reorganisations, the pay increases and the dependency on the Private Finance Initiative to fund capital expenditure, in particular. Nevertheless, this felt for many a proud time to be working in the NHS. Suddenly, there was a bit more money around and scope for local clinicians and managers, starved of resources for so long, to implement the new projects they had been dreaming about and planning for many years.

But in a system that sets out to be universal and comprehensive, there is always a tension between facilitating local, organic growth and the pressure to steer, commission, regulate and manage on a large scale. Local initiatives offer many advantages: projects can be geared to the particular needs of the local community, build on long-standing relationships between key people and benefit from the input of frontline staff and service users from the start of the planning process. From a large-scale perspective, however, local initiatives introduce variation between different areas (the 'postcode lottery'), inequity and troublesome accountability issues.

How can these tensions be resolved? How do we ensure, for example, that all citizens have equitable access to hip replacement operations; that the waiting times for hip operations are the same whether you live in central London, Hartlepool or rural Cornwall; that the technical standard of the operation is the same? How do we ensure lines of accountability are clear and transparent? Such questions have become ever-more pressing since 1948, as technology improves and aspirations increase in parallel.

Let's look back for a moment to the 1950s. One of my motivations for becoming a doctor was watching the very popular TV series *Dr Finlay's Casebook*. For those who weren't around in the early 1960s or don't remember this medical soap, Doctors Finlay and Cameron and their housekeeper, Janet, were part of the community in which they worked. They were loved and revered and knew most of their patients, and often generations of families. They were there at births and deaths, holding their patients' hands and offering comfort in times of need. But, much as I loved them, compared with today, they had very little to offer in those worn, leather doctors' bags: diagnoses tended to rely on bedside acumen; drug treatment was mainly basic antibiotics and pain relief and not much more. Referral on – usually for basic operations – was unusual.

There has been a massive escalation in the intervening decades in what is possible. This has impacted not just on our life expectancy but on the way we organise our health services. Having so much more to offer in terms of investigations, drugs, complex interventions and surgical operations brings the need to manage resources and demand. The management of such a vast and complex system has had to adapt – theoretically, at least – in line with information technology. An underlying principle of the NHS is equity but ensuring that everyone has access to the best and most efficient treatment, no matter where they live, is a complex and challenging task. The concept of evidence-based medicine (critiqued elsewhere in this book) has evolved to this end, as have various regulatory frameworks and management structures. Many readers of this book will feel that such initiatives have gone much too far and, in some cases, become counter-productive, shifting the focus away from caring for individuals and their families to an industrialised system of mass production and excessive accountability. Nevertheless, these changes are part of a massive qualitative change, with its own internal logic and dynamics. They have evolved for a purpose and it is important to understand that, if our critique of the system is to be taken seriously.

Professor Steve Iliffe, a GP academic, was one of the first clinicians to describe and understand the scale of the changes taking place in healthcare provision and the effects of these changes on clinicians and their patients (Iliffe, 2008). In his book on the industrialisation of medicine, *From General*

*Practice to Primary Care: the industrialisation of family medicine*, he wrote:

> The process of change is not a mere reorganisation, but a transformation
> of an activity from a loosely organised enterprise with a poorly
> defined remit and wide scope for individual initiative, interpretation
> and innovation, into a predictable and prescribed series of tasks in
> the management of the public's health. It is creating anxieties among
> professionals about power, autonomy, and patient-centredness as well as
> concern among citizens about the motivation of professionals. (p7)

While Iliffe was well able to see the logic and some advantages of this change – and, indeed, concludes by appealing to GPs to engage and influence the process – he also worried that it could lead to a constricted, impersonal approach, with limited responsiveness to individuals. He described this graphically as 'changing medicine from a craft concerned with the uniqueness of each encounter with an ill person to a mass-manufacturing industry preoccupied with the throughput of the sick' (p3).

Some interventions suit a mass-production, industrial approach better than others. It is easy to see how a primarily technical intervention, such as a hip replacement or cataract operation, can be thought of in this way, but even these become more complicated when you remember that it is elderly patients who most commonly need these interventions, and many will have multiple co-morbidities and social problems that complicate the picture. In our jointly authored book on reforming the culture of healthcare, *Intelligent Kindness: reforming the culture of healthcare* (2011), John Ballatt and I gave IAPT as an example of industrialisation in healthcare, using its implementation to illustrate some of the processes described by Iliffe. We chose IAPT as an example because of what we saw as a glaring misfit between such an industrial model and the task of delivering psychotherapy. Looking back, it seems that many of the fears outlined in the analysis were right, and I update and summarise them below. Many of the themes are taken up in detail in later chapters.

## IAPT as an example of industrial processes

IAPT was inspired by the work of an economist, Professor Lord Richard Layard. He analysed and addressed from an economics perspective the reasons why unhappiness was so prevalent and increasing in our society. He argued (Layard, 2005) that increasing the top rate of tax would have more impact on the nation's mental health than any other measure, but this, and other recommendations in his important thesis – for example, increasing the number of psychiatrists – were ignored. Sadly, this example of a visionary whole-system approach to a problem that then becomes fragmented and undermined from the start is only too common in the NHS: one part of the system is reified as 'the solution' but undermined by lack of change in, or even weakening of, the rest of the system.

Nevertheless, there is no doubt that IAPT was a creative and enlightened idea. It involved the transfer of money from the Department for Work and Pensions to the Department of Health in the hope that money spent on improving the mental health of people off sick due to mental illness could be recouped in savings in sickness and invalidity benefits – an admirable and unusual example of joined-up thinking between government departments. The idea was to intervene psychotherapeutically at an early stage in a depressive episode in the hope that this would prevent the sort of secondary problems (stigmatisation, loss of confidence and status, breakdown in relationships etc) that can render someone unemployable and reliant on secondary care services.

This is an example of what Iliffe, using a term borrowed from the industrial sector, refers to as 'forward integration': an attempt to improve the system by widening it to include and control earlier stages (another example is the reduced incidence of strokes by requiring GPs to monitor and treat high blood pressure). The IAPT scheme addressed problems at a 'macro' level (the effects on the economy), and at the level of mental healthcare (the recurrent complaints from service users about the paucity of talking therapies available on the NHS). The large number of patients that met the criteria for anxiety and depression meant the scheme appeared well suited to *mass production techniques,* with large numbers of staff recruited and trained relatively cheaply to deliver a service designed to produce a *high-volume output* that would make it easy to evaluate significant change.

Iliffe describes how industrial approaches to ensure efficient working practices and manage the organisation of production processes are characterised by six activities (2008: 41). They are listed below, together with discussions of these activities in relation to the IAPT project.

### a) The central codification of knowledge

IAPT has always had at its core a strong commitment to cognitive behavioural therapy (CBT) and CBT has become almost synonymous with IAPT. This focus was driven by early optimism, based on research, that suggested CBT was effective in bringing about relatively rapid change, and that it offered a potentially cheap, easy-to-deliver approach. In fact, the evidence base for CBT having a more beneficial and long-lasting effect than other models of therapy was relatively weak, as subsequently shown by Cuijpers and colleagues (2010: 215–217). This was largely ignored, as CBT's chief advantage is that it is easier to evaluate than most other therapies. Superficially, at any rate, the same product can be delivered in a uniform manner and it is more easily manualised, as it is a technique-based rather than relational therapy. This makes it easier, in theory at least, to control the independent variable and ensure consistency in approach. In other ways, CBT is not such a good fit as it is a very individualistic model of therapy, at odds in some ways with Layard's whole system analysis of why the prevalence of unhappiness is growing in our society. A more systemic-based therapy might have been a better choice.

### b) The standardisation of tools

IAPT practitioners are required to follow a standardised system, from the first telephone contact with the patient through to their discharge from therapy after the requisite, defined number of sessions. Evaluation of that process is extensive – some would say intrusive – and makes use of a number of standardised rating scales. Many psychotherapists take issue with the idea of 'manualised' therapies (where the practitioner literally follows steps in a manual), arguing that they take the focus away from the therapeutic relationship and obstruct a personalised response, tailored and responsive to an individual's needs. The rating scales used for measuring change during and after therapy (PHQ-9 and GAD-7) are also controversial and tend to be skewed towards CBT. There are also issues about validity – ie. whether what is being measured demonstrates real change not just in terms of symptoms but also in overall functioning. Some things are easier to measure than others but this doesn't mean they are necessarily the more important. More nebulous aspects of wellbeing can be fundamental but difficult to capture. It is easy, for example, to measure the rate of return to work, but more difficult to discover if an individual has recovered a sense of meaningfulness, connectedness and agency.

### c) The subdivision of labour

IAPT has been dependent on training up a lot of new therapists in a narrow model very quickly – a pragmatic approach that was attempting to address a gap in services that had been neglected for a long time. It follows a stepped -care structure that enshrines the subdivision of labour, with the least-qualified (the psychological wellbeing practitioners (PWPs)) doing the initial assessment and early work with clients. There are obvious concerns about such a large and inexperienced workforce, trained in such a specific approach, without the wider perspective that a broader training and experience would bring, particularly in services where they are responsible for deciding which clients should be moved up to the next step of more intensive therapy.

There is very good evidence from the literature on counselling and psychotherapy that individual therapist characteristics – particularly experience – and the therapeutic relationship with the client, are more important in predicting outcome than the model of therapy used (see, for example, Wampold & Imel, 2015). Moreover, most research on the effectiveness of psychotherapy comes from academic studies using highly trained staff. A key concern has been the capacity of these inexperienced, minimally trained PWPs, using rigid methods, to recognise patients with more complex problems who require much more complex engagement and assessment, and sophisticated care planning, including the management of many kinds of risk.

More worryingly, specialist psychological therapy resources within secondary mental health care were cut in many areas at the same time as IAPT was introduced. This left the mental health service without psychotherapy resources to work with the people requiring more complex care. This approach is not untypical in the NHS: a gap in service provision or an unmet need is identified, an initiative is introduced in the context of severe financial challenges, with the result that other services, although much needed and vital elements in the overall pathway, are closed.

### d) Machines replace human skills

IAPT relies heavily on telephone and guided self-help techniques, and there is a concerted move towards digital therapies, rather than expensive counselling sessions. Initial assessments are often done on the phone, using tick-box algorithms. While there is evidence that such approaches can help many people with relatively minor needs, there are concerns about the effects of such impersonal contact on people with more severe problems. For many, it is human contact they need and it may be counterproductive to subject them to an impersonal, mechanised system.

### e) Incentive payments

IAPT services do not use incentive payments to motivate individual staff but the whole system is driven from the centre, with tight contracts and national targets that local services have to meet. Locally, fear that the service will lose its NHS contract can drive managers to put individual workers under pressure to get through the required number of clients per day. Peer pressure is used to encourage practitioners to maintain throughput, for fear of being 'named and shamed' for letting down the rest of the team. This pressure can impact negatively on clients who don't recover 'quickly enough'. It can be argued that the scheme is over-monitored, so therapists are more concerned with completing evaluations (and persuading clients to do so) than with meeting the needs of the clients themselves. Demonstrating improvement through bureaucratic measures and facilitating real improvement are not the same thing.

### f) Faster work processes

All IAPT interventions are short and time-limited, allowing a larger number of people to get help. While this may be appropriate for many people, there are few areas in the country where there are properly funded care pathways for patients to move quickly on to if they need further therapy. There is also strong evidence that, for some patients, short-term psychological interventions cause more harm than good – for example, opening up intense and dangerous feelings without the time and psychological containment to work through them (NICE, 2009). The fast throughput and narrow focus is managed by operating strict exclusion criteria, meaning some more severely disturbed patients hoping for therapy are rejected by the system. Such rejection can compound their depression, adding to a sense of hopelessness and helplessness and, in some cases, amplifying their self-harming behaviours.

## Unintended consequences

Thinking about IAPT in this way helps us understand some of the underlying reasons for its strengths and weaknesses. Despite emerging from Layard's whole-system analysis, it was implemented with a narrow remit and little thought about how it would impact on the wider system. Another problem is the way it was rolled out across the country, with little encouragement for local adaptation, despite huge variations in existing services. (In this respect, IAPT is heavily data driven, in that uniformity is essential if the data collected on its effectiveness are to have any validity.)

So, for example, the IAPT schemes were piloted in areas of the country where there was, at the time, little or no psychological therapy available in primary care. Such projects were understandably popular and successful. But in other areas – in my own district of Leicester, for example – the introduction of IAPT meant closing down a good, well-established, existing service that had been built up painstakingly over many years, and redeploying and retraining experienced therapists in very basic, manualised CBT techniques. Staff reported feeling devalued and complained that they spent too much time on the computer, filling in evaluations of a therapy they judged to be far more limited than the model they previously offered. Many of the more experienced therapists chose to leave, infuriated by the narrowness of the approach, feeling that their accrued clinical wisdom was ignored and redundant and regretting the loss of person-centredness. GPs echoed these concerns, complaining that they lost the personal relationship with practice-based therapists that they used to value.

Understanding the pressure on the NHS to mass-produce and standardise a particular intervention is an important prerequisite for actively engaging with the debate, but it is not to be confused with condoning what is being done or an attitude of helpless resignation. The focus on industrial efficiency always carries with it the dangers of depersonalisation and should therefore be held in tension with initiatives to humanise the system. There is no reason why this should not be possible. Some of the most technology-heavy hospital environments – for example, intensive care units (ICUs) – are noted for being particularly sensitive to patients and their families. An example of this is the Stafford Hospital, where the coronary care unit was picked out by families as particularly humane in the otherwise damning report of the Francis Inquiry (Francis, 2010), which catalogued catastrophic failures in the care of elderly patients elsewhere in the same hospital.

However, there have been many examples in the NHS where the industrialising process has been idealised, misunderstood and implemented in rigid ways that have damaged services and people and would concern an expert industrialist or manufacturer. IAPT, with its rigid thinking about therapeutic models and the lack of thought to the impact on the rest of the mental health system, is a prime example. At its worse, the technocentric process has created an impersonal, de-skilled, rule-driven environment, where staff feel treated like machines and patients feel objectified.

What seems to have got lost in the process of implementation and pressure to achieve the promised results is the reality that all mental health work, and therapy in particular, is a relational enterprise. Of course, this is a critique of the system as a whole; there are numerous individual practitioners who struggle to keep the therapeutic relationship at the heart of what they do, and there may well be parts of the country where local leaders are managing to sustain teams of reflective, patient-centred clinicians who still feel they have some autonomy to help the person in front of them to the best of their ability. What I am suggesting is that the system is loaded against them, that there are perverse incentives in the system that draw away IAPT workers from the deep connecting and holding in mind that is necessary for healing to take place.

## Regulating healthcare – the importance of balance

Some of these perverse incentives are to do with the marketisation of healthcare, which I will return to later in the chapter. Another driver of the system that can so easily skew priorities is regulation. Like industrialisation itself, regulation is inevitable and largely desirable, although the view of work as a set of processes requiring regulation and performance management has to be balanced with a holistic view of the client and a focus on the clinical/ therapeutic relationship. Getting this balance right is important and takes skill and nerve. How regulation is constructed and managed has a huge impact on those being regulated. The nature of regulation inevitably evokes feelings and attitudes as well as behaviours and directly influences both the culture and the outcomes of the organisation. Essentially, it is a question of how staff are enabled to manage the balance between the demands of accountability on the one hand and attentive response to the patient/client on the other.

Sadly, those responsible for regulating the NHS – ultimately, the Secretary of State for Health – seem to have no understanding of balance in this regard; the system seems to respond to any untoward incident by heaping yet more regulation onto frontline staff. As regulatory bodies continue to multiply and clinical staff spend a higher percentage of their working hours uploading data on computers, it seems clear that a sensible balance is not being achieved. The system is over-reactive, driven by panic and an unrealistic fantasy of control. Regulation needs to be intelligently applied and proportionate. To understand why this is so difficult in relation to the public sector, we need to understand how mistrustful we have become as a society.

During a recent visit to Berlin, I was interested to read about the regime in the former German Democratic Republic (GDR) (Leo, 2013) and the deep mistrust those in power felt towards their citizens. The leaders of the GDR were German communists (some of them Jewish) who had escaped the Nazis by moving to Moscow or other parts of Europe during the Second World War.

Some of them had fought for the French Resistance. They settled back in East Germany for ideological reasons but were, in effect, governing those they had been at war with, those they had been persecuted by, those who had driven them out, those they saw as the enemy. This context of mistrust seems to me fundamental to understanding why it became such a persecutory culture.

Although it is not of the same order, mistrust also seems to be one of the defining characteristics of 21st century Britain. We are governed by people who profoundly mistrust the public sector and seem to have a need to denigrate the poor and the vulnerable (Jones, 2011).

The philosopher Onora O'Neill spoke about this issue of trust in her Reith lectures back in 2002, but things seem to have continued to get worse. O'Neill argued that we have got the problem wrong: we behave as if there is a crisis in trustworthiness when there is, in fact, no evidence that people are less trustworthy than they were in the past. The real crisis is about the lack of trust, the growing culture of suspicion, linked to excessive accountability regimes. It is difficult for people who are micro-managed, who are constantly watching their back, to develop into discerning professionals who can rely on the wisdom they have gained through experience.

> We have misdiagnosed what ails British society and we are now busy prescribing copious draughts of the wrong medicine... requiring those in the public sector and the professions to account in excessive and sometimes irrelevant detail to regulators and inspectors, auditors and examiners. (2002: 16)

O'Neill points to the need to give up 'childish fantasies that we can have total guarantees of others' performances' and urges us to 'free professionals and their public services to serve the public' (p59).

If only! Many years on, this regulatory system has reached a dangerous level. It's distracting, interfering, disempowering and creates a culture of fear.

Importantly, at a systemic level, monitoring and regulation are not the same as cultivating quality and success. At an individual level, *being* a good therapist is not necessarily the same as complying with the systems that supposedly *show* one is a good therapist. Moreover, there are important questions about who we are accountable to. Being accountable to regulators, to funders, to government departments, is not the same as being accountable to the public.

All this can reach particularly crazy levels in the field of mental health, where there is so much uncertainty around. Being a high profile, innovative service, IAPT had to succeed. It couldn't be allowed to fail, and the uncertainty around this has been managed by tightening the central control on staff behaviour. There is a large body of opinion that considers IAPT was an over-regulated service from the start, the economic argument driving the enterprise over-determining both the highly structured, manualised models of therapy and the outcome measures used. Moreover, the narrow view of 'evidence' and the fact that IAPT has to be shown to work, means the research framework is experienced more like heavy-handed regulation than the pursuit of learning in a genuine spirit of enquiry.

## The competitive market in healthcare

Another driver in the system that creates perverse incentives that pull us away from kind, attentive care of the client is the active promotion of a competitive market economy based on a commodified view of need, skills and service. Such an economy works against the idea of an integrated service that prioritises the needs of vulnerable clients, and can insidiously affect the attitudes, feelings and relationships of staff. This is not a simple matter of debating whether healthcare delivery should be through a mixed economy of public, third-sector and private organisations. A competitive market approach influences how every part of the system – patient, illness, staff member, research, treatment, location – is defined, framed, valued and managed. It is founded in a worldview of commodities, customers, prices and competing technologies and providers.

In his book, *What Money Can't Buy: the moral limits to markets*, Michael Sandel (2012) talks of 'squeezing out altruism'. Markets, he argues, are not neutral; they change us, becoming part of the way we feel about ourselves and each other. He warns about moving from *having* a market economy to *being* a market society as we increasingly find ourselves thinking in terms of the monetary cost of things in a way that crowds out other meanings, often with perverse results.

In healthcare, a competitive market has created a relentless 'more-for-less' culture on the crazy assumption that we can continue to squeeze more out of the system, year on year, ad infinitum. In IAPT, this means squeezing more out of its staff, as they are the main resource. This attitude in the system changes us. Marketisation invades people's thinking and language. Staff begin to see themselves as costed commodities, their work as a series of costed procedures, their clients as products. An expensive commissioning structure drives and amplifies this process.

IAPT was brought into being at a time when there was money around for new initiatives in the NHS, although (as described above) there was evidence from the start that local commissioners and providers were closing secondary care psychotherapy services at the same time. Although initial funding for the project was ring-fenced and adequate – some would say, generous – the competitive pressure on provider services was there right from the start, with services put out to competitive tendering within three years. The ideology behind this time-consuming, resource-heavy process is that competition raises standards. However, pressure to price the service lower than other bidders means the provider must squeeze ever more productivity out of a smaller and increasingly poorly paid workforce, with inevitable consequences for quality.

All this has got worse since 2010, when the Coalition government came to power, followed in 2015 by a Conservative government, both of which have relentlessly implemented a policy of 'austerity' in public sector spending. Despite government claims that NHS spending has been protected from the cuts that other government departments faced, when the increasing percentage of elderly patients and the known extra-inflationary costs of health spending are taken into account, there is clear evidence that healthcare spending has been proportionally lower than at any time since the 1970s, and markedly lower than other countries, such as France, Germany, Sweden and the Netherlands (Office for National Statistics, 2016).

This is not a good financial environment for a developing service such as IAPT. Despite all the rhetoric about moving money from acute services into the community, the percentage of spending on mental health and primary health care continues to shrink, alongside an increasingly desperate recruitment problem within NHS mental health services (Campbell, 2018) and in general practice (Bostock, 2018).

## Anxiety in the system

The NHS is driven by anxiety in a way that few people can understand, let alone articulate. At every level, there is a manic, reactive response to problems. Service managers reach for quick-fix solutions that tend to overload and fragment the system, making things worse.

One person who understood and documented the effects of anxiety on organisations was Isabel Menzies Lyth. Her famous study of nurses in the 1950s (Menzies Lyth, 1960) sought to understand why they resigned from their profession in such high numbers. She proceeded to show how an organisation (the hospital in this case) can be seen as consciously and unconsciously structured around the evasion of anxiety. Menzies Lyth went on to study many other types of organisation and proposed that the success and viability of a social institution was intimately connected with how it contains anxiety.

These ideas have been developed, looking at the 'goodness of fit' between organisational structures on the one hand and the emotional demands of the work on the other. Unfortunately, they have made little impact on the system as a whole, and there is little understanding or attempt to contain the primitive anxieties that pervade a system and affect all involved, including decision-makers at government level. If anything, there is more disconnection nowadays between organisational policy-making and the emotional reality of frontline work with patients and clients. This disconnect is very obvious in the IAPT service. There seems to be little understanding of the experience of being with desperately vulnerable people, or the cost to the individual practitioner of helping people process their pain.

The toll on patient care and outcome has been significant but, long-term, it is the effect on staff morale and retention and recruitment rates that is particularly worrying (Rao et al, 2018). Many staff used to experience the NHS as a benign parent and now feel deeply hurt and betrayed by continual reorganisations and changes. Many staff are at the end of their tether, extremely demoralised and burnt out. Absenteeism is a preoccupation for human resources departments and finance directors but, if you talk to occupational health physicians, they are much more concerned with what has been called presenteeism: the people who continue to work when they should be off sick. A lot of staff are keeping their heads down, concentrating on surviving. 'Getting to the end of the shift without a suicide' is a phrase that frequently comes up when talking to mental health nurses.

IAPT has suffered from being part of this socio-economic system, like every part of the NHS. It is no longer an exciting new project, the recipient of government largesse. Those commissioning and providing IAPT services are always under pressure to make savings and provide the service more cheaply. At the same time, the percentage of patients presenting with common and serious mental health problems is increasing, especially in the younger age groups. Waiting lists and revolving door patients are a growing phenomenon. The result is highly stressed clinical staff, constantly under pressure to process more clients. One of the first things to be sacrificed is time and space for reflection, a process that is generally recognised as being a fundamental part of the psychotherapeutic enterprise.

## Conclusion

In summary, this chapter has explored how the problems that beset IAPT can best be understood in the context of both the pressures that drive the provision of modern healthcare in general and the particular ideologies that have influenced ideas and resource management in the UK over the last two decades. Like so many visionary ideas, the intention and spirit of change has been crushed in its implementation, right from the start.

While there will always be examples of excellent practice, the general picture across the country is one of highly scrutinised, micro-managed, over-stretched staff teams who are trying, against the odds, to create the safe psychological space that is needed for troubled, anxious people to explore their worst fears. To shift this, there would need to be a major change in the culture of care provision: a focus on co-operation rather than competition; a determination not to respond to anxiety with even more fragmented, regulatory bureaucracy, and some serious thinking about how to promote a culture and organising systems that nurture and liberate staff to concentrate on the work of healing.

NHS structures and management systems in general should be seen to succeed or fail by how much they help frontline healthcare staff to work together effectively, focused on and guided by attentive connection with patients. Nowhere is this more important than in IAPT services, where it is the quality of this attention that is of itself therapeutic.

## References

Ballatt J, Campling P (2011). *Intelligent Kindness: reforming the culture of healthcare*. London: RCPsych Publications.

Bostock N (2018). GP workforce falls 4% in two years as shortage continues to grow. [Online.] *GP*; 15 May. www.gponline.com/gp-workforce-falls-4-two-years-shortage-continues-grow/article/1464731 (accessed 22 February 2019).

Campbell D (2018). NHS mental health crisis worsens as 2,000 staff quit per month. [Online.] *The Observer*; 15 September. www.theguardian.com/society/2018/sep/15/nhs-mental-health-crisis-staff-quit (accessed 22 February 2019).

Cuijpers P, Smit F, Bohlmeijer E, Hollon SD, Andersson G (2010). Efficacy of cognitive-behavioural therapy and other psychological treatments for adult depression: meta-analytic study of publication bias. *British Journal of Psychiatry 196*: 173–178.

Francis R (2010). *Independent Inquiry into Care provided by Mid Staffordshire NHS Foundation Trust January 2005–March 2009.* London: the Stationery Office.

House of Lords Select Committee on the Long-term Sustainability of the NHS (2017). *The Long-term Sustainability of the NHS and Adult Social Care.* Report of session 2016-2017. HL Paper 151. London: House of Lords. https://publications.parliament.uk/pa/ld201617/ldselect/ldnhssus/151/151.pdf (accessed 5 February 2019).

Iliffe S (2008). *From General Practice to Primary Care: the industrialisation of family medicine. Oxford*: Oxford University Press.

Jones O (2011). *Chavs: the demonization of the working class.* London: Verso.

Layard R (2005). *Happiness: lessons from a new science.* London: Penguin Books.

Leo M (2013). *Red Love: the story of an East Berlin family* (Whiteside S, trans.) London: Pushkin Press.

Menzies Lyth I (1960). A case-study in the functioning of social systems as a defence against anxiety: a report on a study of the nursing service of a general hospital. *Human Relations 13*(2): 95–121.

National Institute for Health and Care Excellence (2009). *Borderline Personality Disorder: recognition and management.* Clinical guideline CG78. London: NICE.

Office for National Statistics (2016). *How does UK healthcare spending compare internationally?* [Online.] Newport: Office for National Statistics. www.ons.gov.uk/peoplepopulationandcommunity/healthandsocialcare/healthcaresystem/articles/howdoesukhealthcarespendingcompareinternationally/2016-11-01 (accessed 5 February 2019).

O'Neill O (2002). *A Question of Trust: the BBC Reith Lectures.* Cambridge: Cambridge University Press.

Pollock AM (2004). *NHS PLC: the privatisation of our healthcare.* London: Verso.

Rao A, Clarke J, Bhutani G, Dosanjh N, Cohen Tovee E, Neal A (2018). *Workforce Wellbeing Survey 2014–2017.* [Online.] London: British Psychological Society, Division of Clinical Psychology/New Savoy Conference. http://www.newsavoypartnership.org/2018presentations/amra-rao.pdf (accessed 5 February 2019).

Sandel M (2012). *What Money Can't Buy: the moral limits to markets.* London: Penguin Books.

Wampold BE, Imel ZE (2015). *The Great Psychotherapy Debate: the evidence for what makes psychotherapy work* (2nd ed). London: Routledge.

# Chapter 3

## Throwing good money after bad: health services without care under marketised welfare

### Marianna Fotaki

We are witnessing remarkable shifts in public policy under neoliberal ideology, as the notions of care, solidarity and responsibility for the other are being replaced by an individualistic and competitive business ethos (Fotaki, 2017). Initiated by Margaret Thatcher's government almost four decades ago, this shift has now colonised all spheres of public life, including health, education and social services, in many developed (Fotaki & Boyd, 2005; Lynch, 2006) and developing countries (Rudra, 2007). Market-based freedom of choice and user autonomy are increasingly becoming more prominent on policy-makers' agendas than equity of access or equality of opportunity. In addition to improving quality, efficiency and responsiveness of services, offering patients choice, particularly in countries where it has previously been unavailable, is in keeping with political declarations and policy commitments to personalised health services (Cacace & Nolte, 2011).

While market-based choice promises to empower service users by giving them a say in what, when and who should provide these services (Le Grand, 2007), the shift toward consumerism often results in toxic attachments between professionals employed in health settings and those in their care, corrupting the institutional and moral fabric of public service organisations (Long, 1999). This is because, for public servants and for healthcare professionals in particular, a strong ethic of care and equality is among the highest ideals (Hughes et al, 2005; Rogers, 2006). However, the logic of consumerist user choice militates against this (Fotaki, 2010a); nor are such policies likely to produce better health outcomes.

Ill health and low socio-economic status are closely related, and there is little evidence that consumerist choice has any impact on improving these, although in some cases it may lead to higher satisfaction with the services (Dixon et al, 2010). Overall, healthcare is hardly, if ever, consumed for pleasure. If we had the choice not to be ill, we would not use health services at all. Moreover, patients' ability, and even willingness, to make choices is influenced by their beliefs, cultural values and expectations, as well as their life circumstances, personal characteristics and previous experiences of healthcare services (Fotaki et al, 2008). This is particularly relevant for mental health services, where patients' needs and abilities differ, and where a market-based approach may lead to the commodification and instrumentalisation of mental suffering (Bell, 2013).

Derived from early 20th century theories of consumer demand and neoclassic economics, the prevailing logic of choice in healthcare illustrates how 'practical men' often unwittingly become 'the slaves of some defunct economist' (Keynes, 1936/1973: 383). In this instance, policy makers' enslavement relates to their assumption that patients act as calculating and rational utility maximisers, even though people are not generally known to behave in accordance with the predictions of economic models (Kahneman & Tversky, 1979). If such policies are known to be unworkable and there is evidence of their failure, why are they relentlessly promoted?

In this chapter, I argue that insistence on failed market policies in public healthcare signifies a fundamental rejection of the core principle underlying European post-war welfare states: namely, that offering free public services to all those who need them will transform society for the better (Fotaki, 2011). According to Aneurin Bevan (1952), founder of the UK's National Health Service (NHS):

> Society becomes more wholesome, more serene, and spiritually healthier, if it knows that its citizens have at the back of their consciousness the knowledge that not only themselves, but all their fellows, have access, when ill, to the best that medical skill can provide.

I also argue that public and health policies are driven by deeper and less rational forces and motives that lie both within and outside the domain of conventional political science and economic analyses (Fotaki, 2006, 2010b). Specifically, I discuss how the introduction of the market logic and consumerism into public healthcare services relies on and taps into unconscious dynamics and fantasies of invincibility, focusing on a policy of patient choice while denying the weakness and vulnerability that make us human.

Therefore, my first contention is that the real and ultimate aim of introducing consumerism into healthcare is to replace the notion of dependency on others. This is achieved through attacks on relationality and our links with one another, and on the welfare state, which is a societal arrangement embodying this collective responsibility. At the root of the neoliberal narrative is a refusal to accept inevitable 'facts of human life', such as ageing, disease and death (Money-Kyrle, 1978; see also Cooper & Lousada, 2005; Froggett, 2002). This is a denial of the vulnerability and precariousness that necessitates reliance on others. As I argue elsewhere (Fotaki, 2011), rather than facilitating the conditions necessary for a shift toward empowered citizens who are consumers, choosers and co-producers of services, taken together, these shifts have created responsibilised users who are increasingly expected to deal on their own with issues of ill health, and who have little or no control over the services from which they are expected to 'choose'. With reference to mental health services in England, David Bell (2013) suggests:

> In this new world-view welfare provision is no longer seen as something
> that provides people with the basic necessities of life, as part of the duty
> of the state, but as a mechanism by which people are disempowered,
> creating in them a helpless state of invalidism. Instead of 'getting on
> their bike' and competing in the marketplace, people are seen as staying
> at home and 'whingeing' for the 'nanny state' to do something for them.

In the UK, which is the specific focus of this chapter, the shift to marketised welfare is often combined with intensification of direct control by central or local government in the form of audits, targets and inspections (Newman et al, 2004). This combination of the market and bureaucratic control is then used to tighten the eligibility criteria for state support, which is arguably detrimental to various groups of patients with disabilities, including mental health patients (Rizq, 2013). Moreover, the recent public service retrenchment following the global financial crisis has occurred at a time when, in the aftermath of the financial crisis and accompanying austerity, these patients' needs are greater than ever. Rising unemployment, widening inequality, loss of job security and economic hardship all cause increased psychological morbidity in the population, and those who are already mentally ill are particularly affected (Bell, 2013). Making users and patients responsible for their illness or disability and making health status an issue of lifestyle and choice also originate in a refusal to accept the crucial effect of social inequalities on health outcomes. More affluent groups in society, who see themselves as deserving of their good fortune, even though it often results from accidents of birth or geography, deploy these discourses to sustain their fantasy of invincibility, and to influence policies (such as privatising services and tightening eligibility criteria, often coupled with various measures of intrusive surveillance of both patients and staff) that deny access to services to people who need and rely on them.

To better understand these trends, I argue for the use of psychodynamic frameworks to highlight the aspirational function of public policy-making that frequently diverges from organisational pragmatism and to illustrate the dysfunctional results emerging from the development of unrealistic policies and strategic failures. The application of consumerist, market-based solutions to healthcare is well suited to explore the psychosocial dynamics involved, including the cycle of idealisation, splitting and blame in organisations (Fotaki & Hyde, 2015). Following from this, I demonstrate how organisations respond to these policies by using their own defences to detach themselves from failure, and by blaming various groups within and outside their own immediate settings for any unwelcome consequences. In illuminating these dynamics, I hope that organisations tasked with providing public services will recognise the conflicts generated by unworkable policies and will integrate this understanding into their responses.

Last, to counteract the undesirable effects of the shift toward individualistic approaches to public policy and the progressive abdication of responsibility for caring in organisations and society, I propose an ethics of relational care as the foundation of public services. In doing so, I draw on psychosocial approaches (Hoggett, 2006; Long, 1999; Taylor, 2011) inspired by various strands of psychoanalysis, and by Judith Butler's (2004, 2009) and Bracha Ettinger's (2006; see also Kenny & Fotaki, 2015; Fotaki & Harding, 2018) theory of recognition and affective attachments, as well as feminist theorisation on care. The proposed notion of care is ontological (Puig de la Bellacasa, 2012), and suggests that care is everything one does and extends to all living and non-sentient matter. This understanding of care as the crucial underpinning of public policy aims to speak to and account for the interdependency that is essential for our sustenance as relational social beings.

## Marketised welfare in public services

Over the last few decades, sweeping changes have transformed the organisation, delivery and financing of public services in advanced economies. During the 1990s, conservative governments in Europe and elsewhere adopted neoliberal economics (Scott-Samuel et al, 2014). Their strong commitment to property rights, individual freedom and personal responsibility prompted them to introduce various forms of competition in order to devolve the state's responsibility for the most vulnerable individuals in society and to enable the privatisation of public services (Krachler & Greer, 2015).

These pivotal changes relied on introducing into public services the rather unfamiliar notions of humans as atomised individuals and users as choosers, which replaced the principles of universality, solidarity and equality of access that had underpinned the logic of the welfare state until then. Two rationales were deployed to make widening of consumer choice attractive in public health systems specifically: it was seen both as a means for stimulating providers to improve the quality of services offered, and as having an intrinsic value for patients. While there was no groundswell of demand for greater choice among service users, increased user participation had long been advocated by user movements and by alliances between them and radical professionals (Barnes, 1999; Glendinning, 2008; Newman, Glendinning & Hughes, 2008). According to this line of thinking, choice over the types of service on offer and patient involvement in their provision may potentially empower patients to take better care of their lives. For example, when dealing with long-term health conditions, they may be able to choose different courses of treatment, according to what suits them best. Competition between multiple service providers, who would be freely chosen by users, was actively promoted as a chief means of improving service efficiency, quality and user empowerment (Glennerster & Le Grand, 1995).

However, market-based competitive choice may lead to users being held responsible for making wrong choices, even though they may not possess the necessary information (Allmark, 2006). Choice is often constrained by asymmetry of information between users and knowledgeable providers: nurses, doctors, primary care settings or hospitals. Patients' ability to exercise choice of hospital may be influenced by their age, gender, family obligations and socio-economic status (Burge et al, 2005): for example, people on low incomes (below £10,000 per annum), those with caring responsibilities, and even those who do not own a car and find it difficult to travel (Dixon et al, 2010). In addition, culture, language and education barriers limit patients' access to information and choice (Schyve, 2007; Boyce et al, 2010). Pre-existing inequalities and vulnerabilities distributed across different bodies and lives play an important role in how individuals choose (Fotaki, 2010a). Choice, therefore, has different meanings for different user groups, depending on their specific life circumstances. Finally, patients often prefer to trade choice for trust (Fotaki, 2014), thus overriding their desire to 'shop around'.

Furthermore, users of healthcare services rarely act as the rational utility-maximisers of ideational economic models because experiences of vulnerability and frailty that often accompany their disease limit the fabled self-sufficiency of the autonomous neoliberal subject. As I have argued elsewhere (Fotaki, 2006), freedom of choice framed as consumer sovereignty does not and cannot exist in most health situations because healthcare is not readily analogous to the commercial sector. When faced with ill health, there are often few or no meaningful choices to be made. In the absence of genuine options from which to choose, such users/choosers have little control over their destiny, despite freedom of choice. The choices open to users may also be restricted if they perceive themselves to be involuntary service users (Ferguson, 2007). The logic of continuity of care, rather than one-off choices, infuses some of the best practices in health and social services, making health delivery compatible with care rather than choice (Mol, 2008). Overall, rather than choosing from unlimited alternatives, we tend to be satisfied with the existing options on offer, if they are good enough (Kahneman & Tversky, 1979).

The policies centred around individualistic choice and competition that are relentlessly promoted by policy-makers around the world affect people's lives, organisations and societies in profound and often negative ways. This is a real concern, because underpinning many of the current shifts toward marketisation is a dominant conception of citizenship in which responsibilities are transferred to the individual (Scourfield, 2007). In the UK, throughout the 1990s, this transformation was linked to the New Labour government's modernisation project, which conceived the modern citizen as both managerial and entrepreneurial (Giddens, 1990). This was further accelerated under the Coalition and Conservative governments, with public funds increasingly being used to pay for privatised health service provision (Walpole, 2017), despite its demonstrably adverse effects on safety, quality and efficiency (Leys, 2018). Conventional policy analysis cannot easily explain policy-makers' overriding commitment to ideologies that inevitably fail in healthcare. Cultural studies, sociology and psychoanalysis may offer more profound insights.

For instance, Max Haiven (2014) argues that this is a result of a wider trend whereby popular culture and everyday life are being transformed by the logics of finance capital, which depends on such transformations in the realms of social action, representation and subjectivity. Philosopher Ingerid Straume argues similarly that the consumerist shift in public policy, effected through an association of collectivism with totalitarianism, helps the powerful elite to maintain people's illusion that they are all individuals (Straume, 2011), while obscuring the real issue of reduced availability of care for those who need it (Greener, 2015). The drive to privatise public services promoted by the patient-choice policy may also express a desirable but unattainable fantasy that fulfils other, less obvious, functions. Unrealistic policies that are bound to fail may be tapping into an escapist desire to avert the human predicament of disease and dying (Fotaki, 2010a) or the fear of uncertainty following rapid change. To understand why this happens, we must move beyond simplistic economic frames that point to self-interest as a rational decision-making process and the sole driver of human behaviour. Next, I draw on psychosocial theory inspired by psychoanalysis to explain the failures of marketised welfare in public policy.

## Which choice? Psychoanalysis of market failure in public policy

Susan Long (1999) draws on psychoanalysis to explain how practices emerging from consumerism and economic rationalism often act as unconscious organisational and social defences against anxieties. These defences both arise from and are used against uncertainties and changes occurring in a world increasingly dominated by global markets where the customer is 'sovereign'. Long explicitly argues that the discourse of consumerism encourages, and is encouraged by, economic rationales promoting behaviours that are marked by the conflation of many complex societal roles into the simpler category of 'customer'. This absolute dominance of market-type consumerism in public life, which is now proclaimed to be the only viable alternative, I term 'the tyranny of the customer', after Susan Long (1999). The social cost of shifting to individualised consumerism is a corrupt way of thinking in which any sense of greater good is sacrificed to fulfilling individual wants. This perverse state of mind characterises individuals and groups in corporate life (Long, 2008), encouraging various organisational misdemeanours.

Paul Hoggett (2010), following Long's ideas, suggests that recent social changes have created a perverse culture in all contemporary capitalist societies. These changes prioritise individual wants at the expense of the general good and instrumentality in relationships with others, while turning a blind eye to, and enlisting accomplices in, wrongdoing. This, Hoggett suggests, causes human suffering on an everyday basis for many professional and non-professional workers in the public and voluntary sectors, and increasingly in the private sector (Hoggett, 2010). For example, the ritualistic drive for accountability and the rhetoric of customer empowerment introduce perverse incentives for health professionals to manage their emotions in accordance with commercial requirements or unrealistic performance targets set by the organisation (Rizq, 2013). In such an environment, Rizq suggests, self-preservation and survival often cause health professionals to detach from their patients, to avoid emotional burnout. Healthcare organisations are particularly prone to these dynamics, as they are tasked with averting essential conditions of the human predicament, such as disease, decay and the threat of extinction, giving rise to powerful unconscious emotions among organisational members centred around survival and the necessity to defend themselves against this threat.

Psychoanalytic approaches are also useful for highlighting and explaining how policy-makers, organisations and their members may commit themselves to evidently failing courses of action, sometimes to the extent of 'throwing good money after bad'. Next, I focus on the social fantasies that often underpin apparently rational policy initiatives, in order to highlight the powerful emotions that emerge when they fail. I also draw on the psychodynamic concept of socially-structured organisational defences and the idea of organisational blind spots to analyse examples of escalating commitment to failing public service causes in mental health settings in the UK (Fotaki & Hyde, 2015).

## Failing policies and escalation of commitment in mental healthcare: a psychodynamic explanation

Reasons for maintaining commitment to failing strategies have been investigated by organisational researchers. Their explanations tend to focus on cognitive aspects of decisions that neglect emotions, although some studies have reported that individuals' escalation tendencies are a function of negative affect (Wong, Yik & Kwong, 2006). In such cases, it is argued, a cycle of escalating commitment to a failing strategy is produced, with more resources being dedicated in the hope of recouping previous losses, contrary to the 'objective facts of the situation' (Staw & Ross, 1986). The cognitive-positivist approach remains unchallenged when emotions are seen to be rational and predictable manifestations of organisational problems falling neatly into measurable categories, but they cannot on their own explain continued commitment to failing strategies.

Various alternative approaches have been used to theorise this phenomenon, following Isobel Menzies Lyth's work on dysfunctional organisational defences among nursing staff in the late 1950s (Menzies Lyth, 1960). Writing from a psychodynamic perspective, Fotaki and Hyde (2015) describe 'organisational blind spots' involving denial of a painful reality (in this case, failing health policies), which are institutionalised by mechanisms such as rituals, routines and storytelling. They argue that, in order to maintain their commitment to a failing course of action, individuals engage in 'splitting' as a defence against painful emotions and to shift the blame for potential failure. This involves polarising negative and positive feelings toward something or somebody else, thereby reducing the contradictory and complex emotions it or they arouse. Such an unconscious engagement enables individuals to project unwanted aspects of a situation onto others, and thereby avoid having to confront painful emotions that would be aroused by examining their own role in the failure (Fotaki & Hyde, 2015). In this way, splitting and blaming are used to maintain a fantasy that unrealistic policy objectives can be achieved, despite mounting evidence to the contrary. While these mechanisms provide temporary relief, they may be damaging, insofar as problems are not resolved, failing strategies continue to be pursued and opportunities for learning are absent. Furthermore, at a societal level, citizens' projection of their aspirations onto public institutions (Hoggett, 2006) adds to pressures to pursue unworkable policies. The fact that public organisations serve as 'a receptacle for containing social anxieties' (Hoggett, 2006: 177) makes it uncomfortable for organisational actors openly to acknowledge failure.

Healthcare settings provide fertile grounds for examining social defences against anxiety (eg. Bott, 1976; Menzies Lyth, 1960), specifically in the context of mental healthcare. Many authors describe how psychic mechanisms involving splitting, denial and projection are used to protect against painful emotions in mental healthcare settings (Bott-Spillius, 1990; Hyde & Davies, 2004). Historically, the desirability of containing and segregating 'mad' individuals (Prior, 1988) from the rest of society meant that 'asylums' were set in large grounds, removed from major centres of population. The aim was to rehabilitate and 'cure' patients in a caring environment, yet patients were detained against their will in a regime that applied pressure to comply with therapeutic interventions. Staff working in mental health facilities are hence often described as being torn between societal expectations to manage and contain madness and loyalty to patients (Bott, 1976; Willshire, 1999).

Furthermore, a fear of madness on the part of staff (Bott, 1976) results in a mechanistic quality to care-taking. This puts emotional distance between the staff and the patients, 'whose personalities are in the process of obliteration' (Hinshelwood, 1987: 210) in a system that seeks to radically change them. Despite conscious efforts to improve patients' quality of life, at a subconscious level these are defeated by suspicion of anything that might be viewed as stimulating and enlivening (Hinshelwood, 1987). In a context of heavy workloads, staff often resort to blaming (of patients, other stakeholders and factors such as inadequate resources) to avoid confronting painful realities (Hyde & Davies, 2003; Willshire, 1999).

The shift to a market ethos in mental health services, often combined with implementing excessive assessments aimed at meeting targets to reduce entitlement or do more with fewer resources, exacerbates these phenomena still further. Organisational research shows that, when explicit targets are coupled with strong incentives (and/or disincentives), people will strive to meet them, often even at the expense of common sense (Schwartz, 1987). However, from a psychodynamic perspective, it is important to understand the unconscious emotional processes involved in identifying with an organisational ideal (Schwartz, 1987) that is part of individuals' professional identity, even when the two are conflicting, as is often the case when efficiency at any cost is promoted in the marketised public health services. The drive to demonstrate better performance with fewer resources could then lead to intolerable pressure on staff, causing them to compromise their professional standards of care.

Among many examples is the Mid-Staffordshire NHS Foundation Trust's failures in rudimentary aspects of care, which involved leaving elderly patients starved, soiled and in pain. Demonstrating 'financial health' and having sufficient staff to provide adequate patient care were necessary preconditions for the hospital to achieve foundation trust status, but arguably the patients themselves were ultimately seen as 'getting in the way' of achieving the hospital's strategic goals (Fotaki, 2013). The *Francis Report* on the inquiry into the care failures provides a damning indictment of such an approach:

> While the system as a whole appeared to pay lip service to the need
> not to compromise services and their quality, it is remarkable how
> little attention was paid to the potential impact of proposed savings on
> quality and safety. (Francis, 2013: 44)

In another study of UK public mental health services, which had recently been subject to New Public Management restructuring, Rizq (2013) explores how contemporary preoccupations with regulation, surveillance and governance in such institutions may be characterised as symbolic attempts to gain mastery over feelings unconsciously deemed to be abject reminders of the body. She suggests that the mentally ill or psychologically distressed individual is objectified to help us define our own normality and subjectivity through comparison with a radical or 'monstrous' other, and that this is particularly prevalent in the context of marketised, efficiency-driven services. Faced with relentless pressure to produce quick outcomes, staff caring for mentally ill people find it particularly difficult to contain personal feelings of unease and vulnerability when working with those who unconsciously remind them of their own fragmentation and insufficiency (Shildrick, 2002, quoted in Rizq, 2013). 'Doing something' becomes the dominant response to intractable problems (Fotaki & Hyde, 2015), as it helps professionals to avoid emotional trauma (Carr, 1999). Feelings of being powerful, idealisation and hyperactivity may also be employed to defend against the painful emotions, such as sadness and ambivalence, that the organisational context threatens to arouse (Klein, 1940). Only when it becomes too difficult to deny the painful reality are unworkable policies abandoned (Fotaki & Hyde, 2015).

Strategies that enable tolerance of existential anxiety in a way that forms the basis for learning and development in psychodynamic thinking (Bion, 1967) are likely to be a key part of responding to failure if dysfunctional behaviours and their consequences are to be avoided. However, defence mechanisms that help individuals and groups to cope with anxieties 'tend towards a regressive retreat from a changing reality' (Brown & Starkey, 2000), making such learning and development difficult. They also help to sustain a fantasy of future fulfilment and provide a coping mechanism under challenging circumstances. At the same time, although attachment to an object of fantasy (such as the idea of choice) is life-sustaining, the object is simultaneously a threat to individual and organisational flourishing. I now turn to offering an explanation why this might be so.

## The fantasy of invincibility and disavowal of care in neoliberalism

Fantasy is a term used in psychoanalysis to describe the developmental process in infants' state of mind denoting a projection of our unconscious wishes and desires onto the outside world. Originating with Freud, it has been taken up in Melanie Klein's development of object relations theory and Jacques Lacan's re-reading of Freud's core ideas through the prism of Saussurean linguistics (see Fotaki, 2010b). This psychoanalytic concept has proved valuable in many areas of organisation studies, providing a fruitful avenue for exploring how affective attachments to a desired future influence people's actions. The various permutations of this idea include the notion of ideological fantasy (Gunder, 2010), and the liberating potential of fantasy when linked to imagination (Komporozos-Athanasiou & Fotaki, 2015).

Psychoanalytic theory helps us to consider the role of fantasy in policy-making, and how specific policies such as patient choice are legitimised by politicians and their constituencies. It also stresses the importance of dreams, desires and emotions in policy, politics and social life more generally, in terms of how we affect others and are affected by them. Aspirational policies often mirror unconscious societal desires and dreams. In healthcare, this is manifested as counteracting death by curing all disease (Obholzer, 1994). In the same way, patient choice taps into an illusory desire to free ourselves from the physical bounds of the human predicament, while ignoring the limitations of consumerist patient choice and its potentially conflicting objective of care as intrinsic to health service provision (Mol, 2008), as well as the resource implications involved in making a reality freedom of choice for all. Thus, the impossible tasks that policies often articulate conceal unconscious strife and desires, rather than conveying true aims and objectives that might realistically be pursued. Citizens tacitly support these policies by disowning their own subjectivity (eg. their existential anxieties) and projecting it onto the public institutions (Hoggett, 2006) tasked with containing such ambivalence. This results in contradictions in the policy-making process because, in addition to their declared, normative objectives, public policies also express these tensions and fears (Fotaki, 2010a).

The market shift introduced into health services rejects this complex reality, while promoting a fantasy that competition and choice are neutral non-ideological tools of policy-making that have no distributional consequences. Reliance on the much-touted 'invisible hand' of the market purposely ignores the embodied, relational and affective aspects of healthcare. Instead, it promotes an image of independent and invincible, atomised service users who are both disembodied and socially disembedded in their pursuit of maximising utility through choice, as if people cared more about abstract utility than relations with other people. In reality, the opposite is true: care and relationality are what make us human. We cannot understand ourselves as political and social beings without reverting to our relational attachments. In elaborating why and how relatedness and relationality are the foundation of subjectivity and of our very existence, I now turn briefly to the work of Judith Butler and the feminist thinking of Bracha Ettinger and Maria Puig de la Bellacasa. I foreground some of their ideas to argue for the importance of care as an organising principle in public policy and the foundation of being in the social world more generally.

## Toward developing care-based public policy

The psychoanalytic conception of human development may help us understand why relationality gives meaning to our individual experiences and transforms us into social beings. According to Freud, necessity alone would be insufficient to hold groups and communities together (Gabriel, 1999). In the Freudian ontology, love (or Eros), which is synonymous with the life drive, is essential for humans to survive, grow and flourish. Although Freud distinguishes between different kinds of love, social life depends on individuals' ability to sublimate their sexual instincts and use them to bond within successively larger communal groupings (Freud, 1920/1956).

Jacques Lacan, who has re-read Freud's work through a linguistic prism, adds a different iteration to his theory by elucidating why we do not exist except in relation to an important other. People who care about us early in life and with whom we form libidinal ties are the literal others; social institutions and symbolic values onto which we transfer our affect are the big Other, standing for a given symbolic order (Lacan, 2006). It is in relation to literal (loved ones) and symbolic (community, nation etc) others that we strive to remake the world that surrounds us when we engage in various social and political activities.

Judith Butler, a feminist post-structuralist philosopher, draws on the key Lacanian idea of the individual's desire for recognition in the symbolic order (via Hegel) to explain how our own precarity binds us to others. For Butler, the existence of the other is a pre-condition for our own literal and symbolic survivability:

> If I seek to preserve your life, it is not only because I seek to preserve
> my own, but because who 'I' am is nothing without your life, and life
> itself has to be rethought as this complex, passionate, antagonistic, and
> necessary set of relations to others. (Butler, 2009: 44)

Butler's understanding of the human as a relational social being who craves recognition by others allows us to appreciate the role of social norms in the subject's formation. Her reframing of subjectivity in relational terms also has important implications for understanding and rethinking developments in public policy under neoliberalism, offering ways to incorporate these into public policy (Fotaki, 2017). It does so by urging us to make explicit the role of governments in how people understand, treat and relate to one another and why public policies must emerge from a recognition that all our lives are precarious and that we all depend on society for survival.

This may help us understand the utter failure of consumerist patient choice policies that attempt to replace caring relationships with an individualised, one-off, market-type exchange. However, relational care is a socially-conditioned and dynamic process negating the core premise of patient choice policy in health services provision – that patients are individualistically-minded consumers who are allegedly insatiable and driven predominantly by the need to increase their own benefit. It also brings the issue of freedom of choice and control over our own decisions into an entirely different perspective from that proclaimed by market liberals – compelling us to reconsider them in relation to the other and allowing us to consider how we are all inextricably linked to others and to all lives because our own lives are inevitably precarious (Butler, 2004). Our shared vulnerability therefore obliges us to assign irreducible value to human lives. Overall, it creates an opportunity to rethink the role of public policy in terms of care and the notion of care as the foundation of policy.

The work of psychoanalyst feminist philosopher Bracha Ettinger and feminist sociologist Maria Puig de la Bellacasa (2012) provides us with theoretical frameworks for the ontology of care. Ettinger's major ideas of trans-subjectivity and the matrixial borderspace (which is both symbolic and material) imply an absence of separateness of the subject from the other (Kenny & Fotaki, 2015). Matrixial trans-subjectivity denotes that 'I' is always inextricably linked to the unknown 'non-I' or the Other/(m)other that co-emerges through the process of cohabitation in the womb. The subject is therefore always a partial subject (comprising the symbolic and the material remnant of the mother and that of the baby that cohabited with her). Such conceived subjectivity is always an emerging one, co-constituted by the 'I and unknown non-I', and characterised by the notion of an encounter rather than a lack or split:

> In the matrixial feminine, however, this alternative does not arise
> from the absolute Other (as it does for Lévinas or Lacan) but from
> borderlinking with the Other. (Ettinger, 2006: 85)

Ettinger's idea of the subject co-emerging through an encounter with an unknown other presents us with a compelling ethical proposition that connects Levinasian responsibility for the other with the feminist thought of the other defined as 'becoming together'. A relational reconsideration of subjectivity *vis-à-vis* the other has implications for care. Caring and relating thus share conceptual and ontological resonance (Puig de la Bellacasa, 2012). Puig de la Bellacasa, a sociologist, is even more specific on this point: for her, everything we do involves care, 'for not only do relations involve care, care is itself relational'. She continues:

> In worlds made of heterogeneous interdependent forms and processes
> of life and matter, to care about something, or for somebody, is
> inevitably to create relation. (Puig de la Bellacasa, 2012: 198)

Because care is everything we do and is also a way of knowing, her premise has ontological rather than moral groundings. But how can this care be understood, defined and re-made to underpin public policies?

I suggest that two things are required to achieve this. The first involves being in relation with the other through Eros, with or without the 'irreducible other' necessarily having to be a direct recipient of our compassion. It simply means that all humans have an inalienable right to livable lives and to have their lives protected, irrespective of whether or not we are able to identify with them. Attaching an equivalent value to all human lives is essential for our own survivability. Hence, it is only through developing this fundamental relationality to others that we gain a sense of value and significance, because we do not exist without the other, literally and metaphorically.

The second concerns the creation of new imaginary significations that are at present foreclosed and out of imaginary range (Straume, 2011) because the idea of individualised consumers as the only viable and desirable state to which health service provision should aspire is being promoted. Such an ideological position, which essentially excludes all other possibilities associated with any form of collective action, is enforced by promoting affective attachments to the one and only available representation. That is, consumerist choice that is unproblematically equated with individual freedom becomes the only value worth having and aspiring to in public health services. Overcoming this requires a leap of imagination into 'the future… [that] is the time in which we might not be, and yet we must imagine we will have been' (Rose, 1995: 126) if we are to use these insights to reframe public policy in terms of care. In other words, drawing on the economist views in support of the philosopher's ideas: 'The difficulty lies, not in the new ideas, but escaping from the old ones, which ramify, for those brought up as most of us have been, into every corner of our minds' (Keynes, 1936). Identifying with those whose lives are more fragile and precarious than our own (eg. elderly patients, people who are mentally ill or terminally ill) helps us to imagine the future that might have been or 'will have been'.

Here, psychoanalysis may be of help if we accept that the unconscious role of policy is to contain our survival-related anxieties. As I have argued above, the shift to the market in public policy redefines our engagement with fundamental 'facts of life' such as disease and ageing. It also reframes the terms and conditions of our protection from being overwhelmed by these facts of life. However, the rejection of care under competition and choice has powerful implications. The seductive idea of choice brings the illusion of an absolute control (and responsibility) back to the individual patient. This ideological project serves the neoliberal purpose of removing any obligation to provide support and care on the part of society. Psychoanalytically speaking, neoliberalism encourages and gives moral licence to act out the death drive in the social arena, making us infinitely sentimental about ourselves but methodically ruthless toward others (Evans, 2013). As I have argued elsewhere (Fotaki, 2017), this implies an absence of love for the (precarious) other in organised forms of life that lies at the root of many political and social problems. Under neoliberalism, we are witnessing a rapid increase of various categories of undeserving 'others', such as the new poor, refugees and migrants in affluent Western societies. The disregarding of the lives of 'others' as equivalent enables conspicuous and compulsive consumerism to co-exist with abject poverty. This explains why 'othering' is necessary to allow us to ignore the inevitable facts of life when these do not concern us directly. This allows entire groups of people to be treated instrumentally and disposed of in distant parts of the world. Excluded others are seen as absolute 'monstrous others', with no human rights worth protecting. Butler (2009) illustrates this with the case of civilian casualties in the Iraq and Afghanistan wars, who were labelled as collateral damage rather than as men, women and children.

The concept of relational care offers a way for reconsidering public policies through the prism of our shared precariousness as sentient human beings, shared also with all other forms of life and non-sentient matter, if we are not to reject the life-affirming Eros and be devoured by the competitive death drive of the market. Rethinking public policies on care as including *everything that we do* to maintain, continue and repair "our world" so that we can live in it as well as possible' (Puig de la Bellacasa, 2012: 198, emphasis added) is essential if we are to stop throwing good money after bad. It is even more essential for our survival.

## References

Allmark P (2006). Choosing health and the inner citadel. *Journal of Medical Ethics 32*: 3–6.

Barnes M (1999). Users as citizens: collective action and the local governance of welfare. *Social Policy and Administration 33*(1): 73–90.

Bell D (2013). *Mental Illness and its Treatment Today*. CHPI report. London: Centre for Health and the Public interest. https://chpi.org.uk/wp-content/uploads/2013/12/David-Bell-analysis-Mental-illness-and-its-treatment-today.pdf (accessed 20 February 2019).

Bevan A (1952). *In Place of Fear*. Whitefish, MT: Kessinger Publishing.

Bion W (1967). *Second Thoughts*. London: Heinemann.

Bott E (1976). Hospitals and society. *British Journal of Medical Psychology 49*: 97–140.

Bott-Spillius E (1990). Asylum and society. In: Trist E, Murray H (eds). *The Social Engagement of Social Science, Volume 1*. London: Free Association Books (pp586–614).

Boyce T, Dixon A, Fasolo B, Reustkaja E (2010). *Choosing a High-Quality Hospital: the role of nudges, scorecard design and information*. London: The King's Fund.

Brown A, Starkey K (2000). Organizational identity and learning: a psychodynamic perspective. *Academy of Management Review 25*(1): 102–120.

Burge P, Devlin N, Appleby J, Rohr C, Grant J (2005). *London Patient Choice Project Evaluation: a model of patients' choices of hospital from stated and revealed preference choice data*. Cambridge: RAND Europe.

Butler J (2009). *The Frames of War: when is life grievable?* London: Verso.

Butler J (2004). *Precarious Life: the power of mourning and violence*. London: Verso.

Cacace M, Nolte E (2011). Healthcare services: strategy, direction and delivery. In: Walshe W, Smith J (eds). *Healthcare Management*. Maidenhead: Open University Press (pp145–168).

Carr A (1999). The psychodynamics of organizational change. *Journal of Managerial Psychology 14*(5): 421–436.

Cooper A, Lousada J (2005). *Borderline Welfare: feeling and fear of feeling in modern welfare*. London: Tavistock Institute.

Dixon A, Appleby J, Robertson R, Burge P, Devlin N, McGee H (2010). *Patient Choice: how patients choose and how providers respond*. London: The King's Fund.

Ettinger BL (2006). *The Matrixial Borderspace (Essays from 1994–1999)*. Minneapolis, MN: University of Minnesota Press.

Evans M (2013). *Love in a time of neoliberalism.* [Blog.] Open Democracy; 6 November. www.opendemocracy.net/transformation/mary-evans/love-in-time-of-neo-liberalism (accessed 2 April 2019).

Ferguson I (2007). Increasing user choice or privatizing risk? The antinomies of personalization. *British Journal of Social Work 37*(3): 387–403.

Fotaki M (2017). Relational ties of love: a psychosocial proposal for ethics of compassionate care in health and public services. *Psychodynamic Practice 23*(2): 181–189.

Fotaki M (2014). Can consumer choice replace trust in the National Health Service in England? Towards developing an affective psychosocial conception of trust in health care. *Sociology of Health & Illness 36*(8): 1276–1294.

Fotaki M (2013). *On compassion, markets and ethics of care.* [Blog.] Centre for Health and the Public Interest. https://chpi.org.uk/blog/on-compassion-markets-and-ethics-of-care (accessed 20 February 2019).

Fotaki M (2011). Towards developing new partnerships in public services: users as consumers, citizens and/or co-producers driving improvements in health and social care in the UK and Sweden. *Public Administration 89*(3): 933–955.

Fotaki M (2010a). Equity and choice in health care: can they go hand in hand? Theory and evidence. *Sociology of Health & Illness 32*(6): 898–913.

Fotaki M (2010b). Why do public policies fail so often? Exploring health policy-making as an imaginary and symbolic construction. *Organization 17*(6): 703–720.

Fotaki M (2006). Choice is yours: a psychodynamic exploration of health policy making and its consequences for the English National Health Service. *Human Relations 59*(12): 1711–1744.

Fotaki M, Boyd A (2005). From plan to market: a comparison of health and old age care policies in the UK and Sweden. *Public Money & Management 25*(4): 237–243.

Fotaki M, Harding N (2018). *Gender and the Organization: women at work in the 21st century.* London: Routledge.

Fotaki M, Hyde P (2015). Organizational blind spots: splitting, blame and idealization in the National Health Service. *Human Relations 68*(3): 441–462.

Fotaki M, Roland M, Boyd A, McDonald R, Scheaff R, Smith L (2008). What benefits will choice bring to patients? Literature review and assessment of implications. *Journal of Health Services Research & Policy 13*(3): 178–184.

Francis R (2013). *Report of the Mid Staffordshire NHS Foundation Trust Public Inquiry.* London: The Stationery Office.

Freud S (1920/1955). Beyond the pleasure principle. In: Freud S. *Complete Psychological Works of Sigmund Freud, Volume 18.* London: Hogarth Press.

Froggett L (2002). *Love, Hate and Welfare: psychosocial approaches to policy and practice.* Bristol: Policy Press.

Gabriel Y (1999). *Organizations in Depth: the psychoanalysis of organizations.* London: Sage.

Giddens A (1990). *The Consequences of Modernity.* Cambridge: Polity Press.

Glendinning C (2008). Increasing choice and control for older and disabled people: a critical review of new developments in England. *Social Policy & Administration 42*(5): 451–469.

Glennerster H, Le Grand J (1995). The development of quasi-markets in welfare provision in the United Kingdom. *International Journal of Health Services 25*: 203–218.

Greener I (2015). Wolves and big yellow taxis: how would we know if the NHS is at death's door? *International Journal of Health Policy Management 14*(4): 687–689.

Gunder M (2010). Planning as the ideology of (neo-liberal) space. *Planning Theory 9*(4): 298–314.

Haiven M (2014). *Culture of Financialization: fictitious capital in popular culture and everyday life*. London: Palgrave Macmillan.

Hinshelwood R (1987). The psychotherapist's role in a large psychiatric institution. *Psychoanalytic Psychotherapy 2*(3): 207–215.

Hoggett P (2010). Government and the perverse social defence. *British Journal of Psychotherapy 26*(2): 201–212.

Hoggett P (2006). Conflict, ambivalence, and the contested purpose of public organizations. *Human Relations 59*(2): 175–194.

Hughes B, McKie L, Hopkins D, Watson N (2005). Love's labours lost? Feminism, the disabled people's movement and an ethic of care. *Sociology 39*(2): 259–275.

Hyde P, Davies HTO (2004). Service design, culture and performance: collusion and coproduction in health care. *Human Relations 57*(11): 1407–1426.

Kahneman D, Tversky A (1979). Prospect theory: an analysis of decision under risk. *Econometrica 47*(2): 263–291.

Kenny K, Fotaki M (2015). From gendered organizations to compassionate borderspaces: reading corporeal ethics with Bracha Ettinger. *Organization 22*(2): 183–199.

Keynes J (1936/1973). *Collected Writings of John Maynard Keynes, Volume 7: the general theory of employment, interest and money* (2nd ed). Cambridge: Cambridge University Press.

Klein M (1940). Mourning and its relation to manic-depressive states. *International Journal of Psychoanalysis 21*: 125–153.

Komporozos-Athanasiou A, Fotaki M (2015). A theory of imagination for organization studies using the work of Cornelius Castoriadis. *Organization Studies 36*(3): 321–342.

Krachler N, Greer I (2015). When does marketisation lead to privatisation? Profit-making in English health services after the 2012 Health and Social Care Act. *Social Science & Medicine 124*: 215–223.

Lacan J (2006). *Écrits: the first complete translation in English* (Fink B, trans). New York: WW Norton & Co.

Le Grand J (2007). *The Other Invisible Hand*. Princeton, NJ: Princeton University Press.

Leys C (2018). Risks to the NHS when referring to private hospitals. *Health Service Journal*, 7 May. Reprinted as CHPI blog. https://chpi.org.uk/blog/risks-to-the-nhs-when-referring-to-private-hospitals/ (accessed 20 February 2019).

Long S (2008). *The Perverse Organization and its Deadly Sins*. London: Karnac.

Long S (1999). The tyranny of the customer and the cost of consumerism: an analysis using systems and psychoanalytic approaches to groups and society. *Human Relations 52*(6): 723–743.

Lynch K (2006). Neo-liberalism and marketisation: the implications for higher education. *European Educational Research Journal 5*(1):1–17.

Menzies Lyth I (1960). A case-study in the functioning of social systems as a defence against anxiety: a report on a study of the nursing service of a general hospital. *Human Relations 13*: 95–121.

Mol A (2008). *The Logic of Care: health and the problem of patient choice*. London: Routledge.

Money-Kyrle R (1978). The aim of psychoanalysis. In: Money-Kyrle R (ed). *The Collected Papers of Roger Money-Kyrle*. Strathtay: Clunie Press (pp442–449).

Newman J, Barnes M, Sullivan H, Knops A (2004). Public participation and collaborative governance. *Journal of Social Policy 33*(2): 203–223.

Newman J, Glendinning C, Hughes M (2008). Beyond modernisation? Social care and the transformation of welfare governance. *Journal of Social Policy 37*(4): 531–557.

Obholzer A (1994). Managing social anxieties in public sector organizations. In: Obholzer A, Zagier-Roberts V (eds). *The Unconscious at Work: individual and organizational stress in the human services*. London: Routledge (pp170–175).

Prior L (1988). The architecture of the hospital: a study of spatial organisation and medical knowledge. *British Journal of Sociology 39*(1): 86–113.

Puig de la Bellacasa M (2012). 'Nothing comes without its world': thinking with care. *Sociological Review 60*(2): 196–216.

Rizq R (2013). States of abjection. *Organization Studies 34*(9): 1277–1297.

Rogers WA (2006). Feminism and public health ethics. *Journal of Medical Ethics 32*(6): 351–354.

Rose G (1995). *Love's Work: a reckoning with life*. London: Chatto & Windus.

Rudra N (2007). Welfare states in developing countries: unique or universal? *The Journal of Politics 69*(2): 378–396.

Schwartz H (1987). Anti-social actions of committed organizational participants: an existential psychoanalytic perspective. *Organization Studies 8*(4): 327–340.

Schyve P (2007). Language differences as a barrier to quality and safety in health care: the Joint Commission perspective. *Journal of General Internal Medicine 22*(2): 360–361.

Scott-Samuel A, Bambra C, Collins C, Hunter D, McCartney G, Smith K (2014). The impact of Thatcherism on and health and well-being in Britain. *International Journal of Health Services 44*(1): 53–71.

Scourfield P (2007). Social care and the modern citizen: client, consumer, service user, manager and entrepreneur. *British Journal of Social Work 37*(1): 107–122.

Shildrick M (2002). *Embodying the Monster*. London: Sage.

Staw BM, Ross J (1986). Understanding behavior in escalating situations. *Science 246*(4927): 216–220.

Straume I (2011). The political imaginary of global capitalism. In: Straume I, Humphreys J (eds). *Depoliticization: the political imaginary of global capitalism*. Malmo: NSU (pp27–50).

Taylor D (2011). Wellbeing and welfare: a psychosocial analysis of being well and doing well enough. *Journal of Social Policy 40*(4): 777–794.

Walpole S (2017). *NHS hospital subsidies to private hospitals*. [Blog.] Centre for Health and the Public Interest. https://chpi.org.uk/blog/nhs-hospital-subsidies-private-hospitals/ (accessed 20 February 2019).

Willshire L (1999). Psychiatric services: organizing impossibility. *Human Relations 52*(6): 775–803.

Wong KFE, Yik M, Kwong JYY (2006). Understanding the emotional aspects of escalation of commitment: the role of negative affect. *Journal of Applied Psychology 91*(2): 282–297.

# Chapter 4

# Positive affect as coercive strategy: conditionality, activation and the role of psychology in UK government workfare programmes[1]

## Lynne Friedli and Robert Stearn

*We want to acknowledge the complex developments that have taken place since 2013–15, when this chapter was originally researched and written. Many of the forms of coercion that we discuss have intensified since then or taken on new shapes. These have been documented and analysed in a wealth of recent research, while political organising against psychological coercion in workplaces and throughout the social security system is ongoing. Taking adequate account of these changes would be – indeed, has been – the task of several new papers.[2] We have decided to let the chapter stand as a record of a specific moment in the history of coerced labour, but we ask that readers bear the original date of publication (2015) in mind.*

---

1. This chapter was first published as Friedli L, Stearn R (2015). Positive affect as coercive strategy: conditionality, activation and the role of psychology in UK government workfare programmes. *Medical Humanities 41*: 40–47 and is republished here by CC BY 4.0 license (see: http://creativecommons.org/licenses/by/4.0/).

2. See, for notable examples: Burnett, 2017; Cooper & Whyte, 2017; Duffy & Pupo, 2018; Introna & Casagrande, 2019; Recovery in the Bin, 2019; Southwood, 2019; Taylor, 2018.

Negativity enacts the dissent without which politics disappears. Negativity, in this sense, is inseparable from the struggles of subordinated persons to resist the social conditions of their devaluation. (Berlant & Edelman, 2014: xii)

Three people start today on this 'work experience'. They are to help us for up to 30 hours a week for eight weeks over the Christmas period. I am terrified by the idea that head office think they don't need to pay their staff. I myself am on part-time minimum wage and if they can have workers for free now, what is to stop them making my position redundant and using job centre people to run the store at no cost to themselves (Shoezone employee, November 2012). (Clark, 2013)

The cajoling of individuals into a positive affect and 'motivated' stance with regard to their own subordination. (Ferraro, 2014)

This paper considers the role of psychology in formulating, gaining consent for and delivering neoliberal welfare reform, and the ethical and political issues this raises. It focuses on the coercive uses of psychology in UK government workfare programmes: as an explanation for unemployment (people are unemployed because they have the wrong attitude or outlook) and as a means to achieve employability or 'job readiness' (possessing work-appropriate attitudes and beliefs). The discourse of psychological deficit has become an established feature of the UK policy literature on unemployment and social security and informs the growth of 'psychological conditionality'– the requirement to demonstrate certain attitudes or attributes in order to receive benefits or other support, notably food (Community Shop, 2014).[3] In addition, positive affect is routinely imposed in workfare programmes via the content of mandatory training courses and through job centre or contractor 'messaging': for example, motivational tweets or daily positive emails to claimants (Friedli & Stearn, 2013).

The role of workfare in regulating labour through enforcing low-paid, insecure work – 'creating workers for jobs that nobody wants' – has been widely debated, frequently in connection with increased welfare conditionality (Stewart & Wright, 2014). This literature notes that eligibility

---

3. For example, eligibility to receive cheap food from community shops ('inspiring motivation and confidence in our members') requires beneficiaries to be motivated to make positive change in their lives and to sign up to a personal and professional development programme, the 'success plan' (Community Shop, 2014).

for various benefits is now dependent on unemployed and underemployed people carrying out an expanding range of job search, training and work preparation activities, as well as mandatory unpaid labour (Community Shop, 2014; Deeming, 2014). Our focus on workfare schemes and interventions targeting unemployed people's attitudes is also indebted to the body of feminist and Marxist critical work on emotional and affective labour (Hochschild, 1983; Lazzarato, 1996). However, the concerns of this literature – the management and suppression of feeling in service work and the hire of subjectivity in cognitive and affective labours; the constitutive, personality-forming effects of both – differ from ours (Weeks, 2007). The personality set to work is not the same as the personality seeking employment. What the job centre requires is a good but not particular attitude to work in the abstract and a capacity for adaptability that has no object. As a jobseeker, you are required to accept that what differentiates you, the failed and undeserving jobseeker, from other, more deserving and successful jobseekers is a set of attitudes and emotional orientations. The aim is not a job, but the generic skill, attribute or disposition of employability (Moore, 2012). Focusing on this aspect of governance, there has also been extensive critical attention paid to 'the psyche as a site of power and object of knowledge' (Jones, Pykett & Whitehead, 2013a: iii), and, under the rubric of the government of the self (Dean, 1995, 2002), to the role of strengths-based discourse in the formation of systems of discipline and control and the formulation of active welfare subjectivities (Dwyer, 2004; Wright, 2014).

However, there has been a marked silence about the use and misuse of psychology in public policy on many fronts: especially, the role of psychological institutions and professions in workfare and in the emerging employment services industry, and the coercive and punitive nature of many psycho-policy interventions. The voices of claimants and the disadvantaged and excluded populations who are the primary targets of these enforced programmes are little heard. So, this paper is also an effort to challenge that silence: we aim to stimulate more critical reflection on the relationship of medical humanities to psychology and the wider 'wellbeing' field, and to generate greater debate about professional accountability for these developments.[4] We draw on personal testimonies of people experiencing

---

4. Medical humanities is an emerging field. Some of the central themes of enquiry relevant to our concern with the use of psychology to discipline citizens are explored through the work of the Institute (formerly Centre) for Medical Humanities in Durham. See www.dur.ac.uk/imh (accessed 5 February 2019).

workfare,[5] UK policy and document analysis, and social media records of the activity of campaigns opposed to workfare.

## Conditionality

In the last three decades, welfare reforms in many rich democratic states have led to increased emphasis on the conditionality of social security payments and the 'activation' of their recipients, avowedly to avert or correct ethical and psychological 'dependency' and other forms of debility, depression and etiolated work ethic (Jones, Pykett & Whitehead, 2013a; Dean, 1995; Wright, 2014; Walters, 2000; Cole, 2008), which are widely thought to be both symptom and cause of unemployment (Webster, 2005). Failure to meet conditions placed on eligibility for benefits is punished directly by benefit sanctions (the part or total cessation of social security payments for a given period of time) (Department for Work and Pensions, 2012), as well as indirectly by compulsory 'support' in the form of workfare, 'skills training', psychological referral or psychometric testing. The conditions are diverse in kind as well as wide-ranging: from age and residence criteria, or restrictions on numbers of (paid) hours worked per week, to possession of certain levels of qualifications and the capacity to demonstrate positive opinions on employment (Koksal, 2012; Holehouse, 2014; Ingeus, 2010a). The expansion of conditionality in this way is linked to the continually increasing rate at which Jobseeker's Allowance (JSA) and Employment and Support Allowance claimants are sanctioned (the three months to September 2013 saw JSA claimants sanctioned at a rate of 6% of claimants per month, the highest since the introduction of JSA in 1996 (Webster, 2014)). Failure to participate in a training or employment scheme is the most frequently occurring 'failure' that results in a sanction. These mandatory interventions

---

5. Social media is a primary source of personal accounts of the experience of psychological coercion. Twitter, Facebook and the comments section of online articles and blog platforms represent some of the few opportunities for claimants to speak out about the content of mandatory training courses, psychological 'referrals', receiving daily 'positive' emails and the prevalence of positive psychology 'messaging' by job centres and welfare-to-work subcontractors. Boycott Workfare also receives personal testimonies via email and the 'name-and-shame' forms submitted to the website (identifying business and charity users of workfare schemes). We deal with these forms of personal document in the course of our activities with Boycott Workfare; they can be made public where permission has been granted from the person involved. We have also sought permission before citing experiences detailed in blogs and other social media accounts. The ephemeral nature of social media, the use of pseudonyms, claimants' fears of sanctions and retribution if identified and the painful nature of many of the experiences described raise a number of difficulties in accessing, collecting and selecting these data. Addressing these challenges is an important future research agenda for the medical humanities and formed part of a project on workfare at the Wellcome Trust (see http://hubbubgroup.org).

designed to 'shift attitudes and beliefs' have become an important element of 'activating' the unemployed and are the focus of this paper (Community Shop, 2014; Jones, Pykett & Whitehead, 2013a; Dwyer, 2004; Wright, 2014). Although payments by the state to people without jobs have been tied to desirable patterns of behaviour since their first institution (Walters, 2000; Cole, 2008; Faubion & Foucault, 2000; Levine-Clark, 2006, 2010; Taylor, 2014), the unemployment policies of reformed welfare states now aim at more complete and intimate behaviour change through coercive mechanisms of greater scope (Jones, Pykett & Whitehead, 2013b).

The reorganisation of welfare in the UK accompanying current moves to replace six working-age benefits with Universal Credit (UC) by 2017 is the latest face of this broader trend (Walters, 2000; Eichhorst & Konle-Seidl, 2008). Under UC, each claimant will be issued with a Claimant Commitment (CC) (which has already replaced the Jobseeker's Agreement for new claimants at many job centres). The CC enables job centre staff to check claimants' behaviour against the range of 'work-related requirements' to which they have committed (Dwyer & Wright, 2014). These requirements are sorted into a tiered system of conditionality. UC furthers the Department for Work and Pensions' (DWP) project of personalised behavioural conditionality (Gillies et al, 2013), of which psychological coercion and governance – imposed in and through workfare – is an integral part. For the first time, under UC these forms of conditionality are extended to claimants also in work (Pennycook & Whittaker, 2012a).

## Workfare

By workfare we mean the 'work-for-your-benefits' schemes in which unemployed people are forced to work for a charity, business, social enterprise, public service or government agency in order to continue to be eligible for benefits. We also include the range of skills-building and motivational workshops that are presented alongside such schemes – as part of a range of activities that unemployed people are obliged to undertake – and schemes that are composed of training courses in tandem with unpaid work (skills conditionality is an example of the former; traineeships and sector-based work academies, the latter). The participation of unemployed people in schemes with training elements is secured by the same means as work placement schemes: through the threat – tacit or explicit, indirect or direct – of sanctions. It is important that they be looked at as a group (and that we adopt a definite but not too narrow definition of workfare), since this is both how they are implemented and how they impact on unemployed people.

In the UK, as in many other Western states, workfare is organised within an employment services sector that extensively contracts out services to for-profit and non-profit organisations (Greer & Symon, 2014). Where UK policy differs is in the commissioning practices of the DWP, which has outsourced the procurement, design and arrangement of employment services and unpaid work placements to a small number of large-scale for-profit companies (Greer, Schulte & Symon, 2014). The job centre refers a claimant to a 'prime' contractor (Ingeus, A4e, G4S, Serco) that provides some services and mandatory forms of assistance and contracts out others to smaller contractors, which arrange unpaid work placements at charities and businesses. Government contracts specify little about the details of the services to be provided: what control there is, government exerts through a tiered system of 'payment by results' (Greer & Symon, 2014; Department for Work and Pensions, 2013, 2014a). The fact that most psycho-compulsion occurs within this 'black box' has important implications, since there is virtually no oversight of the content of such compulsions, no professional accountability and no effective means of appeal against them (Work & Pensions Committee, 2013; Citizen's Advice Bureau, 2014; Webster, 2014).

Workfare is central to normalisation of the idea that harsh sanctions should be used to underwrite certain obligations of citizenship, and to singling out as the paramount obligation the enforcement of work, with no regard to the specific character of that work or to a person's other responsibilities (Dean, 1995, 2002). Workfare furthers the separation of work and livelihood and normalises the idea that certain groups of people are not entitled to payment for their labour and that lengthy periods of unpaid labour (for example, internships or 'volunteering') are a precondition for employment. In this way, it undermines the security, pay and conditions of all workers and non-workers (Shildrick et al, 2012). Moreover, it demands that people assent to the idea that paid work as it is currently organised is the only route to both personal fulfilment and public value and obscures the economic reality of a dual labour market that produces and relies upon the stratification of work and the escalating inequalities in income and quality of working life (Gorz, 1989; Pennycook & Whittaker, 2012b).

## Psycho-compulsion

Psycho-compulsion, defined as the imposition of psychological explanations for unemployment, together with mandatory activities intended to modify beliefs, attitude, disposition or personality, has become a more and more central feature of activating the unemployed, and hence of people's experience of unemployment. There has been little debate about the recruitment of psychology –and, by implication, psychologists – into monitoring, modifying and punishing people who claim social security benefits (Friedli & Stearn, 2013; Cromby & Willis, 2014) or research into the impact of mandatory positive affect on an expanding range of 'unproductive' or failing citizens (Howell & Voronka, 2012): those who are out of work, not working enough, not earning enough and/or failing to seek work with sufficient application.

A number of reports produced for the Cabinet Office under both the previous Labour government and the subsequent Coalition government have drawn centrally upon psychology and behavioural economics for the legitimation and direction of behaviour change policy or 'instrumental behaviourism' (Halpern et al, 2004; Knott, Muers & Aldridge, 2008; Halpern et al, 2010). The mission of the Cabinet's Behavioural Insights Team or 'nudge unit'[6] – 'the application of behavioural science and psychology to public policy' – is a recent statement in this tradition. The psychological sciences in combination with behavioural economics provide both an ostensibly scientific model and the means for a positive self-image for policymakers and practitioners within the welfare-to-work sector. This notion has considerable traction, so that even critics of recent UK government active labour market policies who advocate the abolition of benefit sanctions suggest that, 'in so far as it is desirable to attempt to influence claimants' behaviour [...] this should be done through a scientific approach' (Webster, 2013).

Psychology allied to behavioural economics allows the sector to consolidate its self-conception as an industry in its own right that sets its own standards and regulates itself via the Employment Related Services Association (established 2005)[7] and the Institute of Employability Professionals (launched 2012).[8]

In this setting, psychology (and 'therapy discourse' more generally) coproduces and validates the core mythologies of neoliberalism, while simultaneously undermining and eroding alternative discourses – of solidarity, collectivity and interdependence (Peacock, Bissell & Owen, 2014). It functions not only to reinforce the view that achieving the status of (paid) working citizen is 'the pinnacle of human experience' (Cole, 2008: 29) but also to construct a very specific definition of the attitudes, beliefs and attributes that constitute

---

6. Behavioural Insights Team. See www.bi.team (accessed 5 February 2019).

7. See http://ersa.org.uk/about (accessed 5 February 2019).

8. See www.iemployability.org/index.php?option=com_content&view=article&id=69&Itemid=186 (accessed 5 February 2019).

'employability': the 'right kind of subject' (Walkerdine, 2002); the 'right kind of affect' (Friedli & Stearn, 2013). The roll call of valued characteristics familiar from positive psychology, the wellbeing industry and public health – 'confidence, optimism, self-efficacy, aspiration' – are imposed in and through programmes of mandatory training and job preparation. They also feature centrally in the way in which people receiving benefits frame their own experiences (Shildrick & MacDonald, 2013). The duties of citizenship are expanded to include enforced rational self-governance so that liberal subjects' capabilities, inclinations and desires are in accord with values and expectations that are identified as already given by a civil society centred on the labour market (Dean, 1995, 2002). For example, in Labour MP Graham Allen's 2011 report on early-intervention public health and education policy, 'life readiness' is said to consist in:

> having the social and emotional capability to enter the labour market;
> understanding the importance and the social, health and emotional
> benefits of entering work, the impacts of drug and alcohol misuse,
> crime and domestic and other violence. (Allen, 2011: 9)

These kinds of policies, seeking to model in unemployed people the imperatives of the market, are carried out by means of the market, through those who are paid to 'activate' claimants and those who benefit from their unpaid labour.

## Positive affect

The growth and influence of discourses of positive affect in these and other systems of governance and 'technologies of the self' have been widely observed (Howell & Voronka, 2012; Berlant, 2007, 2011; Jones, Pykett & Whitehead, 2013b; Friedli & Stearn, 2013; Cromby & Willis, 2014). 'Strengths-based discourse' is a significant policy imperative in both health and welfare reform. Positive affect plays an important supporting role in policy preoccupations with how best to manage the intersection of long-term conditions and long-term unemployment, exemplified in the shift from rest cure (signified by the sick note), to work cure (signified by the fit note[9]).

The psychological attributes and dispositions of individuals and communities (the ostensible presence or absence of optimism, aspiration, self-efficacy, conscientiousness, sense of coherence) are being used to account for unemployment (and for a range of other social outcomes, notably health

9. See www.gov.uk/government/collections/fit-note (accessed 5 February 2019).

inequalities) and are promoted via psychological interventions that aim to modify cognitive function or emotional disposition/affect (Friedli, 2014). Signing up for these interventions is an explicit or implicit condition for receiving support. These trends intersect with and are reinforced by the parallel rise in brain science – 'reading social problems through understanding the brain' – which correlates outcomes (crime, addiction, health behaviour, educational attainment) with brain structure (Abi-Rached, 2010; Rose, 2013). Conditions of psychological deficit are both scientifically and medically legitimised. A cheerful disposition, in combination with a thankful heart and highly developed 'executive control', is so widely celebrated in the policy literature that the politics of this reification are rarely questioned (Marteau & Hall, 2013). These developments may help to explain what lies behind the marked decline in solidarity with unemployed citizens and welfare claimants and the heightened stigma in daily life and public discourse experienced by people who are poor (Tyler, 2013). They also tend to preclude acknowledgement of the corporate and charitable sector beneficiaries of workfare and the 'low pay, no pay' economy that workfare supports, or the estimated £25 billion per annum paid in benefits to workers receiving wages below subsistence levels (Shildrick et al, 2013; Birn, 2009).

## Boycott workfare: history of a campaign

While there is considerable evidence of this hardening of public attitudes towards benefit claimants, the value of mandatory unpaid work activity and enforced 'volunteering' is strongly contested. There are numerous campaigning and claimant solidarity groups in the UK and the rest of Europe whose activities are concentrated in this area. One is Boycott Workfare,[10] which evolved through the work of people who have experienced workfare in the UK. Formed in 2010, it is a movement that campaigns against the imposition of forced, unpaid work on several levels: by taking action to expose the involvement of companies and other entities in taking or arranging placements or providing mandatory training, and by acting as a point of information for claimants and other claimants' organisations:

> We expose and take action against companies and organisations
> profiting from workfare; encourage organisations to pledge to boycott it;
> and actively inform people of their rights.[11]

---

10. See www.boycottworkfare.org/about-us (accessed 5 February 2019).

11. See www.boycottworkfare.org/about-us (accessed 5 February 2019).

Informing people of their rights means proposing a model of activity opposed to and subversive of the 'activated' welfare subject.

Undoing the legitimacy conferred on workfare, in part by its association with psychology, is a central concern of the campaign, as is counteracting the variously inflected negative stereotype of unemployed people. The 'naming and shaming' of organisations participating in workfare has led large numbers to withdraw and is a central factor in DWP efforts not to publish names of those involved. For example, the DWP argued (in appealing the Information Commissioner's decision that they must publish the names of companies involved in mandatory work activity) that making this information public 'would have been likely to have led to the collapse of the [...] scheme' (Courts and Tribunals Judiciary, 2013, 2014). Concerns that mandatory placements undermine the meaning of volunteering have also led many voluntary agencies to sign a 'keep volunteering voluntary' agreement, undertaking not to take part in workfare schemes.[12]

## Waiting for a wage

It is important to understand the extent to which activities that until very recently would have been classified as 'work' are now rebranded as 'work preparation' and are hence both unpaid and characterised in terms of 'psychological preparation'. The government's traineeship matching service[13] reveals the very wide range of private sector organisations offering 'unpaid' opportunities – which are seen to enable young people to become 'work ready', an attribute that is essentially about 'motivation' and the 'right attitude' to work. Tasks that would once have provided paid Saturday or holiday jobs for young people are now provided free of charge to major employers, often in the absence of any return, apart from an 'exit interview'. One unpaid traineeship opportunity lists the following tasks:

> Check and top up under bonnet levels on a vehicle; check anti-freeze content and recommend action; check and adjust tyre pressures; fit a standard light vehicle tyre; balance steel and alloy wheels; change oil and filter; replace spark plugs on a 4-cylinder engine; replace an air filter; torque up wheel nuts to the correct settings.[14]

12. See for example www.haltonsthelensvca.org.uk/keep-volunteering-voluntary-help-work (accessed 5 February 2019).

13. Find a traineeship. www.gov.uk/find-traineeship (accessed 5 February 2019).

14. Find a traineeship. www.gov.uk/find-traineeship (accessed 5 February 2019).

There are currently around 50 traineeships on offer in the NHS where, for no pay, you can do:

> administration and reception work; hospitality and catering, service areas, including portering and post; assisting in clinical areas.[15]

One gets little in return for working unpaid four days per week, for 30 hours, for up to six months in any of these rebranded jobs:

> We expect all traineeships to offer a guaranteed interview with the work placement host at the end of the placement. Where possible, the young person should receive a real job interview where a post or apprenticeship has become available. However, we recognise that this will not always be feasible and, in these cases, a formal exit interview with the employer who provided their work placement will help the young person to practice and prepare for future opportunities. (Department for Education & Department for Business, Innovation and Skills, 2013)

Like workfare, traineeships contribute to the separation of work activity from wages. An unemployed person creates value and generates income for everyone except themselves. Recent developments show that 'waiting for a wage' has been extended to job applicants, with some employers requiring applicants to undertake 'voluntary shifts' before receiving a job offer:

> I had interview in May for Events job. They wanted me to work 2 week trial for free! UNPAID! 8.30am/10pm. (Thomas, 2014a)

## The lived experience of workfare

The imposition of psychological explanations for unemployment functions to erase the economic realities of the labour market and authorises the extension of state-sanctioned surveillance to psychological characteristics. Compulsory positive affect and psychological authority are being applied in workfare in order to 1) identify ostensible psychological barriers to gaining employment and to inculcate attributes and attitudes said to increase employability; 2) punish people for non-compliance (through conditionality and benefit sanctions), and 3) legitimise workfare and other coercive labour market measures.

---

15. Find a traineeship. www.gov.uk/find-traineeship (accessed 5 February 2019).

These developments mean that positive psychology is now as significant a feature of conditionality in the lives of those who are poor as going to church once was, and they share a common evangelical language: 'something within the spirit of individuals living within deprived communities that needs to be healed' (Scottish Community Development Centre, 2011). Unfortunately, the compulsions of positive affect are not confined to Sundays.

> I am shy and have difficulty speaking to people and I will not do play acting in front of a group of people I am very uncomfortable with [...] I was told I would be sanctioned if I didn't take part, so I said I would get up, but I am not speaking [...] After that, we had to fill out yet another 'benefits of being assertive' sheet. (Day, 2013a)

The consistent failure of workfare interventions to achieve their stated aim of improving work outcomes – both in the UK and internationally – has resulted in a much greater focus on psychological or 'soft outcomes', said to 'move people closer to work' (Grier, Schulte & Simon, 2014; Department for Work and Pensions, 2013, 2014a; Work and Pensions Committee, 2013; Citizen's Advice Bureau, 2014; Crisp & Fletcher, 2008; Thomas, 2014b). A 2012 evaluation of an ineffective three-stranded scheme, on which the DWP's recent 'Help to Work' three-part programme is based, found that (Portes, 2013; Coote, 2014), while there was no significant difference in job outcomes at the end of the programme, the OCM[16] and CAP[17] trailblazer strands were successful in achieving soft outcomes such as increases in motivation, confidence, job-seeking behaviour and a positive change in attitudes to work. These softer impacts may yet translate into job outcomes and sign off from JSA (Rahim et al, 2012: 4).

'Soft outcomes' disarticulate work and wages by treating a job as something that may be gained by possessing the right attitude to work (an attitude for which one must labour) and work as something to be valued because it evinces and activates the right attitude in the (potential) employee – rather than because it allows one to purchase a living. At the same time, the means by which soft outcomes are regulated (sanctions: for failures in attitude and in compliance with the actions demanded by active labour

---

16. Ongoing Case Management: more intense jobcentre-based surveillance, coupled with a range of mandatory activities.

17. Community Action Plan: a six-month-long workfare placement, coupled with supported job search (identical to the Community Work Placement strand of the current 'Help to Work' scheme).

market measures) link together more closely than ever a person's failure to manifest the right attitude and their inability to afford to purchase a living.

Efforts to achieve these 'soft outcomes' are evident in the course content of mandatory training programmes run by major workfare contractors like A4e and Ingeus and are increasingly apparent in the personal testimonies of claimants:

> I've been claiming Jobseeker's Allowance for about 8 weeks. I haven't sworn or shouted at anyone. I have had 3 advisor interviews already; yesterday my adviser asked me to see their psychologist. I did not consent. I've been told that I shouldn't look into things too deeply ... & that I am asking too many questions.[18]

> The choice was to accept psych eval, or go straight to MWA.[19]

> You've got all these hooks on you... it's your way of being... you need to shift the way you look at it. You've got all this anger and frustration and that's stopping you from getting a job. It comes across in your CV. (Koksal, 2012)

> I duly attended the offices of A4e and (along with 6 other 'customers') was treated to INSPIRE. This turned out to be a session on Neuro Linguistic Programming (NLP) run by an outside company claiming to be 'Master Practitioners in NLP'. I was 'mandated' to attend under threat of loss of benefits and was effectively unable to leave the session because of the same ever present threat. (Gissajob, 2012)

> My 'advisor' said I needed to see a psychologist because I was tearful and anxious after having my JSA cut for 4 weeks despite having a young child to look after by myself. When I said I did not trust anyone who finds it acceptable to starve others as a punishment, he told me that I was paranoid and again, needed to see a psychologist. (Buckner, 2013)

The A4e Engage Module states: 'Students will learn how to develop the right mindset which will appeal to employers' (other elements of this module are assertiveness, confidence, benefits of work, motivation and enhance

---

18. Anonymous email to Boycott Workfare, undated.

19. Anonymous email to Boycott Workfare, undated.

your mood). As Esther McVey, then Minister of State for Employment, announced, jobseekers are expected to take steps to make themselves attractive to employers – 'employers looking to fill vacancies want people who are prepared, enthusiastic and job-ready' (Holehouse, 2014). Willingness to submit to coerced labour becomes an index of the (approved) disposition and beliefs possessed by an unemployed person.

Izzy Koksal, in her blog on the experience of A4e training, describes the impact of being surrounded by motivational quotes, with their persistent emphasis on individual responsibility for unemployment and the perils of negative thinking (Koksal, 2014). A sheet full of affirmations, handed out to participants in the 'confidence-building' workshops that form part of Ingeus' delivery of the Work Programme, include such motivational statements as:

> Go hard, or go home.
>
> My only limitations are the ones I set for myself.
>
> Failure is the path of least persistence.
>
> Success is getting up one more time than you fall down.
>
> It's always too soon to quit.
>
> Nobody ever drowned in sweat.
>
> The sin isn't falling down but staying down.
>
> No one can make you feel inferior without your consent. (Ingeus, 2010a)

People have described feelings of anger, humiliation and depression on receiving daily 'positive' emails from welfare-to-work contractors such as A4e: 'Success is the only option'; 'We're getting there'; 'Smile at life'; 'This can be the greatest, most fulfilling day you've ever known. For that to happen, you have to allow it' (Warren Clark, personal communication, 2013; Void, 2014).

Reflecting on the feedback they received from Learn Direct (a major training provider), following a four-week unpaid placement at the Salvation Army, one person wrote:

> attitude to work... no idea why they rated me poor for this, I was willing to work, I travelled by train every day then walked a long walk from Edinburgh station to the store every single day for 4 weeks!, and done everything asked plus more![20]

---

20. Anonymous email to Edinburgh Coalition Against Poverty, undated.

The person is concerned because deficits in attitude and motivation can and do trigger sanctions. Psycho-coercion of this kind is directly contributing to the escalation of the number of sanctions being applied, forcing people off benefits and plunging growing numbers into poverty (Faubion & Foucault, 2000; Citizen's Advice Bureau, 2014; Webster, 2014; Shildrick et al, 2012; Webster, 2013; Cooper & Dumpleton, 2013; MacInnes, 2013): eligibility for both out-of-work and in-work benefits is contingent not only on certain behaviours but also on possession of positive affect; conditionality is linked to the 'employability' mindset. For example, one of the criteria for being sent on Community Work Placements (unpaid work for 30 hours per week, for 26 weeks) is 'lack of motivation', although this is never defined (Department for Work and Pensions, 2014b: 4).

The messages in the course handout for Ingeus's mandatory 'Healthy Attitudes for Living' course (2010a) take these themes a step further, intended, perhaps, to counter any residual yearnings in the jobseeker for either justice or security and to pre-empt reflection on the social gradient in 'bad things happening':

> Sometimes life's just plain unfair. Bad things happen to the nicest of people. On top of being unfair, life's unpredictable and uncertain a great deal of the time. And really, that's just the way life is [...] If you can accept the cold hard reality of injustice and uncertainty, you're far more likely to bounce back when life slaps you in the face. You're also less likely to be anxious about making decisions and taking risks. But remember, you can still strive to play fair yourself. (Ingeus, 2010a)

This Ingeus module argues that one 'common thinking trap' is 'catastrophising': 'you may exaggerate or magnify the negative aspect of an event'; 'you may view the probability of disaster as great'. One is encouraged to '[recognise] the negative thinking error' and take 'calculated risks' (Ingeus, 2010b). Of course, power over certain catastrophes lies with Ingeus staff, who are responsible for raising a 'compliance doubt' against an unemployed person, the first step towards being sanctioned. In addition to mandatory training informed by positive psychology, claimants may also be subjected to strengths-based interventions, including online psychometric testing – 'failure to comply may result in loss of benefits' (skwalker 1964, 2013). And, as Cromby and Willis have noted (2014), every aspect of the Values in Action 'Inventory of Signature Strengths' test recently imposed on claimants contravened the British Psychological Society's ethical code.

Working on psychological deficits becomes the full-time, unpaid labour of millions of people,[21] which, together with mandatory job search activities, ensures that these days people who are poor have no money, no time – and no place:

> Basically what I'm saying in short is that I feel there is no place in society for a quiet, shy, creative person like me. And now I feel I don't even deserve to call myself creative, because I don't even do that anymore, because I am too depressed. (Day, 2013b)

In another scheme, claimants will undergo interviews to assess whether they have a 'psychological resistance' to work, along with attitude-profiling to judge whether they are 'bewildered, despondent or determined' (Coote, 2014). Those deemed 'less mentally fit' will be subject to more intensive coaching, while those who are 'optimistic' – such as graduates or those who have recently been made redundant – can be placed on less rigorous regimes. This classification system will be used to recruit to a new scheme, obliging those who are long-term unemployed to spend 35 hours a week at a jobcentre.

The context in which positive psychology's motivational techniques are deployed, then, is one structured by a regime of tacit and explicit threat and coercion, in which one can never be sure whether or not a sanction will be tagged to a particular instance of behaviour or attitude. As many first-hand accounts witness, job centres and the premises of welfare-to-work contractors are not neutral settings for interventions or decisions about the relative degree of unemployed people's material hardship, 'willingness to work', 'readiness' for work or 'resistance' to work: they are intensely anxiety-inducing and intimidating locations that bear witness to marked imbalances of power (False Economy, undated; Walsh & Guardian readers, 2014; DWP Unspun, 2014).

What is perhaps more noteworthy than all these developments is the response of the professional body responsible for ethics and accountability of psychology and psychologists. BPS has confined itself to saying that such tests must be administered by experienced users of psychometrics under supervision of a chartered psychologist (Haughton, 2014).

---

21. More than 1.6 million people had joined the Work Programme alone as of June 2014 (Department for Work and Pensions, 2014a).

## Conclusions

[T]he voices of resistance against the abjectifying logics of neo-liberal governmentality are growing louder. (Tyler, 2013: 2)

The participation of psychology and psychologists in the delivery of coercive goals in welfare reform clearly raises ethical questions. As Wright (2014: 2) has observed, 'the active welfare subject is a figure of aspiration, a transformation possible only via coerced self-improvement'. Psychology now plays a central and formative role in stigmatising the 'existence and behaviour of various categories of poor citizens' (Slater, 2013: 9) and in legitimating the measures taken to transform and activate them. Personality, disposition and behaviour are abstracted from context, history and political struggle, obscuring the fact that the distinction between those with appropriate levels of 'optimism' and those without is essentially a class distinction (Rahim et al, 2012).

Mandatory work-related activity and 'supported job searches' involve tasks experienced as humiliating and pointless by jobseekers (Day, 2013a; 2013b): the 'grotesque daily practices of condemnation and disenfranchisement' that contribute to the social abjection of the most socially and economically disadvantaged citizens (Tyler, 2013: 170–1). There is no evidence that work programme psycho-interventions increase the likelihood of gaining paid work that lasts any length of time. In perpetuating notions of psychological failure, they shift attention away from the social patterning of unemployment and from wider trends: market failure, precarity, the rise of in-work poverty, the cost of living crisis and the scale of income inequalities (Shildrick et al, 2012; Pennycook & Whittaker, 2012b). They contribute centrally to the reification of paid work and the concomitant devaluing and discounting of all other activities, contributions, values and commitments. Above all, psychology is implicated in what amounts to a 'substitution of outcomes', where the modification of psychological attributes stands in for delivering actual improvements in household income or increasing the availability of real paid work.

## Resistance

In the reification of positive affect, what is absent is any reference to the contested nature of constructs such as personality and attitude, their ideological underpinnings and the processes through which specific characteristics or attributes acquire both social value and economic reward. In other words, the political nature of these issues is evaded (Friedli, 2014). Psychological fundamentalism – also evident in the burgeoning wellbeing industry – together with the rise of psychological conditionality, has a very direct impact on the lives of people claiming welfare benefits. This impact has barely been documented and highlights the need for deeper research scrutiny and more pressing questions about relationships between psychology and the medical humanities. The 'black boxing' to which we have referred also means that – for both political and methodological reasons – independent research is especially important in tracing and making transparent the confluence between medico-corporate interests and manifold forms of labour market governance.

Even so, these questions are being asked elsewhere, in the emergence of multiple forms of resistance to neoliberal definitions of value and worth and to the erosion of hard-won rights of social citizenship. Workfare has become an important site for satire on the fetishisation of paid work, for struggle over definitions of a meaningful and productive life and for attempts to embrace myriad shades of human experience and human subjectivities, with notable contributions from those whose welfare dependency is most decried (Marteau & Hall, 2013; McRuer, 2006; Duffy, 2010; Friedli, 2012). The disability rights movement has played a central role in challenging the discourse of 'no legitimate dependency' and in using direct action to express solidarity and to forge discourses and practices that can shape positive identities for people claiming social security (Peacock, Bissell & Owen, 2014). As the coercive use of positive affect in workfare demonstrates, there are good reasons to prefer the politics of rights and justice to the discourses of positive psychology.

## Acknowledgements

An early version of this paper was presented at the Critical Medical Humanities Symposium at Durham University (4–5 November 2013) and was published as a blog by the Centre for Medical Humanities at Durham University (see http://centreformedicalhumanities.org/whistle-while-you-work-for-nothing-positive-affect-as-coercive-strategy-the-case-of-workfare/.) A critique of 'psycho-compulsion' also appeared in Friedli L. A response: the ethics of psycho-policy – reflections on the role of psychology in public health and workfare. *Clinical Psychology Forum* 2014; 256: 11–16. This work now contributes to Lynne Friedli's collaboration with Hubbub, an interdisciplinary exploration of rest and its opposites funded by the Wellcome Trust (see: http://hubbubgroup.org/). We would like to acknowledge the work and testimony of Boycott Workfare.

# References

Abi-Rached JM (2010). The birth of the neuromolecular gaze. *History of Human Sciences 23*(1): 11–36. doi:10.1177/0952695109352407

Allen G (2011). *Early Intervention: the next steps.* London: HM Government.

Berlant L (2011). *Cruel Optimism.* Durham/London: Duke University Press.

Berlant L (2007). Slow death (sovereignty, obesity, lateral agency). *Critical Inquiry 33*(4): 754–780.

Berlant L, Edelman L (2014). *Sex, or the Unbearable.* Durham/London: Duke University Press.

Birn A (2009). Making it politic(al): closing the gap in a generation: health equity through action on the social determinants of health. *Social Medicine 4*(3): 166–182.

Buckner M (2013). Comment on: Friedli L, Stearn R. *Whistle While You Work (for nothing): positive affect as coercive strategy – the case of workfare.* [Blog.] Centre for Medical Humanities; 13 December. http://centreformedicalhumanities.org/whistle-while-you-work-for-nothing-positive-affect-as-coercive-strategy-the-case-of-workfare/ (accessed 22 February 2019).

Burnett J (2017). Austerity and the production of hate. In: Cooper V, Whyte D. *The Violence of Austerity.* London: Pluto (pp217–223).

Citizens' Advice Bureau (2014). *Response to the Call for Information for the Independent Review of Jobseeker's Allowance Sanctions.* London: Citizens' Advice Bureau.

Clark W (2013). *Workfare: a policy on the brink.* [Blog.] Red Pepper; 14 February. www.redpepper.org.uk/workfare-a-policy-on-the-brink/ (accessed 20 February 2019).

Cole M (2008). Sociology contra government? The contest for the meaning of unemployment in UK policy debates. *Work Employment & Society 22*(1): 27–43.

Community Shop (2014). *Giving surplus food social purpose.* [Online.] Community Shop; 12 December. www.companyshop.co.uk/community-shop/news-and-enquiries/news-centre/giving-surplus-food-social-purpose12 December (accessed 21 February 2019).

Cooper N, Dumpleton S (2013). *Walking the Breadline: the scandal of food poverty in 21st century Britain.* [Online.] Oxford: Oxfam with Church Action on Poverty. https://oxfamilibrary.openrepository.com/bitstream/handle/10546/292978/rr-walking-readline-food-poverty-britain-300513-en.pdf;jsessionid=2FE7D6EB4BD65E06ADC813DEB4BB8596?sequence=1 (accessed 21 February 2019).

Cooper V, Whyte D (2017). *The Violence of Austerity.* London: Pluto.

Coote A (2014). Help to Work? Britain's jobless are being forced into workfare, more like. Opinion. [Online.] *The Guardian;* 28 April. https://www.theguardian.com/commentisfree/2014/apr/28/help-to-work-britains-jobless-forced-workfare-unemployed (accessed 20 February 2019).

Courts & Tribunals Judiciary (2014). *Department for Work and Pensions v Information Commissioner and Frank Zola: decision by the Upper Tribunal (Administrative Appeals Chamber).* [Online.] 15 July. www.judiciary.gov.uk/wp-content/uploads/2014/07/dept-work-pensions-v-info-commioner-and-fz2.pdf (accessed 20 February 2019).

Courts & Tribunals Judiciary (2013). *Department for Work and Pensions v Information Commissioner and Frank Zola: decision by the First-Tier Tribunal General Regulatory Chamber (Information Rights).* [Online.]17 May 2013. www.judiciary.uk/wp-content/

uploads/2014/07/dept-work-pensions-v-info-commioner-and-fz2.pdf (accessed 23 February 2019).

Crisp R, Fletcher D (2008). *A Comparative Review of Workfare Programmes in the United States, Canada and Australia.* Research Report number 533. London: Department for Work and Pensions. https://www4.shu.ac.uk/research/cresr/sites/shu.ac.uk/files/review-workfare-usa-canada-australia.pdf (accessed 22 February 2019).

Cromby J, Willis M (2014). Nudging into subjectification: governmentality and psychometrics. *Critical Social Policy 34*(2): 241–259.

Day K (2013a). *Patronising Teamwork Excersise Number 5,348 (or something): the joy of the Jobcentre Work Programme.* [Blog.] So This Is My Life Now; 16 August. [No longer available online, 23 February 2019].

Day K (2013b). *How Work Programme Makes Me Feel.* [Blog.] So This Is My Life Now; 18 August. [No longer available online, 23 February 2019].

Dean M (2002). Liberal government and authoritarianism. *Economy & Society 31*(1): 37–61.

Dean M (1995). Governing the unemployed self in an active society. *Economy & Society 24*(4): 559–583.

Deeming C (2014). Foundations of the workfare state – reflections on the political transformation of the welfare state in Britain. [Online.] *Social Policy & Administration*; 24 Septemberdoi:10.1111/spol.12096 10.1111/spol.12096 (accessed 20 February 2019).

Department for Education, Department for Business, Innovation and Skills (2013). *Traineeships. Supporting young people to develop the skills for apprenticeships and sustainable employment: framework for delivery.* London: Stationery Office. www.bl.uk/britishlibrary/~/media/bl/global/social-welfare/pdfs/non-secure/t/r/a/traineeships-supporting-young-people-to-develop-the-skills-for-apprenticeships-and-sustainable-employment-framework-for-delivery-updated-july-2013.pdf (accessed 21 February 2019).

Department for Work and Pensions (2013). *Work Programme: programme costs to 31 March 2013.* [Online.] London: Department for Work and Pensions. https://www.gov.uk/government/uploads/system/uploads/attachment_data/file/209260/wp-costs-to-31-march-2013.pdf (accessed 20 February 2019).

Department for Work and Pensions (2012). *New Sanctions Regime for Jobseeker's Allowance.* [Online.] London: Department for Work and Pensions. http://webarchive.nationalarchives.gov.uk/20130627060116/http://www.dwp.gov.uk/docs/jsa-sanction-changes.pdf (accessed 20 February 2019).

Department for Work and Pensions (2014a). *Work Programme Official Statistics to June 2014.* [Online.] Newcastle-upon-Tyne: Department for Work and Pensions. www.gov.uk/government/uploads/system/uploads/attachment_data/file/355896/Work_Programme_Statistical_Release_Sep14_Final.pdf (accessed 20 February 2019).

Department for Work and Pensions (2014b). *Community Work Placements: DWP provider guidance.* [Online.] London: Department for Work and Pensions. https://www.gov.uk/government/publications/community-work-placements-dwp-provider-guidance (accessed 22 February 2019).

Duffy A, Pupo N (2018). Unpaid work, coercion and the fear economy. *Alternative Routes 29*: 14–37. www.alternateroutes.ca/index.php/ar/article/view/22445/18239 (accessed 1 March 2019).

Duffy S (2010). The citizenship theory of social justice: exploring the meaning of personalisation for social workers. *Journal of Social Work Practice 24*(3): 253–267.

DWP Unspun. *A Selection of Especially Stupid Benefit Sanctions*. [Online.] 12 July. https://web.archive.org/web/20180129040456/http://dwpunspun.org.uk/sanctions (accessed 23 February 2019).

Dwyer P (2004). Creeping conditionality in the UK: from welfare rights to conditional entitlements? *Canadian Journal of Sociology 29*(2): 265–287.

Dwyer P, Wright S (2014). Universal credit, ubiquitous conditionality and its implications for social citizenship. *The Journal of Poverty & Social Justice 22*(1): 27–35.

Eichhorst W, Konle-Seidl R (2008). *Contingent Convergence: a comparative analysis of activation policies*. Bonn: Institute for the Study of Labor. Bonn: IZA. http://ftp.iza.org/dp3905.pdf (accessed 20 February 2019).

False Economy (undated). *UK Cuts and Testimonies*. [Online.] http://falseeconomy.org.uk/cuts/uk/all/t2 (accessed 22 February 2019).

Faubion J, Foucault M (2000). Truth and juridical forms. In: Faubion J (ed). *Power* (Hurley R et al, trans). New York, NY: New Press (pp1–89).

Ferraro D (2014). *Two Case Studies in Biopolitics: a critique of CBT as ideology*. [Blog.] Archives of a Divided Subject; 12 February. http://melbournelacanian.wordpress.com/2014/02/12/two-case-studies-in-biopolitics/ (accessed 20 February 2019).

Friedli L (2014). A response: the ethics of psycho-policy – reflections on the role of psychology in public health and workfare. *Clinical Psychology Forum 256*: 11–16.

Friedli L (2012). What we've tried hasn't worked: the politics of asset based public health. *Critical Public Health 23*(2): 131–145.

Friedli L, Stearn R (2013). Whistle while you work (for nothing): positive affect as coercive strategy—the case of workfare. [Blog.] *Medical Humanities*; 10 November. http://medicalhumanities.wordpress.com/2013/12/10/whistle-while-you-work-for-nothing-positive-affect-as-coercive-strategy-the-case-of-workfare/. (accessed 20 February 2019).

Gillies A, Krishna H, Paterson J et al (2013). *Universal Credit: what you need to know*. London: Child Poverty Action Group.

Gissajob (2012). *Re: My Battle with WP*. Unemployment Movement [forum]; 5 March. https://web.archive.org/web/20120629183221/http://unemploymentmovement.com/forum/welfare-to-work/:// (accessed 23 February 2019).

Gorz A (1989). *Critique of Economic Reason*. London: Verso.

Greer I, Schulte L, Symon G (2014). *Inside the 'Black Box': ten theses on employment services in Britain*. [Online.] Paper presented at the University of Greenwich. https://marketizationineurope.files.wordpress.com/2014/07/greer-schulte-symon-2014-uk-report.pdf (accessed 20 February 2019).

Greer I, Symon G (2014). *Comparing Workfare Regimes: similarities, differences, and exceptions*. The Business School Working Paper Series. Greenwich: University of Greenwich. http://gala.gre.ac.uk/11194/ (accessed 20 February 2019).

Halpern D, Bates C, Mulgan G, Aldridge S, with Beales G, Heathfield A (2004). *Personal Responsibility and Changing Behaviour: the state of knowledge and its implications for public policy*. London: Prime Minister's Strategy Unit/Cabinet Office.

Haughton J (2014). Should jobseekers be psychometrically tested? [Online.] *Insights*; 17 September. London: Chartered Management Institute. https://www.managers.org.uk/insights/news/2014/september/should-jobseekers-be-psychometrically-tested (accessed 21 February 2019).

Hochschild A (1983). *The Managed Heart: commercialisation of human feeling*. Berkeley, CA: University of California Press.

Holehouse M (2014). Welfare claimants to get attitude tests employment minister reveals. *Daily Telegraph*; 5 September. http://www.telegraph.co.uk/news/politics/11078359/Welfare-claimants-to-get-attitude-tests-employment-minister-reveals.html (accessed 22 February 2019).

Howell A, Voronka J (2012). The politics of resilience and recovery in mental health care. *Studies in Social Justice* 6(1): 1–7.

Ingeus (2010a). *Healthy Attitudes for Living*. London: Ingeus.

Ingeus (2010b). *Common Thinking Traps*. London: Ingeus.

Introna A, Casagrande M (2019). 'We rebel because We misfit.' In: Frayne D (ed). *The Work Cure: critical essays on work and wellness*. Monmouth: PCCS Books (pp211–228).

Jones R, Pykett J, Whitehead M (2013a). *Changing Behaviours: on the rise of the psychological state*. Cheltenham: Edward Elgar.

Jones R, Pykett J, Whitehead M (2013b). Psychological governance and behaviour change. *Policy Politics* 41(2): 159–182.

Knott D, Muers S, Aldridge S (2008). *Achieving Culture Change: a policy framework*. London: Cabinet Office/Prime Minister's Strategy Unit.

Koksal I (2012). *Adventures at A4e*. [Blog]. Izzy Koksal; 13 April. http://izzykoksal.wordpress.com/2012/04/13/adventures-at-a4e/ (accessed 22 February 2019).

Lazzarato M (1996). Immaterial labor. In: Virno P, Hardt M (eds). *Radical Thought in Italy: a potential politics*. Minneapolis: University of Minnesota Press (pp133–147).

Levine-Clark M (2010). The politics of preference: masculinity, marital status, and unemployment relief in post-First World War Britain. *Cultural & Social History* 7(3): 233–252. doi:10.2752/147800410X12634795054694

Levine-Clark M (2006). The gendered economy of family liability: intergenerational relationships and poor law relief in England's Black Country, 1871–1911. *Journal of British Studies* 45(1): 72–89. doi:10.1086/497056

MacInnes T (2013). *Are sanctions driving people off JSA?* [Blog.] New Policy Institute; 7 November. http://npi.org.uk/blog/social-security-and-welfare-reform/are-sanctions-driving-people-jsa/ (accessed 22 February 2019).

Marteau T, Hall P (2013). Breadlines, brains, and behaviour. *British Medical Journal* 347: 6750. doi:10.1136/bmj.f6750 (accessed 20 February 2019).

McRuer R (2006). *Crip Theory: cultural signs of queerness and disability*. New York, NY: New York University Press.

Moore P (2012). Where is the study of work in critical IPE? *International Politics* 49(2): 215–237.

Peacock M, Bissell P, Owen J (2014). Dependency denied: health inequalities in the neo-liberal era. *Social Science & Medicine* 118: 173–180.

Pennycook M, Whittaker M (2012a). *Conditions Uncertain: assessing the implications of Universal Credit in-work conditionality*. London: Resolution Foundation.

Pennycook M, Whittaker M (2012b). *Low Pay Britain*. London: Resolution Foundation.

Portes J (2013). *The 'Help to Work' pilots: success, failure or somewhere in between?* [Blog.] NIESR; 29 December. http://niesr.ac.uk/blog/help-work-pilots-success-failure-or-somewhere-between#.VDxY1UulmlJ (accessed 22 February 2019).

Rahim N, Kotecha M, Chanfreau J, Arthur S, Mitchell M, Payne C, Haywood S (2012). *Evaluation of support for the very long-term unemployed trailblazer.* Report number: 824. [Online]. London: Department for Work and Pensions. https://www. gov.uk/government/publications/evaluation-of-support-for-the-very-long-term-unemployed-trailblazer-rr824 (accessed 22 February 2019).

Recovery in the Bin (2019). Unrecovery. In: Frayne D (ed). *The Work Cure: critical essays on work and wellness.* Monmouth: PCCS Books (pp227–249).

Rose S (2013). Beware 'brain-based learning'. [Online.] *Times Higher Education*; 12 December. www.timeshighereducation.co.uk/features/beware-brain-based-learning/2009703. fullarticle (accessed 20 February 2019).

Scottish Community Development Centre (2011). *Asset Alliance Scotland: event report.* Glasgow: SCDC.

Shildrick T, MacDonald R (2013). Poverty talk: how people experiencing poverty deny their poverty and why they blame 'the poor'. *Sociological Review 61*: 285–303.

Shildrick T, MacDonald R, Webster C, Garthwaite K (2012). *Poverty and Insecurity: life in low pay, no pay Britain.* Bristol: Policy Press.

skwalker1964 (2013). *DWP: fake psych 'test' training given by unqualified 'experts'.* [Blog.] The Skwawkbox; 4 July. http://skwalker1964.wordpress.com/2013/07/04/dwp-fake-psych-test-training-given-by-unqualified-experts/ (accessed 22 February 2019).

Slater T (2013). *Review of Imogen Tyler, 'Revolting Subjects: Social Abjection and Resistance in Neoliberal Britain'.* [Online.] Antipode: September. http://radicalantipode.files. wordpress.com/2013/09/book-review_slater-on-tyler.pdf 2013 (accessed 22 February 2019).

Southwood I (2019). The black dog. In: Frayne D (ed). *The Work Cure: critical essays on work and wellness.* Monmouth: PCCS Books (pp29–44).

Stewart ABR, Wright S (2014). *Conditionality briefing: unemployed people.* [Online.] Welfare Conditionality; September. http://www.welfareconditionality.ac.uk/wp-content/ uploads/2014/09/Briefing_Unemployment_14.09.10_FINAL.pdf (accessed 20 February 2019).

Taylor N (2018). The return of character: parallels between late-Victorian and twenty-first century discourses. *Sociological Research Online 23*(2): 399–415.

Taylor N (2014). *The Politics of 'Character'.* [Blog.] Politics Reconsidered; 9 March. *https:// politicsreconsidered.net/2014/03/09/character* (accessed 23 February 2019).

Thomas J (2014a). Wirral wedding venue Thornton Manor hit with complaints after claims cleaning job applicants were asked to work for free. [Online.] *Liverpool Echo*; 12 December. www.liverpoolecho.co.uk/news/liverpool-news/wirral-wedding-venue-thornton-manor-8276462 (accessed 20 February 2019).

Thomas I (2014b). *Day One Support for Young People Trailblazer: a preliminary impact analysis.* [Online.] London: Department for Work and Pensions. www.gov.uk/ government/uploads/system/uploads/attachment_data/file/380171/day-one-support-young-people-trailblazer-impact-analysis.pdf (accessed 22 February 2019).

Tyler I (2013). *Revolting Subjects: social abjection and resistance in neoliberal Britain.* London: Zed Books.

Void J (2014). *Pauline got promoted! DWP management psychobabble is turning Jobcentres into cults.* [Blog.] the void; 17 December. http://johnnyvoid.wordpress.com/2014/12/17/

pauline-got-promoted-dwp-management-psychobabble-is-turning-jobcentres-into-cults/ (accessed 22 February 2019).

Walkerdine V (ed) (2002). *Challenging Subjects: critical psychology for a new millennium*. London: Palgrave.

Walsh J, *Guardian* readers (2014). 'Even the sight of a CV would give me an anxiety attack': Guardian readers on benefit sanctions. *The Guardian*; 5 September. www.theguardian.com/society/2014/aug/05/even-the-sight-of-a-cv-would-give-me-an-anxiety-attack-guardian-readers-on-benefit-sanctions (accessed 22 February 2019).

Walters W (2000). *Unemployment and Government: genealogies of the social*. Cambridge: Cambridge University Press.

Webster D (2014a). *Independent review of Jobseeker's Allowance (JSA) sanctions for claimants failing to take part in back to work schemes*. [Online.] London: HM Parliament. www.cpag.org.uk/sites/default/files/uploads/CPAG-David-Webster-submission-Oakley-review-Jan-14_0.pdf (accessed 20 February 2019).

Webster D (2014b). *The DWP'S JSA/ESA Sanctions Statistics Release, 19 February 2014*. [Online.] London: Child Poverty Action Group. Child Poverty Action Group. www.cpag.org.uk/sites/default/files/uploads/CPAG-19-02-D-Webster-19-Feb-2014.pdf (accessed 20 February 2019).

Webster D (2013). *Written Evidence Submitted to the House of Commons Work and Pensions Committee Inquiry into the Role of Jobcentre Plus in the Reformed Welfare System*. [Online.] London: HM Parliament. http://data.parliament.uk/writtenevidence/WrittenEvidence.svc/EvidencePdf/1401 (accessed 20 February 2019).

Webster D (2005). Long-term unemployment, the invention of 'hysteresis' and the misdiagnosis of structural unemployment in the UK. *Cambridge Journal of Economics* 29: 975–995.

Weeks K (2007). Life within and against work: affective labor, feminist critique, and Post-Fordist politics. *Ephemera* 7(1): 233–249.

Work and Pensions Committee (2013). *Work and Pensions Committee: first report. Can the Work Programme work for all user groups?* London: Stationery Office.

Wright S (2014). Conceptualising the active welfare subject: welfare reform in discourse, policy and lived experience. *Policy & Politics* 44(2): 235-252.

# Chapter 5

# CBT's integration into societal networks of power[1]

## Michael Guilfoyle

Like any clinical practice, CBT is a participant in societal networks of power relations. This chapter explores one aspect of this and considers how the success and widespread recognition of this approach may be a function not of its effectiveness *per se*, but of its comfortable integration with and, in certain circumscribed fields (for example, clinical psychology), its assignation of an authoritative role within existing cultural and institutional power arrangements and commonsense discourse. Our Enlightenment heritage calls for a rationalist ordering of the therapies, in accordance with narrow and pre-constructed values and knowledges that correspond with and can take forward those of society's most powerful institutions. I suggest that it is within this context that we should understand CBT's overwhelming emergence as 'the therapy of choice'. The danger of its institutional success is the establishment and legitimisation of a therapeutic hegemony, in which therapists are ranked, therapeutic activities prescribed and clients required to shape their identities in line with particular normalising discourses and practices. All of this, in my view, contributes not only to the diminishment of a once rich landscape of therapeutic possibilities, but also to a curbing of the people, communities and ways of living to which our practices can speak.

---

1. An earlier version of this chapter appeared in the *European Journal of Psychotherapy and Counselling* 2008; 10(3): 197–206. This chapter was first published in Loewenthal D, Proctor G (eds) (2018). *Why Not CBT? Against and for CBT revisited.* Monmouth: PCCS Books (pp19–32).

My argument is that CBT's success as a therapeutic form owes much to its strategic success in the domains of institutional and political power. I suggest that its discourses and practices are both aligned with and subject to many of the dominant *political* requirements of a modern therapy: it *looks* – perhaps more than other therapies – scientific; it has a reasonable – though far from exemplary – 'empirical evidence base'; it sits comfortably with existing dominant mental health and medical discourses, policies and practices; it is apparently time-efficient and therefore economically justifiable, and its language is close enough to that of Western commonsense discourse (for example, consider the popular binaries of positive/negative, rational/irrational) to make its relevance immediately visible to large sectors of the lay public. This is not an approach that will cause too much trouble for existing power structures and ways of coordinating institutional practices. It is a politically convenient technology, whose theoretical tools are not designed to help us critique the political, social and cultural practices of persons' lives, except to the extent that these practices seem unscientific, irrational or lacking in evidence. It tends to stick to solving problems within psychiatrically and medically accepted terms. It changes people's thoughts so that they can get back to an *a priori*, taken-for-granted political landscape, hence adapting their lives to this apparently 'real' world. CBT has managed to manoeuvre itself, more successfully than any other approach, into the policies and decision-making structures of professional psychological bodies and mental health systems internationally.

In this landscape, in order for a therapy to even be in the race – to be in contention for the title 'therapy of choice' – it must satisfy a few simple criteria: it must be amenable to measurement, standardisation and manualisation. If it is not, it cannot hope to be a serious contender. This immediately and substantially reduces the field, barring entry to a host (perhaps the majority) of therapeutic approaches. However, we should be clear that their exclusion is *not in any way* a comment on their effectiveness or lack thereof. All we can say is that excluded therapies do not comply with a particular way of playing the game and deciding on winners. Interestingly, CBT practitioners do not always adhere to the 'science' or the manual in practice. Waller, Stringer and Meyer (2012) have noted that practitioners tend to 'drift' theoretically and practically (p171). What I found most intriguing in these authors' paper is their belief that this is a problem to be resolved. They were less interested in the possibility that 'drift' might *aid* effectiveness and focused more on calling on practitioners to fall back into line – to stick to the script. After all, it is only in this way that these practitioners can really participate in the scientifically and politically sanctioned race. It seems to me that effectiveness, as such, has become less important than scientific compliance.

CBT's complicity with contemporary power arrangements – in, for example, legal, educational, psychiatric, psychological, political, even commonsense institutions – is surely a comfort to its practitioners. This complicity reassures the practitioner of continued support and approval, and permits its alignment with broader social, political, medical, economic and cultural aims and objectives. But what continues to strike me is the extraordinary difficulty of challenging with any effectiveness the taken-for-granted belief that this approach is superior – in almost all scientific respects – to other therapies. It is worth dwelling on this for a moment, because it tells us much about how the therapeutic landscape has evolved and is evolving.

## Impotent critiques of CBT

A series of critiques have been articulated in relation to CBT itself and its alleged superiority over other approaches. But it seems to me they have been largely ineffective in shifting the discourse about how therapies are evaluated.

The first difficulty in effectively critiquing CBT lies in the apparent refusal of its promoters to recognise the enormous complexity of the requirement that our therapies be ranked according to evidence. Certainly, its scientifically 'proven' status – its success in 'the race' – has been challenged on many fronts (see Loewenthal & Proctor, 2018): its selective use of scientific principles; its blurring of efficacy and effectiveness; its skewed research populations and simplistic categorical view of the person; its mechanistic and objectivist orientation to research, despite the availability of alternative models of science that might enable more nuanced accounts of persons (cf. Clarkson, 2003), and there is even much contradictory 'scientific' evidence. A considerable amount of research, for example, supports the notion that common factors contribute more to therapeutic change than specific factors associated with (for example) CBT (Andrews, 2000; Messer & Wampold, 2002; Bohart & House, 2018).

It has been argued that much of the 'evidence' for CBT is actually nothing of the sort. For instance, Wampold and colleagues (2017), who recently conducted an examination of meta-analyses that concluded in favour of CBT over other approaches, found that these studies were built on the foundations of problematic primary studies, and yielded only small, non-significant effects. Similarly, Shedler (2011) reported that some studies found no advantage for CBT (his focus was on psychodynamic therapies in particular), but, as he put it: 'No one took notice' (p152). His argument is that this selectivity indicates that some practitioners (and academics) 'value only evidence that supports an *a priori* agenda, while ignoring, dismissing, or attacking evidence that does not'. He goes on to say: 'This is not science, but ideology masquerading as science' (p154). So problematic is the reading of the 'evidence' – particularly in the UK – that Bolsover (2002) has described CBT's promotion as 'a marketing rather than a research strategy' (p294). On these accounts, CBT's success is more to do with its marketing prowess and with its ideological situation. I refer to such related ways of thinking about CBT's success in terms of its integration with networks of power.

Wampold and colleagues (2017) also raise the issue of *which* CBT is meant when it is advanced as what Tarrier (2002) has termed 'the treatment of choice' (p291). It is by no means one single approach, and different studies incorporate certain techniques and therapies into their definition of CBT (eg. dialectical behaviour therapy, mindfulness, schema therapy), while others do not. It is also evident that many experienced CBT practitioners do not strictly adhere to the manuals supported by the 'science' (Waller, Stringer & Meyer, 2012). Waller and colleagues call for practitioners to look out for this apparently dangerous drifting tendency – as if it were the product of laziness or a lack of rigorous reflection, or worse, of their seduction by other approaches – and to move back to adherence to the manual. Does this not effectively call on experienced practitioners, who might have otherwise learned to practise in ways that attend to the nuances and complexities of their clients' lives – a level of complexity that CBT itself is not designed to notice (Bolsover, 2002) – to act more like novices? For me, this is the worst use of science. It reduces the practitioner to a technician – one who is expected to rigidly, uncritically, and without contextual sensitivity or deviation, apply approved principles and techniques. To their credit, however, Waller and colleagues do at least acknowledge the possibility that deviations from the approved script might not necessarily lead to a compromise in therapeutic effectiveness.

Challenges to CBTs scientific claims have done little to tame the bold, sometimes arrogant and dismissive claims of this approach's superiority. When Jeremy Holmes (2002) argued that CBT's superiority 'may be more apparent than real' (p288) – a view expressed by numerous other scholars, as we have seen – Tarrier (2002) responded that Holmes was simply 'unhappy that those who make policy in the NHS... have become wise' to CBT's 'evidence base' and have begun to 'act on it' (p291). To my mind, this is far from the spirit of questioning, fallibility and openness to critique that I associate with the sciences more broadly.

If the science seems invulnerable to critique, then perhaps we can focus on some of the ethical limitations of this approach. For example, we might argue that CBT focuses on problems instead of people, in its own language rather than that of the client; that it patronises in its educative stance, and that it only works to the extent that the therapeutic common factors are actively put into practice (eg. Castonguay et al, 1996). One possible response to such critiques is the oft-touted claim that CBT is collaborative (eg. Chadwick, Birchwood & Trower, 1996), and that its practitioners are open to the views and experiences of clients. Often, what is meant by 'collaboration' is unclear to me, and certainly does not tally with the way the term is understood in some other approaches. For example, Harlene Anderson (eg. 1997) situates her postmodern, collaborative approach very carefully at a theoretical level. She draws on the theoretical linkage between power and knowledge, on Bakhtin's distinction between monologue and dialogue, and on Shotter's notion of 'joint action' to build a deep understanding of what collaboration can mean. Similarly, for the narrative therapist, collaboration might be thought of in terms of an honouring of the client's values, hopes and beliefs, and of his or her very way of making sense of self and the world. In other words, in such approaches, the term 'collaboration' has a particular meaning and entails far more than paying attention to the client's experience, getting agreement on a procedure, or allowing the client to have a say.

Precisely what does 'collaboration' mean in CBT? I wonder, sometimes, when I read CBT literature and case studies, is collaboration here anything more than a belated recognition that *any* interpersonal situation is inevitably a two-way street, and that a client should be consulted on what happens in the room? The practitioner hears a client's account, and – *influenced* by her stories, and attending to her hopes – goes on to formulate it in terms of negative automatic thoughts, schemas etc. So too, the medical doctor listens to our list of symptoms and uses them to come to a diagnosis or obtains agreement from us to pursue a particular medicinal or surgical strategy. Is this what is meant by collaboration? It seems to me that this approach has a rather minimalistic and misleading take on the term.

Consider the idea of 'collaborative empiricism', intended to combine the empiricism of CBT with a collaborative therapeutic spirit. Merali and Lynch (1997) explain it thus:

> ... client perceptions of the etiological and maintaining factors underlying their presenting problems may be impoverished or erroneous... If a counsellor relies exclusively on the client's self-reports of his/her situation,

the wrong intervention may be implemented, thus compromising therapeutic efficacy. In order to prevent such errors, the counsellor must guide the client in collecting data surrounding the presenting problem and the counsellor and client must work together in examining the data. This technique is called collaborative empiricism. (pp287–288)

Where is the collaboration here? Well, from the authors' perspective, it seems to lie in the fact that the client's report on his or her situation is considered, but not trusted, as it 'may be impoverished or erroneous', and so the therapist must 'guide' the person to yield error-free data before they 'together' examine what emerges. The authors go on to argue that part of this collaboration entails the therapist 'explaining' to the person why this or that intervention is appropriate and how it should be done (eg. homework exercises), clarifying 'instructions' for these tasks to prevent 'errors', and 'giving praise for homework completion' (p290). Aside from the patronising tone – in a paper designed *specifically* to show off CBT's collaborative credentials – it seems that there is only a minimalist, certainly hardly persuasive, understanding of collaboration.

Merali and Lynch's (1997) account takes me to the views of Proctor (2002, 2017), who has argued that CBT practices tend to confuse collaboration with client compliance and docility, and that this effectively conceals power and what she considers to be the 'paternalism' of its practices (p79). She notes that this paternalism is underscored by the educative style associated with the approach. Here, on the one hand, we have the 'well-motivated intentions' (Allison, 1996: 156) of the therapist posing as a naïve guarantee of the practice's ethical standing, and, on the other, a client 'relegated to the role of the ignorant pupil' (Proctor, 2002: 77).

In a defence of CBT, Kazantis and colleagues (2013) say that collaboration is evidenced by 'balanced decision-making, balanced contributions to the session, and the extent to which client and therapist are respectful, interested, and responsive to each other's contributions' (p458). What 'balance' means is unexplained. Does it mean each person has equal time? Or that they take turns making decisions? Indeed, can CBT even function if the client's way of looking at self and world – which may *not* be in terms of CBT discourse of rationality, the primacy of cognitions etc – has an 'equal' chance of shaping the therapy process? To what extent can the client's words count as truth?

Still, the term persists. Tarrier (2002) insists that CBT is 'collaborative – the patient is an equal, and information is shared' (p292). He goes on to quote South in this respect: the practitioner must 'produce evidence and… share their knowledge with their patients' (p292). But such claims ring hollow. One wonders how much 'sharing' (balance, equality, collaboration) is really possible when it is scientific knowledge that is most highly valued, and yet it is the practitioner – *not* the client – who invariably holds this knowledge. It requires that clients accept not only the science paradigm as the best way to approach their lives, but also the therapist's claims to represent such truths.

This defensive self-labelling – CBT is collaborative – could possibly be symptomatic of a broader dishonesty in the therapeutic professions, as Goldberg (2001) once argued. But perhaps this criticism is too harsh. Perhaps it is associated more with simplistic conceptualisations of issues like collaboration, ethics and power. Perhaps the lack of nuanced explorations into such concerns can blind practitioners to the ways in which we exercise our expert knowledge, minimise that of our clients, and use this imbalance to shape people's visions of how they should think about themselves and their problems. Under such circumstances, one wonders how nuanced ethical questions concerning the subtleties of power operations and the constructive power of language can be appropriately addressed.

The troubling science issue persists, as does the collaboration claim. We might then turn to examine CBT's collusion with psychiatric power structures, and the manner in which it has, in the process, summarily dismissed decades of meticulous attempts by psychologists and others to question these very systems. Well-known critiques of this power network – of which the CBT practitioner cannot in good conscience claim ignorance – include the concern that forms of subjectivity are imposed upon clients (and related 'labelling' critiques), that clinical categories can have self-fulfilling effects, that clinical interactions lean toward monologue rather than dialogue, and that there is a press for normative and cultural compliance rather than resistance (eg. Kirk & Kutchins, 1997). Considering that CBT functions within this network, what more can be said on these issues? What benefits might accrue from a reiteration of such concerns, or from the production of new ones? Indeed, is there any real sense of compulsion within the CBT community to seriously engage with these challenges, and will such dialogue make any difference?

It seems that challenges against CBT on scientific, ethical, or political grounds are likely to be fruitless. This relative impotence is itself already an indication that something very significant – and very troubling – has happened in the therapeutic world. It seems that the title of 'most important' therapy – or, more medically, the 'first-line treatment of choice' (Wilson, 1996: 197) – can be awarded without any serious consideration of the numerous philosophical, ethical and political formulations that have been designed to give us pause in how we think about therapy. I do not argue with the claim that CBT can sometimes be an effective approach. But even its scientific basis, apparently the biggest weapon in its armoury, is unconvincing to many academics and practitioners. Our best objections and cautions, which include some of the issues already touched on, are more easily dismissed out of hand than ever before. Indeed, what is most alarming is that they do not even have to be addressed.

This did not matter so much when therapists were given space to practise in any number of ways, and toward a range of different ends; to make choices about how to work instead of having practices prescribed by professional bodies and other crystallisations of power. But it matters a great deal now, as many therapists find their approaches delegitimised to the extent that they are not represented on centralised lists of approved therapies. The voice of the dissenting therapist, or even that of the client who might not appreciate CBT discourses and practices, can be ignored. In at least one study, drop-out from CBT interventions was a major feature (Leff et al, 2000). To be acknowledged, one must learn to speak in the prescribed language, act in accordance with pre-constructed and independently developed priorities and measure one's work using prescribed methods. The psychoanalyst's concerns about CBT's inattention to unconscious forces (Milton, 2018) need not be heard unless there is a specific sort of evidence to support his claims; the feminist therapist's questions about the role of subtle forms of gender discrimination in producing distress can be ignored if they are based only on case studies, or if there aren't enough meta-analytic studies to justify her claims. It has become legitimate to dismiss critique that is not couched in the discourse of science, or even to disregard critique altogether. Thus, we might challenge CBT's narrow version of science, its complicity with psychiatry and so on, but these critiques are, in any case, no longer on the agenda for dialogue over what shall be counted as a valid therapy.

I aim here to develop some ideas about how this agenda is constructed and maintained. In the process, I discuss CBT's institutionalisation as the 'most important' therapy, and the marginalisation of its competitors.

## Managing the therapeutic horizon

In order to understand CBT's political situation, I think it is useful to situate it briefly in relation to its strategic competitors: the full range of therapies aiming for recognition, circulation and reproduction. This aggregate, comprising hundreds of approaches, can be seen as a therapeutic discursive horizon in that they constitute a kind of store of culturally available ideas and practices from which therapists are, in principle, able to draw. In what is sometimes described as a 'postmodern age' (cf. Lyotard, 1984), in which difference and choice are celebrated (eg. Sampson, 1993) and essentialism and grand narratives are treated with suspicion, some might have hoped to find in the therapeutic industry a proliferation of creative ideas and practices. Different therapies speak to different people, to different concerns and values, to different ways of life.

Indeed, Safran and Messer (1997) noted precisely such a multiplication of therapeutic approaches in the second half of the 20th century, broadly enabled by the pluralism and contextualism of postmodernism. In recent years, however, many Western societies have begun to aim once more, with renewed vigour, to fulfil a more convergent, consensually orientated, rationalist vision of the world that is our Enlightenment heritage (eg. Habermas, 1987/1972; Brazier, 2018; Lees, 2018), and from which we have been unable to escape. Difference and diversity in the therapeutic landscape have become constructed as a danger, as a threat to the wellbeing of the broader populace.

Safran and Messer (1997) have noted in the therapeutic domain a move toward convergence in the last few decades (which they see approvingly as integrationism), as attempts are made to organise and manage this seemingly unwieldy therapeutic diversity. Under the influence of this privileging of agreement, consensus, unification and convergence, and perhaps out of a fear of the alterations of power that a truly inclusive, postmodern social system – which embraces a range of values, religions, hopes and ways of living – might bring, certain ideas have become entrenched as absolutes, despite the avowed respect for difference and choice so intrinsic to the rhetoric of modern societies. All societies must adopt specific versions of democracy; consensus must overcome difference at a fundamental level; consensus is to be established around objective, absolute truths, and we should not be satisfied with diverse opinions/perspectives; science is the only proper means for knowing the truth, and scientists are the only valid truth tellers.

With such assumptions in place, a normative, closely regulated and ultimately authoritarian system is created, posing as a protector of our rights and promising to rescue us from charlatans by steering us to the approved therapeutic 'officer' (Hook, 2003) – that person deemed qualified, and awarded the authority, to diagnose our thoughts and guide us on what is in our best interests and how we should think, act, interact and live our lives.

It is in such circumstances that the proliferation of therapeutic approaches seems to be grinding to a halt and pulled into reverse. Under the influence of Enlightenment principles of rationalism and consensus, it appears that we feel the need to suppress this therapeutic variation in order to discover the objectively 'best' treatments. This, our Enlightenment principles inform us, is the most responsible and ethical thing to do. Exemplifying this stance, King and Ollendick (1998), for example, make the often-cited twin assertions that the identification of empirically validated treatments facilitates protection of clients and ensures the survival of the profession. It was originally rationalised in the National Institute for Health and Care Excellence (NICE) system of guidelines as a way of overcoming the 'lottery' model of healthcare provision. In these terms, the quest for the 'best' and most scientific therapy is easily constructed as a noble undertaking. Thus, each approach must be evaluated according to absolute scientific methods and principles, and once those principles are in place, a kind of consensus can be generated.

Under the influence of such consensus – and the positive valuation placed on consensus as such, in contrast to difference – the critical therapist starts to doubt his or her own ideas, as the impression is created that 'right-thinking' practitioners recognise the importance of having therapeutic work monitored and legislated, of evidence-based practice, of meeting economic needs, insurance company demands, and psychiatric and forensic requirements of clear diagnoses, categorical interventions and unequivocal recommendations. Not all therapies satisfy these demands and so the multitude of approaches – of *choices,* for clinician and client alike – that we might have expected begins to dwindle as the therapeutic landscape is gradually overtaken by a few selected approaches, of which CBT is the most salient example. A therapeutic hegemony sets in.

What I have referred to as the therapeutic horizon has already begun to take on a new shape, although it is noteworthy that alternative views continue to be expressed, and new practices continue to be developed. Still, the shape of the therapeutic world is strongly influenced by forces inside and outside the therapeutic industry itself. The American Psychological Association (APA) has drawn up lists of approved therapies and is joined by insurance companies in expecting psychologist practitioners to use psychiatry-like diagnostic categories and to match these up with their corresponding validated interventions. The APA is a world leader among psychological bodies, moreover, and so others are closely following suit. Training courses in the Western world, in clinical psychology in particular, are increasingly advocating the use of such 'evidence-based' practice, drawing from such lists (usually headed by CBT) to inform training and practice.

Clearly, many therapies are not represented on such lists because they do not play the 'games of power' (Foucault, 1980: 298) at which CBT has proven itself so adept. Many therapies are simply not amenable to standardisation and manualisation, and they might conceptualise problems, measure change and construct objectives in ways that do not suit the criteria laid out by the APA and other governing bodies. Narrative therapy, psychoanalysis, systemic therapy, collaborative therapy and many others tend to be scientifically awkward. This does not mean they are therapeutically ineffective, only that their ways of working, and the concerns of the people they aim to assist, are more nuanced than the hard sciences are able to assess. But their awkwardness is potentially costly. It may have the longer-term effect of their delegitimisation and eventual disqualification as reputable therapies. It is these approaches, adjudged to be unscientific and based on conjecture rather than fact, whose opinions can be ignored and whose concerns are increasingly absent from the agenda of the dialogue on valid therapies.

Under the force of such pressures, the training of clinical psychologists is increasingly dominated by CBT, with other therapeutic approaches relegated to the periphery (Lloyd, 2009). Indeed, the profession of clinical psychology itself seems to be increasingly conflated with CBT, confusingly implying that cognition can stand alone in representing the breadth and depth of human psychological processes (Gilbert, 2009).

Further, CBT has been prescribed at government level in the UK (Pilgrim, 2018). Economist and former prime ministerial adviser Lord Richard Layard (2004) called for the training of 10,000 CBT specialists for the UK health services. This call received support from different sources (eg. the Body Dysmorphic Foundation (2017); the Centre for Mental Health (2006)). CBT continues to be recommended for use in the UK's National Health Service by NICE and the Department of Health for numerous designated problem 'types'. CBT – above all other approaches – is systematically being called forth as the Western world's 'therapy of choice', and this is beginning to give the therapeutic landscape a decidedly skewed appearance.

The therapeutic horizon, in other words, is managed, ostensibly, in the name of truth, but it would be more accurate to say that it is in the service of prevailing power arrangements. Political and economic forces are dictating that only certain therapies will be allowed to remain in place – therapies that are, for instance, time-limited and 'scientific', but which more fundamentally speak into, rather than away from, the linguistic and practice contexts of relevant institutions. Therapies are to be arranged in terms of their capacity to meet the needs of societal systems of power.

Thus, the plethora of available approaches is given an order, and each therapy assigned a place along a narrowly constructed continuum of proven effectiveness. This ordering is then advertised directly or indirectly by such bodies as NICE, the APA, and other psychological and therapeutic governing bodies, by government departments of health and other interested officials, by media talk-show hosts, and sometimes by those therapists who find their favoured approach catalogued on the approved therapies list and who are thereby given permission – it seems one is merely telling the objective truths of science, after all – to express disapproval of other therapies in their writing, in their engagements with other professionals, and of course very persuasively (given the power imbalance) in sessions with clients. With all of this public activity, CBT's name and its ideas have now entered mainstream commonsense discourse.

## Therapeutic dominance and political serviceability

In any society that values consensus and absolute truth, competition will inevitably involve a differentiated 'natural' selection of participants. At present, as I have argued, this is moving toward a situation of therapeutic hegemony and a reduction of available therapies. This may not be the final result, and we may not be witnessing an end to therapeutic history, since we cannot know what new developments might be ushered in by changes in politics (for example, reduced intervention in the therapeutic industry), or in the 'science' of therapy (for example, via an acknowledgement of the limitations of scientific methods in answering questions of how people should live or think about themselves or their lives, or a growing respect for research into the so-called 'common factors', which might once more open up the field (Bohart & House, 2018). But at present, various forms of government – from public officials, to insurance and mental health industries, to therapy's governing bodies – seem to have converged to promote specific therapeutic practices (of which CBT is the exemplar), and to demote others. But then, we must ask, if CBT has been selected from the universe of therapeutic possibilities as 'the single most important… approach' (Salkovskis, 1996: xiii), what has it been selected to do?

If we consider the range of forces that have converged to establish a broad-based (though not universal) consensus on the issue, then we cannot simply assume that therapies are chosen on the basis of their scientific merits or their capacity to improve happiness, minimise distress, or even advance mental health. This is not to suggest that CBT practitioners do not strive at precisely these goals. Rather, my question concerns CBT's institutionalised selection as the best therapy – the status it is granted by powerful bodies of public, economic, and professional governance. It is surely reasonable to suspect that there are likely factors involved in CBT's success that transcend those that therapists and clients tend to value the most.

To take an obvious instance, Professor Lord Layard advocates CBT in the UK at least in part because it will aid the economy: it will get people back to work more quickly than other therapies, and thereby reduce strain on the benefit system (Layard, 2005). This call has even been followed up by attempts to integrate into CBT practices what Wesson and Gould (2010) call a 'return-to-work' agenda. These authors argue that the 'RtW' (return-to-work) component of therapy should not be 'a hidden agenda item' but brought into the open and included as part of the therapeutic goals (p32). And if the client does not raise this issue as an explicit concern, then the authors suggest that – in order to avoid imposition and to protect CBT's 'collaborative spirit' – it should be integrated into 'the social domain of a client's formulation' (p33). It is stunning how easily economic arguments can come to shape therapeutic practices and objectives; how easily therapeutic practices become tools for the promotion of political and economic objectives. It seems to me naïve to believe that economists, governments, insurance companies and so on – primary shapers of the therapeutic landscape – are more invested in the population's happiness than in its productivity and its maintenance of societal institutions. And yet many practitioners continue to find ways to align their activities with the interests of those forces.

On the question of CBT's serviceability to society's institutions, let us consider a hypothetical scenario. If science is the defining criterion for a selected therapy, then what would happen if it emerged – scientifically – that the most effective therapies were those that *challenged* many of society's institutions: those that proactively put on hold the drive for economic growth in order to prioritise psychological wellbeing; that challenged psychiatry's centrality in mental health practice, or that pointed toward unjust economic, educational and foreign policies, rather than cognitive distortions, as key factors in maintaining distress? One wonders if such a therapy would be afforded the same marketing and promotion avenues that we have witnessed in the case of CBT over the last couple of decades. As it is, such therapies (for example, narrative, feminist, and some psychoanalytic approaches) do not, in any event, fit the shape desired by official society, although numerous efforts are under way to reshape them so that they lose their critical edge and become more serviceable to existing power arrangements (Guilfoyle, 2005).

Different therapies do different things. They embody different visions, not just of the narrow tasks that have been assigned to professional therapists: diagnose, understand what facilitates 'mental health', formulate and solve problems in the domains of private thoughts and emotions. The range of therapies also speaks to a range of visions of what is important in life, of how life should or could be lived. Diversity in the therapies enables us to make space for multiple ways of being a person and positions us – as a body of therapists – so that we are better able to speak to diverse cultural and societal values and practices, not all of which assume the primacy of science, rationality and testable and measurable thoughts. It seems to me that such questions are not high on the agenda for bodies such as NICE. We are given a narrowly defined job to do: a job that intersects with and contributes just so to social, political and economic institutions. The suppression of its variation might mean that it becomes accomplished at a narrow range of practices that are authored, ultimately, by external forces. It is the significance of these external influences that we should question – more, perhaps, even than the fact that CBT is winning the race they want us to run. The more pertinent question is how the rules for competition are constructed, and which institutions stand to gain.

As therapists, we must be alert to being reduced to government agents. CBT practitioners face this quandary imminently. It is not our job to reproduce existing power arrangements, or to satisfy the needs of society's most powerful institutions. Yet the political reality is that therapies that perform such a reproductive function are useful institutional partners, and thereby more likely than others to become successful, popular and recognised, and even to become part of commonsense discourse (which itself then enhances the likelihood of effectiveness). All therapists risk becoming inadvertent agents of 'social control' (Hare-Mustin, 1994: 20) – a position that we should surely resist. But CBT's popularity is such that we practitioners – especially at the point of training – are inundated with very tempting invitations to become part of the fold – to find a place in the havens that such belonging provides. One would like to think these invitations will be in some way refused. Very often they are. But that is a risky strategy for the practitioner. It not only calls on us to critique the games of power to which CBT's technologies are so well suited; it also puts us in a position of being subject to the normalising judgements of our colleagues, the professional bodies of which we are a part, our referral networks, and perhaps even our clients.

Have a look at the NICE guidelines: being something other than a CBT practitioner might not be a good career move.

# References

Allison A (1996). A framework for good practice: ethical issues in cognitive behavioural therapy. In: Marshall S, Turnbull J (eds). *Cognitive behaviour therapy*. London: Balliere Tindall (pp155–180).

Anderson H (1997). *Conversation, Language and Possibilities: a postmodern approach to therapy*. New York, NY: Basic Books.

Andrews HB (2000). The myth of the scientist-practitioner: a reply to R King (1998) and N King and Ollendick (1998). *Australian Psychologist* 35(1): 60–63.

Bohart A, House R (2018). Empirically supported/validated treatments as modernist ideology, part 1: the dodo, manualisation and the paradigm question. In: Loewenthal D, Proctor G. *Why Not CBT? Against and for CBT revisited*. Monmouth: PCCS Books (pp286–303).

Body Dysmorphic Foundation (2017). Getting help. [Online]. http://bddfoundation.org/helping-you/getting-help-in-the-uk/ (accessed 8 February 2017).

Bolsover N (2002). Commentary: The 'evidence' is weaker than claimed. *British Medical Journal* 324(7332): 288–294.

Brazier D (2018). CBT: a historico-cultural perspective. In: Loewenthal D, Proctor G. *Why Not CBT? Against and for CBT revisited*. Monmouth: PCCS Books (pp146–151).

Castonguay LG, Goldfried MR, Wiser S, Raue PJ, Hayes AM (1996). Predicting the effect of cognitive therapy for depression: a study of unique and common factors. *Journal of Consulting and Clinical Psychology* 64(3): 497–504.

Centre for Mental Health (2006). *We need to talk*. [Online.] www.centreformentalhealth.org.uk/we-need-to-talk (accessed 5 February 2019).

Chadwick PD, Birchwood MJ, Trower P (1996). *Cognitive Therapy for Delusions, Voices and Paranoia*. Chichester: Wiley.

Clarkson P (2003). *Citrinitas* – therapy in a new paradigm world. In: Bates Y, House R (eds). *Ethically Challenged Professions: enabling innovation and diversity in psychotherapy and counselling*. Ross-on-Wye: PCCS Books (pp60–74).

Foucault M (1980). *Power/Knowledge: selected interviews and other writings 1971–1977* (C Gordon ed). New York, NY: Harvester Wheatsheaf.

Gilbert P (2009). Moving beyond cognitive behaviour therapy. *The Psychologist* 22(5): 400-403.

Goldberg C (2001). Influence and moral agency in psychotherapy. *International Journal of Psychotherapy* 6(2): 107–115.

Guilfoyle M (2005). From therapeutic power to resistance? Therapy and cultural hegemony. *Theory & Psychology* 15(1): 101–124.

Habermas J (1972/1987) *Knowledge and Human Interests*. Shapiro J (trans). Oxford: Polity Press.

Hare-Mustin RT (1994). Discourses in the mirrored room: a postmodern analysis of therapy. *Family Process* 33(1): 19–35.

Holmes J (2002). All you need is cognitive behaviour therapy? *British Medical Journal* 324: 288–290.

Hook D (2003). Analogues of power: reading psychotherapy through the sovereignty–discipline–government complex. *Theory & Psychology* 13: 605–628.

Kazantzis N, Tee JM, Dattilio FM (2013). How to develop collaborative empiricism in cognitive behavior therapy: conclusions from the *C&BP* special series. *Cognitive and Behavioral Practice 20*: 455–460.

King NJ, Ollendick TH (1998). Empirically validated treatments in clinical psychology. *Australian Psychologist 33*(2): 89–95.

Kirk S, Kutchins H (1997). *Making Us Crazy – DSM: the psychiatric bible and the creation of mental disorders*. New York, NY: Free Press.

Layard R (2005). *Mental Health: Britain's biggest social problem?* Paper presented at No 10 Strategy Unit seminar on mental health, 20 January 2005. London: London School of Economics. http://eprints.lse.ac.uk/47428 (accessed 4 February 2018).

Lees J (2018). Cognitive behavior therapy and evidence-based practice: past, present and future. In: Loewenthal D, Proctor G. *Why Not CBT? Against and for CBT revisited*. Monmouth: PCCS Books (pp152–161).

Leff J, Vearnals S, Wolff G, Alexander B, Chisholm D, Everitt B, Asen E, Jones E, Brewin CR, Dayson D (2000). The London depression intervention trial. *The British Journal of Psychiatry 177*(2): 95–100.

Lloyd J (2009). Threats to clinical psychology from the CBT stranglehold. *Reformulation 33*: 8–9.

Loewenthal D, Proctor G. *Why Not CBT? Against and for CBT revisited*. Monmouth: PCCS Books.

Lyotard JF (1984). *The Postmodern Condition: a report on knowledge*. Minneapolis, MN: University of Minnesota Press.

Merali N, Lynch P (1997). Collaboration in cognitive behavioural counselling: a case example. *Canadian Journal of Counselling 31*(4): 287–293.

Messer SB, Wampold BE (2002). Let's face facts: common factors are more potent than specific therapy factors. *Clinical Psychology: Science and Practice 9*(1): 21–25.

Milton J (2018). Psychoanalysis and cognitive behaviour therapy: rival paradigms or common ground? In: Loewenthal D, Proctor G. *Why Not CBT? Against and for CBT revisited*. Monmouth: PCCS Books (pp181–200).

Pilgrim D (2018). Happiness: CBT and the Layard thesis. In: Loewenthal D, Proctor G. *Why Not CBT? Against and for CBT revisited*. Monmouth: PCCS Books (pp52–66).

Proctor G (2002/2017). *The Dynamics of Power in Counselling and Psychotherapy: ethics, politics and practice*. Ross-on-Wye: PCCS Books.

Safran JD, Messer SB (1997). Psychotherapy integration: a postmodern critique. *Clinical Psychology: Science and Practice 4*(2): 140–152.

Salkovskis PM (1996). Preface. In: Salkovskis PM (ed). *Frontiers of Cognitive Therapy*. London: Guilford Press (ppxi–xiv).

Sampson EE (1993). *Celebrating the Other: a dialogic account of human nature*. San Francisco, CA: Westview Press.

Shedler J (2011). Science or ideology? *American Psychologist 66*(2): 152–154.

Tarrier N (2002). Commentary: yes, cognitive behaviour therapy may well be all you need. *British Medical Journal 324*: 291–292.

Wampold BE, Fluckiger C, Del Re AC, Yulish NE, Frost ND, Pace BT, Goldberg SB, Miller SD, Baardseth TP, Laska KM, Hilsenroth MJ (2017). In pursuit of truth: a critical examination of meta-analyses of cognitive behavior therapy. *Psychotherapy Research* 27(1): 14–32.

Waller G, Stringer H, Meyer C (2012). What cognitive behavioral techniques do therapists report using when delivering cognitive behavioral therapy for the eating disorders? *Journal of Consulting and Clinical Psychology* 80(1): 171–175.

Wesson M, Gould M (2010). Can a 'return-to-work' agenda fit within the theory and practice of CBT for depression and anxiety disorders? *The Cognitive Behaviour Therapist* 3: 27–42.

Wilson GT (1996). Treatment of bulimia nervosa: when CBT fails. *Behaviour Research and Therapy* 34(3): 197–212.

# PART 2

The State of the NHS

# Chapter 6

# IAPT and the flawed ideology of diagnosis

## Sami Timimi

Initially widely welcomed for its promise to expand access to psychological therapies for people with common mental disorders, the Improving Access to Psychological Therapies (IAPT) programme has also prompted economic and conceptual critiques and remains controversial. In 2011, the UK government extended IAPT to services provided for children and young people, with the aim of 'transforming' the way mental health services are delivered to them.

In this chapter I will critically reflect on the problems associated with both IAPT and the Children and Young People's Improving Access to Psychological Therapies (CYP-IAPT) and trace the root of the problems back to the programme's reliance on technical and diagnostic-based, process-driven ideologies that contribute to commodifying, reifying, and internalising personal distress. The chapter will present evidence that demonstrates the failure of both the adult and CYP IAPTs to improve the mental health of the nation's young and adult population.

## The IAPT model

In 2007, the UK government announced a substantial expansion of funding for psychological therapies in England to provide better support for people with conditions such as anxiety and depression. For those who believe that psychological therapies help people, there was much to celebrate in this plan to dramatically increase access to these therapies with the aim of decreasing waiting times and allowing more people with common mental health problems access to the means to help them recover.

However, from the start, IAPT came with considerable baggage, in terms of both ideology and results – although its mixed reputation and results have not dented its continued expansion across England. There are several reasons why IAPT is a problematic project.

First, there is a 'fetishisation' of certain therapeutic modalities (particularly cognitive behavioural therapy (CBT)), resulting from an adherence to a primarily technical understanding of the nature of mental health problems and their solutions. This stance marginalises the evidence base that points to the limitations of the technical paradigm (Bracken et al, 2012), sets up an artificial hierarchy of desirability and efficacy for psychotherapies (and therefore psychotherapists), encourages medicalisation, and leads to claims about efficiency that have not been matched by the available evidence.

A second problem relates to its origins in an economic model promoted by the economist Professor Lord Richard Layard. Layard envisaged common conditions such as anxiety and depression as broadly naturalistic phenomena that are concrete and quantifiable and that result in significant loss of productivity through days lost by sickness (Layard et al, 2006). In this model, he envisages that scaling up treatments for these conditions leads to more people returning to work, resulting in increased national productivity, thereby more than paying back the government's investment in the programme (Boseley, 2006). In this way, some of the problems of the national economy (ie. those relating to a perceived disproportionately high burden of welfare payments to people off sick due to mental health problems) can be 'magicked' away by treating these 'ill' people faster and more effectively (Summerfield & Veale, 2008). However, not only does this obscure the social origins of many people's anxiety and depression (for example, in poor working conditions or chronic job insecurity); it also paves the way to individualising economic woes and psychologising the economic consequences of inequality in social conditions under capitalism as due to psychological/psychiatric dysfunction of individuals.

A third and related issue is that IAPT is based on a model of mental health that proposes individualised, medicalised and industrialised solutions to a variety of psychosocial stresses that have been shown to be associated with increased likelihood of developing a mental health problem. The result is an upside-down strategy to improving wellbeing where Lord Layard, who was advising the government on mental health at the time, could declare, without challenge, that mental illness had now taken over from unemployment as our greatest social problem (Layard, 2005). Whether intended or not, the political and economic order benefits when distress or dysfunction that may connect to its policies and practices is relocated from the socio-political space (a public and collective problem) to the mental space (a private and individual problem) (Summerfield, 2007). Not only does it risk obscuring and supporting a cruel political and economic system; it can obscure other sources of powerlessness and oppression, such as those connected with child abuse and other adversities, where formulaic therapies on offer may accidentally reinforce some people's conviction that the adversities they experience are their fault.

IAPT, along with the rest of mainstream mental health services in the UK, relies on a technical model for understanding people's distress. This assumes that mental health problems arise from faulty mechanisms or processes involving abnormal physiological or psychological events occurring within the individual. It also assumes that these mechanisms or processes can be modelled in causal terms, are not context-dependent, and that treatments can be designed and delivered in a manner that is independent of relationships, contexts and values (Bracken et al, 2012). Thus, IAPT's foundational paradigm follows a pathway that assumes that a correct diagnosis (of mild to moderate depression, for example) will enable the correct choice of a technical intervention (for example, treatment with CBT) that will reliably achieve the desired recovery outcome. In this linear formatting, process-driven protocols are central and relational and other contextual issues are of secondary importance – issues to be negotiated to enable satisfactory compliance with the required 'correct' treatment.

The diagnostic model IAPT uses is derived from National Institute for Health and Care Excellence (NICE) guidelines. NICE guidelines rely on diagnostic concepts and the results of randomised controlled trials, and are presented as 'evidence based'. If the relevant NICE guidelines have serious flaws, then so will the IAPT services based on them. In mental health (unlike the rest of medicine), NICE guidelines are based on eminence, not evidence: in other words, they rely more on the individuals on the expert group gathered to produce the guidelines than on what the evidence says (Moncrieff & Timimi, 2012; Timimi, 2014a). NICE guidelines focus on process adherence, but have little to say about outcomes. They derive from diagnostic constructs that have done little to advance scientific knowledge or clinical practice in psychiatry and have no capacity to match treatments to aetiology, thus failing the basics required of a technical model (Timimi, 2014b, and see below).

Randomised controlled trials of mental health treatments use exclusion criteria that often mean that patients with multiple problem and complex diagnostic overlap, typical of those who use mental health services, are not adequately represented. These guidelines are based on the fantasy that expertise in technique is king. However, this is one of the factors that got us into the mess we are in with our mental health services in the first place. This ideological commitment to NICE guidelines bypasses simple logic. If the outcomes with a patient show improvement, does it matter what model you used to help achieve this? If outcome isn't improving, then it surely does matter and, irrespective of what your manual says, you may need to rethink together what you are doing.

The use of NICE guidelines relies on faith in the validity and reliability of the psychiatric diagnostic constructs the guidelines are built around. Therefore, I will next consider the problematic nature of using a psychiatric diagnostic template.

## Are diagnostic-based guidelines valid in mental health?

While prognosis for most conditions dealt with by the rest of medicine has improved, often reflecting genuine technical advances, no such progress has been seen for those who use mental health services. The figures on outcomes from treatment in real-world mental health settings in the developed world are nothing short of shocking. A number of studies in the US have concluded that as little as 20–25% of patients improve in routine mental health services (Lambert, 2010; Hansen, Lambert & Forman, 2002). In England, a review of the effectiveness of IAPT services found only 15% of referrals were achieving 'recovery' by the time they left (Centre for Social Justice, 2012). Likewise, in Australia, despite massive investment in mental health services in the past two decades, no corresponding improvement in the adult mental health of the population has been found (Jorm & Reavley, 2012).

A similar picture of poor outcomes in real-world child and adolescent mental health services has also been found. Weisz and colleagues (1995) reported that, for traditional treatment in the community, the overall effect size of change for those attending community child and adolescent health services, compared with those who weren't, was close to zero – a finding replicated in further studies (Weiss, Catron & Harris, 1999; 2000). Jörg and colleagues (2012) also found that, across a variety of measures, those who continuously attended community CAMHS had higher levels of self-rated distress/problems when compared with a matched community sample with similar levels of initial distress/problems who did not access CAMHS. Warren and colleagues (2009; 2010) also found a deterioration rate of 24% among children in public community mental health settings.

In the US, Whitaker (2010) has documented a tripling of the number of people categorised as disabled mentally ill over the past two decades. Similarly, the numbers of young people there categorised as having a disability because of a mental condition leapt from around 16,000 in 1987 to 560,000 in 2007. Mental disorders have also become the most common reason for receiving benefits in the UK, with the number of claimants rising by 103% between 1995 and 2014, while numbers of claimants with other conditions fell by 35% (Viola & Moncrieff, 2016).

The above is a snapshot of the deteriorating outcomes from mental health treatment witnessed throughout much of the Western world, despite a rise in spending on and uptake of mental health services.

One common feature in the service models used in Western mental health care is that services are built around technical/diagnostic concepts. While those desperately poor figures are likely to reflect many things, including the toll inflicted on populations from neoliberal individualisation, diagnostic models can be said, at the very least, to have failed to contribute to the picture of improved outcomes achieved in most other branches of medicine.

So, what are the problems with diagnosis in mental health and why should we conclude that diagnostic thinking lacks validity? It is fairly straightforward to demonstrate that the concept of psychiatric diagnosis lacks real-world validity, as from a logical/technical perspective there is no such thing as a psychiatric diagnosis (apart from some forms of dementia and a few other known organically based conditions that are sometimes encountered by psychiatrists).

In medicine, diagnosis is the process of determining which disease or condition explains a person's symptoms and signs. Diagnosis therefore points to causal processes. Making an accurate diagnosis is a technical skill that enables effective matching of treatment to address specific pathological processes. Pseudo-diagnoses – for example, 'bipolar disorder' – cannot explain behaviours or experiences as the 'symptoms' are only descriptions (not explanations). Even using the word 'symptom' may be problematic as, in medicine, 'symptoms' usually refer to patients' suffering/experience as a result of an underlying disease process and are therefore associated in our minds with an explanation for the 'symptom', which then leads to a medical procedure to correct it.

But psychiatric diagnoses do not explain symptoms. Consider the following example. If I were to ask the question 'What is depression?', it is not possible for me to answer it by reference to a particular known pathological abnormality. Instead, I will have to provide a description: 'Depression is the presence of low mood and negative thinking,' for example. Contrast this with asking the question 'What is diabetes?' If I were to answer this question in the same manner, by simply describing 'symptoms' such as needing to urinate excessively, thirst and fatigue, I could be in deep trouble as a medical practitioner: there are plenty of other conditions that may initially present with these symptoms, and diabetes itself may not present with these symptoms in a recognisable way. In order to answer the question 'What is diabetes?' I have to refer to its pathology – its abnormalities of sugar metabolism. To move from a hypothesised to a confirmed diagnosis, I would need to obtain independent (to my subjective opinion), empirical data to support or otherwise my hypothesis about what may be causing the patient's described experiences (such as testing the urine and/or blood for levels of glucose). In the rest of medicine, therefore, my diagnosis explains and has some causal connection with the behaviours/symptoms that are described. Diagnosis in that context sits in a 'technical' explanatory framework.

The problem of using a classification like 'depression' to *explain* an experience (ie. as a diagnosis) can be illustrated by asking another set of questions. If I was to ask *why* someone is feeling low and I were to answer that it is *caused* by depression, then a legitimate question to ask is 'How do you know that?' The only answer I can give is that I know it's depression because the person is feeling low. In other words, if we try to use a classification that can only describe in order to explain, we end up with what philosophically is known as a 'tautology'. It is troubling when doctors use a descriptive category like depression to explain and cannot see this problem of tautological circularity. Using depression to explain low mood is like saying the pain in my head is caused by a headache. In psychiatry, therefore, what we are calling diagnosis will only describe but is unable to explain.

The failure of decades of basic science research to reveal any specific biological or psychological marker that identifies a psychiatric diagnosis is well recognised. Unlike the rest of medicine, which has developed diagnostic systems that build on an aetiological and pathophysiological framework, psychiatry has failed to connect diagnostic categories with aetiological processes. Thus, there are no physical tests referred to in any mental health diagnostic manual that can be used to help establish a diagnosis. Despite the belief that psychiatric disorders have a significant genetic loading, molecular genetic research is failing to uncover any specific genetic profile for any psychiatric disorder. Possible genetic abnormalities appear to account for only a small percentage of causal factors, and whatever genetic contribution has been found crosses diagnostic categories rather than having a distinct profile for each diagnostic category (Cross-Disorder Group of the Psychiatric Genomics Consortium, 2013; Timimi, 2014b).

There is also a poor correspondence between levels of impairment and having the required number of symptoms for many psychiatric diagnoses. Thus, many people who are deemed below the threshold for a diagnosis have higher levels of impairment than those above, and many who reach the cut-off for a diagnosis have relatively low levels of impairment (Kendler, 1999).

The development of diagnostic manuals in psychiatry has not followed accepted scientific protocol and instead the diagnoses that have appeared in them have been literally imagined into being by a few influential (mostly male and white) individuals (Davies, 2013). Not only does the concept of psychiatric diagnosis lack validity, it is also unreliable (in other words, many psychiatrists would disagree about what the 'correct' diagnosis would be for any given presentation). Analysis of the studies involved in developing the first psychiatric diagnostic manual that took the approach of 'operationalising' psychiatric diagnosis through the checklist of symptoms approach, the third edition of the US *Diagnostic and Statistical Manual of Mental Disorders* (DSM-III) (American Psychiatric Association, 1980) found no diagnostic category for which reliability was uniformly high. Ranges of reliability were found to be broad, and in some cases ranged the entire spectrum from chance to perfect agreement, with the case summary studies (in which clinicians are given detailed written case histories and asked to make diagnoses – an approach that most closely approximates what happens in clinical practice) producing the lowest reliability levels (Kirk & Kutchins, 1994).

In field trials of the most recent edition, *DSM-5* (American Psychiatric Association, 2013), Freedman and colleagues (2013) found that the kappa coefficients (a statistical measure of inter-rater agreement) were uniformly poor. Some common diagnoses, such as major depressive disorder and generalised anxiety disorder, had such poor levels of inter-rater agreement that diagnosis was determined more by who was doing the diagnosis than by what the problem was.

With regards to the relationship between treatment and outcome, the evidence for psychotherapeutic interventions finds that 'common factors', such as developing a strong therapeutic alliance with the practitioner, are much more important than technique (Duncan et al, 2009; Wampold, 2001).

Decades of outcome research have concluded that the majority of variance in treatment outcome in therapy is accounted for by extra-therapeutic factors, while the quality of the therapeutic alliance accounts for most of the within-therapy variance (Duncan, Miller & Sparks, 2004; Wampold & Imel, 2015). This is also evident in 'real-life' clinical encounters. For example, in a review of over 5,000 cases treated in a variety of NHS settings in the UK, only a very small proportion of the variance in outcome could be attributed to psychotherapeutic technique, as opposed to non-specific factors such as the therapeutic relationship (Stiles et al, 2008). Unlike most other branches of healthcare, outcome studies have not shown reliable improvements from treatments for adult or child presentations in the decades since they were first undertaken (Shedler, 2018; Weisz et al, 2018). In fact, some studies suggest that treatment outcomes for some presentations were better several decades ago, despite the availability these days of a plethora of new psychotherapies and other treatments from which to choose (Weisz et al, 2018).

The importance of non-specific factors is also found with psychoactive drug treatments. The evidence supports the view that pharmacological agents are best conceptualised as inducing particular psychological states, rather than correcting chemical imbalances, and that, while this effect is not specifically related to the diagnosis, it is the basis for their usefulness (Moncrieff, 2009). So, for example, alcohol is able to reduce social anxiety in many people, not because it corrects some chemical imbalance, but because it induces a state of mind that can reduce shyness, regardless of whether or not they have a diagnosis of social anxiety. The lack of treatment specificity is not limited to the more common and less severe presentations. Thus, patients who live outside the US and Europe and experience a psychotic episode have much lower relapse rates and are significantly more likely to make a 'full' recovery and show lower degrees of impairment when followed up over several years, despite mostly having limited or no access to 'anti-psychotic' medication (Hopper et al, 2007). Evidence is also accruing that, particularly in terms of functional outcomes, those who come off antipsychotic drugs have better long-term outcomes than those who stay on them (Harrow, 2007; Wunderink et al, 2013), adding further support to the importance of psychosocial approaches in treating psychosis.

Diagnostic thinking has had a significant impact on service provision and public and professional beliefs about mental distress. It is widely argued that a large proportion of the population suffers from mental illness, that this amounts to a significant economic burden, and that there is a strong case for investing in improved mechanisms of screening, detection and treatment for these disorders. In order to increase rates of diagnosis and treatment, a variety of campaigns have been undertaken. For example, in the early 1990s in the UK, the Royal College of Psychiatrists and Royal College of General Practitioners launched their 'Defeat Depression' campaign (Paykel & Priest, 1992). Evaluations of this campaign found no evidence that it led to any significant improvements in clinical outcomes, but instead was associated with a rapid increase in antidepressant prescribing (Croudace, Evans & Harrison, 2003).

Similarly, research evaluating the 'Beyond Blue' campaign in Australia (Goldney et al, 2010), which aimed to increase awareness about depression and other mental disorders, demonstrated an increase in medical model beliefs about depression and an increase in rates of diagnosis of major depression between 1998 and 2008. It also noted a decrease in mental health-related quality of life over this decade, and that having only 'poor' or 'fair' levels of 'mental health literacy' (defined as a belief that depression is a medical diagnosis requiring medical treatment) was a significant protective factor for recovery from major depression – in other words, those who rejected the idea that their mental suffering was the result of a disease that needed an expert to 'diagnose' and treat it were more likely to recover.

The likelihood of positive outcomes for those with mental disorders is also further hampered by the stigma associated with the medical model (Sayce, 2000). Nearly all studies that have looked at public attitudes towards mental illness have found that the medical model for mental illness ('mental illness is an illness like any other illness') is associated with increased negative attitudes, greater fear of people with a mental illness diagnosis, and a greater likelihood of wanting to avoid interacting with them (Angermeyer et al, 2011).

As reviewed, there is much evidence to suggest that the spread of the scientifically untenable concept of 'diagnosis' in psychiatry is likely to have caused significant harm, rather than being helpful. The reliance of national programmes like IAPT on diagnostic thinking and pathways thus renders it vulnerable to contributing to, rather than alleviating, harms at the population level. While psychological therapies are associated with less immediate and obvious physical harms, available evidence, as I will now show, suggests that, at the very least, the enormous expenditure involved in developing, implementing and running IAPT, is not associated with population level improvement in mental health.

## The fading promise of IAPT

As discussed, factors external to therapy, such as the real-life challenges and histories that patients carry, have by far the biggest impact on outcomes, regardless of treatment. Within treatment, the factor that has the biggest impact on outcomes is the therapeutic alliance (as rated by the patient); matching treatment model to diagnosis has a clinically insignificant impact (Duncan et al, 2009; Wampold 2001). This relationship between the alliance and outcome seems remarkably robust across treatment modalities and clinical presentations (Castonguay & Beutler, 2005). The search for the 'active ingredients' of a psychological therapy is likely to be doomed to failure anyway because it depends on the false assumption that such ingredients are delivered by therapists in a uniform manner, regardless of the state, requirements and input of the patient (Shapiro et al, 1994). After all, the utterances of a patient may not have a direct impact on the chemical activity of a drug, but they will in the two-way process of a well-delivered talking therapy. Thus, we should not be surprised that attempts to find the active ingredients of, for example, CBT have failed, as studies have shown that most of the specific features of CBT can be dispensed with, without adversely affecting outcomes (Jacobson et al, 1996; Longmore & Worrell, 2007). Countless reviews and meta-analyses have found that no clear pattern of superiority for any particular treatment model has emerged (Budd & Hughes, 2009; Cooper, 2008).

As a result, the IAPT process, which insists on following manualised treatment protocols for limited modalities, ends up limiting choice for patients, despite the lack of evidence supporting such a stance. It is possible, of course, that choice has had to be sacrificed to maximise the efficiency that may come from standardisation, but the evidence here provides no encouragement either.

Not surprisingly, the national IAPT programme leaders have reported favourable results from their services (Clark, 2011; Gyani et al, 2013). However, their reports do not include comparisons with the costs and outcomes of non-IAPT services. Nor do they have a 'natural' comparison group; therefore, we don't know how many patients would have got better with time anyway. Finally, their figures do not account for what happens to those refused treatment or who drop out after one session. A report in 2014 (Wise, 2014) found that only a half of referrals to IAPT in England resulted in the patient actually entering treatment (see also Scott Steen's Chapter 8 for a detailed critique of IAPT statistics).

The first independent evaluation of the initial IAPT pilot sites found little difference between them and comparator services. What differences there were in outcomes were not significant four months after treatment and had disappeared at eight months, but the IAPT treatments had cost more per patient than those provided in neighbouring boroughs (Hawkes, 2011). According to reports compiled by the Artemis Trust (Evans 2011a, 2011b), which evaluated data from the subsequent national roll-out, the average number of patients achieving recovery for a fixed expenditure of £100,000, when treated by an IAPT service was far lower (49) than for pre-IAPT primary care counselling services (115) or voluntary sector counselling services (78). In addition, recovery rates, as a percentage of patients referred, was lower for IAPT services than comparable services (pre-IAPT primary care therapy services, university counselling services and Employee Assistance Programme counselling services). Most recently, Scott (2018) independently assessed 90 IAPT clients post-treatment, using a standardised semi-structured interview, and concluded that only 9.2% fully recovered from their disorder – a finding likely to reflect a basic failure at the heart of IAPT methodology (Timimi, 2018). Looking at IAPT's own data also reveals considerable variation between services. Using their national data, Delgadillo and colleagues (2015) found that the prevalence of mental health problems was greater in poorer areas and that these areas had lower average recovery rates from IAPT treatment. Predictably, IAPT has little to say on the association between the stressed lives of those living in greater poverty and deprivation, given that it is built on the belief that poor mental health contributes to poor economic wealth, not the reverse (Layard & Clark, 2014; Clark et al, 2016).

Perhaps training in the delivery of IAPT-approved therapies led to a more skilled and confident workforce able to better deliver properly structured therapies, leading to their achieving better outcomes once they completed such training? There is no evidence to support this possibility either. Branson and colleagues' (2015) study of 43 therapists treating 1,247 patients found little support for an association between CBT competence and patient outcome following completion of IAPT-CBT training.

Perhaps IAPT has helped reduce medicalisation? Again, the answer is no. In the years of IAPT's national roll-out, prescriptions for antidepressants have risen steadily. There is no evidence that the introduction of IAPT has had any meaningful impact on these trajectories. Spence and colleagues (2014) found a 165% increase in the prescribing of antidepressant drugs in England between 1998 and 2012 (an average increase of 7.2% a year), with the increase accelerating after 2008, coinciding with the financial recession. Access to the much-vaunted IAPT programme was not significantly associated with the extent of antidepressant prescribing – in other words, availability of IAPT services has had no impact on the continuous increase in antidepressant prescribing rates.

Perhaps more people being treated, whether by psychological or medicinal means, is a good thing of itself, leading to national reduction in the burden of mental illness? Again, the evidence isn't reassuring. As mentioned earlier, mental disorders have become the most common reason for receiving benefits in the UK, with the number of claimants rising by 103% from 1995 to 2014 (with continuing year-by-year increases recorded since 2007, at the time of IAPT's initial introduction), while numbers of claimants with other conditions fell (Viola & Moncrieff, 2016). Numbers of people claiming the main disability benefit (Disability Living Allowance) in the UK for a mental health problem rose from 30.9% of claimants in 2000 to 44.8% in 2013, with the biggest sub-category (over 50%) being for people given a diagnosis of depression (Timimi, 2014c).

If current national models of mental health service delivery were effective, we would not see this picture of steadily worsening long-term outcomes and greater psychosocial disability in parallel with steadily increasing expenditure and numbers receiving treatment. Layard's original economic model now appears naïve and mistaken. IAPT had little chance of improving the wellbeing of the nation; instead it acts as another mechanism for individualising social suffering, hiding the social origins of much distress and thus implicitly making broken/dysfunctional brains/psychologies responsible for psychosocial suffering. As discussed extensively by Philip Thomas and other contributors to this book, IAPT has all the hallmarks of a neoliberal-friendly project.

## Children and Young People's Improving Access to Psychological Therapies (CYP-IAPT)

Turning now specifically to the mental health of children and young people, IAPT gave birth to the CYP-IAPT programme in 2011. CYP-IAPT had a different remit to adult IAPT: rather than establishing a completely new service, it has focused on improving the skills of the existing CAMHS workforce by training staff in the manualised implementation of particular therapies. In addition, CYP-IAPT has the more ambitious aim of transforming the whole CAMHS service in England. Unlike adult IAPT, which was designed as a separate project operating alongside standard community mental health services, CYP-IAPT was designed to become *the model* for delivering community child and adolescent mental health services. Although it claimed to have a 'bottom-up' philosophy because it included consultation with some young people, it conformed to the principles of IAPT and imposed (ultimately, by April 2016) on all CAMHS in England a complex and bureaucratic structure based around NICE-inspired diagnostic 'care pathways'.

However, as with the adult outcome literature, there appears to be little evidence to support the claim that matching this treatment model to a diagnosis differentiates between successful and unsuccessful treatments for children and young people (Miller, Wampold & Varhely, 2008; Timimi et al, 2013). It seems that 'evidence-based' treatments for young people tend to come out as superior to usual care only if the 'evidence-based' treatment was developed by the researcher (Weisz, McCarty & Valeri, 2006). As with adults, technical factors appear irrelevant when it comes to the relationship between specific presentations and treatment outcome. Thus, a meta-analysis of component studies found that the theoretically-derived ingredients deemed critical to CBT are not specifically ameliorative for child and adolescent depression and anxiety, as full CBT treatments offered no significant benefit over treatments with only components of the full model (Spielmans, Pasek & McFall, 2007).

As mentioned earlier, clinical outcomes from real-life CAMHS have been consistently poor. Attempts to 'transform' CAMHS using diagnostic-based guidelines do not appear to improve outcomes either. The Fort Bragg evaluation in the US (Bickman et al, 1995, 2000) described the implementation, quality, costs and outcomes of a $94 million demonstration project designed to improve mental health outcomes for children and adolescents who were referred for mental health treatment. As with CYP-IAPT, the Fort Bragg experiment used a technical diagnostic care pathway model to 'transform' the new service. Outcomes in the experimental service were no better than those in the treatment-as-usual group, despite the considerable extra costs incurred. This finding was replicated in the Stark County evaluation study, where again there were no differences in outcomes when compared with care received outside the new system, despite the extra expenditure (Bickman et al, 1997).

These are sobering findings, suggesting that, just as with adults, traditional, medical/technical model approaches do not appear to provide much 'added value' in terms of improving the outcomes and efficiency of services.

In a debate with the national programme leads for IAPT and CYP-IAPT, I pointed out the poor evidential basis and questioned the legitimacy of the paradigms they were using (Timimi, 2014c, 2015). In their reply, Peter Fonagy and David Clark (2015) fail to address the problem of their reliance on NICE guidelines and instead argue that their technical approach supports collaborative working. However, theirs is an expert-led concept of this alliance; it ignores the problem of patients who do not want the model of therapy that the IAPT protocol has told them they should have. They quote all sorts of largely irrelevant data (such as percentage of services working to IAPT principles, percentage of clinicians using routine outcome data and so on) to support their claim that CYP-IAPT is improving services. Tellingly, they do not reference any patient outcome data, even though collecting this is a core feature of the IAPT and CYP-IAPT programmes. The data they do quote come from a report that was at the time not yet in the public domain. Published subsequently and quietly in September 2015 (Edbrooke-Childs et al, 2015), it found rates of clinical 'improvement' (as a result of a CYP-IAPT service treatment) of between one and 31% across the different treatment pathways. No wonder Fonagy and Clark chose not to mention this.

Here you can see the difference between reported outcomes for adult IAPT, which provides services separate from the standard community mental health services and doesn't accept anyone deemed to have anything more serious (such as a history of suicidal thinking) and the outcomes achieved when trying to implement such an approach across a whole, national CAMHS. If overblown claims about outcomes for adult IAPT services formed a specious basis for IAPT's implementation across CAMHS, clearly children's services could not live up to these unrealistic expectations.

The service I work in implemented CYP-IAPT across our county in April 2016. Up until then, we were using a positive and award-winning model (Outcome Orientated CAMHS – OO-CAMHS – see Timimi et al, 2013). This was kicked into the long grass when CYP-IAPT came along. We had implemented OO-CAMHS in my current team in 2012. OO-CAMHS is a whole-service model that draws on the 'common factors' evidence base and takes a non-diagnostic approach, emphasising collaborative practice and a focus on outcomes rather than process. Two years after implementation of OO-CAMHS, the number of children attending the service for more than two years had reduced from 38% of the caseload to 18% and the number receiving our help for more than one year had reduced from 59% to 29%. Non-attendance rates at the outpatient clinics had dropped significantly, with some clinicians having a three per cent non-attendance rate; the outpatient average non-attendance rate in other services in the trust was 19%. Of those discharged from our service at that time, 77% had achieved a clinically significant positive change and/or were above the clinical cut-off on the outcome rating scale we used. Since implementation of CYP-IAPT across the county, non-attendance rates in my team have gone up to between 15% and 18% of follow-up appointments. Outcomes are not being properly monitored since the implementation of CYP-IAPT and introduction of diagnostic care pathways. However, based on the partial information we have been able to collect, our previous 77% rate appears to have dropped to 66% achieving significant positive change and/or above the clinical cut-off.

## Beyond diagnosis, NICE and IAPT

The main message from outcome research is that diagnosis-driven models do not improve outcomes and services can improve outcomes by concentrating on developing meaningful relationships with service users that fully include them in decision-making processes (Bracken et al, 2012). Using flexible treatment models where there is regular testing through service-user feedback of whether or not a particular intervention is proving helpful for them has also been shown to improve outcomes and reduce the likelihood of becoming a 'long-term' patient (Duncan, 2014).

Hegemonic mental health service approaches stress the need for 'accurate' diagnosis in order to understand what the correct 'treatment' should be. As reviewed above, there is little evidence to suggest that such an approach leads to improved mental health outcomes. There is much evidence to suggest that, instead, it can cause significant harm. Furthermore, I argue that the individualisation of distress and its amelioration serves the functioning of neoliberal politics well. Not only does it help deflect from the effects of social distress and disempowerment on populations; it also allows for commodification of 'treatments' for distress (Timimi, 2017). Diagnoses can operate like 'brands', with an industry attached to them (pharmaceutical, psychotherapy, training institutions, books, courses, researchers etc). IAPT and CYP-IAPT fit perfectly into that neoliberal marketisation model where social, political and economic causes of suffering are obscured and technical 'brand' solutions for broken minds are offered instead.

# References

American Psychiatric Association (APA) (2013). *Diagnostic and Statistical Manual of Mental Disorders* (5th ed*)*. Washington, DC: APA.

American Psychiatric Association (APA) (1980). *Diagnostic Statistical Manual of Mental Disorders* (3rd ed). Washington, DC: APA.

Angermeyer MC, Holzinger A, Carta MG, Schomerus G (2011). Biogenetic explanations and public acceptance of mental illness: systematic review of population studies. *British Journal of Psychiatry 199*: 367–372.

Bickman L, Guthrie PR, Foster EM (1995). *Evaluating Managed Mental Health Services: the Fort Bragg experiment.* New York, NY: Plenum.

Bickman L, Lambert EW, Andrade AR, Penaloza R (2000). The Fort Bragg continuum of care for children and adolescents: mental health outcomes over five years. *Journal of Consulting and Clinical Psychology 68*: 710–716.

Bickman L, Summerfelt WT, Firth J, Douglas S (1997). The Stark County Evaluation Project: baseline results of a randomized experiment. In: Northrup, D, Nixon C (eds). *Evaluating Mental Health Services: how do programs for children 'work' in the real world?* Newbury Park, CA: Sage (pp231–259).

Boseley S (2006). Depression is UK's biggest social problem, government told. [Online.] *The Guardian;* 28 April. www.theguardian.com/money/2006/apr/28/1 (accessed 25 February 2019).

Bracken P, Thomas P, Timimi S, Asen E, Behr G et al (2012). Psychiatry beyond the current paradigm. *British Journal of Psychiatry 201*: 430–434.

Branson A, Shafran R, Myles P (2015). Investigating the relationship between competence and patient outcome with CBT. *Behaviour Research and Therapy 68*: 19–26.

Budd R, Hughes I (2009). The dodo bird verdict – controversial, inevitable and important: a commentary on 30 years of meta-analyses. *Clinical Psychology and Psychotherapy 16*: 510–522.

Castonguay LG, Beutler LE (eds) (2005). *Principles of Therapeutic Change That Work.* Oxford: Oxford University Press.

Centre for Social Justice (2012). *Completing the Revolution: commissioning effective talking therapies.* London: Centre for Social justice.

Clark A, Fleche S, Layard R, Powdthavee N, Ward G (2016). *Origins of Happiness: evidence and policy implications.* [Online.] VOX: CEPR Policy Portal. https://voxeu.org/article/origins-happiness (accessed 6 February 2019).

Clark DM (2011). Implementing NICE guidelines for the psychological treatment of depression and anxiety disorders: the IAPT experience. *International Review of Psychiatry 23*: 318–327.

Cooper M (2008). *Essential Research Findings in Counselling and Psychotherapy: the facts are friendly.* London: Sage.

Cross-Disorder Group of the Psychiatric Genomics Consortium (2013). Identification of risk loci with shared effects on five major psychiatric disorders: a genome-wide analysis. *The Lancet 381*: 1371–1379.

Croudace T, Evans J, Harrison G (2003). Impact of the ICD-10 Primary Health Care (PHC) diagnostic and management guidelines for mental disorders on detection and outcome in primary care. *British Journal of Psychiatry 182*: 20–30.

Davies J (2013). *Cracked: why psychiatry is doing more harm than good*. London: Icon Books.

Delgadillo J, Asaria M, Ali S, Gilbody S (2015). On poverty, politics and psychology: the socioeconomic gradient of mental healthcare utilisation and outcomes. *British Journal of Psychiatry 209*: 429–430.

Duncan BL (2014). *On Becoming a Better Therapist: evidence-based practice one client at a time* (2nd ed). Washington, DC: American Psychological Association.

Duncan B, Miller S, Sparks J (2004). *The Heroic Client*. San Francisco, CA: Jossey-Bass.

Duncan BL, Miller S, Wampold B, Hubble M (eds) (2009). *The Heart and Soul of Change: delivering what works in therapy* (2nd ed). New York, NY: American Psychological Association.

Edbrooke-Childs J, Calderon A, Wolpert M, Fonagy P (2015). *CYP IAPT: rapid internal audit national report*. London: Evidence-Based Practice Unit, the Anna Freud Centre.

Evans R (2011a). *Comparing the Quality of Psychological Therapy Services on the Basis of Number of Recovered Patients for a Fixed Expenditure*. Chichester: The Artemis Trust.

Evans R (2011b). *Comparing the Quality of Psychological Therapy Services on the Basis of Patient Recovery*. Chichester: The Artemis Trust.

Fonagy P, Clark D (2015). Update on the Improving Access to Psychological Therapies programme in England. Commentary on: CYP IAPT. *Psychiatric Bulletin 39*: 248–251.

Freedman R, Lewis DA, Michels R, Pine DS, Schultz SK et al (2013). The initial field trials of DSM-5: new blooms and old thorns. *American Journal of Psychiatry 170*: 1–5.

Goldney RD, Eckert KA, Hawthorn G, Taylor AW (2010). Changes in the prevalence of major depression in an Australian community sample between 1998 and 2008. *Australia and New Zealand Journal of Psychiatry 44*: 901–910.

Gyani A, Shafran R, Layard R, Clark DM (2013). Enhancing recovery rates: lessons from year one of IAPT. *Behaviour Research and Therapy 51*: 597–606.

Hansen N, Lambert M, Forman E (2002). The psychotherapy dose-effect and its implications for treatment delivery services. *Clinical Psychology: Science and Practice 9*: 329–343.

Harrow M (2007). Factors involved in outcome and recovery in schizophrenia patients not on antipsychotic medications. *Journal of Nervous and Mental Disease 195*: 406–414.

Hawkes N (2011). Talking therapies: can the centre hold? *British Medical Journal 342*: 578.

Hopper K, Harrison G, Janka A, Sartorius N (eds) (2007). *Recovery from Schizophrenia: an international perspective*. Oxford: Oxford University Press.

Jacobson NS, Dobson KS, Truax PA, Addis M, Koerner K, Gollan JK, Gortner E, Prince SE (1996). A component analysis of cognitive-behavioural treatment for depression. *Journal of Consulting and Clinical Psychology 64*: 295–304.

Jörg F, Ormel J, Reijneveld SA, Jansen DE, Verhulst FC, Oldehinkel AJ (2012). Puzzling findings in studying the outcome of 'real world' adolescent mental health services: the TRAILS study. *Public Library of Science 7*: e44704.

Jorm AF, Reavley NJ (2012). Changes in psychological distress in Australian adults between 1995 and 2011. *Australian and New Zealand Journal of Psychiatry 46*: 352–356.

Kendler KS (1999). Setting boundaries for psychiatric disorders. *American Journal of Psychiatry 156*: 1845–1848.

Kirk S, Kutchins H (1994). The myth of the reliability of DSM. *Journal of Mind and Behavior 15*: 71–86.

Lambert MJ (2010). *Prevention of Treatment Failure: the use of measuring, monitoring, and feedback in clinical practice*. Washington, DC: American Psychological Association.

Layard R (2005). *Mental Health: Britain's biggest social problem?* Paper presented at No 10 Strategy Unit seminar on mental health, 20 January 2005. London: London School of Economics. http://eprints.lse.ac.uk/47428 (accessed 4 February 2018).

Layard R, Clark DM (2014). *Thrive: the power of evidence-based psychological therapies*. London: Penguin.

Longmore RJ, Worrell M (2007). Do we need to challenge thoughts in cognitive behaviour therapy? *Clinical Psychology Review 27*: 173–187.

Miller S, Wampold B, Varhely K (2008). Direct comparisons of treatment modalities for youth disorders: a meta-analysis. *Psychotherapy Research 18*: 5–14.

Moncrieff J (2009). *The Myth of the Chemical Cure*. Basingstoke: Palgrave MacMillan.

Moncrieff J, Timimi S (2012). The social and cultural construction of psychiatric knowledge: an analysis of NICE guidelines on depression and ADHD. *Anthropology and Medicine 20*: 59–71.

Paykel ES, Priest RG (1992). Recognition and management of depression in general practice: consensus statement. *British Medical Journal 305*: 1198–1202.

Sayce L (2000). *From Psychiatric Patient to Citizen: overcoming discrimination and social exclusion*. London: Macmillan.

Scott MJ (2018). Improving Access to Psychological Therapies (IAPT) - the need for radical reform. *Journal of Health Psychology 23*(9): 1136–1147.

Shapiro DA, Startup M, Harper H, Reynolds S, Suokas A (1994) The high-water mark of the drug metaphor: a meta-analytic critique of process-outcome research. In: Russell RL (ed). *Reassessing Psychotherapy Research*. New York, NY: Guilford Press (pp1–35).

Shedler J (2018). Where is the evidence for 'evidence-based' therapy? *Psychiatric Clinics of North America 41*: 319–329.

Spence R, Roberts A, Ariti C, Bardsley M (2014). *Focus On: antidepressant prescribing: trends in the prescribing of antidepressants in primary care*. London: The Health Foundation/ Nuffield Trust.

Spielmans GI, Pasek LF, McFall JP (2007). What are the active ingredients in cognitive and behavioral psychotherapy for anxious and depressed children? A meta-analytic review. *Clinical Psychology Review 27*: 642–654.

Stiles WB, Barkham M, Mellor-Clark J, Connell J (2008). Effectiveness of cognitive-behavioural, person-centred, and psychodynamic therapies in UK primary-care routine practice: replication in a larger sample. *Psychological Medicine 38*: 677–688.

Summerfield D (2007). The invention of post-traumatic stress disorder and the social usefulness of a psychiatric category. *British Medical Journal 322*: 95–98.

Summerfield D, Veale D (2008). Proposals for massive expansion of psychological therapies would be counterproductive across society. *The British Journal of Psychiatry 192*: 326–330.

Timimi S (2018). The diagnosis is correct, but National Institute of Health and Care Excellence guidelines are part of the problem not the solution. *Journal of Health Psychology 23*: 1148–1152.

Timimi S (2017) Critical cultural theory. In: Cohen B (ed). *Routledge International of Handbook of Critical Mental Health*. London: Routledge (pp56–63).

Timimi S (2015). Update on the Improving Access to Psychological Therapies programme in England: author's reply. *Psychiatric Bulletin 39*: 252–253.

Timimi S (2014a). Children's behaviour problems: a NICE mess. *International Journal of Clinical Practice 68*: 1053–1055.

Timimi S (2014b). No more psychiatric labels: why formal psychiatric diagnostic systems should be abolished. *International Journal of Clinical and Health Psychology 14*: 208–215.

Timimi S (2014c). Children and Young People's Improving Access to Psychological Therapies: inspiring innovation or more of the same? *Psychiatric Bulletin 39*: 57–60.

Timimi S, Tetley D, Burgoine W, Walker G (2013). Outcome Orientated Child and Adolescent Mental Health Services (OO-CAMHS): a whole service model. *Clinical Child Psychology and Psychiatry 18*: 169–184.

Viola S, Moncrieff J (2016). Claims for sickness and disability benefits owing to mental disorders in the UK: trends from 1995 to 2014. *British Journal of Psychiatry Open 2*: 18–24.

Wampold BE (2001). *The Great Psychotherapy Debate: models, methods and findings.* Hillsdale, NJ: Lawrence Erlbaum.

Wampold BE, Imel Z (2015). *The Great Psychotherapy Debate* (2nd ed). London: Routledge.

Warren JS, Nelson PL, Burlingame GM (2009). Identifying youth at risk for treatment failure in outpatient community mental health services. *Journal of Child and Family Studies 18*: 690–701.

Warren JS, Nelson PL, Mondragon SA, Baldwin SA, Burlingame GM (2010). Youth psychotherapy change trajectories and outcomes in usual care: community mental health versus managed care settings. *Journal of Consulting and Clinical Psychology 78*: 144–155.

Weiss B, Catron T, Harris V (2000). A two-year follow-up of the effectiveness of traditional child psychotherapy. *Journal of Consulting and Clinical Psychology 68*: 1094–1101.

Weiss B, Catron T, Harris V (1999). The effectiveness of traditional child psychotherapy. *Journal of Consulting and Clinical Psychology 67*: 82–94.

Weisz JR, Donenberg GR, Weiss B (1995). Bridging the gap between laboratory and clinic in child and adolescent psychotherapy: efficacy and effectiveness in studies of child and adolescent psychotherapy. *Journal of Consulting and Clinical Psychology 63*: 688–701.

Weisz JR, Kuppens S, Yi Ng M, Vaughn-Coaxum,RA, Ugueto AM. Eckshtain D, Corteselli KA (2018). Are psychotherapies for young people growing stronger? Tracking trends over time for youth anxiety, depression, Attention-Deficit/Hyperactivity Disorder, and conduct problems. [Epub ahead of print]. *Perspectives in Psychological Science*; doi: 10.1177/1745691618805436

Weisz JR, McCarty CA, Valeri SM (2006). Effects of psychotherapy for depression in children and adolescents: a meta-analysis. *Psychological Bulletin 132*: 132–149.

Whitaker R (2010). *Anatomy of an Epidemic.* New York, NY: Crown.

Wise J (2014). Only half of patients referred for talking therapies enter treatment. *British Medical Journal 348*: g295.

Wunderink L, Nieboer R, Wiersma, D, Sytema S, Nienhuis F (2013). Recovery in remitted first-episode psychosis at 7 Years of follow-up of an early dose reduction/discontinuation or maintenance treatment strategy. *Journal of the American Medical Association: Psychiatry 70*: 913–920.

# Chapter 7

## Staying afloat: hope and despair in the age of IAPT

### Andy Rogers

When I was first practising as a therapist in the late 1990s, we talked a lot about the stigma attached to counselling and psychotherapy. The principal organisational concern for the college counselling service I ran was how to 'get people through the door', how to help them overcome the awkwardness or shame, the sense of failure or weakness in talking to a counsellor. I thought a lot about the wording of leaflets, the tone of posters and the best ways to raise awareness of the service among students and staff.

Twenty years on, I am still working in a college of further and higher education (FE/HE), and generally the young people we see are more comfortable with the idea of counselling. As society has gradually embraced discussion of 'mental health' and its 'treatment', there has been a shift in the perception of the 'talking therapies'. Many of our clients have had some form of therapy already, either at school or in NHS mental health services, and even among those seeing a counsellor for the first time, there is a greater sense of familiarity with the form, no doubt absorbed from peers, family members, teachers and other professionals, as well as the media and culture. Tellingly, we now worry less about how to encourage students to access our service than how to meet the growing demand.

Sadly, though, this change has not been entirely benign; while the stigma around attending counselling is dissipating, psychological distress has become subject to a deepening medicalisation. We hear this in the way young people sometimes speak about their concerns. As our culture has learned to be more open about mental health, so the idea has proliferated that it is 'just like physical health'. Encouraged by well-meaning, celebrity-endorsed media campaigns that reiterate this reductionist message, all manner of human experiences are now pathologised as discrete 'disorders' or 'illnesses'.

Is this anything to worry about? Well, yes and no. While psychological distress is as important as physical illness – as potentially restricting, debilitating, isolating, disturbing and ultimately life-ending – it is not the same thing. The erosion of stigma and shame around mental health is welcome, of course, particularly where it enables people to access support, but it is highly problematic to adopt the language, values and practices of medicine in how we understand and respond to the concerns that lead people to seek out therapy, not least because these experiences are rooted in complex interactions between subjectivity, meaning, past experience, embodiment, relationships and the cultural and socio-economic environments.

The notion of 'illness' in this context is at best a somewhat dated metaphor. At worst, it is an unscientific myth that can disempower and alienate people from their own experience, while simultaneously advancing the power and status of health professionals. Historically, the wildly heterogeneous field of counselling and psychotherapy has both courted and opposed the medical model, from the 'patients', 'symptoms', 'treatment' and 'cure' of psychoanalysis, to the de-medicalised potentiality models of humanistic psychology. Yet many contemporary therapists from across the theoretical spectrum would now reject a dogmatically medicalised understanding of the difficult edges of human experience, instead viewing their clients' thoughts, feelings and behaviours as idiosyncratic human responses to the sometimes-toxic conditions of life; not illnesses or deficiencies but subjective, embodied, relational attempts to navigate adversity and find meaning amid confusion and overwhelm. Somewhat ironically, this account is at odds with the dominant narratives in the mental health sector, where workers routinely adopt the medicalised language of psychiatry, passing on to service users a set of questionable, culturally-determined assumptions as if they were scientific truths, which then accompany people into therapy, like linguistic poltergeists that disrupt the articulation of experience with external distractions.

In one sense, this hardly matters. Whatever the person-in-therapy's relationship with psychiatric diagnosis – whether it is comforting, disempowering, ambivalent or enlightening – the therapeutic task, as ever, is to listen deeply and to tentatively open up a space for exploration, relational engagement and meaning-making, so that clients may find their own, unique voices with which to articulate the things that matter most. Given the freedom to do so, the significance of hastily applied or authoritatively imposed labels may evaporate or recede, to form just one of many threads that weave in and out of the work.

So perhaps the challenge is simply to go on providing such freeing spaces? We have been here before, of course. From the middle of the 20th century, anti-psychiatry and the humanistic/existential approaches transformed psychological theory and practice with liberating alternatives, seemingly for good. But power has a way of reasserting itself. At the expense of explorative, relational therapies and the people who value them, the medical model of distress has been resurgent, facilitated by a convergence of powerful influences: Big Pharma's desire to sell psychiatric drugs; biomedical psychiatry's obsession with genetics and neuroscience; the therapy profession's pursuit of mainstream acceptance via an alignment with healthcare, and the cultural capital acquired by cognitive behavioural therapy (CBT), which expediently marketed itself as a cheap, 'evidence-based treatment' at exactly the right moment to prosper from endorsement by the state in the Improving Access to Psychological Therapies (IAPT) programme.

It would be a mistake, then, to assume we can just hunker down in our therapy rooms, safe in the comforting belief that the space we offer is radical or liberating. For one thing, the values and culture of IAPT are intruding upon, contaminating and actively closing down that very space.

## The IAPT delusion

Initially, many therapists seemed to view CBT's dominance in IAPT as the project's only real problem. Despite decades of research suggesting that there is little to distinguish the outcomes of the main therapies – with client resources, external factors and the therapeutic relationship found to be more important than treatment model (Wampold, 2015) – CBT nonetheless accumulated masses of flawed but NHS-satisfying data to support its alleged technique-specific effectiveness, which, in an intensely competitive mental health sector, left other therapies desperately playing catch-up. The main counselling and psychotherapy organisations – anxious to appease both policy-makers and job-hunting members – largely played along with the perception that IAPT was a force for good in need of a little tinkering, and politely lobbied for the inclusion of other therapies in its offer. Meanwhile, in a parallel move, factions of both the person-centred and psychoanalytic schools gained some limited access to the programme by developing heavily manualised and compliantly researched versions of practice (person-centred experiential counselling for depression and interpersonal psychotherapy, respectively).

But these interventions have had little success in changing the overall CBT monoculture in IAPT. Despite eager appeals to 'science' in the debates, in truth it is impossible to disentangle the arguments on all sides from professional self-interest and political ideology. As we traverse the newly marketised professional landscape, therapists and their organisations are compelled to respond to the shifting cultural forces around mental health. In the process, therapy has been drawn away from its emancipatory values and towards the more controlling intentions of the state. Professional self-interest obviously fuels these dynamics – as individuals and groups vie for influence, legitimacy, jobs and funding – but political ideology plays a leading role too.

IAPT, we should remember, is a deeply politicised project. From its early development by CBT zealots and right-wing economists, to its implementation in England from 2008 by the New Labour government, IAPT has been driven by an unambiguous ideological agenda. Its goal is to reduce the welfare bill by rolling out 'cost-effective' (cheap, fast), NHS-based talking therapy in order to get depressed and anxious benefits claimants back to work – a rationale that reached its coercive nadir with the Conservative government's 2015 plan to put IAPT therapists directly into jobcentres (Meikle & Campbell, 2015). These policies conveniently ignore both the damaging effects of certain types of work and the socio-economic conditions that give rise to unemployment in the first place. Instead, the person is reduced to an atomised unit of potential labour. Work (any work) is viewed as a health goal and unemployment a matter of individual, personal – and even moral – deficiency. If we fix these deficiencies by curing mental ill health, the argument goes, the welfare bill will go down and the economy will prosper.

This toxic mix of political ideology, therapy practice, professional self-interest and health and welfare policy – and the rejuvenated medicalisation of distress that runs through it – has had a huge impact in the NHS, where psychotherapy departments in secondary mental health services have been cut and existing primary care counselling decimated. It is understandable that counsellors and psychotherapists should be outraged by CBT's flourishing in IAPT, not least on behalf of the prospective clients who have little, if any, choice about the therapy they end up with. But it is in many respects entirely appropriate that a project driven by such a blatantly neoliberal mindset would reject relational, explorative therapies – with their valuing of subjectivity and connectedness, their critical approach to expertise, their respect for the right to self-determination, and their inherent protest at the dehumanising conditions of contemporary life – and instead favour an instrumental method of non-relating that fits easily into a politically driven system of treatment targets and self-justifying data generation.

Whatever the intentions and efforts of its thousands of employees, IAPT is functioning as an act of state intrusion into the field of psychological suffering, powered by neoliberal values around health and work, with therapy co-opted as a tool for the maintenance and advancement of capitalism. These priorities are also visible in the IAPT behemoth's scandalous malfunctioning, within which critical thinking, authenticity and compassion are subordinated to the appearance of efficiency. What matters is getting people through the system. The pressures this imperative places on poorly supported staff, confronted daily with the complexity of psychological distress in such an industrialised working environment, is evident in the high rates of burnout (Westwood et al, 2017). Those using the service are also subject to its demoralising production-line culture. It is now a regular occurrence in my college counselling service for students to report poor experiences in IAPT. Young people's highly tuned radars for hypocrisy, judgement and inauthenticity instantly grasp the charade they are asked to take part in, even if they don't feel sufficiently empowered to challenge the professionals delivering it. Long waiting lists, short-term availability, highly manualised (to the point of feeling scripted), therapist-led interactions, meaningless bureaucracy masquerading as insight and evidence, referral to computerised self-help, cancelled sessions, lack of continuity in practitioners and high staff turnover all add to the sense of not being really listened to, respected or understood as a person. The burden of the system too often crushes the possibility of human acknowledgement and connection.

And if this picture of mental health provision in the NHS is not disturbing enough, IAPT's reductionist, mechanistic and technocratic culture is leaking out into areas beyond its own remit, contaminating therapeutic practice in other sectors and infiltrating our everyday understanding of psychological distress.

## 'Restructuring' relationships

The FE/HE counselling sector – my professional home for two decades – played an important role in the development of counselling in the UK. From the middle of the 20th century, as therapy grew in popularity, university counselling services emerged alongside courses in person-centred, psychodynamic and other therapies. In the late 1970s, trailblazers in HE and the Association for Student Counselling helped form what would become the UK's largest therapy organisation, the British Association for Counselling and Psychotherapy (BACP) (Aldridge, 2017). By the turn of the century, when I graduated from therapy training, university counselling was well established, but the picture in FE was rather different. In my own college, I was employed originally to develop a coherent service from the existing ad hoc provision. Over time, the service grew to meet increasing demand, as did many other services in the sector, but it still remained congruent with the therapeutic values I held in my own practice. Tensions between organisational agendas and counselling sometimes arose, usually around funding for an area that was not the college's core business, but generally the holistic, pastoral and developmental values of FE seemed a relatively nourishing environment for the provision of counselling.

Over the last few years, however, as services have become busier and the mental health of young people – and students particularly – has appeared to deteriorate (Thorley, 2017), student counselling has been undermined, to the extent that it now exists in a state of extreme precarity. Counsellors in both universities and colleges – but especially in FE – have lost their jobs as services have been restructured out of existence or drastically cut back to skeletal levels of provision. While writing this chapter, my own long-established service narrowly escaped a proposal to shut it down and replace the staff with lower-paid and less well trained 'wellbeing practitioners' offering short-term, solution-focused support. At precisely the time when it seems to be most needed, student counselling is in danger of being destroyed.

Part of what is going on here comes down to cold, hard cash. Since the 2008 global financial crisis and the UK Coalition government's decision to implement a programme of economic 'austerity', funding in FE has been in steady decline (Belfield, Farquharson & Sibieta, 2018; Jeffreys, 2018). Arguably, this neglect is itself political, as the culture of FE – aside from its role as a servant of local business – is not well understood by a political class who progressed through private school sixth-forms into Russell Group universities (Harris, 2015). But whatever prejudices are manifesting in government funding decisions, the impact of austerity on our colleges has been devastating. The sector is now riddled with a stress-inducing and ultimately unsustainable 'do more with less' culture, with yearly restructures thinning out staff and spreading division and anxiety, while long-term pay freezes mean many of us earn less in real terms than we did a decade ago.

But this economic context does not fully explain what is happening in student counselling. For one thing, the savings from axing counselling services are relatively small – indeed, non-existent, if we factor in the impact on student retention (Wallace, 2012). But even in universities, with their larger student support departments, better economies of scale and more funding than colleges, therapeutic counselling has been scaled back or cut completely, to be replaced by so-called 'wellbeing' teams. Any surviving counsellors in these services have usually had to make substantial concessions, often sacrificing the possibility of offering clients longer-term work just when the rising levels of severe distress would seem to warrant precisely the opposite (Lightfoot, 2018). University managers might believe they are modernising support through such changes but, for students themselves, the wellbeing model invariably means less opportunity for in-depth therapeutic work.

So where has this come from and why has the therapy field not challenged its emergence more vigorously, when restructuring student support into wellbeing teams seems to be having such a detrimental effect on the practice of counselling and psychotherapy on the ground? No doubt money is a key driver here – a 'wellbeing practitioner' can be paid less than a counsellor – but there are ideological forces at work too. While colleges might have fared worse financially under austerity, the HE sector has not been immune to a political climate dominated by neoliberal values. The New Labour-inspired explosion in university admissions and the Conservative government-derived policy to make students pay for their own higher education have turned those students into consumers and their courses into commodities, remodelling HE as a highly competitive marketplace. So, buzzwords, corporate branding and organisational reputation management begin to trump critical thinking and personal development.

One response we might expect to this changing ethos is that students, enabled by their newfound identity as consumers, would demand the best services – including access to more counselling – and that our professional organisations would back them up. There have been glimmers of hope in this regard (BACP, 2018; Weale, 2018), but this is also where medicalised tropes around mental health swoop in to quash dissent, with wellbeing services basking in the glow of NHS legitimacy by modelling themselves on IAPT and being seen to offer 'evidence-based treatments', even though in reality that often means less counselling and more superficial levels of support.

Frustratingly, these developments have been accelerated by the therapy field's own self-defeating collusion with the evidence-based regime (House, 2010), as the profession struggles to respond to the emperor's-new-clothes omnipotence of CBT, the pseudo-success of IAPT, and the burgeoning power of the NHS in how we make sense of psychological distress. Rather than resist and critique these dominant narratives, the temptation for therapists and their organisations – pressured to justify themselves in an increasingly cut-throat market in psychological treatment – has been to seek mainstream endorsement as a means of survival, giving in to the audit culture's demands for standardisation, medicalisation and bureaucratisation. This has always been something of a tense dynamic in the field, where the urge to make therapy as accessible as possible carries the risk that pragmatic compromise with powerful social institutions, such as the NHS, tips over into an expedient but corrosive incongruence of values, but it is surely at its most fraught right now.

As the state's biggest investment in the psychological therapies, IAPT is influencing our culture far beyond the boundaries of the health service. The authority bestowed by government endorsement and the high status of both the NHS and the medical model, coupled with the sheer scale of the programme, gives IAPT considerable power to dictate the language, values and acceptable ('best') practices within counselling and psychotherapy, potentially delegitimising anything that strays from its own medicalised blueprint.

One of the most striking examples of this incursion happened in my own sector when BACP introduced a 'competency framework' for university and college counselling (Hill & Roth, 2016), a document that expediently aligned the work of student counsellors with the values of the healthcare system. The very act of compiling 'competences' is itself not a neutral or objective thing to do, as it relies upon and promotes an instrumental understanding of therapeutic relationships in which predictable outcomes are thought to be ensured by adherence to manuals and the compliant implementation of specific techniques. This might be how some practitioners attempt to operate, but it ignores others who see therapy as a meaning-making dialogical encounter or principled 'way of being'. The competency framework thus purports to describe practice but in fact redefines it through a narrowing of its articulation, distorting or denying other ways of understanding the work that still thrive in the sector.

It is important to note here that CBT does not currently dominate student counselling, within which person-centred, integrative and psychodynamic approaches are still common (Wallace, 2013). Yet the competency framework structure, methodology and one of the principal authors were lifted straight from University College London's (UCL) earlier work on a competency framework for CBT, which was developed as part of the evolution of the IAPT programme (IAPT, 2007; Roth & Pilling, 2008). Indeed, the CBT framework was commissioned by IAPT, part-funded by Skills for Health, part-sponsored by the British Association for Behavioural and Cognitive Psychotherapies, and the final documents were published by the Department for Health, with IAPT named as the author (IAPT, 2007: 2).

So, while it is true that the methodology has been used since to define competences for other therapies (not without criticism from within those approaches – for example, CP-UK, 2009), the culture the competency project emerges from is clear to see: its core assumption being that therapy is – or should be – a manualised, instrumental, rigidly evidence-based branch of healthcare. In BACP's university and college counselling framework, this bias is most obvious in some of the language employed. The document refers to therapists as 'clinicians', to therapy as an 'intervention' or 'treatment', and to the work of counselling services as the 'delivery of healthcare'. But, for many of us, counselling is not healthcare, nor is it ancillary to healthcare. We do not 'deliver interventions' or 'treatments' and we do not understand our clients' experiences to be 'symptoms', as the framework calls them. Elsewhere in the document, 'behaviour regulation', 'corrective emotional experience' and 'cognitive mastery' are listed as 'factors common to all therapeutic approaches', when these phrases and the assumptions underpinning them are deeply problematic for some therapies.

In adopting this approach, the competency framework contributes – unwittingly perhaps – to the delegitimising of soundly researched, theoretically interrogated and philosophically consistent approaches to human distress that have been valued by students in counselling for decades. And if it was intended to support counsellors in the sector, the initiative certainly had no impact on the government's current plans for addressing young people's mental health, which involve importing the IAPT model directly into schools and colleges by lightly training existing academic and pastoral staff in CBT, with supervision from local NHS-based IAPT practitioners (Department of Health/Department for Education, 2017). What hope then of any remaining counsellors being kept on and resisting the medicalisation of their students' experiences?

As these developments testify, the deification of the IAPT model puts everything else at risk of extinction, particularly when the trajectory gathers momentum from forces within the therapy field itself. Organisational power moves; individual professional self-interest; the desire for endorsement by state institutions; the fear of being cast aside in the therapy marketplace; the search for professional status and bureaucratic certainties to mitigate the anxiety of the unquantifiable elements of therapeutic practice – all these tributaries feed into the IAPT surge as it washes away the diverse ecologies of practice in its path.

Witness here the closure of the University of East Anglia's (UEA) internationally renowned person-centred counselling training and its attached student counselling service (Rogers, 2017). I trained on the UEA postgraduate diploma in the late 1990s and it was rare, even then, for the person-centred approach (PCA) to be taught in a university setting. Yet the UEA programme remained defiantly congruent with person-centred values: deeply experiential; highly focused on the personal development of the practitioner; the spiritual and political dimensions of therapy were core themes, and completion of the course was through self- and peer-assessment. This congruence between theory, principle and practice was also expressed through its embeddedness within the campus and city communities: trainees had placements in the student counselling service and were encouraged to take up linked placements in a diverse range of settings outside the university, from an insurance company to Norwich prison.

The Centre for Counselling Studies, which ran the training within the School of Education, was a respected presence in the wider counselling and psychotherapy community. Led by prominent academics, it staged a number of international conferences, developed a successful masters and PhD programme, and, towards the end of the 2000s, was undertaking qualitative and quantitative research into therapeutic outcomes. But, by 2014, funding cuts had reduced the Centre to little more than a teaching operation, with no research or enterprise remit, and in 2017 it was closed completely.

Why would such a well-regarded and over-subscribed programme, which supported a large university counselling service, be axed? The courses might have been relatively costly to run – due to the intensive, experiential element, which required high levels of contact time between staff and students – but this is only part of the picture. Crucially, the philosophy of both the training and the counselling service were incongruent with the emerging ideologies in education and mental health. The radically de-medicalised and highly relational PCA, with its deep respect for freedom, self-determination and interconnectedness, not to mention its tendency towards social critique, was – and still is – a living, breathing challenge to the neoliberal values that were coming to occupy our institutions. Perhaps, at some level, the ongoing promotion of such a counter-cultural force in the university became intolerable.

Whatever the machinations that led to the decision, it has been a blow to the academic life of the PCA and curtailed the training plans of a cohort of future person-centred counsellors. It has also wiped out the availability of longer-term relational counselling at UEA, with the thriving counselling service replaced by a wellbeing team offering mostly short-term, CBT-based mental health support and group work. Meanwhile, across the campus in the clinical psychology department of the School of Medicine, the university has maintained its CBT training programme, which feeds directly into IAPT (UEA, 2018a), supplying the system with more willing agents of the state's wellbeing agenda.

A year and a half after I first looked at these courses on UEA's website, the link to the department's IAPT training in 'Other Modalities' still leads to an otherwise blank page that promises, 'Coming soon' (UEA, 2018b). So, whatever the intentions, for now it is CBT or nothing. A possibility we face here is that relational, exploratory, meaning-making counselling and psychotherapy could be all but erased from our culture, because fewer and fewer people will experience it, either as clients or practitioners. Instead, those who seek therapy or who have a calling for working with distress will be funnelled through a narrowing chamber of thought and practice, which sucks out anything that transgresses its prescriptive, medicalised dogma.

## Hope and despair

As a former client of the closed UEA counselling service made clear in a moving Facebook post (Keep Counselling, 2017), these changes are having a devastating effect on the provision of time and space for severe distress to be heard and witnessed and tentatively explored in a trusting therapeutic relationship. Instead, it must be packaged up, medicated, put through its paces by short-term, solution-focused interventions, sent away to other agencies providing much the same thing, and ultimately submerged; 'wellbeing' is in grave danger of coming to mean little more than emotional compliance with the narrow expectations of anxious, overwhelmed services.

It seems to me that there is an incremental tragedy occurring, not just in IAPT or in student counselling but across the whole sphere of human psychological suffering and how we respond to it as individuals, families, communities, professionals, institutions and as a society. While important, meaningful work no doubt continues to occur in all sorts of therapy settings, we are also witnessing a creeping dehumanisation in the structures that are built around these unpredictable and idiosyncratic interactions. As the IAPT/wellbeing model expands, carpet-bombing our culture with its medicalised view of unhappiness, we must register the losses.

This is not about the survival of favoured therapy brands, although we might well mourn them, but about the demise of key principles in encountering the pain of another human being. Compassion, empathy, self-determination, subjectivity, connectedness, meaning-making, growth, critical thinking, self-reflection, openness, diversity, trust, hope... love? These barely figure in the new order emerging around the talking therapies, which is obsessed instead with manuals, outcomes, risk management, haste, efficiency, surveillance, uniformity, status and, of course, data.

Why are we not marching in the streets about this? Why are we allowing our organisations to stumble on, compliantly eking out the odd concession from the state but never really standing up to the cultural forces corrupting our field? After a century of counsellors and psychotherapists doing their imperfect best to work with the complexity of the human condition, are we suffering from a form of collective compassion fatigue, a profession-wide burnout that seeks solace in the simplistic reassurances of State Therapy? Do this thing, get that outcome. Do it for more people, more cheaply. Get a salary, and don't think too hard about it. How comforting.

But, as this book and others like it attest, there is growing resistance to the neoliberal forces in and around mental health, from service users, therapists, activists, writers and even state-regulated psychologists (Johnstone & Boyle, 2018). We are pushing back against the medicalisation of distress and the industrialisation of care in a bid to create a new kind of space, where the person is no longer an isolated and sick individual in need of superficial cure but a complex social being, emerging from their own history and intimately connected to others within shared cultural and socio-economic environments.

So, while there might not be much cause for optimism, there is always hope. In my own practice, I am reminded regularly that, whatever mechanistic solutions are served up elsewhere, you only have to invite a person to tell their story and then listen closely to what they have to say, setting aside your own agenda for a time, for the value of us all to each other to be so strikingly obvious that it rings like a bell. It is heartening that young people readily embrace this opportunity for a deeper kind of engagement with their experiences of distress, when their lives are constantly flooded with infinitely scrolling reams of instruction about how to live.

As one young person said to me in counselling recently, while pondering the clunky interventions of the NHS in their search for meaning and hope amid ongoing despair: 'I don't want to just function, I want to live or not live.'

It really is that simple, that complicated and that important.

# References

Aldridge S (2017). Forty years of BACP: 1977-2017. *Therapy Today* 28(8): 22–27.

BACP (2018). *Campaign briefing: looking after our students' mental health – University and FE counselling services*. [Online.] BACP. www.bacp.co.uk/media/4159/bacp-student-mental-health-briefing.pdf (accessed 21 February 2019).

Belfield C, Farquharson C, Sibieta L (2018). *Annual Report on Education Spending in England*. London: Institute for Fiscal Studies/Nuffield Foundation.

CP-UK (2009). *Response from The College of Psychoanalysts UK to Skills for Health Briefing Sheet for 'Psychological Therapies National Occupational Standards Development Project' (May 2009)*. [Online.] London: College of Psychoanalysts UK; June. www.psychoanalysis-cpuk.org/HTML/RegulationArchive/Response0609.htm (accessed 16 July 2018).

Department of Health & Social Care/Department for Education (2017). *Transforming Children and Young People's Mental Health Provision: a Green Paper*. Norwich: HM Stationery Office.

Harris J (2015). Further education provides a lifeline. But try telling the government that. [Online.] *The Guardian*; 18 June. www.theguardian.com/commentisfree/2015/jun/18/further-education-lifeline-colleges-skills-cut (accessed 16 July 2018).

Hill A, Roth A (2016). *The Competences Required to Deliver Effective Counselling in Further and Higher Education: counsellor's guide*. Lutterworth: BACP. www.bacp.co.uk/media/2043/bacp-competences-working-in-further-higher-education-counsellors-guide.pdf (accessed 16 July 2018).

House R (2010). *In, Against and Beyond Therapy: critical essays towards a post-professional era*. Ross-on-Wye: PCCS Books.

IAPT Programme (2007). *The Competences Required to Deliver Effective Cognitive and Behavioural Therapy for People with Depression and with Anxiety Disorders*. London: Department of Health. www.ucl.ac.uk/drupal/site_pals/sites/pals/files/migrated-files/Backround_CBT_document_-_Clinicians_version.pdf (accessed 16 July 2018).

Jeffreys B (2018). Further education college finances face double whammy. *BBC News Online*; 17 September. www.bbc.co.uk/news/education-45524935 (accessed 17 September 2018).

Johnstone L, Boyle M, with Cromby J, Dillon J, Harper D, Kinderman P, Longden E, Pilgrim D, Read J (2018). *The Power Threat Meaning Framework: overview*. Leicester: British Psychological Society. www.bps.org.uk/sites/bps.org.uk/files/Policy%20-%20Files/PTM%20Main.pdf (accessed 16 July 2018).

Keep Counselling (2017). *Keep Counselling Facebook page*. Anonymous post; 2 May. www.facebook.com/keepcounselling/posts/287013121709313 (accessed 16 July 2018).

Lightfoot L (2018). Universities outsource mental health services despite soaring demand. *The Guardian*; 17 July. www.theguardian.com/education/2018/jul/17/universities-outsource-mental-health-services-despite-soaring-demand (accessed 16 July 2018).

Meikle J, Campbell D (2015). Hundreds of mental health experts issue rallying call against austerity. *The Guardian*; 17 April. www.theguardian.com/society/2015/apr/17/hundreds-of-mental-health-experts-issue-rallying-call-against-austerity (accessed 16 July 2018).

Rogers A (2017). Standing on the edge. *Therapy Today* 28(7): 30-33 [Adapted from: Rogers A. UEA Course Closures – an attack on values. [Blog.] Alliance for Counselling & Psychotherapy. https://allianceblogs.wordpress.com/2017/05/22/uea/ (accessed 16 July 2018).]

Roth AD, Pilling S (2008). Using an evidence-based methodology to identify the competences required to deliver effective cognitive and behavioural therapy for depression and anxiety disorders. *Behavioural and Cognitive Psychotherapy 36*: 129–147.

Thorley C (2017). *Not By Degrees: improving student mental health in the UK's universities*. London: IPPR. www.ippr.org/research/publications/not-by-degrees (accessed 16 July 2018).

UEA (2018a). *Training in Cognitive Behavioural Therapy*. [Online.] Norwich: University of East Anglia. www.uea.ac.uk/medicine/departments/psychological-sciences/cognitive-behavioural-therapy-training (accessed 17 September 2018).

UEA (2018b). *IAPT Other Modalities Training*. [Online.] Norwich: University of East Anglia. www.uea.ac.uk/medicine/departments/psychological-sciences/cognitive-behavioural-therapy-training/iapt-and-cbt-resources/iapt-other-modalities-training (accessed 17 September 2018).

Wallace P (2013). *Survey of Counselling Approaches in FE/HE*. Unpublished internal report. Lutterworth: BACP Universities & Colleges.

Wallace P (2012). The impact of counselling on academic outcomes: the student's perspective – final research findings, implications and future developments. *University & College Counselling (November)*: 6–11.

Wampold BE (2015). *The Great Psychotherapy Debate: the evidence for what makes psychotherapy work*. New York, NY: Routledge.

Weale S (2018). Bristol University faces growing anger after student suicides. [Online.] *The Guardian*; 26 May. www.theguardian.com/education/2018/may/26/bristol-university-faces-growing-anger-after-student-suicides (accessed 16 July 2018).

Westwood S, Morison L, Allt J, Holmes N (2017). Predictors of emotional exhaustion, disengagement and burnout among improving access to psychological therapies (IAPT) practitioners. *Journal of Mental Health 26*(2): 172–179.

# Chapter 8

# A critical appraisal of the economic model underpinning the Improving Access to Psychological Therapies (IAPT) programme

## Scott Steen

Despite recommendations from the National Institute for Health and Care Excellence (NICE, 2011) that psychotherapeutic interventions are effective for treating common mental health problems, such as depression and anxiety disorders, it was the cost-savings first proposed by Layard, Clark, Knapp and Mayraz (2007) that arguably catalysed what became the Improving Access to Psychological Therapies (IAPT) programme. The initial proposal quantified the scale and burden of mental health problems and the benefits of treating them not only as a moral imperative but also, crucially, on an economic basis. The calculation itself was relatively straightforward. It claimed that, given that NICE-approved therapies are effective for at least half of those treated, making them more available would substantially improve the nation's mental wellbeing and productivity (Layard et al, 2007). This economic case was and continues to be referenced.

Layard and Clark (2014) went on to estimate the economic cost of poor mental health as at least £70 billion, due to losses in work productivity, plus an additional £10 billion in physical healthcare costs. Estimates itemising the cost burden of poor mental health are almost equivalent to the entire budget of the NHS, at around £105 billion per year in England (Mental Health

Taskforce to the NHS in England, 2016). What's more, the overall investment in mental health treatments is far outweighed by the actual NHS activity costs incurred (Mental Health Taskforce to the NHS in England, 2016). The implications are self-evident: effectively treating poor mental health would generate massive cost-benefits, not only for healthcare services but also for workplaces and, by extension, the economy.

Over the course of its existence, there have been huge investments in the IAPT programme, including most recently a share of the £1.3 billion promised to mental health services in England by the government (Department of Health, 2017). Considering how central the economic model is to the IAPT programme, it stands to reason that evaluating its cost impact is central to its appraisal. It is 10 years since IAPT began to be rolled out nationally in England, and it therefore seems particularly timely to evaluate its overall economic impact. This chapter will consider whether the claim that IAPT would effectively 'pay for itself' (Layard et al, 2007: 8) can be substantiated.

I will start by considering the main theoretical critiques aimed at the programme and its economic rationale. Following this, I will appraise each of the main arguments, as set out by Layard and colleagues (2007), drawing on relevant and up-to-date research and publicly available data. In so doing, I will highlight any gaps in knowledge and potential false economies that emerge from my analysis. Given that most of the programme's work is focused on adults of working age and this activity is most commonly the subject of the research literature, I will only include sources focusing on this group.

Before starting on the economic appraisal, however, I want to acknowledge the opportunity afforded by the IAPT programme's emphasis on data collection. While not without its critics, one of the most significant achievements of the programme has been its collection and use of outcomes data. The decision to mandate the collection of outcomes measures at every client session has meant that 98% of all patients completing therapy with an IAPT service will have valid pre-and-post treatment outcome data (Clark et al, 2017). This not only provides enhanced transparency and accountability; it also means the data are highly representative of the population treated. This helps minimise confounding issues such as missing data, possible biases and exaggerated uncontrolled treatment effects (Clark, Fairburn & Wessely, 2008). Most notably, its ability to report such high-quality data is presented as crucial to the continued implementation and dissemination of psychological therapies within the NHS (McHugh & Barlow, 2012). The IAPT programme represents one of the largest practice-based evidence models ever incepted, if not the largest. That researchers can closely scrutinise its outcomes – as is the case here – is a unique strength that should be acknowledged.

## Theoretical critiques

There have been numerous theoretical critiques of the IAPT programme, many of which are relevant to its economic justification. The first of these refers to its epistemological understandings about the nature of mental health. Given the programme's close alignment with a positivist and biomedical ideology, many contend it over-simplifies and medicalises complicated psychosocial issues (Guy et al, 2012; Marzillier & Hall, 2009; McPherson, Evans & Richardson, 2009; Mollon, 2009; Pietroni et al, 2008; Samuels & Veale, 2009; Williams, 2015). This ideology is most notable in the original economic proposal, in which mental conditions are defined as discrete and quantifiable and something to be 'cured' with an appropriate dose of treatment (Layard et al, 2006, 2007). Consequently, the ideology underpinning IAPT disregards the philosophically and empirically disputed issue of defining what is meant by a mental health problem – a concept that, by its very nature, is subjectively constructed (Ingleby, 2004). A loosely defined concept risks pathologising everyday negative emotions as in need of treatment, leading to a somewhat paradoxical increase in perceived need, not reduction (Summerfield, 2018). It is notable that the incidence of common mental health problems across England over the last decade, far from decreasing, might have actually increased (Jorm et al, 2017).

IAPT is also criticised for an underpinning positivist philosophy that favours research methodologies that are considered inappropriate for determining the effectiveness of psychological therapies (Guy et al, 2012; Williams, 2015). Controlled methodologies, which NICE prioritises, can be limited to a non-clinically representative population that is less complex and diverse and less likely to have co-morbid conditions (Goddard, Wingrove & Moran, 2015; Guy et al, 2012; Hepgul et al, 2016). This risks further exacerbating care inequalities as the outcomes from such trials tend to come from a select minority who respond to treatment (Williams, 2015). Similarly, there is growing evidence that treatment-specific interventions have very little impact on outcomes, and that broader contextual factors such as client expectations, social determinants and individual therapist effects are far more influential (Wampold & Imel, 2015). The notion that some psychological therapies are superior to others in effectiveness is also being increasingly challenged in light of evidence for general treatment equivalence, both in meta-analyses (Barkham, Moller & Pybis, 2017; Cuijpers, 2016; Cuijpers et al, 2013; Wampold & Imel, 2015) and across IAPT services (NHS Digital, 2018a; Pybis et al, 2017). Championing this ideology, therefore, risks undermining the development of alternative and perhaps more suitable approaches.

Proponents of the IAPT programme point to cross-disciplinary support throughout its continued implementation, yet this incorrectly assumes that mental health professionals, commissioners, economists and politicians are all working towards the same goal of productivity and happiness (Cooper, 2009). Many criticise the programme for embracing a neoliberal philosophy of individualism and personal responsibility and neglecting more influential societal factors and economic policies (Marzillier & Hall, 2009; Rizq, 2012; Scanlon, 2015; Scanlon & Adlam, 2013). In line with this, some criticise the inherent assumption within IAPT that paid employment is an absolute good, of itself beneficial to health (Scanlon, 2015; Scanlon & Adlam, 2013; Slaney, 2016). Stable employment can indeed be positive for mental wellbeing (Black 2008; Waddell & Burton, 2006). However, as Scanlon (2015) argues, the programme effectively replaces socio-economic and political issues with imagined individual psychological failings (see also Lynne Friedli and Robert Stearn's Chapter 4 in this book). A consequence is that individual patients' problems are exacerbated and they are shamed and ostracised further for not finding suitable work, when in reality employment opportunities are simply not available (Viola & Moncrieff, 2016). What's more, the way in which mental health problems are classified by the Department for Work and Pensions (DWP) do not align with official clinical classification systems (Viola & Moncrieff, 2016), further demonstrating a lack of joined-up thinking.

Further compounding this issue, interventions that were never intended to improve work-related productivity or occupational status are being rolled out despite little or no empirical evidence to support this (McPherson, Evans & Richardson, 2009; Wesson & Gould, 2010). Rather, the evidence for IAPT's effectiveness is based mostly on symptom reduction, as measured by brief, disorder-specific outcome metrics, such as the PHQ-9 (Kroenke, Spitzer & Williams, 2001) and GAD-7 (Spitzer et al, 2006); the data do not include measures of improvements in quality of life, acceptability to patients and cost-effectiveness (Cooper, 2009; McPherson, Evans & Richardson, 2009). Furthermore, these measures, which were only ever meant to act as an indicator of disorder-specific conditions, are conflated for the purposes of financial remuneration, which they were also never designed or validated to do (Griffiths et al, 2013). Thus, costing treatment impact is complicated by the broad conceptualisation of mental health problems and the varied, multidisciplinary nature of interventions (Shearer, McCrone & Romeo, 2016).

Common interventions such as cognitive behavioural therapy (CBT) are a very general term used to refer to a group of similar therapeutic techniques (BABCP, 2012). Outcomes measured using symptom-oriented metrics, especially for specific diagnostic categories, are devalued by the common incidence of multiple co-occurring conditions, including personality disorders, substance misuse and physical health problems, among those seen by IAPT services (Goddard, Wingrove & Moran, 2015; Hepgul et al, 2016). Outcomes and engagement can vary widely between services and practitioners (Delgadillo et al, 2015; Gyani et al, 2013; NHS Digital, 2018b; RCP, 2013), even where interventions are highly protocolised and intensively case-managed (Firth et al, 2015; Green et al, 2014a).

Evidence has demonstrated the value of geographically adjusted benchmarking for areas with higher levels of deprivation that, due to various socio-demographic challenges, report lower treatment engagement and overall clinical outcomes (Delgadillo et al, 2015; Finegan et al, 2018). Given the wide variability not only between service settings but between treatments themselves, the suitability of the economic model for improving access to specific treatments is open to interpretation. For that reason, any claim about outcomes and, ultimately, their cost-association as attributable to a specific intervention is debatable.

## Challenges of costing mental health

Although psychotherapeutic interventions might show evidence of effectiveness, most research often lacks cost-benefit analyses. Very expensive treatments are unlikely ever to be integrated into clinical practice (Emmelkamp et al, 2014). Accordingly, any intervention should be studied in terms both of their clinical- and their cost-effectiveness. Indeed, many of the interventions available in IAPT services can point to evidence of cost-effectiveness in other settings (Biesheuvel-Leliefeld et al, 2012; Bosmans et al, 2012; Hollinghurst et al, 2010, 2014; McCrone et al, 2008; Richards et al, 2016; Shimodera et al, 2012). Nevertheless, direct economic evaluations of the IAPT programme have been limited, with most research focusing on service evaluations of clinical effectiveness, with little consideration for their cost (Clark et al, 2009; Glover, Webb & Evison, 2010; Hepgul et al, 2016; Royal College of Psychiatrists, 2013). Those evaluations that have considered costs have reported mixed findings on IAPT's cost-efficiency savings (de Lusignan et al, 2012; Griffiths & Steen, 2013;

Mukuria et al, 2013; Radhakrishnan et al, 2013; Sreeharan et al, 2013), with any effects found to disappear at follow-up (Mukuria et al, 2013).

Early economic evaluations reported considerable uncertainty about cost comparator outcomes (McCrone, 2013; Mukuria et al, 2013). Elsewhere, research has reported higher costs-per-treatment than the Layard and colleagues' (2007) original estimates (Mukuria et al, 2013; Radhakrishnan et al, 2013). A payment-by-results model has been trialled previously, with less than desirable results, due to significant data limitations and exclusion of influential factors such as measures of deprivation (Griffiths et al, 2013; IAPT, 2013). Regardless of the limited evidence for cost-benefit analyses and concerns about research that has already been done, the roll-out of the programme has continued, along with the introduction in April 2018 of an outcomes-based payment model (NHS Improvement, 2016).

## Tackling unemployment and incapacity benefit

While the original economic case for investing in psychological therapies promised savings in healthcare use, social services, crime, substance abuse and additional social support, it was the promise of tackling the numbers of people claiming incapacity benefit that was and continues to be given high credence (Layard et al, 2007; 2015). The case, put simply, was that costs to the exchequer for someone claiming incapacity benefit rather than working were roughly equivalent to a full course of CBT (on average), and treatment would therefore effectively cost nothing, as the expenditure would be recovered by welfare benefits savings (Layard et al, 2007). Indeed, such was their confidence in this claim, Layard and colleagues asserted that, even if these assumptions were halved, IAPT would still 'pay for itself' (2007: 8). These claims are, indeed, important, as employment circumstances have been linked with treatment outcomes (Finegan et al, 2018).

On that account, it is worth revisiting what has become of the proportions of people claiming incapacity benefit due to mental ill health over the decade since the programme's implementation. Starting with the initial demonstration sites, the claim that employment status can improve as a result of engaging with IAPT treatment appeared initially to be supported, with a five per cent improvement overall – a remarkable achievement, given that these services were just starting up and the short courses of treatment provided (Clark et al, 2009). However, since 2013/14, IAPT annual reports and data tables (NHS Digital, 2014a; 2014b; 2015; 2016; 2018a; 2018b) have shown that, while there have been signs of improvement for those who were unemployed or claiming incapacity benefit when they entered treatment, overall there are little to no differences before and after treatment in absolute numbers across each category. This suggests that any gains in employment among IAPT patients are countered by those who have to stop working because of mental health problems, despite this also being something that the programme is supposedly designed to address. Nonetheless, it should be noted that some, if not all, of this pattern can be accounted for by patients not stating their employment status at the end of treatment.

To obtain an alternative perspective, it is necessary to consider the overall trends in benefit claimants during the programme's inception. UK national trends in disability claims between 1995 and 2014 show that, although overall the number of claimants has fallen by 6.4%, and those classified as having conditions other than a mental disorder fell by 35.0%, the number of those whose claim is attributable to a mental health problem has more than doubled, rising by 103.4% (from 571,600 in 1995 to 1,136,360 in 2014) (Viola & Moncrieff, 2016). Almost half of all these mental health claims were due to 'depressive disorders', which accounted for 44.2% in 2014, rising to 66.8% when combined with anxiety disorders – almost seven in 10 of all claimants (Viola & Moncrieff, 2016). While these trends should be set in the context of the 2007/08 economic recession, the overall and relative downward trend in all other types of claimant suggest IAPT's influence was minimal.

With respect to gains in numbers of patients who returned to employment and reductions in incapacity benefit payments, it seems that the cost-benefit is lower today than it was in the original economic proposal. In 2008, all new benefit claims were replaced by the Employment and Support Allowance (ESA), paying between £57.90 and £73.10 a week for the first 13 weeks, and then £102.15 to £109.30 per week thereafter (Grange, 2018). The median annual income in the UK during the 2015/16 financial year was £26,300 (Office for National Statistics, 2017), which, at a basic tax rate of 20% (excluding personal allowance of up to £11,500), would mean a loss to the exchequer of £56.92 per week. Assuming a claimant has been receiving ESA for more than 13 weeks, today's costs to the exchequer would be between £689.30 and £720.29 per month, about £30 to £60 less than the estimated cost of a course of therapy provided by Layard and colleagues (2007) over a decade earlier. What's more, this estimate excludes any adjustments for inflation, so absolute financial implications are likely to be higher. Consequently, the remuneration provided by IAPT returning people to work has in effect reduced. When scaled at a national level, this further calls into question the claim that psychological therapies can, on their own, improve employment prospects at a beneficial cost.

Employment advisers and co-ordinators are employed in IAPT to help people with employment issues (Steadman & Thomas, 2015). Services use a variety of models, including contracting out this work to specialist employment advisers, usually based in DWP job centres or other, external organisations. However, the optimal model for providing this advice and support is not known, and evidence for comparative effectiveness is currently limited (Steadman & Thomas, 2015). Work-directed, clinical interventions for depressed people, including telephone and online CBT, have been shown to improve sickness absence rates (Nieuwenhuijsen et al, 2014; Reme et al, 2015; Steadman & Thomas, 2015). However, interventions such as these have also been identified as potentially opening the door to coercive practices aimed at getting unemployed people back into work (BABCP, 2015; see also Lynne Friedli and Robert Stearn's Chapter 4 in this book). Overall, then, it is unclear whether the national roll-out of these interventions has produced any significant impact on work absenteeism and, by extension, if the rates of returns to work support the economic justification.

## Reducing healthcare use

The economic case for the IAPT programme identified potential savings to the NHS, including through reduced healthcare use and fewer prescriptions for medication (Layard et al, 2007). There is evidence to suggest that engagement with psychological therapy leads to improved adherence to medication and an overall reduction in healthcare costs (de Lusignan et al, 2012; Layard et al, 2007; Mukuria et al, 2013; Parsonage, Hard & Rock, 2014). Similarly, meta-analytical evidence reports an association between engagement with psychological therapies and more sustained benefits to mental health over time (Cuijpers et al, 2013), with patients preferring talking treatments to medication (McHugh et al, 2013). Recent epidemiological evidence reports an improved treatment rate for adults with common mental health problems, increasing from 24% in 2007 to 39% in 2014 (McManus et al, 2016), probably due to investment in IAPT services. Studies evaluating healthcare use rates in relation to engagement with IAPT services have found subsequent reductions in accident and emergency department attendance and sickness certification, improved adherence to drug treatment (de Lusignan et al, 2012) and fewer GP appointments (Mukuria et al, 2013). Similarly, evidence suggests quicker access to adequate treatment can lead to reductions in the use of secondary and tertiary care services (Tosh et al, 2013), generating significant cost-savings overall (Saeidi & Wall, 2018).

Nonetheless, these studies are limited by inconsistent coding practices between service settings and short periods of data collection. A lack of joined-up service provision also restricts the potential gains in healthcare use. Equally, the wider impact of IAPT services on antidepressant prescribing appears negligible. While the incidence of mental health problems, care-seeking and diagnosis by GPs have remained stable, rates of antidepressant prescribing have increased by 10% every year since 1998 (Ilyas & Moncrieff, 2012; NHS Digital, 2017a). When these data are focused specifically on the local implementation of IAPT services, no significant effect on prescribing rates has been found (Sreeharan et al, 2013). The costs of increased antidepressant use are high, and rising, with recent findings reporting an NHS spend of £266.6 million per year (NHS Digital, 2017a). Antidepressant prescribing is clearly a complicated issue and one that cannot be resolved by simply providing more psychological therapy. Similarly, increased prescribing could be the result of other factors, such as increased recognition, and thus treatment, of depression, and reduced stigma. However, given that the incidence of mental health problems remains generally unchanged (Jorm et al, 2017), the data would seem to suggest that the impact of IAPT on healthcare use and prescription rates has been minimal.

Healthcare use is a complex issue, with particular patient groups using more resources than others. Factors such as co-morbidity, personality, socio-demographics and previous service use have been shown to increase uptake of services and affect treatment outcomes (Bower et al, 2013; Delgadillo et al, 2015; Goddard, Wingrove & Moran, 2015; Hepgul et al, 2016; Mukuria et al, 2013; Twomey et al, 2015). Nevertheless, the acknowledgement of these complex and interweaving factors is nominal when compared with the continued emphasis on symptom-focused outcome scores, especially with regard to remuneration (NHS Improvement, 2016). This is concerning as there is evidence to suggest that, when IAPT outcomes are evaluated using more in-depth and longitudinal approaches, the rates for improvement decrease (Scott, 2018). Therefore, a more robust and comprehensive consideration for these broader elements is necessary for appropriately determining the overall impact of the programme.

## Increasing pressures and service inefficiencies

IAPT's emphasis on targets and performance management is accused of creating perverse solutions to the realities of suffering (Rizq, 2012; Scanlon, 2015), which the programme's advocates strongly refute (Fonagy & Clark, 2015). Due to the pressures on the programme to treat an increasing number of patients, there has been an escalation of throughput in recent years (NHS Digital, 2014a;

2014b; 2015; 2016; 2018a). It took three years for the programme to see its first one million patients (Department of Health, 2012), but it saw almost this many in 2017/18 alone (NHS Digital, 2018a). By 2020/21, the programme plans to increase the numbers accessing services to 1.5 million per year, representing a 25% prevalence access rate (Mental Health Taskforce to the NHS in England, 2016). The pressure to see large volumes of patients reduces the opportunity to appropriately explore an individual's needs, difficulties and experiences at assessment. Many IAPT services conduct their initial assessments over the phone, using their least experienced practitioners for this work (Emmelkamp et al, 2014; Jones, Bale & Morera, 2013; Rizq, 2012). This is a concern when IAPT services are known to be taking referrals for people with highly complex difficulties, including personality disorders and multiple co-morbidities (Bower et al, 2013; Goddard, Wingrove & Moran, 2015; Hepgul et al, 2016).

To cope with these increased numbers, services are likely to have to provide other forms of treatment, such as online or group therapies. That is not to say these interventions are ineffective – indeed, there is evidence to support their real-world utility (NHS Digital, 2018b) – rather, it is to highlight that the allocation of treatment may be determined by these external pressures, more than by actual need. To illustrate this point, there is evidence of variable access to high-intensity treatments across IAPT services (Gyani et al, 2013; Richards et al, 2012), poor rates for stepping-up patients who don't improve from the treatment to which they have been allocated (Delgadillo, Gellatly & Stephenson-Bellwood, 2013; Richards et al, 2012), early drop-out from treatment (Emmelkamp et al, 2014; NHS Digital, 2018a; Richards et al, 2012; Richards & Borglin, 2011), high rates of re-referral (Cairns, 2013; Di Bona et al, 2014; Hepgul et al, 2016), and little differentiation between the intake scores for patients allocated to low- and high-intensity treatments (Bower et al, 2013; Chan & Adams, 2014). These findings suggest patients are commonly referred to inappropriate treatment, suggesting these decisions are influenced by pressures beyond the individual's presenting needs.

The stepped-care model and in particular the provision of low-intensity therapies, delivered principally by psychological wellbeing practitioners (PWPs), are central to the IAPT model. These interventions comprise a broad range of treatments that are typically short in length, with minimal practitioner input. Based on evidence that they can be effective for mild-to-moderate common mental health problems (Bennett-Levy, Richards & Farrand, 2010; Cuijpers et al, 2010, 2011; Haug et al, 2015; Zhou et al, 2016), IAPT has been able to use them to treat increasing numbers of patients year on year. Some of these therapies report recovery rates of around 53–57%

(guided self-help and computerised-CBT) (NHS Digital, 2018b), and some patients prefer less intensive treatments (Bennett-Levy et al, 2010), although findings can vary (Brown et al, 2011).

Low-intensity interventions that can be delivered without practitioner input offer great potential from a cost-benefit perspective. However, when treatments are unsupported, particularly in the case of self-help interventions, recovery rates are up to 10% lower (NHS Digital, 2018b). Moreover, these interventions, particularly computer-based therapies, have high attrition and limited uptake, even when there is additional support (Duarte et al, 2017; Gilbody et al, 2015). There is also a gap in the literature on the effectiveness of low-intensity interventions with black and minority ethnic (BME) groups (Birmingham Healthy Minds 2017). This is a problem, given the IAPT workforce is predominantly white, female and aged 26–45 years, and therefore not always representative of local populations (de Lusignan et al, 2011; NHS England/Health Education England, 2016).

Other low-intensity treatments report recovery rates of around 45% (NHS Digital, 2018b), but the evidence for their relative cost-effectiveness in clinical settings is mixed. Some studies have found technologically mediated low-intensity interventions to be equally effective and also cheaper than those supported by a therapist (Hammond et al, 2012; Radhakrishnan et al, 2013), although other evidence reports general cost equivalence (Duarte et al, 2017). Research to support the clinical and cost-effectiveness of low-intensity interventions for preventing relapse and recurrence of depression is limited (Rodgers et al, 2012). Indeed, research on the longer-term benefits of low-intensity interventions is lacking (Zhou et al, 2016), although there is evidence that the durability of their effects is negligible beyond one year (Ali et al, 2017). This might explain why returning patients are common in IAPT, with at least a third being re-referred (Hepgul et al, 2016), sometimes as many as seven times (Cairns, 2013). This, therefore, challenges the claim that treatment by IAPT is 'a one-off cost' per person (Layard, 2015: 5).

Given that the cost-benefit and longer-term effects of low-intensity treatments are unknown, it is interesting how extensive their roll-out across the IAPT programme has been. Low-intensity treatments represent only one component of an effective and responsive service model and serve as an entry to care for those perhaps unable or initially unwilling to engage with higher-intensity treatments. Nevertheless, as evidence has shown, procedures for stepping-up patients and allocating them to appropriate levels of care can be less than optimal within IAPT (Bower et al, 2013; Chan & Adams, 2014; Delgadillo et al, 2013; Richards et al, 2012), and the pathway from low- to high-intensity provision is far from clear, with wide variations between services in practices and protocols (Gyani et al, 2013; Richards et al, 2012). Furthermore, evidence for the superiority of stepped care over other delivery models, including stratified care, is notably lacking (van Straten et al, 2015). The variation in outcomes and delivery models across services suggest the possibility that this model may widen inequalities in care (Glover et al, 2010; Royal College of Psychiatrists, 2013; Richards et al, 2012).

## Engagement rates

Access and engagement studies are limited mainly to investigating differences between IAPT services and not by comparison with other, non-IAPT services (Binnie & Boden, 2016; Di Bona et al, 2014; Marshall et al, 2016). Research in this area has only focused on a small number of variables, mainly to do with access (de Lusignan et al, 2012; Mukuria et al, 2013). National data report the number of sessions that are not attended to be 12%, with a range of between five and 27% (Binnie & Boden, 2016; Clark, 2015; South West Expert Reference Group, 2015). Other sources report non-attendance rates as high as 45–48% for initial assessment and treatment sessions (Byng et al, 2011; Di Bona et al, 2014; NHS Digital, 2018a; Murphy et al, 2013; Richards & Borglin, 2011). Experiential research tells us that patient expectations about assessment and treatment, service and practitioner rigidity and dissatisfaction with the service can influence early engagement (Binnie & Boden, 2016; Cairns, 2014; Marshall et al, 2016). A consistent finding across IAPT services is that a large proportion of patients tend to end their therapy much sooner than the NICE guidelines recommend (Royal College of Psychiatrists, 2013; NHS Digital, 2018b). What's more, patients who prematurely terminate their therapy have been found to attend, on average, three sessions only (Royal College of Psychiatrists, 2013). Although session-by-session measures provide more representative outcome data, the claim that IAPT services deliver genuine NICE-recommended therapies appears disingenuous in the light of the actual number of sessions most clients attend.

## Assessment, one-session only referrals

As I acknowledge at the start of this chapter, the model adopted by IAPT services, including session-by-session measures, has generated more representative data than has ever been achieved previously in the NHS (Clark, Fairburn & Wessely, 2008; Clark et al, 2017). Nearly every client completing treatment (defined as at least two treatment contacts) is included in the national analysis of treatment effectiveness. Crucially, however, this fails to account for those attending one session only. In the latest annual report (2016/17) (NHS Digital, 2018a), there were 965,379 referrals who entered treatment (defined as attending at least one treatment session) and 567,106 who completed treatment (defined as at least two treatment contacts). This would suggest that around 40% of those entering IAPT do not complete treatment – a substantial proportion. Admittedly, there are caveats to this interpretation: namely, the referrals entering and completing treatment are not necessarily within the same year, given the process nature of service data. Also, a head-count of referrals is not strictly a head-count of patients, as a patient may be referred several times. Nevertheless, these figures have been consistent in previous annual reports (NHS Digital, 2014a; 2014b; 2015; 2016) and research findings (Di Bona et al, 2014; Radhakrishnan et al, 2013; Richards & Borglin, 2011). Moreover, referrals are counted in the same way for recovery and improvement calculations.

Given that referrals could be receiving advice/information, that this group attends just one session need not be a negative. However, excluding them from the data analysis serves to narrow the interpretation of service effectiveness. From the perspective of referrers, commissioners and policy-makers, all individuals accessing the service are important, providing data to appropriately inform and assign the allocation of resources. Not engaging in initial treatment can be due to a range of internal and external factors, including waiting times, patient expectations and perceived unacceptability of the service and practitioner (Marshall et al, 2016). In the NHS Digital (2018b) annual 2016/17 data, around 43% of referrals were deemed suitable for the service at assessment but declined the treatment offered, while 23% were deemed not suitable, and only nine per cent were discharged by mutual agreement after being given advice and support. According to NHS Improvement (2016/17), assessments for IAPT adult mental health cluster activity totalled 726,002, at an average cost of £127 each, or around £92.5 million in total. Consequently, the 40% of referrals who attend just one session appear to incur a substantial cost of approximately £37 million.

## Considering the cost-benefit of IAPT services

Given the IAPT programme's economic justification, the levels of engagement and the proportion of referrals who attend one session only, I undertook a brief analysis to assess to what extent the money spent on IAPT services is achieving its target benefits. Using publicly available data on costs and outcomes, it is possible to generate an overall figure for cost per clinical outcome. While, understandably, this will mask huge variation between and within services, it is a useful indicator of how efficient the programme is as a whole in terms of what it delivers for the total money invested. This calculation represents a small part of a broader cost-benefit analysis published in the *Journal of Health Psychology*, which reviewed the cost-benefits in greater detail, including estimated session costs and sensitivity analyses (Steen, 2018).

### IAPT annual reports

The IAPT programme publishes national annual data tables on the use of its services, including overall figures on the numbers of new referrals, referrals entering treatment, referrals finishing a course of treatment (at least two treatment contacts), and recovery and reliable improvement. Data are submitted regularly to NHS Digital and are then summarised to inform stakeholders about activity and outcomes at national and local levels. To allow the most up-to-date information, data are reported up until the last time point available and this single data point is taken to represent the whole referral. Referrals are included if they have an end date within that year, regardless of when the referral was first added, so some activity will have begun in the preceding year. As already stated, while not strictly a true snapshot of activity and outcomes, given that the national reporting adopts this approach, I will too.

Categories of completing treatment, reliably improving, moving to recovery and reliably recovering are included, as per the programme's definitions (NHS Digital, 2018a). The primary source of these data on IAPT service activity and outcomes is *Psychological Therapies: annual report on the use of IAPT services (2016/17)*, published February 2018, representing data from 1 April 2016 to 31 March 2017 (NHS Digital, 2018a; 2018b). Outcomes data completeness during this period was of high quality, with the latest estimates reporting pre-and-post outcome measures for 98% of those completing treatment (Clark et al, 2017).

### NHS reference costs

In April 2018 an outcomes-based payment model was implemented across IAPT services with the aim to incentivise service delivery to enhance quality and efficiency. It follows publication of the 2017/18 and 2018/19 national tariff payment system (NHS Improvement, 2016), which includes a set of prices and rules for providers and commissioners to use as a basic service price and payment guide. Although prices are agreed locally, the system stipulates that they must be linked to outcomes. Each submission is mandated and supported by detailed guidance on costing and collection, to reduce the variation in practices. A secondary source of data therefore includes the NHS reference costs (2016/17) – that is, the average unit costs of providing specifically defined services in a given financial year. It is the responsibility of providers to improve processing systems to ensure there are accurate reference cost data for delivering services. NHS references costs are submitted annually by providers and are used to inform national tariff prices. During this period, total activity, unit costs and total costs are provided for adult IAPT mental health care clusters episodic care and initial assessments. A unit cost is the cost incurred by providing a single unit of care and the cost of the initial assessment is per patient assessed and can cover multiple attendances. This activity and the unit costs have been extracted and are reported in Table 1 below.

**Table 1: Extracted NHS reference costs for adult IAPT activity and total costs 2016/17**

| Description | Total Activity | Unit cost | Total cost |
|---|---|---|---|
| Adult IAPT mental health care clusters | 886,645 | £309.78 | £274,664,758 |
| Adult IAPT mental health care clusters – initial assessments | 726,002 | £127.49 | £92,554,434 |
| **Total overall costs** | | | **£367,219,192** |

The analysis aimed to assess, based on the amount invested in IAPT services, how many people completed, reliably improved, recovered and reliably recovered, to help determine how beneficial IAPT treatment is as a cost-per-category. To generate an estimated cost-per-patient, overall costs were divided by the number of patients who completed treatment, reliably improved, recovered and reliably recovered, each of which is reported in Table 2. Overall costs were calculated using the total NHS reference costs (2016/17) for care treatment clusters and initial assessments. Given that initial assessments can involve advice, signposting and assessing for unsuitability, the cost-per-patient relative to each outcome category is provided with and without overall assessments costs. I have included assessment costs as necessary, given that a large proportion of patients entering treatment do not attend at minimum two contact sessions. Finally, given that the recovery and reliable recovery calculation depends on how many referrals enter the system at caseness (that is, considered to be sufficiently unwell to need treatment), I also report a proportional figure based on this rate of above-caseness.

Table 2: Overall cost-per-referral completed, reliably improved, recovered and reliably recovered relative to IAPT NHS reference costs 2016/17 (including and excluding overall assessment costs)

| | Number of referrals (IAPT 2016/17) | Relative to IAPT total overall NHS reference costs (2016/17) | Relative to IAPT NHS reference costs (2016/17) (excluding overall assessment costs) |
|---|---|---|---|
| Completed | 567,106 | £647.53 | £484.33 |
| Reliably improved | 369,254 | £994.49 | £743.84 |
| Recovered* | 258,884 | £1,418.47 | £1,060.96 |
| Reliable recovered* | 246,456 | £1,490.00 | £1,114.46 |
| | | | |
| *Started at caseness | 524,730 | £1,312.48 | £981.68 |
| Proportion | 93% | | |

The calculation demonstrates large differences in costs, depending on whether the assessment costs are included or excluded. This further supports the need to consider all referrals entering treatment in IAPT services and not just those who complete at least two treatment contacts, given it risks skewing the interpretation of effectiveness. Based on these figures, the overall cost per patient completing treatment is £648, reliably improving is £994, recovering is £1,419 and reliably recovering is £1,490. The national recovery rate target is 50% and has been since the programme's inception over a decade ago (Department of Health, 2012). Although this rate was not achieved nationally during 2016/17 (49.3%), it was for the first time in early 2017 (National Collaborating Centre for Mental Health, 2017). If a 50% recovery rate of all those completing treatment was assumed during this period, then the cost per recovered referral would be £1,295, or £969 if we exclude overall assessment costs.

At first glance, the cost of completing treatment (£648) compares favourably with the original economic analysis of £750 per person treated. Indeed, it is lower than Mukuria and colleagues' (2013) figure of £1,042 (using national unit costs as per this calculation) and Radhakrishnan and colleagues' (2013) £877. Given their costs are based on data collected from 2007 to 2009 and 2009 to 2010 respectively, any gains in cost-benefit per patient completing treatment appears to have slowed proportionally year on year. The cost per patient recovered (£1,419) also compares favourably with the £1,766 figure reported by Radhakrishnan and colleagues (2013) and the reliable recovery cost (£1,490) is substantially less than the cost-per-patient reliably recovering of £3,800 reported by Mukuria and colleagues (2013).

Nevertheless, it is worth putting these figures in context. Both the Radhakrishnan et al (2013) and Mukuria et al (2013) papers cite significant start-up costs and use of inexperienced trainees as limitations. Also, crucially, the figure presented in this analysis does not take into consideration the number of sessions needed to deliver these cost-benefits. For Radhakrishnan and colleagues (2013), the median number of sessions received was five for low-intensity and eight for high-intensity treatments. Mukuria et al (2013), who uses an average and possibly includes the assessment session, reports three sessions attended overall and, although not providing any direct costs-per-intensity level, specifies that the majority (more than 90%) were initially assigned to low-intensity interventions.

In the annual figures for 2016/17, IAPT (NHS Digital, 2018b) reported an average overall attendance of 6.6 sessions, with its largest proportion of low-intensity treatments ranging from around 2.7 to 3.6, and high-intensity ranging from around 5.4 to 7.2 sessions. Layard and colleagues' (2007) original estimate of £750 was broadly based on 10 sessions delivered at an assumed cost of £75 per session. If this were updated to include the 6.6 average, the cost per patient completed would be £495. Even at a 7.2 session attendance average – the longest high-intensity treatment session attendance, for interpersonal psychotherapy (NHS Digital, 2018b) – this works out at £540, still short of the figure reported here (£648). Using existing literature sources and national data, Barkham, Moller and Pybis (2017) use average session attendance and recovery rates data to demonstrate potential savings can be achieved upwards of £30 million should patients receiving high-intensity CBT have less costly counselling instead, translating to a £212 saving per patient. The PSSRU (2017) estimates the cost of a course of CBT to be around £450 per person within the first year, or around £280 for six sessions, again all lower than the cost reported here (£648). Across 21 studies, Barrett and Petkova (2013) found the cost per hour of individual CBT ranged from £31 to £133, at 2012 pricing. The cost per completed treatment overall divided by an average of 6.6 sessions would work out at £98 per session, or £108 per CBT session, based on a 6.0 average, as per the annual report figures for CBT (NHS Digital, 2018b). This suggests that, while encouraging at first, these figures must be regarded in the context of a lower session attendance average. At a session-level, the cost-efficiency of interventions in IAPT services appears to be at the higher end, although admittedly they are not strictly the most expensive (Barrett & Petkova, 2013).

## Staff training and retention

Much of the discussion so far has focused on service-level factors; I have not yet considered the impact of IAPT on its workforce. The ambitious new access rate targets will require extensive funding and training (NHS England Mental Health Taskforce, 2016). However, regarding mental health, there can be wide variation in local spending decisions (Martin, Rice & Smith, 2008), highlighting a potential risk of increased care inequalities. Currently, the programme has over 6,000 newly trained CBT workers practising at both low- and high-intensity levels, as well as non-CBT modality therapists who have undergone a short training programme (NHS England/Health Education England, 2016). Although NICE (2011) recommends that interventions should be delivered by trained and competent practitioners, the latest audit of psychological therapies (Royal College of Psychiatrists, 2013), involving mostly IAPT services, reported that more than 30% of practitioners had no formal training or accreditation for the interventions they were delivering, and around one in six supervisors had not received any formal training. What's more, as Barkham and colleagues (2017) point out, there was a 35% decrease in the number of qualified counsellors working as high-intensity therapists between 2012 and 2015, despite the total IAPT workforce growing by up to 18%. A notable reason for the incidence of mental health problems not decreasing in the population, despite IAPT investment, appears to be the less-than-optimal standards of the treatments being delivered, combined with a failure to reduce disparities in access to treatment (Jorm et al, 2017).

Work-related stress, depression and anxiety represent a significant challenge for IAPT services. Intensified workforce pressures can create stressful working experiences (Black, 2008; West, 2016), leading to increased sickness absence rates (West, 2016). Improved workforce engagement is linked with lower staff turnover and reduced sickness absence rates (Black, 2008). In 2017, a national survey of 1,678 NHS psychological services staff (including IAPT workers) reported high levels of anxiety, stress, depression, burnout and low morale (BPS, 2018). While levels of depression showed signs of decreasing, in comparison with previous years, experiences of stress and pressure in response to increasingly ambitious targets appeared to be on the increase (BPS, 2018; Rao et al, 2016). Furthermore, a culture of bullying and harassment is reportedly common (BPS, 2018). This emulates a historical pattern within IAPT services, in which reports of an overly-stretched workforce and high-pressure roles are common (BPS, 2018; Johnson et al, 2018; Rao et al, 2016; Rizq, 2012; Steel et al, 2015). Many of the stressors relate to a top-down fixation on targets, lack of management/supervision support, additional administrative demands, unpaid overtime and insufficient resources. The pressure of the audit culture within IAPT, with its emphasis on targets and performance management, is intensified by management scrutiny of practitioners within the programme (Rizq, 2012). This can lead to depersonalisation and the development of negative or cynical attitudes towards clients (Rizq, 2012; Steel et al, 2015). Increased pressure and focus on targets can undermine compassionate care and engagement, affecting treatment quality and patient experience (Delgadillo, Saxon & Barkham, 2018; Johnson et al, 2018; Rizq, 2012; see also Penny Campling's Chapter 2 and Rosemary Rizq's Chapter 9 in this book).

Pressures such as these have been seen elsewhere in the NHS, most notably in Mid-Staffordshire NHS Foundation Trust, where the needs of the system were put before the needs of the patients (Francis, 2013). That said, the IAPT programme's documentation does attempt to remind its workforce of their ethical duty (National Collaborating Centre for Mental Health, 2017). However, the direct link between financial income and treatment outcomes introduced by the new outcomes-based payment model (NHS Improvement, 2016) could complicate this.

The number of NHS mental health staff taking long-term stress leave increased by 22% between 2012/13 and 2016/17 (Greenwood, 2017). Considering the salary bandings of IAPT staff, from Band 4 trainee PWPs to Band 8 high-intensity therapists, the cost among the IAPT workforce would be between £74 to £319 per lost working day, assuming the lowest and highest hourly wage rates and a 37.5-hour working week (NHS Employers, 2017). A sickness absence rate of 4.8% was recorded for all mental health services during 2016/17 (NHS Digital, 2017b), which, when applied to 6,000 newly trained therapists, would translate to an estimated loss of up to £21,000–£92,000 per day. There is also notable turnover among IAPT PWPs, with reported leaver rates of up to 22% on average (NHS England/ Health Education England, 2016). While explanations for this suggest these are individuals moving to other IAPT services for career progression, rather than leaving the programme entirely, this has yet to be empirically verified. Moreover, there are direct experiential accounts from PWPs that illustrate stressful working practices and a perceived undervaluing of the role (Bogart, 2015; Westwood et al, 2017). Keeping trained PWPs in their post is necessary for the IAPT delivery model and for reaching its ambitious access targets rate. Concerns about the safety and effectiveness of services were also highlighted in the latest NHS psychology services staff survey (BPS, 2018), with approximately three-quarters of respondents citing low staffing levels as a primary reason for a loss of confidence in standards of treatment.

## Implications and potential solutions

A review of the available evidence seems to indicate a potential misrepresentation of the true costs of IAPT service delivery and efficiency. The evidence needed to accurately cost mental health services, and in particular for determining the cost-effectiveness of IAPT services, is limited to only a handful of studies (de Lusignan et al, 2012; Delgadillo et al, 2017; Griffiths & Steen, 2013; Mukuria et al, 2013; Radhakrishnan et al, 2013). That rates of mental health problems have not decreased in the population (Jorm et al, 2017) and mental health-related benefit claims have increased (Viola & Moncrieff, 2016) contests the notion that IAPT is succeeding in its intended effect. Cost-effectiveness studies in this regard are therefore much needed.

That the costs are below £1,500 per successful patient treatment is reassuring at first, but cost-benefit figures must be set in context of a lower average number of sessions than originally predicted, which in turn increases the individual cost-per-category estimates. It appears that the programme is achieving its access, engagement and outcome targets by offering more low-intensity therapy. Potentially, the recently increased access rate target to 25% (Mental Health Taskforce to the NHS in England, 2016) may exacerbate service efficiency issues, which is concerning, given the notable rates of relapse for those receiving these treatments (Ali et al, 2017). This high rate of relapse could explain the sizeable rate of re-referrals (Cairns, 2013; Di Bona et al, 2014; Hepgul et al, 2016). Again, it is worth restating evidence of the high levels of complexity among IAPT referrals (Bower et al, 2013; Goddard et al, 2015; Hepgul et al, 2016), as well as the less than optimal treatment allocation and stepping-up practices (Bower et al, 2013; Chan & Adams, 2014; Delgadillo et al, 2013; Richards et al, 2012). There is potential for inefficient systems and false economies emerging, where services treat and re-treat referrals in the interests of short-sighted outcome targets. This again highlights the need for more longitudinal and follow-up research, particularly with respect to low-intensity treatments.

Cost-effectiveness doesn't just mean providing cheaper interventions; rather, it considers whether the gains made clinically, personally and societally are less than the direct treatment costs (Cohen & Reynolds, 2008). It is encouraging that greater attention is being paid to organisational factors, as opposed to solely seeking to improve treatment fidelity. Clark and colleagues (2017) demonstrate how influential service-level factors are in determining patient outcomes, including enhanced data quality, increased attendance, improved engagement and reduced waiting times. Widening access to a range of non-therapy services, implementing techniques to enhance service management, focusing on prevention of drop-out, and increasing follow-up opportunities have all been shown to improve outcomes from therapy (Tosh et al, 2013). The findings from the field of implementation science are revealing how important the context is when integrating evidence-based techniques in real-world clinical settings (Proctor et al, 2009; Shidhaye, 2015). More real-world data on cost-effectiveness can now be collected via IAPT services and used to complement existing evidence from controlled methodologies (Barkham et al, 2017). Future IAPT reports are expected to include funding information that could be used to better inform statistical models and cost-benefit analyses (Clark et al, 2017). The cost aspect of effectiveness is clearly important and future research in this area should make efforts to include this where possible.

Part of the problem stems from using single indicators for complex processes. Therefore, a promising opportunity is the greater embrace of pluralistic techniques that consider multiple research methodologies, including an increased emphasis on evidence founded in clinical practice (Barkham, Hardy & Mellor-Clark, 2010; Barkham et al, 2017). Although the update to the NICE guidelines on depression has been delayed, the draft (in press) incorporates a greater scope to include research beyond controlled methodologies and meta-analyses, although it still preferences these methods (Barkham et al, 2017). This broadened scope will bring within NICE's remit other interventions previously excluded by its reliance on controlled methodologies. Moreover, it acknowledges the accumulating body of evidence demonstrating treatment equivalence between psychological therapy modalities (Barkham et al, 2017; Cuijpers, 2016; Cuijpers et al, 2013; Wampold & Imel, 2015). Furthermore, it should be noted that a quarter of the IAPT workforce now classifies themselves as non-CBT specialists (Fonagy & Clark, 2015), indicating improving treatment choice for patients. There are also promising avenues of research that offer the opportunity to enhance service delivery through more practice-based and relevant methods, including practice research networks (Lucock et al, 2017), collaborative care models (Green et al, 2014b), outcome feedback technology (Delgadillo &

Overend, 2017), outcome adjusted benchmarking (Delgadillo et al, 2015) and improved record linkage (de Lusignan et al, 2011, 2013; Parsonage et al, 2014). These will allow for more practical and meaningful solutions to be disseminated and so help to determine the actual effectiveness and, ultimately, cost-effectiveness of interventions.

## References

Ali S, Rhodes L, Moreea O, McMillan D, Gilbody S, Leach C, Lucock M, Lutz W, Delgadillo J (2017). How durable is the effect of low intensity CBT for depression and anxiety? Remission and relapse in a longitudinal cohort study. *Behaviour Research and Therapy* 94: 1–8.

BABCP (2015). *'Coercive' Therapy Proposals for Jobcentres - Statement from BABCP Board.* [Online.] BABCP; 25 June 2015. www.babcp.com/files/Press/'coercive'-therapy-proposals-for-jobcentres-statement-from-babcp-board.pdf (accessed 25 February 2019).

BABCP (2012). *What is CBT?* [Online.] BABCP: British Association for Behavioural & Cognitive Psychotherapies. www.babcp.com/files/Public/what-is-cbt-web.pdf (accessed 25 February 2019).

Barkham M, Hardy GE, Mellor-Clark J (2010). *Developing and Delivering Practice-Based Evidence: a guide for the psychological therapies.* Chichester: Wiley-Blackwell.

Barkham M, Moller NP, Pybis J (2017). How should we evaluate research on counselling and the treatment of depression? A case study on how the National Institute for Health and Care Excellence's draft 2018 guideline for depression considered what counts as best evidence. *Counselling and Psychotherapy Research* 17(4): 253–268.

Barrett B, Petkova H (2013). Cognitive behaviour therapy: a comparison of costs. In: Curtis L. *Unit Costs of Health and Social Care 2013.* Canterbury: Personal Social Services Research Unit, University of Kent (pp16–20). www.pssru.ac.uk/pub/uc/uc2013/full-with-covers.pdf (accessed 1 March 2019).

Bennett-Levy J, Richards DA, Farrand P (2010). Low intensity CBT interventions: a revolution in mental health care. In: Bennett-Levy J, Richards DA, Farrand P et al (eds). *Oxford Guide to Low Intensity CBT Interventions.* Oxford: Oxford University Press (pp3–19).

Biesheuvel-Leliefeld KEM, Kersten SMA, van der Horst HE, van Schaik A, Bockting CL, Bosmans JE, Smit F, van Marwijk HWJ (2012). Cost-effectiveness of nurse-led self-help for recurrent depression in the primary care setting: Design of a pragmatic randomised controlled trial. *BMC Psychiatry* 12(1): 59. https://doi.org/10.1186/1471-244X-12-59

Binnie J, Boden Z (2016). Non-attendance at psychological therapy appointments. *Mental Health Review Journal* 21: 231–248.

Birmingham Healthy Minds (2017). *Innovative Ways of Engaging with Black and Minority Ethnic (BME) Communities to Improve Access to Psychological Therapies.* [Online.] London: NICE. www.nice.org.uk/sharedlearning/innovative-ways-of-engaging-with-black-and-minority-ethnic-bme-communities-to-improve-access-to-psychological-therapies (accessed 1 March 2019).

Black C (2008). *Working for a Healthier Tomorrow: Dame Carol Black's review of the health of Britain's working age population.* Norwich: the Stationery Office.

Bogart K (2015). 'Sometimes, I feel that the psychological well-being practitioner role is undervalued'. *British Psychological Society 28*: 236–239.

Bosmans JE, Schreuders B, Van Marwijk, HW, Smit JH, Van Oppen P, Van Tulder MW (2012). Cost-effectiveness of problem-solving treatment in comparison with usual care for primary care patients with mental health problems: a randomized trial. *BMC Family Practice 13*(1): 98.

Bower P, Kontopantelis E, Sutton A, Kendrick T, Richards DA, Gilbody S et al (2013). Influence of initial severity of depression on effectiveness of low intensity interventions: meta-analysis of individual patient data. *BMJ 346*: f540.

British Psychological Society (2018). Survey of mental health workforce finds many services compromised by staff vacancies. [Online.] *British Psychological Society News*; 21 March 2018. www.bps.org.uk/news-and-policy/survey-mental-health-workforce-finds-many-services-compromised-staff-vacancies (accessed 1 March 2019).

Brown JSL, Sellwood K, Beecham JK, Slade M, Andiappan M, Landau S et al (2011). Outcome, costs and patient engagement for group and individual CBT for depression: a naturalistic clinical study. *Behavioural and Cognitive Psychotherapy 39*(3): 355–358.

Byng R, Newbold L, Qureshi A, et al (2011). *The South West Improving Access to Psychological Therapies (IAPT) Evaluation Study.* Plymouth: Primary Care Research Group, Institute of Health Services Research, Plymouth University.

Cairns M (2013). Patients who come back: clinical characteristics and service outcome for patients re-referred to an IAPT service. *Counselling and Psychotherapy Research 14*(1): 1–8.

Chan SW, Adams M (2014). Service use, drop-out rate and clinical outcomes: a comparison between high and low intensity treatments in an IAPT service. *Behavioural and Cognitive Psychotherapy 42*(6): 747–759.

Clark D (2015). *Improving Access to Psychological Therapies (IAPT): background, strengths, weaknesses and future directions. Conference proceedings.* [Online.] Leicester: British Psychological Society.

Clark DM, Canvin L, Green J, Layard R, Pilling S, Janecka M (2017). Transparency about the outcomes of mental health services (IAPT approach): an analysis of public data. *The Lancet 6736*(17): 1–8.

Clark DM, Fairburn CG, Wessely S (2008). Psychological treatment outcomes in routine NHS services: a commentary on Stiles et al (2007). *Psychological Medicine 38*(5): 629–634.

Clark DM, Layard R, Smithies R, Richards DA, Suckling R, Wright B (2009). Improving access to Psychological Therapy: initial evaluation of two UK demonstration sites. *Behaviour Research and Therapy 47*(11): 910–920.

Cohen DJ, Reynolds MR (2008). Interpreting the results of cost-effectiveness studies. *Journal of the American College of Cardiology 52*(25): 2119–2126.

Cooper B (2009). Strange bedfellows: economics, happiness and mental disorder.

*Epidemiologia E Psichiatria Sociale – an International Journal for Epidemiology and Psychiatric Sciences 18*(3): 208–213.

Cuijpers P (2016). Are all psychotherapies equally effective in the treatment of adult depression? The lack of statistical power of comparative outcome studies. *Evidence-Based Mental Health 19*(2): 39–42.

Cuijpers P, Berking M, Andersson G, Quigley L, Kleiboer A, Dobson KS (2013). A meta-analysis of cognitive-behavioural therapy for adult depression, alone and in comparison with other treatments. *Canadian Journal of Psychiatry 58*(7): 376–385.

Cuijpers P, Donker T, van Straten A, Li J, Andersson G (2010). Is guided self-help as effective as face-to-face psychotherapy for depression and anxiety disorders? A systematic review and meta-analysis of comparative outcome studies. *Psychological Medicine 40*(12): 1943–1957.

Cuijpers P, Donker T, Johansson R, Mohr DC, van Straten A, Andersson G (2011). Self-guided psychological treatment for depressive symptoms: a meta-analysis. *PLoS ONE 6*(6): e21274.

de Lusignan S, Chan T, Arreal MCT, Parry G, Dent-Brown K, Kendrick T et al (2013). Referral for psychological therapy of people with long term conditions improves adherence to antidepressants and reduces emergency department attendance: controlled before and after study. *Behaviour Research and Therapy 51*(7): 377–385.

de Lusignan S, Chan T, Parry G, Dent-Brown K, Kendrick T (2012). Referral to a new psychological therapy service is associated with reduced utilisation of healthcare and sickness absence by people with common mental health problems: a before and after comparison. *Journal of Epidemiology & Community Health 66*(6): e10.

de Lusignan S, Navarro R, Chan T, Parry G, Dent-Brown K, Kendrick T (2011). Detecting referral and selection bias by the anonymous linkage of practice, hospital and clinic data using Secure and Private Record Linkage (SAPREL): case study from the evaluation of the Improved Access to Psychological Therapy (IAPT) service. *BMC Medical Informatics and Decision Making 11*: 61. https://doi.org/10.1186/1472-6947-11-61

Delgadillo J, Asaria M, Ali S, Gilbody S (2015). On poverty, politics and psychology: the socioeconomic gradient of mental healthcare utilisation and outcomes. *British Journal of Psychiatry 209*(5): 429–430.

Delgadillo J, Gellatly J, Stephenson-Bellwood S (2013). Decision making in stepped care: how do therapists decide whether to prolong treatment or not? *Behavioural and Cognitive Psychotherapy 43*: 1–14.

Delgadillo J, Overend K, Lucock M, Groom M, Kirby N, McMillan D et al (2017). Improving the efficiency of psychological treatment using outcome feedback technology. *Behaviour Research and Therapy 99*: 89–97.

Delgadillo J, Saxon D, Barkham M (2018). Associations between therapists' occupational burnout and their patients' depression and anxiety treatment outcomes. *Depression and Anxiety 35*(9): 844–850.

Department of Health (2012). *IAPT Three-Year Report: the first million patients.* London: Department of Health.

Department of Health (2011). *No Health without Mental Health: a cross-government mental health outcomes strategy for people of all ages.* London: HM Government.

Department of Health and Social Care (2017). *Thousands of New Roles to be Created in Mental Health Workforce Plan.* [Online.] News story. (accessed 25 February 2019).

Di Bona L, Saxon D, Barkham M, Dent-Brown K, Parry G (2014). Predictors of patient non-attendance at Improving Access to Psychological Therapy services demonstration sites. *Journal of Affective Disorders 169*: 157–164.

Duarte A, Walker S, Littlewood E, Brabyn S, Hewitt C, Gilbody S, Palmer S (2017). Cost-effectiveness of computerized cognitive-behavioural therapy for the treatment of depression in primary care: findings from the Randomised Evaluation of the Effectiveness and Acceptability of Computerised Therapy (REEACT) trial. *Psychological Medicine 47*(10): 1825–1835.

Emmelkamp PM, David D, Beckers T, Muris P, Cuijpers P, Lutz W, Andersson G et al (2014). Advancing psychotherapy and evidence-based psychological interventions. *International Journal of Methods in Psychiatric Research 23*(1): 58–91.

EuroQol Group (1990). EuroQol: A new facility for the measurement of health-related quality of life. *Health Policy 16*: 199–208.

Finegan M, Firth N, Wojnarowski C, Delgadillo J (2018). Associations between socioeconomic status and psychological therapy outcomes: a systematic review and meta-analysis. [Online.] *Depression and Anxiety.* https://doi.org/10.1002/da.22765

Firth N, Barkham M, Kellett S, Saxon D (2015). Therapist effects and moderators of effectiveness and efficiency in psychological wellbeing practitioners: a multilevel modelling analysis. *Behaviour Research and Therapy 69*: 54–62.

Fonagy P, Clark DM (2015). Update on the Improving Access to Psychological Therapies programme in England: commentary on… Children and Young People's Improving Access to Psychological Therapies. *BJPsych Bulletin 39*(5): 248–251.

Francis R (2013). *Report of the Mid Staffordshire NHS Foundation Trust Public Inquiry.* 3 Volumes. Norwich: The Stationery Office.

Gilbody S, Littlewood E, Hewitt C, Brierley G, Tharmanathan P, Araya R et al (2015). Computerised cognitive behaviour therapy (cCBT) as treatment for depression in primary care (REEACT trial): large scale pragmatic randomised controlled trial. *British Medical Journal 351*: h5627.

Glover G, Webb M, Evison F (2010). *Improving Access to Psychological Therapies: a review of the progress made by sites in the first roll-out year.* Stockton on Tees: North East Public Health Observatory.

Goddard E, Wingrove J, Moran P (2015). The impact of comorbid personality difficulties on response to IAPT treatment for depression and anxiety. *Behaviour Research and Therapy 73*: 1–7.

Grange G (2018). *Employment and Support Allowance.* [Online.] Patient; 18 June 2015. https://patient.info/health/personal-health-budgets/employment-and-support-allowance (accessed 1 March 2019).

Green H, Barkham M, Kellett S, Saxon D (2014a). Therapist effects and IAPT Psychological Wellbeing Practitioners (PWPs): a multilevel modelling and mixed methods analysis. *Behaviour Research and Therapy 63*: 43–54.

Green C, Richards DA, Hill JJJ, Gask L, Lovell K, Chew-Graham C et al (2014b). Cost-effectiveness of collaborative care for depression in UK primary care: economic evaluation of a randomised controlled trial (CADET). *PloS One 9*(8): e104225.

Greenwood G (2017). Mental health staff on long-term stress leave up 22%. *BBC News*; 22 September. www.bbc.co.uk/news/health-41172805 (accessed 25 February 2019).

Griffiths S, Foster J, Steen S, Pietroni P (2013). *Mental Health's Market Experiment: commissioning psychological therapies through any qualified provider*. Report No 1. Chester: Centre for Psychological Therapies in Primary Care, University of Chester.

Griffiths S, Steen S (2013). Improving Access to Psychological Therapies (IAPT) programme: scrutinising IAPT cost estimates to support effective commissioning. *Journal of Psychological Therapies in Primary Care 2*(2): 142–156.

Guy A, Loewenthal D, Thomas R, Stephenson S (2012). Scrutinising NICE: the impact of the National Institute for Health and Clinical Excellence guidelines on the provision of counselling and psychotherapy in primary care in the UK. *Psychodynamic Practice 18*(1): 25–50.

Gyani A, Shafran R, Layard R, Clark DM (2013). Enhancing recovery rates: lessons from year one of IAPT. *Behaviour Research and Therapy 51*(9): 597–606.

Hammond GC, Croudace TJ, Radhakrishnan M, Lafortune L, Watson A, McMillan-Shields F, Jones PB (2012). Comparative effectiveness of cognitive therapies delivered face-to-face or over the telephone: an observational study using propensity methods. *PLoS ONE 7*(9): e42916.

Haug T, Nordgreen T, Öst L-G, Kvale G, Tangen T, Andersson G et al (2015). Stepped care versus face-to-face cognitive behavior therapy for panic disorder and social anxiety disorder: predictors and moderators of outcome. *Behaviour Research and Therapy 71*: 76–89.

Hepgul N, King S, Amarasinghe M, Breen G, Grant N, Grey N et al (2016). Clinical characteristics of patients assessed within an Improving Access to Psychological Therapies (IAPT) service: results from a naturalistic cohort study (Predicting Outcome Following Psychological Therapy; PROMPT). *BMC Psychiatry 16*(1): 52.

Hollinghurst S, Carroll FE, Abel A, Campbell J, Garland A, Jerrom B et al (2014). Cost-effectiveness of cognitive-behavioural therapy as an adjunct to pharmacotherapy for treatment-resistant depression in primary care: economic evaluation of the CoBalT Trial. *British Journal of Psychiatry 204*(1): 69-76.

Hollinghurst S, Peters TJ, Kaur S, Wiles N, Lewis G, Kessler D (2010). Cost-effectiveness of therapist-delivered online cognitive-behavioural therapy for depression: randomised controlled trial. *British Journal of Psychiatry 197*(4): 297–304.

Ilyas S, Moncrieff J (2012). Trends in prescriptions and costs of drugs for mental disorders in England, 1998-2010. *British Journal of Psychiatry 200*(5): 393-398.

IAPT (2013). *IAPT Payment by Results: pilot feasibility study – final report*. London: Department of Health.

IAPT (2012). *Improving Access to Psychological Therapies: guidance for commissioning IAPT training 2012/2013*. London: Department of Health.

Ingleby D (2004). Understanding 'mental iIllness'. In: Ingleby D (ed). *Critical Psychiatry: the politics of mental health*. London: Free Association Books (pp23–71).

Johnson J, Hall LH, Berzins K, Baker J, Melling K, Thompson C (2018). Mental healthcare staff well-being and burnout: a narrative review of trends, causes, implications, and recommendations for future interventions. *International Journal of Mental Health Nursing 27*(1): 20–32.

Jones EA, Bale HL, Morera T (2013). A qualitative study of clinician's experiences and attitudes towards telephone triage mental health assessments. *The Cognitive Behaviour Therapist 6*: e17.

Jorm AF, Patten SB, Brugha TS, Mojtabai R (2017). Has increased provision of treatment reduced the prevalence of common mental disorders? Review of the evidence from four countries. *World Psychiatry 16*(1): 90–99.

Kroenke K, Spitzer RL, Williams JB (2001). The PHQ-9: validity of a brief depression severity measure. *Journal of General Internal Medicine 16*(9): 606–613.

Layard R (2015). *A New Priority for Mental Health.* London: Centre for Economic Performance, London School of Economics and Political Science.

Layard R, Centre for Economic Performance's Mental Health Policy Group (2006). *The Depression Report: a new deal for depression and anxiety disorders.* London: Centre for Economic Performance, London School of Economics and Political Science.

Layard R, Clark D (2014). *Thrive: the power of evidence-based psychological therapies.* London: Allen Lane.

Layard R, Clark D, Knapp M, Mayraz G (2007). Cost-benefit analysis of psychological therapy. *National Institute Economic Review 202*(1): 90–98.

Lucock M, Barkham M, Donohoe G, Kellett S, McMillan D, Mullaney S et al (2017). The role of Practice Research Networks (PRN) in the development and implementation of evidence: the Northern Improving Access to Psychological Therapies PRN case study. *Administration and Policy in Mental Health and Mental Health Services Research 44*(6): 919–931.

Marshall D, Quinn C, Child S, Shenton D, Pooler J, Forber S, Byng R (2016). What IAPT services can learn from those who do not attend. *Journal of Mental Health 25*(5): 410–415.

Martin S, Rice N, Smith PC (2008). *The Link Between Health Care Spending and Health Outcomes for the New English Primary Care Trusts.* Working paper. CHE research paper. York: Centre for Health Economics, University of York.

Marzillier J, Hall J (2009). Boldly going forward on IAPT. *Psychologist 22*(7): 564–565.

McCrone P (2013). IAPT is probably not cost-effective. *British Journal of Psychiatry 202*(5): 383.

McCrone P, Dhanasiri S, Patel A, Knapp M, Lawton-Smith S (2008). *Paying the Price: the cost of mental health care in England to 2026.* London: The King's Fund.

McHugh RK, Barlow DH (2012). *Dissemination and Implementation of Evidence-based Psychological Interventions.* Oxford: Oxford University Press.

McHugh RK, Whitton SW, Peckham AD, Welge JA, Otto MW (2013). Patient preference for psychological vs. pharmacological treatment of psychiatric disorders: a meta-analytic review. *Journal of Clinical Psychiatry 74*(6): 595–602.

McManus S, Bebbington P, Jenkins R, Brugha T (2016). *Mental Health and Wellbeing in England: adult psychiatric morbidity survey 2014.* Leeds: NHS Digital.

McPherson S, Evans C, Richardson P (2009). The NICE Depression Guidelines and the recovery model: is there an evidence base for IAPT? *Journal of Mental Health 18*(5): 405–414.

Mental Health Taskforce to the NHS in England (2016). *Five Year Forward View for Mental Health for the NHS in England.* London: NHS England.

Mollon P (2009). The NICE guidelines are misleading, unscientific, and potentially impede good psychological care and help. *Psychodynamic Practice 15*(1): 9–24.

Mukuria C, Brazier J, Barkham M, Connell J, Hardy G, Hutten R et al (2013). Cost-effectiveness of an Improving Access to Psychological Therapies service. *British Journal of Psychiatry 202*(3): 220–227.

Murphy E, Mansell W, Craven S, Menary J, McEvoy P (2013). Pilot study of an investigation of psychological factors associated with first appointment nonattendance in a low-intensity service. *Behavioural and Cognitive Psychotherapy 41*(4): 458–469.

National Collaborating Centre for Mental Health (2017). *The Improving Access to Psychological Therapies Manual.* London: NHS England.

NHS Digital (2018a). *Psychological Therapies: Annual report on the use of IAPT services England, 2016–17.* Leeds: NHS Digital.

NHS Digital (2018b). *Psychological Therapies: Annual report on the use of IAPT services England, 2016–17 – data tables.* Leeds: NHS Digital.

NHS Digital (2017a). *Prescriptions Dispensed in the Community 2006-2016.* [Online]. Leeds: NHS Digital. https://digital.nhs.uk/data-and-information/publications/statistical/prescriptions-dispensed-in-the-community/prescriptions-dispensed-in-the-community-statistics-for-england-2006-2016-pas (accessed 1 March 2019).

NHS Digital (2017b). *NHS Sickness Absence Rates: January 2017 to March 2017 and Annual Summary 2010-11 to 2016-17.* [Online.] Leeds: NHS Digital. https://digital.nhs.uk/data-and-information/publications/statistical/nhs-sickness-absence-rates/nhs-sickness-absence-rates-january-2017-to-march-2017-and-annual-summary-2010-11-to-2016-17 (accessed 1 March 2019).

NHS Digital (2016). *Psychological Therapies: annual report on the use of IAPT services England, 2015–16.* Leeds: NHS Digital.

NHS Digital (2015). *Psychological Therapies: annual report on the use of IAPT services England, 2014–15.* Leeds: NHS Digital.

NHS Digital (2014a). *Psychological Therapies: annual report on the use of IAPT services England, 2012–13.* Leeds: NHS Digital.

NHS Digital (2014b). *Psychological Therapies: annual report on the use of IAPT services England, 2013–14.* Leeds: NHS Digital.

NHS Employers (2017). *Agenda for Change Pay Scales – Hourly.* Leeds: NHS Employers. http://www.nhsemployers.org/your-workforce/pay-and-reward/agenda-for-change/pay-scales/hourly (accessed 1 March 2019).

NHS England/Health Education England (2016). *2015 Adult IAPT Workforce Census Report. Version 1.* London: NHS England.

NHS Improvement (2018). *National Cost Collection guidance 2018.* London: NHS England/NHS Improvement.

NHS Improvement (2017). *Combined Costs Collection: education and training costs collection guidance 2016/17.* London: NHS England/NHS Improvement.

NHS Improvement (2016). *2017/18 and 2018/19 National Tariff Payment System.* London: NHS England/NHS Improvement.

NHS Improvement (2016/17). *NHS Reference Costs 2016/17: highlights, analysis and introduction to the data.* London: NHS Improvement.

NICE (in press). *Depression in Adults (update).* London: NICE. www.nice.org.uk/guidance/indevelopment/gid-qs10057 (accessed 1 March 2019).

NICE (2011). *Common mental health problems: identification and pathways to care.* Clinical guideline CG123. London: NICE.

Nieuwenhuijsen K, Faber B, Verbeek JH, Neumeyer-Gromen A, Hees HL, Verhoeven AC et al (2014). Interventions to Improve Return to Work in Depressed People. *Cochrane Database of Systematic Reviews* 3(12):CD006237. doi: 10.1002/14651858.CD006237. pub3.

Office for National Statistics (2017). *Household Disposable Income and Inequality in the UK: financial year ending 2016.* Statistics bulletin. [Online.] Newport: Office for National Statistics. www.ons.gov.uk/peoplepopulationandcommunity/personalandhousehold finances/incomeandwealth/bulletins/householddisposableincomeandinequality/ financialyearending2017 (accessed 1 March 2019).

Parsonage M, Hard E, Rock B (2014). *Managing Patients with Complex Needs: evaluation of the City and Hackney Primary Care Psychotherapy Consultation Service.* Discussion Paper. London: Centre for Mental Health.

Pietroni P, Martin M, Wilkinson M, Griffiths T, Goodwillie G (2008). Psychological therapies in primary care where we were – where we are – where are we going? *Journal of Psychological Therapies in Primary Care* 1(1–2): 19–31.

Proctor EK, Landsverk J, Aarons G, Chambers D, Glisson C, Mittman B (2009). Implementation research in mental health services: an emerging science with conceptual, methodological, and training challenges. *Administration and Policy in Mental Health and Mental Health Services Research* 36(1): 24–34.

PSSRU (2017). *Unit Costs of Health and Social Care 2017.* Canterbury: Personal Social Services Research Unit, University of Kent.

Pybis J, Saxon D, Hill A, Barkham M (2017). The comparative effectiveness and efficiency of cognitive behaviour therapy and generic counselling in the treatment of depression: evidence from the 2nd UK National Audit of psychological therapies. *BMC Psychiatry* 17: 215.

Radhakrishnan M, Hammond G, Jones PB, Watson A, McMillan-Shields F, Lafortune L (2013). Cost of Improving Access to Psychological Therapies (IAPT) programme: an analysis of cost of session, treatment and recovery in selected Primary Care Trusts in the East of England region. *Behaviour Research and Therapy* 51(1): 37–45.

Rao AS, Bhutani G, Dosanjh N, Clarke J, Hacker J, Easton S et al (2016). *Psychological Wellbeing and Resilience: resetting the balance.* Leicester: British Psychological Society/ New Savoy Partnership.

Royal College of Psychiatrists (2013). *Report of the Second Round of the National Audit of Psychological Therapies for Anxiety and Depression (NAPT) 2013.* London: Royal College of Psychiatrists.

Reme SE, Grasdal AL, Løvvik C, Lie SA, Øverland S (2015). Work-focused cognitive– behavioural therapy and individual job support to increase work participation in common mental disorders: a randomised controlled multicentre trial. *Occupational & Environmental Medicine* 72(10): 745-752.

Richards DA, Borglin G (2011). Implementation of psychological therapies for anxiety and depression in routine practice: two-year prospective cohort study. *Journal of Affective Disorders* 133(1–2): 51–60.

Richards DA, Bower P, Pagel C, Weaver A, Utley M, Cape J et al (2012). Delivering stepped care: an analysis of implementation in routine practice. *Implementation Science* 7(1): 3.

Richards DA, Ekers D, McMillan D, Taylor RS, Byford S, Warren FC et al (2016). Cost and Outcome of Behavioural Activation versus Cognitive Behavioural Therapy for Depression (COBRA): a randomised, controlled, non-inferiority trial. *The Lancet* 388(10047): 871–880.

Rizq R (2012). The perversion of care: psychological therapies in a time of IAPT. *Psychodynamic Practice* 18(1): 7–24.

Rodgers M, Asaria M, Walker S, McMillan D, Lucock M, Harden M et al (2012). The clinical effectiveness and cost-effectiveness of low-intensity psychological interventions for the secondary prevention of relapse after depression: a systematic review. *Health Technology Assessment* 16(28): 1.

Saeidi S, Wall R (2018). The case for mental health support at a primary care level. *Journal of Integrated Care* 26(2): 130–139.

Samuels A, Veale D (2009). Improving access to psychological therapies: for and against. *Psychodynamic Practice* 15(1): 41–56.

Scanlon C (2015). On the perversity of an imagined psychological solution to very real social problems of unemployment (work-lessness) and social exclusion (worth-lessness): a group analytic critique. *Group Analysis* 48(1): 31–44.

Scanlon C, Adlam J (2013). Knowing your place and minding your own business: on perverse psychological solutions to the imagined problem of social exclusion. *Ethics and Social Welfare* 7(2): 170–183.

Shearer J, McCrone P, Romeo R (2016). Economic evaluation of mental health interventions: a guide to costing approaches. *PharmacoEconomics* 34(7): 651–664.

Shidhaye R (2015). Implementation science for closing the treatment gap for mental disorders by translating evidence base into practice: experiences from the PRIME project. *Australasian Psychiatry* 23(6): 35–37.

Shimodera S, Furukawa TA, Mino Y, Shimazu K, Nishida A, Inoue S (2012). Cost-effectiveness of family psychoeducation to prevent relapse in major depression: results from a randomized controlled trial. *BMC Psychiatry* 12(1): 40.

Slaney C (2016). We don't even have a name for it. *Psychotherapy and Politics International* 14(2): 97–106.

Spitzer RL, Kroenke K, Williams JB, Löwe B (2006). A brief measure for assessing generalized anxiety disorder: the GAD-7. *Archives of Internal Medicine* 166(10): 1092–1097.

Sreeharan V, Madden H, Lee JT, Millett C, Majeed A (2013). Improving Access to Psychological Therapies and antidepressant prescribing rates in England: a longitudinal time-series analysis. *British Journal of General* 63(614): e649–653.

Steadman K, Thomas R (2015). *An Evaluation of the 'IPS in IAPT' Psychological Wellbeing and Work Feasibility pilot.* Lancaster: The Work Foundation, University of Lancaster.

Steel C, Macdonald J, Schröder T, Mellor-Clark J (2015). Exhausted but not cynical: burnout in therapists working within Improving Access to Psychological Therapy Services. *Journal of Mental Health* 24(1): 33–37.

Summerfield D (2018). NHS antidepressant prescribing: what do we get for £266m a year? [Online.] News and views. *BMJ* 360: k1019. www.bmj.com/content/360/bmj.k1019 (accessed 1 March 2019).

South West IAPT Expert Reference Group (2015). *Data quality & new developments.* [Online.] Mayden. www.swscn.org.uk/wp/wp-content/uploads/2015/12/South-West-IAPT-Expert-Reference-Group-Mayden.pdf (accessed 1 March 2019).

The New Savoy Partnership (2016). *Charter for Psychological Staff Wellbeing and Resilience.* [Online.] New Savoy Partnership. www.healthcareconferencesuk.co.uk/news/newsfiles/ charter-2016_1314.pdf (accessed 1 March 2019).

Tosh J, Kearns B, Brennan A, Parry G, Ricketts T, Saxon D et al (2013). Innovation in health economic modelling of service improvements for longer-term depression: demonstration in a local health community. *BMC Health Services Research 13*(1): 150.

Twomey CD, Baldwin DS, Hopfe M, Cieza A (2015). A systematic review of the predictors of health service utilisation by adults with mental disorders in the UK. *BMJ Open 5*(7): e007575.

van Straten A, Hill J, Richards DA, Cuijpers P (2015). Stepped care treatment delivery for depression: a systematic review and meta-analysis. *Psychological Medicine 45*(2): 231– 246.

Viola S, Moncrieff J (2016). Claims for sickness and disability benefits owing to mental disorders in the UK: trends from 1995 to 2014. *BJPsych Open 2*(1): 18.

Waddell G, Burton AK (2006). *Is Work Good for Your Health and Well-being?* Norwich: The Stationery Office.

Wampold BE, Imel ZE (2015). *The Great Psychotherapy Debate: the evidence for what makes psychotherapy work.* (2nd ed). London: Routledge.

Wesson M, Gould M (2010). Can a 'return-to-work' agenda fit within the theory and practice of CBT for depression and anxiety disorders? *The Cognitive Behaviour Therapist 3*(1): 27–42.

West M (2016). *Engagement is up according to the NHS staff survey, but at what cost?* [Online.] The King's Fund. www.kingsfund.org.uk/blog/2016/03/nhs-staff-survey (accessed 1 March 2019).

Westwood S, Morison L, Allt J, Holmes N (2017). Predictors of emotional exhaustion, disengagement and burnout among improving access to psychological therapies (IAPT) practitioners. *Journal of Mental Health 26*(2): 172–179.

Williams CHJ (2015). Improving Access to Psychological Therapies (IAPT) and treatment outcomes: epistemological assumptions and controversies. *Journal of Psychiatric and Mental Health Nursing 22*(5): 344–351.

Zhou T, Li X, Pei Y, Gao J, Kong J (2016). Internet-based cognitive behavioural therapy for subthreshold depression: a systematic review and meta-analysis. *BMC Psychiatry 16*(1): 356.

# PART 3

## The State of the Workplace

# Chapter 9

# Perverting the course of therapy: IAPT and the fetishisation of governance[1]

## Rosemary Rizq

A middle-aged woman came to see me for psychotherapy in the IAPT service where I spent some years working as a psychologist. When she arrived, she was asked by the receptionist at the front desk to complete a number of questionnaires routinely required by the service before the start of our appointment. These questionnaires included brief, standardised self-report measures of her mood over the previous week, her employment status and a rating scale of how her difficulties were affecting her ability to manage at home and in her close relationships.

My patient duly completed the various forms and handed them to me when I came to collect her for our appointment. When we arrived at my consulting room, she not unreasonably asked why she had to answer all these questions. I replied that the service was required to demonstrate weekly outcomes to the government in order to continue being funded. After a pause, my patient said, somewhat dryly, that she didn't really think that the 'outcomes' on the form were the outcomes she was interested in – and would I mind if she didn't fill in the forms? 'Not at all,' I replied, putting them down

1. This chapter is an edited version of Rizq R (2014). Perverting the course of therapy: the fetishisation of governance in public sector mental health services. *Psychoanalytic Psychotherapy* 28(3): 249–266 © The Association for Psychoanalytic Psychotherapy in the NHS, reprinted here by permission of Taylor and Francis Ltd, http://www.tandfonline.com, on behalf of the Association for Psychoanalytic Psychotherapy in the NHS.

on the table. 'Actually,' she said after a pause, now looking at me sideways with a smile, rather like a naughty child, 'I don't want to make trouble. Let's have them there – but not really. I'll fill in my name and the date, but I won't fill in the rest. I'll give you blank forms to keep on file – and at least that'll keep the government happy.' We both laughed heartily at this, and thereafter each week she solemnly handed me a blank form, index of her unwillingness to comply with service governance requirements.

When I raised the matter at a subsequent clinical supervision group, there was some disagreement about the best way to deal with this rather delightful piece of what is often referred to, in the psychoanalytic field, as 'acting out'. One colleague thought that, if my patient wasn't willing to complete the questionnaires, then she shouldn't be offered psychotherapy. Another thought I was secretly colluding with the patient's lack of co-operation. A third argued heatedly that, as we all 'knew' the scores were irrelevant to understanding our patients, it was perfectly reasonable for my patient to refuse to comply. Indeed, after a while, the discussion turned into a more general debate about the nature of the service and the recent imposition by management of what many felt were therapeutically intrusive and clinically inappropriate outcome measures on those referred to the service. Finally, perhaps in response to what was fast becoming a rather fractious mood in the group, the supervisor intervened to suggest that, as the funding of the service was now unfortunately dependent on receiving data from our patients, perhaps I should consider completing the scores myself on the basis of how I felt my patient was progressing.

I later found myself rather thoughtful about this notion of things being 'there… but not really'. For it seemed to me that our group, my patient and the supervisor were all part of a system that had recruited us into a very particular position in relation to reality: one in which we were being asked to subscribe to something while, at the same time, undermining it. This mental feat clearly involved everyone in an act of disavowal that entailed the acceptance of something – in this case, the requirement for clinical outcome measures – being 'there… but not really': we had been conscripted, it seemed, into what might be termed a lying relationship to reality. Indeed, the outburst of wry laughter in the group following our supervisor's suggestion was, I think, testament to our recognition of precisely this perverse position we found ourselves adopting as clinicians.

The psychoanalytic term 'perversion' has been used in many different ways. It was originally identified by Freud (1927) in the rather narrow context of the sexual perversions or fetishism, but in subsequent literature has been regarded either as a solution to developmental conflict (eg. Stoller, 1986; Khan, 1987) or as a disavowal of castration and lack (Lacan & Granoff, 1956). It has since been accorded a wider significance in the psychosocial and organisational literature, which has attempted to illuminate how systemic failures within institutions (Long, 2009) and perverse social defences (Hoggett, 2010; Rizq, 2012) disavow and undermine the work of an organisation. Building on the rich tradition of psychoanalytic theorising about organisations (eg. Jaques, 1952; Menzies Lyth, 1960), I want to consider notions of perversion and fetishisation within the context of contemporary UK public mental health services, such as IAPT, which have been subject to New Public Management (NPM) restructuring since the 1980s. Indeed, deployment of NPM strategies in the work of teachers, police officers, doctors and social workers has been evident for some time where rationalist philosophies of transparency, effectiveness and accountability prevail, resulting in an audit culture pervading all levels of the organisation.

We have all become familiar with stories about how the 'tick-box culture' characteristic of these NPM strategies lies at the heart of serious problems within the NHS, including failings at the Mid-Staffordshire NHS Foundation Trust, abuse at Winterbourne View Hospital and the deaths of 'Baby P', Ayeeshia-Jane Smith and Victoria Climbié, to mention only a few exceptionally high-profile examples. These were all cases where attention to government targets, clinical outcomes and paperwork took precedence over what Ballatt and Campling (2011) call 'intelligent kindness' (see also Penny Campling's chapter in this book), resulting in perverse organisational dynamics that ultimately led to terrible suffering and unnecessary deaths.

Gabriel and Carr (2002) suggest that psychoanalysis 'opens valuable windows into the world of organisations and management, offering insights that are startlingly original, have extensive explanatory powers and can find ample practical implementations' (p348). In this chapter, I use a psychoanalytic lens to illuminate how IAPT services that exemplify neoliberal regulatory and performance management systems sponsor a perverse organisational solution to the anxieties and difficulties of dealing with psychologically distressed patients. I will first offer a brief theoretical outline of psychoanalytic views of perversion and fetishism, drawing on Freud and Lacan, before suggesting that the current marketisation of the NHS and the pressure on staff and managers to conform to ever-increasing clinical governance requirements both result from and defend against anxieties aroused by contact with those in psychological distress. Drawing on my clinical and supervisory work in an IAPT service, I then offer a case vignette to illustrate how perverse dynamics percolate throughout an organisation in ways that undermine the very care these services set out to provide.

## Psychoanalytic views of perversion and fetishism

In his early essay, 'Fetishism', Freud (1927) argues that the little boy is unable to accept the fact that a woman has no penis. Using the term 'Verleugnung', Freud proposes that an unconscious process of disavowal takes place whereby the child is able both to know and to not-know about this absence at one and the same time:

> It is not true that, after the child has made his observation of the woman, he has preserved unaltered his belief that women have a phallus. He has retained that belief, but he has also given it up. (1927: 154)

Freud's early example points to the significance of the individual's relationship to absence – a loss that is disavowed, with consequent implications for the possibility of its symbolic representation. Thus, for Freud, the disavowal of loss is seen as a central obstacle to the construction of inner psychic reality. Indeed, the trauma of the loss is what can trigger fetishism, where the fetish object – the shoe, the silk dress – becomes the symbolic substitute for the mother's missing penis. It masks a gap or an absence that cannot be symbolised.

While Freud sees perversion and fetishism largely as a process of sexual substitution that results in aberrant sexual behaviour, Lacan weaves the notion of disavowal into a more complex theoretical account of personality structure, in which a constitutive lack or fragmentation at the heart of subjectivity is perceived as fundamental. In Lacan's (1949) 'mirror stage', his template for the Imaginary order, the child's primordial anxiety is seen as a response to its lack of physical coherence and motor co-ordination. Identification with its mirror image thus confers a subjective feeling of wholeness, completeness and self-mastery, allowing the child triumphantly to assume a narcissistic ideal, an anticipated sense of self-unity and control that it does not yet possess.

By contrast, the Symbolic order is represented by the Law of the Father, a symbolic Father and symbolic phallus that fulfil a function independent of the existence or behaviour of the actual flesh and blood father and his penis. The symbolic Father imposes the Law and regulates desire in the Oedipal configuration of mother and child. It is acceptance of the Law of the Father – ie. acceding to castration or lack – that separates the child from an Imaginary identification with the desire of the mother. It is this that precipitates the child into the Symbolic order where relationships are regulated within the larger socio-symbolic system of language, rules, gender differences and cultural ideals. However, while repression and foreclosure are the fundamental operations by which the neurotic and the psychotic respectively manage their knowledge of lack, Lacan sees disavowal as the main mechanism by which the pervert relates to his or her knowledge of castration: by simultaneously denying and recognising it.

What is disavowed here, according to Lacan (1962), is the notion that lack causes desire. The perverse individual constitutes him or herself as the subject that plugs up the desire in the (m)Other so that there can be no lack and no castration. However, this process of disavowal paradoxically engenders intense anxiety:

> What provokes anxiety? Contrary to what people say, it is neither the rhythm nor the alternation of the mothers' presence-absence. What proves this is that the child indulges in repeating presence absence games: security of presence is found in the possibility of absence. What is most anxiety producing for the child is when the relationship through which he comes to be – on the basis of lack which makes him desire – is most perturbed: when there is no possibility of lack, when his mother is constantly on his back. (Lacan, 1962)

Lacan and Granoff's (1956) reworking of Freud's (1927) original paper suggests that fetishism occurs when these anxieties are transferred to the social images and ideals of the Symbolic order: in particular, the Name of the Father or his representatives such as the state, the government, the police or the law. For this reason, perversion – or fetishism – always involves an attempt to buttress the paternal function, to bring the Law into being so that the anxiety-relieving separation from the (m)Other can occur. Indeed, Lacan writes perversion as 'pere-version', to emphasise the way in which the pervert appeals to the father, trying to make the symbolic Other exist via the perverse act:

> [T]he perversion (that is, the fetish) serves to multiply the force of the father's symbolic action (putting the mOther's lack into words), to supplement or prop up the paternal function. The name given by the father is a start, a first step, but does not go far enough. It needs support, it needs amplification. (Fink, 1997: 183)

In perversion then, there is a staging of the Law, an attempt to bring the Law into being. However, Lacan argues that the fetish object can never be fully functioning; the subject can never entirely 'be' the longed-for symbolic phallus. This is because the order of the Real, the realm of that which cannot be symbolised, ensures there is always a lack that escapes the subject and therefore the symbolic Other. It is this lack that engenders the subject's ceaseless search for the lost jouissance of unity with the (m)Other and ensures the perpetuation of desire.

## Perversion and anxiety

Before we turn to how these unconscious dynamics play out within mental health services in general, and IAPT services in particular, it is important to recognise how Western society has historically viewed, defined and treated those deemed to be 'mad'. Foucault's (1972) notion of mental disorder as a social construction in the service of exclusion and social control is often conveniently forgotten in the contemporary drive to label, treat and cure those thought to be mentally ill. Indeed, the transformation of what was once a space of exclusion into a medical space is what, according to Foucault, enabled mental illness to become the object of scientific observation and experimentation. Currently, the so-called scientific basis of psychological treatment takes for granted the object that it has, in fact, itself constructed. The uncritical acceptance of this assumption is central to current mental health policies, whose implementation depends on psychiatric diagnoses that are presumed to index preferred forms of government-approved therapeutic and pharmacological treatments. Foucault reminds us that:

> The positivist psychiatry of the nineteenth century, like our own...
> secretly inherited the relationship that classical culture as a whole had
> set up with unreason. They were modified and displaced, and it was
> thought that madness was being studied from the point of view of an
> objective pathology; but despite those good intentions, madness was
> still haunted by an ethical view of unreason, and the scandal of its
> animal nature. (1972/2006: 159)

I want to suggest that public sector organisations offering psychological care are still subject to this 'secret inheritance'; they are still haunted by a fear of 'unreason' and the 'animal nature' of those deemed mentally ill. Indeed, the psychosocial literature, drawing on Kleinian psychoanalytic theory and Menzies Lyth's (1960) view of social defences against anxiety, conveys precisely this view by suggesting that institutions develop strategies and defences to protect staff from the emotional difficulties aroused by contact with vulnerability, illness and death. The difficulties, stresses and strains of working with those who have been diagnosed as mentally ill have also been documented in an extensive clinical literature. This commonly deploys psychoanalytic concepts such as splitting, projection and projective identification to understand the often paradoxical ways in which organisations aiming to help those in distress fail to help those most in need of their care (eg. Cooper & Lousada, 2005; Obholzer & Roberts, 1994; Scanlon & Adlam, 2011).

From a Lacanian perspective, however, anxiety is not simply an affect subject to repression: anxiety is, rather, something that arises when the subject is confronted with the ineluctable fragmentation and instability of the self (Lacan, 1962). The Imaginary nature of the self's sense of unity and identity is disrupted by any reminder of its constitutive lack of cohesion, which would result in a confrontation with the traumatic Real. It is this that sponsors an anxiety that can never be contained or dissipated, although the gap between the illusory ego and the alienated subject may be temporarily filled with language, forming the basis of social projects unconsciously designed to recapture a lost fantasy of unity and wholeness. Those deemed mentally ill, then, whose vulnerability and dependence confront us with a fragmentation that is the basis of a shared humanity, may be said to arouse particular anxieties in society, which governments and welfare institutions are tasked with managing. In line with Foucault, MacCallum (2002) and Peternelj-Taylor (2004) have referred to a process of 'othering', by which means we establish clear boundaries between those who are 'normal' and those who are deemed to be different, damaged or deformed (Shildrick, 2002). In this way, I suggest, mental health services unconsciously operate to organise and sustain an Imaginary sense of unity and 'normality' within society, keeping painful subjective reminders of lack and division at bay.

Following Long (2009) and Hoggett (2010), we can now understand the current marketisation of the NHS, the fragmentation and privatisation of its services and the pressure on staff and managers to conform to ever-increasing clinical governance requirements as resulting from, as well as productive of, anxieties aroused by contact with those in psychological distress. It is here that I think we can see the emergence of a perverse organisational solution, where these anxieties are concealed and disavowed beneath a fetishised 'target culture' offering an idealised picture of the work of a mental health service while simultaneously undermining and subverting the very care that it is mandated by government to provide. To develop this idea, I will draw on the way in which the government's IAPT programme has resulted in extensive changes to how mental health services are commissioned, organised, implemented and evaluated.

These changes are described in other chapters in this book and I will not rehearse them here. The particular feature of IAPT that I want to emphasise is the one that most clearly defines it as a mental health programme exemplifying the NPM ideals of transparency, accountability and governance: the requirement for clinical staff to record multiple clinical outcome measures on a computer software system. Staff are closely monitored to ensure they record every contact with patients and evaluate clinical progress according the full IAPT dataset. This is used to inform local and national reporting, to demonstrate adherence to 'best-practice' guidelines and to justify the use of what are assumed to be 'evidence-based' approaches to psychological therapy recommended by the National Institute for Health and Clinical Excellence (NICE).

The following case example, based on a period of work as a senior psychologist and clinical supervisor in a primary care IAPT service, is intended to be illustrative of the complex intersection between unconscious perverse dynamics, staff behaviour and the specific regulatory procedures to which both I and my colleagues were subject.

## Organisational case example

The IAPT programme, incorporating the 'stepped care' approach advocated by the NICE guidelines for treating anxiety and depression (2009), has introduced large numbers of newly trained junior mental health workers into the NHS (psychological wellbeing practitioners, or PWPs), who offer 'low-intensity' guided self-help, computerised cognitive behavioural therapy (cCBT), psycho-education and signposting to voluntary sector services. The PWPS are the first step in the IAPT model of stepped care and form the gateway to 'high-intensity', face-to-face therapy delivered by qualified counsellors and psychotherapists, based mainly on cognitive-behavioural principles.

This particular primary care service had been through a long period (two years) of upheaval and change. Due to the planned restructuring of all services within the NHS, including the abolition of strategic health authorities and primary care trusts, it had been decided that the service and its staff should be re-employed by a local NHS mental health trust. During this period, managers of the service were under increasing pressure to demonstrate its compliance with activity targets and recovery rates in order to establish the viability and legitimacy of the service. As part of the validation process, the most junior staff in the service, the PWPs, came under renewed pressure to increase their caseloads to meet the required target of 5,000 referrals a year. However, during this time, a number of the PWPs decided to leave after only a very short time, and it became apparent to managers that these young and, in many cases, very inexperienced staff were finding the demands of high-volume, high-turnover clinical work very challenging. There was concern that the planned handover to the mental health trust would be placed in jeopardy due to the loss of staff and the resulting reduced activity levels in the service.

For some years previously, a system of monthly support groups or 'reflective practice' groups had been in place, facilitated by senior counsellors and psychotherapists in the service. They had been set up to provide a space where the PWPs could reflect on and discuss salient professional and personal issues arising from their clinical work. The groups were voluntary; staff attended unless they had unavoidable clinical commitments and, over time, they had become a regular part of the service. As a senior psychologist and psychotherapist in the service, I was asked to offer individual supervision to the counsellors who facilitated these groups. Over a period of two or three years, it had become clear to me that the counsellors felt these groups served an important function in the service. They seemed to enable the PWPs to share difficulties, particularly those arising from some of the more complex cases in which they frequently found themselves involved. It was also clear that the groups served as a safety valve for the venting of complaints and grumbles, usually relating to the increasing demands of their caseloads, the lack of time permitted for joint clinical discussion, the problems associated with individual caseload management, and the reluctance on the part of management to consider their training and development needs.

During a supervision session with one of the counsellors, I was told that a letter of complaint about a PWP had recently been received by the head of the service. This young PWP had been given the letter, which she had brought and read out to her reflective practice group. It was clear, my supervisee said, that the patient who had made the complaint against the PWP was very angry and upset. She had been seeking counselling from the service to help support her with a profoundly disabled child and, following her referral, had received the offer of a telephone consultation to discuss the problem. The patient had written to complain about the way this PWP had handled the discussion: by telephoning her when she had expected a 'proper' face-to-face' appointment; by asking her to complete a number of what she felt were irrelevant questionnaires over the telephone; by telling her that, if she was unwilling to complete these questionnaires, she would be unable to access the service at all, and, finally, by offering to refer her on to a voluntary sector service when she had specifically asked for NHS counselling. In the letter, the patient wrote: 'I felt utterly uncared for, I was treated like a number,' and went on to say that she was shocked that an NHS service could dismiss her legitimate needs in such a way.

The counsellor I was supervising explained that the PWP, for her part, had clearly felt guilty and defensive. In explaining the case to the group, she made it clear that she had treated this very depressed and anxious patient with great care and courtesy, and that she had carefully followed all the relevant protocols for a telephone assessment. What else was she supposed to do? She felt that she had done everything she could – including the onward referral of the patient to a service that could offer her respite care for her disabled child. 'I didn't take this job to be complained about,' she said rather tearfully to the group, 'I can't care for everybody!' At this point, group members, who had initially tried to help their colleague think about how else she might have dealt with the situation, all rallied round, agreeing that she had certainly done everything she could reasonably do in the circumstances; indeed, they reasoned, given the numbers of people on their caseloads, of course she wasn't able to care for everybody.

There seemed to be, my supervisee said, a growing anxiety and indignation in the group about this accusation from a patient of being 'utterly uncared for', as if group members felt that following the correct procedure, doing everything 'right', should be sufficient. It was as if, he said, rather worriedly, 'there's no need actually to care; the policies and protocols will do the work instead'. When my supervisee invited the group to think more closely about what this undoubtedly very angry patient had wanted from the PWP, he was met with much protest about the impossibility of managing the intense emotional demands of such 'fragile' patients, about the lack of training provided for coping with 'difficult' members of the public, and about the many other patients that remained on caseloads waiting for attention. It was clear that the complaint had created enormous anxieties for the group and that their ability to think about the feelings generated by such an event was limited.

Two weeks later, the head of the service sent an email to all staff announcing that the reflective practice groups were to become compulsory. No explanation was given for this blanket directive and no link was made with the patient's complaint. As supervisor, I was summoned by the clinical lead and asked to ensure that each facilitator kept a group attendance register and notes on what was discussed at each session. I too would be required to keep a supervision register and notes on what was discussed with each of my supervisees. When I queried the necessity to undertake the additional work and administration involved, I was rather briskly told that the service needed to ensure it was 'covered in case of complaints' and therefore, along with all other aspects of the service, what took place within the reflective practice groups should be recorded and kept on file. This would demonstrate 'good practice' and 'transparency', in line with what the service's prospective employers expected. When I subsequently discussed these procedural changes with the counsellors, it was clear that we were all uncomfortable and worried about the change from what had hitherto been a fairly relaxed and informal setting, a space that was free of impingement by management, to yet another bureaucratised space, one that was being watched and reported on.

The few PWPs who had not so far shown an interest in attending the groups were now required by their managers to participate. Some of them were initially unwilling to come and several counsellors noticed that this changed the atmosphere of the groups over the next few months from one of enthusiasm, goodwill and interest to one that was, for a time at least, characterised by a degree of covert resistance. I now started to hear from my supervisee how he struggled to manage PWPs who expressed impatience with having to make time to attend when they had so many assessments to undertake. Over time, however, these difficulties seemed to recede and I became increasingly aware of a more subtle shift in the work he reported. For example, I heard less about the PWPs' difficulties, mistakes and problems and more about examples of clinical work that group members felt had been particularly innovative or successful. The groups also started to discuss administrative matters and to provide detailed examples of how they had managed to find short-cuts on the computer system that enabled them to input activity data and clinical outcomes more efficiently.

My supervisee, relieved to find these discussions reviving what he felt to be the group's flagging interest, recounted with satisfaction several occasions where, spurred on by their colleagues, group members appeared to 'compete' with each other in offering accounts of how they had successfully managed 'tricky' patients or manoeuvred the software system to their advantage in different ways. Grumbles and complaints in the group seemed to reduce, and I now heard how the PWPs were rather ambitiously extolling the virtues of 'best practice' and their successful use of an 'evidence base' in their work. Group members were keen to talk about how well the service was faring relative to other services in the locality and were excited at the planned recruitment of new staff to replace those who had left. Over time, my supervisee started to joke that the group didn't really seem to need him anymore, and that it could perhaps 'run by itself now'.

It was during this period that I found myself uncharacteristically seized with a sudden sleepiness during our supervision sessions. My supervisee and I met in the afternoons, and for several weeks I told myself it was a post-lunch dip in my metabolism. Much as I tried to rationalise it, it quickly became clear to me that I was not able to pay proper attention to what he was saying. I felt tired, muzzy and overpoweringly drowsy, and on several occasions I even had to ask him to repeat what he had said. I became increasingly concerned – and ashamed – about what I felt was my lack of interest in the supervision, and I redoubled my attempts to demonstrate attention and interest. However, it was not until he unprecedentedly failed to attend a session, ostensibly because he had forgotten to put the date in his diary, that matters came to a head. On finding him absent at the usual time, I sent a text asking where he was. I received a profuse apology and we arranged to meet a week or so later. When I subsequently asked him what had happened, I found to my surprise that he appeared unwilling to discuss our missed session, reiterating that it was simply a timetabling mistake and 'wasn't important'. At the end of the supervision session, however, he asked in a rather offhand way whether I intended to record his absence on my own supervision record: it was obvious to me that he didn't want management to know about his 'timetabling mistake'. Anxious to reassure him about something that evidently was important now, I said that of course I would simply be recording the current date as the one originally agreed. 'Thanks for covering for me,' he said, clearly relieved, and left the room.

## The fetishisation of bureaucracy

The above organisational case illustrates how a letter of complaint pointing to a lack within the service – a perceived lack of caring – is experienced as a devastating attack by the individual concerned, the group and the organisation. The PWP's initial feelings of doubt and shame quickly give way to comforting reminders of how service policies and protocols should be sufficient to demonstrate care and the group moves to reassure their colleague that, by following these directives, she has done all that can be expected in the circumstances. Indeed, the fact that she 'can't care for everyone' – that there are limits to what such young and inexperienced mental health workers can be expected to manage, given their extremely high caseloads and the nature of the short, protocol-based IAPT training they undertake – is not something that appears to be considered at an organisational level. The perceived lack of emotional care raised by the complaint is not discussed by management at all, but instead appears to be addressed by recourse to increased bureaucracy and surveillance. By pursuing imaginary objectives such as demonstrating 'transparency' and 'accountability', by insisting on compulsory attendance at the group as well as access to registers and process notes, management aims to 'cover' itself: there is a 'staging' of the Law as it were, which is invoked as a means of disavowing the lack of care brought to light by the patient's complaint.

My supervisee's use of the term 'cover' is important in this context, and it is here that the notion of the fetish becomes relevant. Lacan (1994) uses metaphors such as the 'veil' or 'curtain' to refer to the masked or disguised qualities of the fetish. Indeed, its 'fig-leaf' qualities draw attention to its unconscious function in misrepresenting reality. This is taken up by Chasseguet-Smirgel (1971) in her discussion of Hans Andersen's 'The Nightingale and the Emperor of China', a story about how the Emperor prefers the mechanical tinkling of an artificial bird over the song of the real nightingale. Chasseguet-Smirgel draws a parallel between the artificial bird in the story and a fetish, noting that, in both cases, admirers are enthralled by what is false. She contrasts the mechanical bird, which is covered with glittering jewels, with the more 'modest' plumes of the real, living nightingale, pointing out that:

> ... the true one does not need to hoodwink anybody or make any display to the world, because it has nothing to conceal. At the same time the mechanical nightingale by its radiance will have to try to make people forget that it is 'fabricated' and only an assemblage of mechanics. (1971: 201)

I have previously (Rizq, 2012) taken Hans Andersen's fairy-tale as a rich metaphor for the IAPT programme's fascination with NPM strategies of governance and proceduralism. Like the admirers of the mechanical nightingale, managers in the service appeared to be gripped not only by the glittering 'virtual reality' displayed in the activity data required by the service but more generally by the possibility of measuring, labelling, quantifying and calculating its activities and outcomes. These 'technologies of representation'

(Power, 2004: 778) are, of course, part and parcel of a wider discourse generated recently by the requirements of what has been called 'evidence-based practice' in the psychotherapeutic field. As such, it is those services that demonstrate models of therapeutic practice and systems of care that conform to the demand for comprehensive performance monitoring systems demonstrating efficiency and effectiveness that attract continued funding and investment by the government. For this reason, I suggest, such systems generate a level of excitement and energy that undoubtedly constitutes a fetish, an attractive fabrication serving to conceal what is felt to be an unbearable lack within the organisation.

In the case example above, it can be seen that management's insistence on the marshalling of evidence – the directive to make the groups mandatory, to keep attendance registers and to open the group's process to scrutiny by management – was not only an extension of the performance monitoring system characteristic of the service, but in fact sponsored further perverse dynamics. In response to the increased surveillance following the letter of complaint, the group reacted by idealising their work. Difficulties, problems and complexity were increasingly glossed over, as were the feelings of shame, guilt and inadequacy that had initially been expressed. Instead, a 'glittering' version of the work started to emerge, one in which the very real difficulties in providing sufficient care and concern were ignored and replaced with a discourse of excellence, ready-made rules, regulations and 'short-cuts', all of which seemed to absolve members from any responsibility for thinking about what had happened. My supervisee too seemed to become swept up in the fabrication that was being constructed, led astray by the perverse dynamics being played out in the group, in which his own role and function – in fact, to provide care and concern to staff – was increasingly diminished and marginalised.

I subsequently examined my relationship with my supervisee in a little more detail with my own supervisor. Somewhat reluctantly, I noticed how I too had been increasingly marginalised in the supervision sessions. Just as my supervisee felt redundant in the face of the group's increasingly self-celebratory language (leading him to feel the group could 'run by itself now'), so I had felt redundant, emotionally removing myself through boredom and sleepiness. I realised that I had been losing interest in our work for some time; indeed, in a perverse dynamic akin to the one with which I started this paper, perhaps I had been 'there… but not really', unconsciously allowing my supervisee to 'run by himself'. In this sense, it was not surprising that he had 'forgotten' to come to the session.

At a wider level, then, it seems that an unconscious perverse organisational dynamic had been percolating through the service, culminating in the missed supervision session that indexed and enacted the very lack (of care) within the service that had been noticed by the complaining patient. It seemed to me that my colleague had himself disavowed the lack of care I had been showing, as well as, perhaps, his own unconscious anger, by refusing to discuss his absence in any detail. Instead, he had recruited me as willing accomplice (Long, 2009) into 'covering' the absence (thereby ensuring that he too was 'there... but not really'), using the service's 'rituals of verification' (Power, 1999) to conceal something felt to be shameful – something that could not be spoken or thought about.

## Discussion

What is it that the fetishisation of bureaucracy within mental health services disavows? Obholzer and Roberts (1994) argue that a national health service is used as an unconscious receptacle for the nation's anxieties about frailty, illness and death, suggesting that, quite apart from its acknowledged, normative healthcare aims, the NHS has always performed a symbolic or existential role in society. Hinshelwood (1994: 42) too argues that: 'Our institutions are set up with the prime purpose of dealing with unwanted anxiety'. He goes on to propose that mental health staff are tasked by society to carry out 'anxiety work' that demands an exceptionally high degree of emotional resilience in those who have to cope with the psychological stress of managing 'madness', vulnerability and mental illness.

The continuing – and escalating – demand for the care of those thought to be mentally ill was, of course, something the IAPT programme was explicitly designed to address; as a flagship mental health initiative, it has received the highest level of investment by any UK government since the inception of the NHS. However, the prevailing neoliberal philosophies from which IAPT has emerged have successfully sponsored forms of selfhood and subjectivity that are characterised by omnipotent fantasies of invulnerability and security, alongside a repudiation of weakness, dependency and a reduced capacity for empathy. Layton (2009), in the US, points to the lack of secure, containing authorities and institutions as well as the failure of governments to offer adequate social provision, resulting in a traumatic decline in people's sense of safety, security and trust. These reactions speak vividly to the UK experience, where, for many years, there has been increasing disavowal of the need for social and institutional containers. Obvious examples here include the abolition of universal child support, the instigation of 'parent-led' schools, the demise of final-salary pension schemes and swingeing cuts to welfare services and benefits. Within public healthcare services too, the Coalition government's Health and Social Care Act, passed into legislation in 2012, points to a political decision absolving government from their responsibilities for service provision in favour of service commissioning.

How might this decline in symbolic authority, together with its repudiation of citizens' dependency needs, intersect with healthcare policy, organisational structure and the emergence of the above perverse dynamics in mental health services? Fotaki (2010) argues that one of the difficulties in understanding the impact of public policy-making is that contemporary theorising is generally based on assumptions of rational reflexivity. She goes on to suggest, from a Lacanian perspective, that policy-making expresses not only rational objectives but also 'societal fantasies originating in the imaginary strivings of the subject' (2010: 704). Applying Fotaki's arguments to the hugely ambitious scale of the IAPT programme, we can view its overtly optimistic agenda to 'improve not only the health and well-being of the population but also promote social inclusion and improve economic productivity' (Department of Health, 2007: 4) as more aspirational than achievable. Indeed, Fotaki (2006) goes on to argue that policies based on 'semi-utopian' ideas must ultimately fail – in reality, of course, we 'can't care for everybody'.

I suggest that the government's response to this unwelcome piece of reality – its evident failure to 'care for everybody' – was the emergence of what might be termed a perverse solution: the implementation of a large-scale mental health policy based on improving financial productivity in a time of unprecedented global austerity. This has not only allowed successive governments to turn a blind eye to contemporary global socio-economic realities; it has also permitted the dependency and psychological distress of patients, as well as the anxieties and limitations of those tasked with caring for them, to be simultaneously disavowed and concealed beneath overwhelming bureaucratic and governance systems.

I suggest that the construction of this 'virtual' system of psychological care constitutes a fetish, a fabricated Symbolic father, where attention to targets, activity data, risk assessments, measurable clinical outcomes and so on 'covers' or substitutes for the failure of government to install thoughtful, containing institutions and services. Like the song of the mechanical nightingale, the signifiers of care thus become more important, more real – and more attractive – than the actual care they signify. In this way, as

Hoggett (2010) suggests, 'welfare governance takes on the form of a virtual reality' (p5), perverting the course of therapy and leaving patients feeling 'utterly uncared for', while the organisation remains duped by its own illusory competence.

Indeed, I suspect it was no coincidence that the patient who made the complaint about the PWP was herself struggling to cope with a profoundly disabled child, whose total dependence on her maternal care and support was clearly overwhelming, exhausting and draining. As exemplar of the disavowed suffering and dependency of patients (recall that this patient was in fact refused counselling and referred to another service), I suggest the letter of complaint, which may be seen as part of a Symbolic order structured by loss and lack, acted to blow the service's Imaginary 'cover', exposing, articulating and driving home the unwelcome reality of its limitations in caring for such mentally distressed patients. The fetishisation of governance within the organisation thus provides a managerially sanctioned route to the disavowal of limitations intrinsic to the care of those deemed mentally ill (Cooper & Lousada, 2005), via the staging of 'evidence' intended to demonstrate an idealised view of the organisation's work.

## Conclusion

Power (2000: 118) writes:

> Finally, the 'audit society' can be understood as a label for a loss of confidence in the central steering institutions of society, particularly politics. So it may be that a loss of faith in intellectual, political and economic leadership has led to the creation of industries of checking which satisfy a demand for signals of order. In the UK auditing and inspection will be set to work in the name of 'best value' and 'joined-up' government, but we may be forced to understand auditing as part of a general language of decline which attempts to bridge the widening gulf between plans and achievements.

These comments speak to the way in which systems of governance act to 'prop up' or support failing trust in the Symbolic role of government. This is particularly evident within the IAPT programme, where an emphasis on regulation, evaluation and performance measurement systems are unconsciously deployed by services to buttress the paternal function of a government deemed by the public to be increasingly weak and uninterested in welfare provision. At the same time, these systems undermine and subvert the very care they are mandated to ensure. Theorising the paradoxical effects of the audit culture in this way expands our understanding beyond the more traditional psychoanalytic Kleinian literature on unconscious social defences within organisations (Jaques, 1955; Hinshelwood, 1994; Hoggett, 2006; Menzies Lyth, 1960) by recasting NPM strategies of audit, evaluation and performance as fetishistic constructions unconsciously designed to mask or conceal a subjective sense of lack and fragmentation sponsored by contact with psychological pain and suffering.

The 'tyranny of transparency' (Strathern, 2000) characteristic of IAPT is, of course, now endemic in public sector services. The Francis Inquiry was commissioned by the government in 2010 to investigate the hundreds of deaths at the Mid-Staffordshire NHS Foundation Trust Hospital during the period 2005–2009. It was outspoken about the way in which hospital staff reacted to the pressure to meet targets, trenchantly concluding that:

> People must always come before numbers. Individual patients and their treatment are what really matters. Statistics, benchmarks and action plans are tools, not ends in themselves. They should not come before patients and their experiences. This is what must be remembered by all those who design and implement policy for the NHS. (Francis, 2010: 4)

Today, Francis's words are still apposite, particularly in the current context of continued changes to the structure of the NHS and the promises made by successive governments to establish mental health services on an equal footing with physical health. The *Five Year Forward View for Mental Health*, produced in 2016 by an independent taskforce for the Conservative government (Mental Health Taskforce to the NHS in England, 2016), suggests that NHS England should increase access to evidence-based psychological therapies to reach 25% of need so that at least 600,000 more adults with anxiety and depression could access IAPT services (and 350,000 complete treatment) each year by 2020/21. Understanding the complex intersection of neoliberal governmentality, mental health policy and the resulting unconscious dynamics of perversion and fetishism may enable us to predict the likely psychic, clinical and organisational consequences of such operational, strategic and financial decision-making. As the NHS is pushed through yet more reforms, we will need to develop such understanding if we are to implement and sustain effective and empathic clinical work in the future.

# References

Ballatt J, Campling P (2011). *Intelligent Kindness: reforming the culture of healthcare*. London: RPsych Publications.

Chasseguet-Smirgel J (1971). Le rossignol de l'Empereur de Chine. In: *Pour une Psychoanalyse de l'Art et de la Creativité*. Paris: Payot (pp183–216).

Cooper A, Lousada J (2005). *Borderline Welfare: feeling and fear of feeling in modern welfare*. Tavistock Clinic Series. London: Karnac Books.

Department of Health (2007). *Commissioning a Brighter Future: Improving Access to Psychological Therapies. Positive practice guide*. London: Department of Health.

Fink B (1997). *A Clinical Introduction to Lacanian Psychoanalysis: theory and technique*. Cambridge, MA: Harvard University Press.

Fotaki M (2010). Why do public policies fail so often? Exploring health policy making as an imaginary/symbolic construction. *Organisation 17*(6): 703–720.

Fotaki M (2006). Choice is yours: a psychodynamic exploration of health policy-making and its consequences for the English National Health Service. *Human Relations 59*(12): 1711–1744.

Foucault M (1972/2006). *History of Madness* (J Murphy, J Khalfa, trans). London: Routledge.

Francis R (2010). *Independent Inquiry into Care provided by Mid Staffordshire NHS Foundation Trust January 2005–March 2009 (volume I)*. Norwich: the Stationery Office.

Freud S (1927/1968). Fetishism. In: *Standard Edition of the Complete Psychological Works of Sigmund Freud Vol XX1: The future of an illusion, civilization and its discontents and other works*. London: Hogarth Press (pp147–158).

Gabriel Y, Carr A (2002). Organisations, management and psychoanalysis: an overview. *Journal of Managerial Psychology 17*(5): 348–365.

Hinshelwood RD (1994). The relevance of psychotherapy. *Psychoanalytic Psychotherapy 8*: 283–294.

Hoggett P (2010). Government and the perverse social defence. *British Journal of Psychotherapy 26*: 202–212.

Hoggett P (2006). Pity, compassion, solidarity. In: Clarke S, Hoggett P, Thompson S (eds). *Emotion, Politics and Society*. Basingstoke: Palgrave Macmillan (pp145–161).

Jaques E (1955). Social systems as a defence against persecutory and depressive anxiety. In: Klein M, Heimann P, Money-Kyrle R (eds). *New Directions in Psychoanalysis*. London: Tavistock (pp478–498).

Khan M (1987). *Alienation in Perversions*. London: Hogarth Press.

Lacan J (1994). *Le Seminaire IV: la relation d'objet* [Seminar IV: The object relation]. Paris: Seuil.

Lacan J (1962). *The Seminar of Jacques Lacan. Book X: anxiety, 1962-1963* (C Gallagher, trans). [Translated from unedited manuscript.] Cormac Gallagher.

Lacan J (1949/1977). The mirror-phase as formative of the function of the I as revealed in psychoanalytic experience. In: *Écrits: a selection* (A Sheridan, trans). London: Tavistock (p1–7).

Lacan J, Granoff W (1956). Fetishism: the symbolic, the imaginary and the real. In: Lorand S, Balint M (eds). *Perversions: psychodynamics and therapy*. New York, NY: Random House (p265–276).

Layton L (2009). Who's responsible? Our mutual implication in each other's suffering. *Psychoanalytic Dialogues 19*: 105–120.

Long S (2009). Greed. *Psychodynamic Practice 15*: 245–259.

MacCallum E (2002). Othering and psychiatric nursing. *Journal of Psychiatric and Mental Health Nursing 9*: 87–94.

Mental Health Taskforce to the NHS in England (2016). *The Five Year Forward View for Mental Health: a report from the independent Mental Health Taskforce to the NHS in England*. London: NHS England.

Menzies Lyth I (1960). The functioning of social systems as a defence against anxiety. *Human Relations 13*: 95–121.

National Institute for Health and Care Excellence (NICE) (2009). *Depression in adults: recognition and management*. Updated April 2018. London: NICE.

Obholzer J, Roberts N (1994). *Managing the Unconscious at Work*. London: Routledge.

Peternelj-Taylor C (2004). An exploration of othering in forensic, psychiatric and correctional nursing. *Canadian Journal of Nursing Research 36*(4): 130–146.

Power M (2004). Counting, control and calculation: reflections on measuring and management. *Human Relations 57*(6): 765–783.

Power M (2000). The audit society: second thoughts. *International Journal of Auditing 4*: 111–119.

Power M (1999). *The Audit Society: rituals of verification*. Oxford: Oxford University Press.

Rizq R (2012). The perversion of care: psychological therapies in a time of IAPT. *Psychodynamic Practice 18*(1): 7–25.

Scanlon C, Adlam J (2011). Who watches the watchers? Observing the dangerous liaisons between forensic patients and their carers in the perverse panoptican. *Organisational and Social Dynamics 11*(2): 175–195.

Shildrick M (2002). *Embodying the Monster*. London: Sage.

Stoller R (1986). *Perversion: the erotic form of hatred*. London: Karnac Books.

Strathern M (2000). The tyranny of transparency. *British Educational Research Journal 26*: 309–321.

# Chapter 10

# The industrial relations of mental health

## Elizabeth Cotton

This chapter will explore industrial relations in today's mental health services and current workforce trends, based on the Surviving Work Survey, which I led in 2016–2017. The research was motivated by the current lack of workforce data and industrial relations perspectives in the debates about how to deal with the crisis in mental health services. Despite a majority of mental health workers now practising within a complex and insecure employment relations context – employed in a range of clinical jobs, in multiple settings, on multiple contracts – there is still an assumption in public and policy debates that this workforce is made up of professionally distinct roles that are protected and privileged. As a result of this lack of data and understanding about the systemic trends in the service, the current national workforce strategy, most recently articulated in the *Stepping Forward to 2020/21: the mental health workforce plan for England* (Health Education England, 2017), is not underpinned by informed industrial thinking. This feeds into a lack of awareness within the workforce about the impact of the introduction of the NHS's largest mental health programme, Increasing Access to Psychological Therapies (IAPT), in relation to the downgrading of clinical care and jobs right across the mental health service.

The central argument of this chapter is that IAPT has introduced a rigid system of performance management that has led to a downgrading of mental health jobs that now threatens genuine psychological therapies. IAPT is one of the largest and expanding sources of employment in the mental health sector, in particular for counsellors and psychotherapists, and also psychologists in training, at a point when other sources of paid employment are drying up correspondingly, which explains the fear of clinicians to raise their concerns about the impact of the IAPT model on patient care. This may also explain why the IAPT model has been introduced without much internal resistance. When the entire talking therapies system has been moved towards an IAPT model, with a shrinking independent psychotherapeutic sector and limited sustainability of private practice, securing paid work as a counsellor is largely dependent on an acceptance of the IAPT model, whatever your views as a practitioner.

At the end of this chapter, I outline the organising challenge ahead and a framework for how mental health workers might challenge the IAPT model and build collective responses to it.

## The Surviving Work survey

The Surviving Work Survey was carried out during 2016–17 to try to get a current picture of working conditions in the mental health sector as a whole (including but not exclusively psychology and talking therapies services), including pay, promotion prospects and problems at work. The survey was motivated by the deficit of data and research into the working conditions of mental health workers, as well as the reluctance of clinicians to raise concerns, for fear of victimisation.

The research involved an online survey, using Survey Monkey, comprising 50 multiple-choice and open-answer questions. The survey ran from January to July 2016 and received 1,500 responses. A further 68 one-hour, semi-structured telephone interviews were carried out to explore in more detail interviewees' experiences of work and workplace issues, including their own mental health. Because of the sensitivity of the issues covered and the reluctance of people working in the profession to disclose mental health problems, the interviews were conducted on speaker phone, so that the responses could be typed up verbatim, and were not recorded. All the data and quotes used in this chapter come from the survey.

To reach potential participants, the survey took a long run-up, involving a campaign of discussion events under the title 'Do you have to marry a rich man to be a therapist in the UK?', as well as blogs and social media. This engagement was carried out through www.survivingwork.org, an online network of an estimated 30,000 people that I founded in 2012 to create a safe and critical space where people could talk about their experiences of work.

Information about the survey was disseminated through mental health professional, training, academic, trade union and allied networks, including the Royal College of Nursing (RCN), Unison, Unite, the British Association for Counselling and Psychotherapy (BACP), the British Psychoanalytic Council (BPC), the British Psychological Society (BPS), the Association of Child Psychotherapists (ACP), the UK Council for Psychotherapy (UKCP), WPF Therapy, the Association of Psychosocial Studies and the Tavistock & Portman NHS Trust.

I led the Surviving Work team, in my role as academic at Middlesex University. The data analysis was completed collaboratively with Professors John Grahl (Middlesex University) and Ahmet Suerdem (Istanbul Bilgi University). The public engagement activities and promotion of the survey were supported by Clare Gerada, Medical Director of the Practitioner Health Programme, and Leanne Stelmaszczyk, Association for Child Psychotherapists, who had both been active supporters of Surviving Work for some years.

The findings reported here relate to the whole survey sample, unless otherwise specified. The survey respondents included the full range of mental health workers. The highest percentage were mental health nurses, who continue to dominate mental health jobs in the NHS, followed by psychotherapists, trainees, CAMHS workers and counsellors. However, the majority of respondents held qualifications in psychotherapy and counselling, and many worked in a number of roles and used a variety of therapeutic modalities.

Most worked in IAPT services, followed by the third sector, private practice, psychiatric hospitals and community mental health services. However, the majority (54%) worked across multiple settings, rising to 91% among self-employed workers.

The percentage of respondents working as self-employed was high at 30%, consistent with labour market trends in the UK. Forty-five per cent of these were providing services to the NHS and 22% to the voluntary sector. While only 13% were currently working directly for IAPT services, 24% had some experience of working within IAPT services. In addition, due to the short-term nature of many employment contracts and use of self-employed practitioners and contractors to deliver IAPT services, it is likely that a larger percentage of respondents had experience of working within IAPT services, directly and indirectly, since 2008, although this number was not captured.

Many respondents, although not currently working in IAPT, could give detailed information about working conditions in the service. Because of the distribution of the survey through unions and professional bodies and networks, there was an over-representation within the IAPT sample of senior clinicians, such as counsellors and high intensity cognitive behavioural therapists (HICBT), and an under-representation of lower grades and clinical roles, such as psychological wellbeing practitioners (PWPs).

Due to the length of time that academic publication requires, the survey results were published online at the end of 2017, on a dedicated website, The Future of Work.[1] The website comprises a series of infographics on core themes, such as the downgrading of clinical work and raising concerns, as well as reporting the experiences of people working in various functions. It includes a video summarising the research findings, an eBook, *The Future of Therapy* (Cotton, 2017a), and guidance on setting up 'survival surgeries', which is also summarised at the end of this chapter.

## What the data show

Although it is true to say that working life in mental health is diverse, with teams and individuals trying to build sustainable services everywhere and many experienced clinicians able to influence how work is done, the trends that our survey highlights are uniform across the UK. I have selected representative quotes from IAPT workers specifically, which relate only to England (IAPT is not implemented in any of the three other UK countries).

### Trend 1: Dominance of precarious work and low pay

> I was trained in all the low-intensity training. I wasn't allowed to take 'risk' clients but actually all the people I saw were moderate to severe on PHQ-9. I had initially six to 12 sessions and by the time I left we were expected to get recovery rates with four sessions. It was very stressful for the people there full time. I was only there only one day a week. That's how I coped.
>
> Honorary unwaged IAPT counsellor, Kent

A clear picture of 'flexible' work emerged in the research – a picture of a growing majority of people working in multiple settings using different modalities,

---

1. www.thefutureoftherapy.org

increasingly providing generic rather than specialist care. Although 74% of respondents said they worked for the NHS, many reported that they worked on short-term contracts, for multiple employers, both directly for third-sector or private providers or indirectly, on self-employed contracts.

In the survey and interviews, it emerged that people were often confused about who they worked for and what their employers' responsibilities were. When asked about their employer, 20% said they were self-employed, but when asked what kind of contract of employment they had, 30% said they were self-employed. Further, eight per cent of respondents did not know what kind of contract they had and another eight per cent had no written contract at all.

The 24% of respondents who worked in IAPT services reported the same issues of precarity as the wider group: 19% were employed indirectly and worked for external contractors, 14% for third-sector organisations, four per cent for agencies, and 28% were self-employed. A high number of people worked in IAPT services as honoraries (unpaid), as part of their clinical training (20%).

The nature of flexible work means that many respondents were working across a range of services, including the 22% of NHS workers who had multiple employers. Part-time work was common (29% of survey respondents). Of these part-timers, 59% worked in the NHS and 38% were self-employed. Many respondents, particularly the NHS workers and more senior clinicians, reported that going part-time was how they coped with work intensification. Among newly qualified workers and trainees who had set up in private practice, part-time working was often to do with low patient numbers. Nobody I interviewed from this group was optimistic that they could earn a living from working in private practice.

Another issue that emerged from the findings was that many of the therapists were earning low wages. The average income across all respondents was £401–£500 a week after tax. But 14% of therapists working in the NHS and 28% working in other sectors or in private practice earned less than £300 a week; only 17% of those employed in the third sector were earning the average rate. This may be partly explained by the one third of people working part-time but may also relate to the widespread practice of using honorary (unpaid) workers to deliver services.

Some 21% of therapists worked unwaged in 'honorary' positions – a system that traditionally has been part of most psychotherapy and counselling training courses as well as a requirement for gaining sufficient clinical hours for membership of and registration/accreditation with the psychotherapy and counselling professional bodies. Honoraries worked across the range of public and private mental health employers, with 50% working in the third sector and 45% in the NHS.

However, a significant finding was that one third of honoraries were qualified practitioners, not trainees, yet still worked many hours, without pay, both in the NHS and the third sector. In the interviews, one explanation for this was the widespread policy of not replacing senior roles in services and cuts in funding, so some senior clinicians continued to work for free post-retirement, in order for services to continue.

## Trend 2: Downgrading and de-professionalisation of clinical jobs

> The PWP role is high volume low intensity, just churn them out. It's
> viewed as an unskilled job. The managers would say 'Don't take on
> counsellors in this role because they are just trouble and not prepared
> to do tick-box services.' It's an uncomfortable dynamic with the young
> PWPs straight from universities, who are naively prepared to do as
> required by the service. In reality, most of our patients have lots of
> life problems. We work in a really deprived area, lots of housing and
> drugs problems and severe depression and anxiety. That's kind of
> ignored by the service providers because they have to answer to their
> commissioning group. There's a big gap between the data and the reality
> of what we're trying to do.
>
> Psychological wellbeing practitioner, Liverpool

Two further trends emerged in the survey: the disparity between the practitioners' qualifications and clinical roles, through the downgrading of jobs, and the implications of the ageing workforce in the sector, as outlined in the next section.

In relation to qualifications, 78% of respondents working in IAPT services had postgraduate clinical qualifications as counsellors, cognitive behavioural therapists and psychotherapists prior to entry into the service. Only 25% had received the specialist IAPT training in high-intensity CBT.

To measure the gap between qualifications and clinical role, we asked for information on qualification seniority: all respondents registered with a psychotherapy professional association and all those with a clinical qualification at doctorate level or in psychoanalysis. This may not have captured the level of qualifications of a small number of respondents who had gained postgraduate qualifications but had not yet completed their registration process. We also took clinical seniority to include respondents working as psychotherapists or counsellors but with additional roles/responsibilities, such as supervision, teaching, clinical/team lead, management or providing a specialist service. Because of the downgrading of jobs in the NHS, the work required may be of a high clinical standard but the clinical role/job title itself may not recognise this. In the interviews, a number of IAPT counsellors reported that they would use their psychotherapeutic training and experience to support clients, but this required going 'off script', so they would not divulge this to their teams or management, for fear of reprisals.

The survey identified a significant gap between the qualification seniority of IAPT workers and the clinical level of the job they were employed to do – 48% of IAPT respondents were working below their clinical qualification levels.

## Trend 3: The age gap

> Therapists are in the main worried about their jobs but that's bizarre because nobody wants their jobs. We're not the happiest of working groups. The newcomers are very compliant and over eager to please.
>
> IAPT worker, Coventry

In our survey, 60% of respondents were older than 47 years and 21% were older than 58, rising to 29% in London. Only 19% of respondents were younger than 37. Within the UK working population, the percentage in this age group is nearly double, at 35%. Among the IAPT respondents, 80% were born in 1970 or earlier.

Table 1: Age and job type

|  | Born 1950 and earlier (%) | Born 1980 and later (%) |
|---|---|---|
| Mental health nurse | 17 | 32 |
| Counsellor | 13 | 5 |
| Support worker | 5 | 13 |
| Cognitive behavioural therapist | 8 | 8 |
| CAMHS worker | 14 | 12 |
| Psychotherapist | 39 | 8 |

Although many experienced therapists were working in a combination of private practice and NHS work, the demography suggests that they are only able to survive financially because they have spent most of their working lives in the NHS, so have pensions and own their own homes. A third of respondents said that the best thing they could do to improve their working lives was to retire.

One of the significant problems raised in the survey and interviews was the lack of progression available to clinicians, principally because services were not replacing senior staff when they retired and there was no opportunity for clinicians to progress into more senior grades as they gained experience and qualifications.

Although it is the case that trainees in psychotherapy and counselling are generally older than most people just starting out on their professional career (they are often in their 40s and 50s, pursuing a second career), there is a growing concern that services are failing to recruit the next generation of mental health workers into training and retain them through career progression. If the trend continues, the costs of clinical training and securing professional registration will not be balanced by paid and secure employment in the long term, inevitably affecting recruitment into the sector.

The future this suggests is one in which the psychotherapy and counselling professions are persistently stripped of senior, experienced practitioners, who are considered too expensive for IAPT services. This should be of major concern to the profession and has worrying implications for our mental health services if talking therapies are to be provided primarily by inexperienced practitioners with limited training in delivering short-term, highly manualised CBT interventions. The demography of the profession, in which unusually high numbers of practitioners are aged 50 and older, can only exacerbate this trend. Our survey suggests many of these more experienced, older practitioners are considering if it is worthwhile to continue to work such long hours and in such stressful conditions, where they do not feel able to practise ethically to meet their patients' needs.

In both the survey and interviews, respondents raised concerns about the standards and quality of services in IAPT. The principal concern was the limited number of sessions offered to patients, the pressure on throughput and the rigidity of the CBT model offered, which is manualised, often scripted (especially in the case of low-intensity treatments) and increasingly provided remotely, either by telephone (assessments) or online (guided CBT).

The main reason for poor therapeutic care is timescale. 'When are they going to be fixed?' They want to see the evidence for progress in 12 weeks.

There's no understanding of what it takes to build people's mental health.

IAPT counsellor, Essex

There were also concerns about the number of people with ambiguous clinical status working in mental health services. PWPs were introduced through IAPT to provide manualised, short-term interventions and carry out initial phone assessments. However, as the next generation of IAPT workers enter the profession, there is little clarity about the clinical framework, including training and supervision, within which they are working.

Respondents in IAPT services also reported high caseloads, ranging from five to eight patients per day, and consequent problems with work intensification, particularly for the more senior staff, with more complex patients, in order to complete the requisite performance data forms.

Our senior manager is very much focused on the contract – push, push, push, more contacts, getting us on Facebook, advertisements on buses – but he's removed from the experience of the patient. Apparently, he described high intensity workers as 'the workhorse of the psychological world' – well, they end up in the knacker's yard, don't they.

HICBT worker, Midlands

This is not a debate about status and the niceties of clinical practice; it is a real concern about the standards of treatment offered to patients who are not able or willing to access short-term CBT interventions and those who require long-term, interpersonal work. From a therapeutic perspective, the demands of the IAPT model on both the clinician and patient radically undermine the possibility of establishing a therapeutic relationship that allows for working in depth with underlying issues. In our interviews, many clinicians regarded IAPT as 'sub-therapy', and many risked reprisals by offering psychotherapeutic interventions and going 'off script'.

It is notable that IAPT workers were more likely than those working in other NHS services to raise concerns about working conditions – 55%, compared with a survey average of 36%, and 58%, compared with a survey average of 38%, in relation to patient care.

## The industrial relations of mental health

People are put into management positions to pressure clinicians into reaching targets. Clinicians didn't have anyone they could talk to about it. They just had to shut up. I had confidential chats with colleagues – to be honest, the staff needed counselling.

Honorary counsellor, IAPT service, Kent

Ironically for therapists who are in the business of talking and thinking, they are not doing much talking together about the future of jobs in the mental health sector. With the notable exception of critical networks such as the Alliance for Counselling and Psychotherapy, the Mental Wealth Alliance, Psychotherapists and Counsellors for Social Responsibility and the Psychotherapy and Counselling Union (PCU), the debates so far about the future of jobs in mental health have been mainly institutionally and professionally territorial.

Part of the reason for this is the lack of industrial relations perspective among practitioners in the sector, including a lack of awareness of the strategic use of performance management techniques to increase 'productivity' right across the public sector. What follows in this section is a brief outline of performance management in mental health services and the specific impact on mental health services, jobs and workers.

Performance management was a central component of the political argument in favour of the creation of the NHS (Cutler, 2011). However, the current model of New Public Management (NPM) was introduced across the public services in the UK in the 1980s, as part of a shift towards introducing competition and privatisation of public services, promoted through neoliberal economic policies adopted internationally (Bach, 2016). This financial logic in the healthcare sector has been reinforced by the 'austerity logic' (Pollitt, 2013), introduced following the financial crisis in 2008 (Lynch, 2015) in an attempt to address the tension between budgets and clinical priorities. NPM's characteristics include marketisation and a 'results-oriented' culture, performance management based on targets and performance measurement regimes, including performance-related pay, and decentralisation of decision-making to allow managers to prioritise organisational performance (Verbeeten & Speklé, 2015).

In the UK, healthcare reform has been coupled with a programme of quasi-market modernisation, with decentralisation of commissioning and service planning implemented since the late 1990s (Bach, 2016) and enshrined in the 2012 Health and Social Care Act. The motivation for the breaking down of public services and encouraging privatisation through the introduction of 'any qualified provider' into NHS tendering processes follows the neoliberal ideology that, by breaking up monopolistic public sector organisations into business units, the sector will run competitively and more efficiently. This involved a rapid decentralisation of decision-making right across the NHS, with the introduction of new, localised structures at commissioning and contracting levels. It has led to a mix of both centralising and decentralising tendencies within the NHS, with a resulting increase in management control by virtue of their enhanced operational discretion, including shaping employment relationships. At the same time, the government has taken a greater role in setting national performance targets, such as waiting times and access, as well as performance monitoring mechanisms, auditing and regulation (Levy, 2010). Within this model, there is a clear tension between decentralised decision-making and deregulation, such as team working or democratic leadership, and centralised performance management, with its bureaucratic requirements for collecting and auditing performance data.

One of the 2012 Health and Social Care Act's objectives was also to reduce management costs by 45% (Bresnen et al, 2017) – a saving that was later compounded by the NHS England (2014) *Five Year Forward View*, which proposed £22 billion efficiency savings by 2020. The impact in the NHS has been complex, with fewer management jobs and the 'transformation' of clinical roles to cover frontline management functions, thus embodying the tension between the financial and clinical logics (Bresnen et al, 2017).

In the context of austerity, performance management has become an ideological and moral approach to managing public resources, in response to what is considered 'irresponsible' overspending in the public sector (Lynch, 2015). In this way, the use of performance data and management to 'evidence' the value of public spending has become a narrow debate about market efficiencies, rather than one about quality of care and the needs of an ageing population (Bach, 2016). Additionally, the demands of performance measurement have greatly increased the bureaucratic workload within the NHS, making management more a question of ticking boxes than based on a real understanding of performance within the organisation.

The evolution of the IAPT programme has taken place within this context, to the extent that its funding is significantly predicated on a parallel reduction in welfare benefits costs, such as disability unemployment benefits through Universal Credit and getting people back into work. This linking of mental health with work has been graphically reinforced with the introduction of IAPT counsellors in job centres and the presence of employment advisers in health settings (GP surgeries as well as mental health), the phenomenon of psycho-compulsion to 'motivate' claimants to find work, the application of sanctions on those who fail to comply adequately, and the resulting reduction in the welfare benefits bill (see Lynne Friedli and Robert Stearn's Chapter 4 in this book). The use of mental health treatments to reduce welfare costs is not just a clinical problem; it is a political one. As mental health services are co-opted into implementing successive governments' attacks on welfare provision, the lack of informed debate within the mental health sector means that mental health workers have not been able to respond meaningfully and in any concerted way to this misuse of their therapeutic role.

Additionally, the way in which performance is measured is highly problematic. The targets and measures used may have dysfunctional consequences (Lynch, 2015), including misplaced incentives and sanctions that can undermine quality of care (Keogh, 2013). That is, performance measurements may not lead to improved performance (Cutler, 2011) because of a potential 'performance paradox' (Pollitt, 2013) where data does not capture either the strengths or weaknesses of the care system. For example, in the case of mental health, the way that recovery outcomes are formulated assumes a linear process of change and recovery (Blackman et al, 2006) – a far cry from the dynamic and complex experiences of patients engaged in the talking therapies.

One of the under-articulated consequences of this centrally defined model of performance data collection is the problem of 'gaming'. Organisations are forced to misrepresent outputs in order to achieve performance targets (Bevan, 2006). The emergence of gaming as an 'alternative logic' (Politt, 2013) within the NHS is one of the most serious problems with the performance management system. Although there may be a distinction between a deliberate misrepresentation of performance and reporting data using an inadequate measurement, the results may be equivalent. In addition to misrepresenting the efficiency of services, the gaming of data can also lead to a lack of engagement with the consequences of poor services, such as suicide rates. Using the current measures, it is quite possible for a service to be considered to be performing well in terms of waiting times and discharging patients, as reflected in Care Quality Commission audits, but at the same time have serious problems with patient safety (Zhinchin & Shah, 2013).

Within IAPT services, the way performance is measured has led to a preoccupation with targets and performance indicators that reflect efficiency within the service rather than clinical outcomes (Cotton, Kline & Morton, 2013). An economic imperative is driving the 'evidence base' for IAPT interventions. Recovery rates (a 50% target), waiting times and numbers of people discharged from IAPT are the primary performance indicators used to establish the effectiveness of the IAPT model that now dominates policy decisions about mental health services and funding. Where in all this is the patient experience? Quality of care? Drop-outs? Re-referrals?

This 'evidence base' for IAPT starts with the baseline assessment, usually done on the telephone by PWPs, with no training in diagnosis, using scripted questionnaires that allow only minimal discussion between therapist and patient and requiring the practitioner to select from a limited range of broad-brush diagnostic categories. Patients with complex needs may find themselves referred to short-term interventions that are not designed to treat their needs, or having to go through several hoops and re-referrals before they can access the intensive, one-to-one psychotherapy that would be of benefit. This question over the evidence base for IAPT was taken up by the National Audit Office (NAO) in an inquiry into its performance data on recovery rates and waiting times in 2017. A high volume of submissions were made by IAPT workers and researchers, including the Surviving Work Survey, but the NAO decided not to publish the inquiry report. Despite repeated Freedom of Information requests, no explanation for this decision has been given.

Clinicians consistently raise concerns about the ethics of the IAPT model but, because of the dominance of the IAPT performance data regime, providers within the NHS and in the independent and third sectors alike are forced to adopt these measurements in order to provide 'evidence' of their value for money and secure funding and contracts.

> The culture is budget conscious and very much 'do as we say'. There's a lot of disillusionment – more among ward-level staff. I don't think the senior managers really feel anything. It's about appearances – if it looks good, it's OK. It's horrible because, for someone who feels very passionate about mental health and loves working in it, to feel that the trust you're working for has a lack of interest in patient care and experience, it's very disheartening.
>
> NHS psychotherapist, Essex

A direct consequence of the dominance of this model of performance management has been the establishment of a 'command-and-control' management culture within the NHS (Ghoshal & Bartlett, 1995), outlined in detail in the Francis reports into the high number of unexplained fatalities at the Stafford Hospital (Francis, 2010; 2013; see also Penny Campling's Chapter 2 in this book). Research indicates that managers under pressure to deliver targets typically default to a command-and-control style, become insensitive and defensive, and put a downward pressure on quality of care

(Alimo-Metcalfe & Alban-Metcalfe, 2005). This in turn is linked to the emergence of a culture of bullying (Cotton et al, 2013), with staff reluctant to raise concerns for fear of victimisation (Cotton, 2017b) – a concern reinforced by the treatment of NHS whistleblowers (Holt & Kline, 2012). This management culture has led to a widespread silencing of staff, both within mental health services and more broadly in healthcare, and the establishment of the National Guardian's 'Freedom to Speak Up' initiative (Hammond & Bousefield, 2011; Francis, 2015).

> Then organisational problems get located in the individual. There's a kind of pseudo-competency that is being privileged at the moment and asking for help is seen as a weakness. With job insecurity, people are less open about their struggles. It's so dangerous. That feels more pronounced than it did.
>
> Consultant psychotherapist, Manchester

It is important to understand that this industrial relations strategy is not an accident. There is a strategic objective behind this promotion of manualised/non-clinical/virtual therapies, combined with the growth of self-employment, in that it opens up the mental health sector to private, third-sector and non-clinical providers. Based on the experience in the public and other sectors, we will see the rise of private employment agencies (PrEAs) and large-scale contractors supplying mental health workers to the NHS and, with it, the risk of failed contracts and lack of corporate accountability. From the survey responses and interviews, there appears to be a particular growth in private employment agencies providing IAPT services in Child and Adolescent Mental Health Services (CAMHS) as the Child and Young People's IAPT (CYP-IAPT) is rolled out in England. There is also a strategic growth of jobs that do not require clinical training or registration with professional bodies – such as IAPT PWPs – and therapies, such as computerised CBT programmes, that don't even require clinicians to deliver them. This downgrading of clinical requirements across the mental health sector is a strategic invitation to private providers, including private employent agencies who operate in other healthcare professions such as nursing, to enter the mental health service.

## The organising challenge ahead

The Surviving Work Survey findings raise some questions about how we can influence the way mental health services are delivered in the future. How do mental health workers get to the point of organised industrial activity where they can make demands about wages and working conditions across the mental health sector? Which institutions are going to offer us the support and protection we need to do this organising work?

In the long term we know that mental health services deserve an independent public inquiry into the current regime of performance management – one that is run by people with no financial investment in the outcome. Inevitably, public and publicly accountable structures need to be fought for, but we are a long away from achieving this because of the absence of workplace organising in the sector.

Something that stood out in our survey responses was the low number of people who sought help with their workplace problems from a trade union or directly from colleagues. Outside the NHS, only four per cent of therapists spoke to a colleague about problems at work. The question I have been repeatedly asked throughout this research is whether I know of a group in the area that mental health workers can join to get support. There are several large trade unions in the sector, but strangely, for people trained to increase relationality, we do not seem to be applying this with the people with whom we work. The dual meaning of free association seems important here in describing both our right to collectivise at work and our skills in developing deep relationality with the people around us.

Traditionally, workplace organising is practised using some powerful educational methods based on the work of Paulo Freire (1970) and the workers' education traditions developed in Western Europe (Croucher & Cotton, 2011). These methods provide a framework of three connected stages of learning: problem identification, getting information (particularly identifying what resources are available), and planning concrete next steps. In the TUC education system, this became known as the PIP framework – problems, information and planning (Cotton, 2017c). Emancipatory education is underpinned by a number of principles, including confidentiality and solidarity, and activities aim to provide a safe space for expressing and processing diverse and often difficult workplace experiences. Because the methods open up debate, they can, if used well, support the inherently political processes of consciousness raising and collective planning, in order to identify and mobilise collective interests – the basis of putting solidarity into action.

These methods have been exported internationally through solidaristic programmes and offer us a methodology that has important parallels with the psychoanalytic project, as well as the capacity to build relationality at work (Cotton, 2017c). They can be understood as psychosocial, looking at both internal and external realities, and require raising consciousness, collectivisation and praxis, understood as understanding reality and taking action to transform it. These methods aim to promote a dialogue between participants, looking at their experiences of the real world, reflecting on them and making material changes (Vella, 2002), particularly in relation to wages and working conditions.

In a context of downgraded mental health services, the fact that mental health workers are unorganised and silenced is a matter of both professional and personal ethical concern. Sometimes working in healthcare forces you to walk a very thin line between the personal and the political, to allow you both to defend ethical and clinical principles and negotiate the conditions in which those principles can survive. To do any of this ordinary organising work requires us to challenge the performance management systems within which we work and, maybe more importantly, support each other in doing that. This rests entirely on our capacities to build relationships with the people we actually work with.

Despite the troubling picture presented by my survey findings, they also offer hope. One of the privileges of a trade union is that we are one of the practical solutions that emerge when working people have reached a point where they cannot accept their working conditions. We know that people can and do organise successfully in the most precarious environments – often self-organising, when their institutions fail to represent their interests. This is not principally an ideological response; it is one of necessity.

It is the importance of this ordinary organising work that often gets missed. The principle objective of this research is to open up a debate about the dual purpose of organising: how to make real changes in our working conditions and pay while at the same time sustaining ourselves in the current climate.

The next section is a guide to building collective action. The 'survival surgery' is based on emancipatory principles and has been piloted with health workers and trade unionists in various settings since 2012. It does not offer a magic solution to the complex problems of working in today's mental health services, but it does save time by showing you how to engage with colleagues in a way that is more likely to result in action.

## Survival surgeries: working on the healthcare frontline

Whether you're a self-employed psychotherapist or a nurse working in old-age care, survival surgeries are a simple way for you to build your capacity to address workplace problems. We developed this model, working with health workers in diverse settings, based on the principles of adult education and using tried-and-tested activities that have brought about real change in workplaces all over the world.

These methods can be used in formal and informal meetings, workshops and group events, wherever workers want to develop an agenda for change.

Survival surgeries follow three core steps: establish what the real problems are, get more information and plan collectively. The process is acronymed as the **LAUGH** approach:

**Stage 1:** Start where you are by **L**istening and **A**ssessing what is actually going on at work.

**Stage 2:** **U**nderstand your environment and identify the resources you individually and collectively hold.

**Stage 3:** **G**et **H**elp from the people around you and collectively solve problems.

## Getting started

How you start very much depends on your working environment. It may be that you are part of an existing group or team that wants to try this model for managing discussions. If you want to establish a group yourself, you can do this as part of a professional development, team-building, supervisory or social activity. Surgeries can be described in any way you think will get people to join – from book clubs to reflective groups. Use whatever language you think people will be receptive to; the key is to create a safe and containing space where people can say what they think.

On a pragmatic note, if you ask your workplace for permission to start a new 'project', often the answer will be no. You do not need permission to set up an informal group or safe space for the people you work with. In fact, it is worth having a go at creating a space informally a few times before going public with what you want to do. It's much easier to get people to sign up to something that already exists, and much harder to block it too.

It's better (more efficient) if just two or more people initially drive the process, recruit participants and facilitate the initial survival surgeries. Over time, you will build up capacity and will be able to rotate the responsibility for facilitation. New people will emerge who want to run sessions. When you're starting a group, it is often easier to start small, with regular meetings, usually with monthly or six-week gaps.

Because of the likelihood that conflict and anger will arise in surgeries, you need to set some clear ground rules. These are:

- confidentiality of content
- anonymising workplace issues to reduce scapegoating
- respect and equality for everyone's experience
- voluntary attendance but a commitment to attend regularly
- no lectures, posturing or power points.

You will also have to think about whether you invite managers and supervisors to your surgeries. You should think carefully about whether their participation will help or hinder collective action and dialogue within the group.

# Activities

Following the LAUGH model, here are three activities that you can use to run a survival surgery. This session can take 2–3 hours, about the length of a staff meeting, which most people can generally commit to. Group size can vary from eight to 30 – even larger if you're comfortable with that, but if you're starting a new group, around 15 people is ideal.

**First set your ground rules** – it helps if you introduce them and write them up on a flip chart.

## Activity 1: Listening swap (30–45 minutes)

Ask participants to work in pairs, preferably with someone they don't know well. One person will be the speaker and will talk for about five minutes about what is on their mind. The listener should just listen – no prompting, questions or normalising, just listening. After five minutes ask the pairs to swap roles.

It's best to leave this activity open, but if you want to focus it, use an open question such as 'What is the real issue you're facing at work today?'

Depending on the size of the group, you can ask participants to report back to the group what came up in the Listening Swap and write this down on a flip chart. The issues raised here become the focus of the discussions during the survival surgery. If you are working with a larger group (over 20), you can ask people to initially work in groups of five or six and discuss the key themes that came up for 15 minutes, and then have a whole group discussion (another 15 minutes).

## Activity 2: Understanding workplace issues (30 minutes)

You can do this activity as one group if you have fewer than 15 members. If you are working in a larger group, ask people to work in small groups of 5–6 people.

Ask if there is a case/issue at work from the previous activity that one of the participants would like to discuss with the group. Normally people are willing, but this may take some encouragement from the facilitators. This person will spend five minutes introducing the problem they are facing at work. It works better if the person speaking uses the flip chart to draw a map of the issue, so that participants can see it from an organisational perspective. Participants will then reflect back what struck them about the case and collectively identify what the issues behind it are.

Small groups should be asked to write on a flip chart the issues that emerge from this discussion. In a larger group, the facilitator should summarise the issues around the case. Take a five-minute break here if needed.

## Activity 3: Collective problem solving (30 minutes)

Continuing with this case study, ask people to work in groups of three to five people to identify three or more actions that could be taken to address the issues raised. It is important here to work in smaller groups to allow for a real exchange of experiences. It can help focus discussions to ask people to come up with three things that could be done, but if there are more, try to capture them. After 20 minutes, ask each group to report back on their proposed lines of action and write them on a flip chart. The next stage is a whole-group discussion to identify the actions that the participants think are realistic and can commit to in the short and long term.

Whatever is agreed by the group during this activity is the plan of action for the group, so if the usual suspects end up with all the tasks allocated to them, you will need to address that in the group. It is important to review the plan of action at each subsequent surgery and discuss any issues that have arisen since the previous one. You can do this using an amended version of Activity 2.

## Summarise the survival surgery

Normally you will use the last 15 minutes to review what has been agreed and set the date for the next survival surgery.

## Why survival surgeries work

Survival surgeries are a highly effective method that can, in a short period, organise collective responses to workplace problems. Having a clear three-stage model and activities to guide discussions can be containing for participants, who are likely to be anxious about talking about difficulties at work for the first time. Dialogic methods are really effective in building relationships with the people we work with as they are based on real understanding and an appreciation of other people's experiences. The collective problem-solving at the end of each surgery focuses participants on the real job of work ahead and their collective responsibilities for bringing about change.

Surgeries do not have to go on forever – they often work well for six months, after which the focus can drift. This is not a failure, if relationships within the group have been strengthened. The main thing is to keep the energy and pace of the group going for as long as people feel it is useful. Surgeries can also shift in their focus and membership – again, as long as the surgery is responsive to what people actually want, this is a good thing. Surgeries work if they are useful, so the key is to respond to the needs that come up, rather than to stick rigidly to the original plan.

## Working with group dynamics

Health workers are experienced at dealing with anger and distress but most of us feel a lot more about problems at work than we normally express, and if a Survival Surgery is going well, people will raise difficult issues. If participants become angry or distressed during discussions, it is important to acknowledge this and allow the group to process strong emotions and the issues that trigger them.

The following is a simple process of containment that you can use to manage your own or other people's overwhelming feelings, either in survival surgeries or more broadly at work.

First aid provides some very simple and immediate steps to contain overwhelming feelings. You can use five steps, which we are calling **CABIN** (a nice mental picture of a safe place in a wood, with birds and Bambi).

Contain: remove yourself from whatever is making you anxious and find somewhere where you feel safe. If you can, call a friend or find someone at work you trust to help you.

Acknowledge: don't try to ignore what has just happened – acknowledge the anxiety.

Body: try to control your breathing. Lengthen your breath and, if it helps, count one-two-three slowly in your head. Keep going until your breathing has normalised. If you're around someone you like, ask them to give you a hug or even a little squeeze. Human contact really works.

Identify: work out what you are worried about right now – the immediate, real source of the anxiety, rather than the nameless dread that sometimes creeps up on us.

Next steps: work out what the next steps should be. Find at least one concrete thing that you're going to do right now to make sure the fear doesn't pop back. This stage is always better if you can find a friend to do this with.

## If you do one thing

It may be that you're not able to run a survival surgery right away. But you can use these activities in your meetings and working life to stimulate a real discussion with the people you work with. If you do one thing, start each discussion or meeting with colleagues by asking what is on their mind and genuinely listening to the answer.

## Survival resources

There are loads of free online resources about how to survive working in healthcare at www.survivingworkinhealth.org

# References

Alimo-Metcalfe B, Alban-Metcalfe D (2005). Leadership: time for a new direction? *Leadership* *1*(1): 51–71.

Bach S (2016). Deprivileging the public sector workforce: austerity, fragmentation and service withdrawal in Britain. *Economic and Labour Relations Review 27*(1): 11–28.

Bevan G (2006). Setting targets for health care performance: lessons from a case study of the English NHS. *National Institute Economic Review 197*(1): 67–79.

Blackman T, Elliott E, Greene A, Harrington B, Hunter DJ, Marks L, McKee L, Williams G (2006). Performance assessment and wicked problems: the case of health inequalities. *Public Policy and Administration 21*(2): 66–80.

Bresnen M, Hodgson D, Bailey S, Hyde P, Hassard J (2017). Mobilizing management knowledge in healthcare: institutional imperatives and professional and organizational mediating effects. *Management Learning 48*(5): 597–614.

Cotton E (2017a). *The Future of Therapy.* [ebook.] Surviving Work. www.thefutureoftherapy. co.uk (accessed 11 March 2019).

Cotton E (2017b). *Surviving Work in Healthcare: helpful stuff for people on the frontline.* London: Routledge.

Cotton E (2017c). Constructing solidarities at work: relationality and the methods of emancipatory education. *Capital & Class 41*(2). DOI: 10.1177/0309816817723284.

Cotton E, Kline R, Morton C (2013). Following Francis: reversing performance in the NHS from targets to teams. *People & Strategy 36*(1): 63–65.

Croucher R, Cotton E (2011). *Global Unions, Global Business: global union federations and international business* (2nd ed). London: Libri Publishing.

Cutler T (2011). Performance management in public services 'before' new public management: the case of NHS acute hospitals 1948–1962. *Public Policy and Administration 26*(1): 129–147.

Francis R (2015). *Freedom to Speak Up: a review of whistleblowing in the NHS.* London: Freedom to Speak Up. https://webarchive.nationalarchives.gov.uk/20150218150953/ https://freedomtospeakup.org.uk/wp-content/uploads/2014/07/F2SU_web.pdf in the NHS (accessed 12 February 2019).

Francis R (2013). *The Report of the Mid Staffordshire NHS Foundation Trust Public Inquiry HC 947.* Norwich: the Stationery Office.

Francis R (2010). *Independent Inquiry into Care Provided by Mid Staffordshire NHS Foundation Trust January 2005 – March 2009, vol 1.* Norwich: the Stationery Office.

Freire P (1970). *Pedagogy of the Oppressed.* New York: Continuum Books.

Ghoshal S, Bartlett CA (1995). Changing the role of top management: beyond structure to processes. *Harvard Business Review 73*(1): 86–96.

Hammond P, Bousfield A (2011). Shoot the messenger: how NHS whistleblowers are silenced and sacked. A *Private Eye* special. *Private Eye 1292*(8–22 July): 15–22.

Health Education England (2017). *Stepping forward to 2020/21: the mental health workforce plan for England.* London: Health Education England.

Holt K, Kline R (2012). Whistle while you work – if you dare. *Health Service Journal*, 25 October.

Keogh B (2013). *Review into the Quality of Care and Treatment Provided by 14 Hospital Trusts in England: overview report*. London: National Health Service.

Levy R (2010). New Public Management: end of an era? *Public Policy and Administration* 25(2): 234–240.

Lynch T (2015). What is the problem with health economics? a critique of health system performance measurement. *International Journal of Health Services* 45(4): 743–761.

Pollitt C (2013). The logics of performance management. *Evaluation* 19(4): 346–363.

Vella J (2002). *Learning to Listen, Learning to Teach: the power of dialogue in educating adults*. San Francisco, CA: Jossey Bass.

Verbeeten FHM, Speklé RF (2015). Management control, results-oriented culture and public sector performance: empirical evidence on new public management. *Organization Studies* 36(7): 953– 978.

Zhinchin G, Shah A (2013). The relationship between NHS performance indicators and suicide rates. *Medicine, Science and the Law* 53(4): 223–226.

# Chapter 11

# At what cost? The impact of IAPT on third-sector psychological therapy provision

## Jude Boyles and Norma McKinnon Fathi

This chapter reflects on our experience of managing counselling and therapy services during a period of major transformation in NHS primary and community mental health services, and the effects of these changes on the third sector, in the context of an emerging dominant ideology for how best to respond to the mental health needs of communities.

The roll-out of the Improving Access to Psychological Therapies (IAPT) programme across England from 2008 has had a huge impact on the mental health landscape, but not just within the NHS; it has also impacted on the third sector. Many third-sector services have benefited from the new funding that became available through NHS contracts to deliver IAPT services. But this, as we argue here, is at a potential very great cost. NHS England, in its *Five Year Forward View* (NHS England, 2014: 14), notes that the third sector often has 'an impact well beyond what statutory services alone can achieve'. It observes that the third sector has unique strengths in relation to its commitment to specific missions: a 'rich range of activities on offer in response to mental health, often under the one roof', and many examples of 'service user led or influenced initiatives'. It recognises that the third sector is 'better able to reach underserved groups'.

We want to explore if and how IAPT, with its neoliberal ethos and New Public Management (NPM) practices, has influenced access to and the delivery of talking therapies in the third sector, and the impact of that on the diverse client groups it – often uniquely – serves.

We are both therapists and have worked as managers in third-sector clinical services for many years. In the past decade we have experienced shifts in the ways we were expected to practise and to lead our teams. Our personal concern about the changes in the third sector and its ability to work with marginalised communities motivated us to write this chapter.

As reported in several chapters in this book, IAPT's methodology includes the introduction of NPM techniques. We have since seen these same management approaches crossing into the third sector, our services included, even where the services concerned did not receive IAPT contract funding, and how language from the business world has crept into the narrative of clinical practice. The focus has shifted away from client problems and needs to 'meeting targets' and 'evidencing impact' and how to do more with less; to discussions about how to reduce 'care spells' and move people through the system faster. We felt we were essentially doing less for people, but with much more paperwork. We found it changed how we practised as managers and therapists, in ways we did not like.

To investigate what influence, if any, IAPT was having on third-sector provision, we undertook a small-scale, qualitative, thematic analysis study. Using a semi-structured interview format, we spoke with 10 practitioners working in 10 different third-sector organisations in England that delivered counselling and psychotherapy to marginalised communities. They included therapists practising a range of different modalities as well as managers. We also spoke with an experienced IAPT practitioner.

The chapter contains our personal reflections and the insights shared by these interviewees on the influence of IAPT on third-sector counselling and therapy provision.

To recruit participants for the study, we posted an open invitation on the Facebook pages of several professional bodies and networks, asking therapists working in third-sector talking therapy services to get in touch if they would like to participate in a semi-structured interview about the impact of IAPT. We asked particularly about the influence of IAPT on the delivery of accessible services to marginalised communities and if they had experienced any changes in the sector's ability to adapt the design and delivery of services to meet clients' cultures, preferences and needs. The respondents were all self-selected.

We chose to anonymise the participants to protect everyone and enable interviewees to speak openly and honestly. The participants were interviewed individually. Interviews lasted approximately one hour and began with participants sharing with us their professional backgrounds and training, before describing their understanding of the IAPT model (the descriptions were all quite similar, which was interesting in itself), before reflecting on whether it had changed the services where they worked, and for better or worse. Our sample included a senior executive officer, a clinical director, a clinical lead, service managers and psychological therapists (sometimes they held a dual role) working in third-sector black and minority ethnic (BME), refugee, young people's and women's services, and other specialist services such as HIV/AIDS and brain injury teams. The experienced IAPT practitioner had been working for the programme since its introduction in their locality.

The interviews took the form of dynamic dialogues. It was clear that we had hit a raw nerve with some of the people we talked to. The main themes to emerge inevitably included sustainability, resourcing and funding in a precarious economic landscape. However, other more philosophical themes also emerged, including changing values within the sector, a shift in the focus of mental health provision, the scope of services and concerns about the third sector's continued ability to reach the communities these counselling and support organisations had been set up to serve. Interestingly, more subtle themes were also present in people's narratives: themes of power and control, conformity and uniformity, constraint and pressure, fear and survival.

Throughout the chapter, there are anonymised quotes from the people we interviewed. It would be difficult to draw conclusions from a small qualitative study, but we conclude our chapter with a discussion on areas that may need further research and reflection.

We have both worked with refugees in a variety of settings for many years and are acutely aware that the prevalence of depression, anxiety and post-traumatic stress disorder (PTSD) is higher among people seeking asylum than in the general UK population (Turner & Gorst-Unsworth, 1990; Van der Veer, 1998; Lavik et al, 1996; Fazel, Wheeler & Danesh, 2005). Despite the need among this population, our experience was that third-sector services were becoming increasingly reluctant to work with refugees.

We have frequently debated with colleagues in the third sector about transcultural working and the limitations of PTSD as a diagnosis. We have discussed the systemic, structural violence faced by our clients and how to address it so that they have some influence over the social factors that can impede their recovery. We chose to work in the third sector because it offered us the clinical freedom to practise holistically and in ways that acknowledge the wider causes of people's suffering. This is who we are as practitioners; it is what we believe in. The third sector is generally perceived to be independent of the state and driven by its own, unique values, blending advocacy on behalf of its users with direct service delivery to marginalised communities (National Audit Office, 2010).

We each had our own moment of revelation when the scale of how much the landscape had changed hit home. For one of us, it was a chance conversation with a long-standing colleague working from a feminist perspective in a women's service that provided counselling and support to women who have experienced sexual violence. The colleague described how they offered a 'stabilisation service of six weeks counselling' to women who had been raped or sexually violated. It was new and shocking to hear someone describe this service's work with women in this manner and illustrated to us just how much the language of IAPT and the widespread acceptance of brief interventions as a legitimate response to distress has pervaded the third sector. This service offered no long-term work, and this was not questioned by the worker. Given what we know about the long-term impact of sexual abuse and rape, and the history of feminist responses to male violence against women, we were curious as to why the service had evolved in this way.

For the other, it was a request for a job reference from an LGBTQ service. The request arrived with the job description attached that specifically sought a therapist working from a humanistic perspective. How did they manage that? Cognitive behavioural therapy (CBT) was the predominant, if not only modality being sought across all sectors at that time; that this service was able to explicitly seek to recruit a practitioner from a humanist modality was intriguing and inspiring. That this was our response signified to us the insidious changes we were witnessing across the third sector. We felt out of place in a neoliberal epoch.

In recent years, too, our experience has been that much of our management work was focused on responding to repeated restructures. Peers and colleagues in the third sector worked under the constant threat of redundancy. The very people who were often holding the highest clinical risks on the frontline had no secure base from which to practise. In this anxiety-provoking context, what did it really matter if clinical psychologists, systemic family therapists, psychotherapists and counsellors from different modalities had their job titles relabelled as 'psychological therapists' to create uniformity? What mattered was that they still had jobs. Yet, with this uniformity, we experienced an erosion of our professional identities, and with that, we would argue, our clinical voices and influence were lessened and, in some cases, erased.

## 'Hit by the IAPT juggernaut'

Most of the therapists we spoke with were now delivering services funded by IAPT (although their organisations may have been delivering other services alongside). Sadly, not one of the interviewees, apart from one manager who worked in a young people's service, talked positively about the changes wrought by IAPT's arrival within their organisations. This one manager said it had been a positive experience overall, as they had found a way to retain their organisational ethos and were using other sources of funding to deliver a range of support services over and above what the IAPT contract allowed. Other than this, perceived negative changes to organisational values and ethos were a dominant theme. Some practitioners were deeply disillusioned by what they had experienced. Many talked with sadness about how their practice and organisations had profoundly altered; some said they no longer enjoyed their work or took no pride in where they worked:

> We are not proactively investing in the future of individuals. It's sad looking back at my charity, I was so proud of what we did, it was holistic, and it's been sad to see that go, the choices went for us and our clients.

One of the key characteristics of IAPT is its short-term focus: numbers of sessions are strictly limited in most services. Interviewees told us that, to meet the IAPT contract requirements, their services had to adhere to tight service specifications. For some organisations, this had meant their service had to abandon its holistic approach – one of the very things that NHS England (2014) highlighted as being a defining positive characteristic – in order to conform to the funding body's requirements.

A psychotherapist and service manager told us:

> IAPT is not a panacea for mental health. I don't want to degrade it, and I think IAPT works for the worried well, people with very specific problems faced in adulthood, but if there is something developmental, trauma related or long-term systemic, then IAPT is too constrained to allow the evolution of the person to develop and their needs to be met. It's like trying to fit square pegs in round holes.

A clinical lead told us: 'The brief, goal-directed model is everywhere. It is spreading to become the default process.' The perceived danger was that third -sector services, both established and emerging, were being influenced to only offer time-limited therapy that was primarily goal-orientated – the perceived 'gold standard'. The IAPT practitioner noted:

> It's all about moving people on. A lot of my colleagues now talk in terms of 'how I can move this person on' as their first question on meeting the person. It's not like delivering therapy, it's like feeding the machine.

The people we interviewed had almost all been practising for over two decades but, sadly, only one therapist was still practising in their chosen theoretical model. This was shocking. We were told that organisations are now working in a context where just one theoretical approach is favoured (CBT), and one model of delivery (IAPT's stepped model of talking therapy) across England. One therapist reflected that getting therapy was now like shopping in any UK high street: 'All the shops are the same, you could be anywhere.' The IAPT service practitioner reflected that: 'You get the therapy that the politics allows, and I think CBT fits a political way of thinking about the work.'

Thus, an approach that values uniformity and conformity has been adopted to engage with diversity. Some of the therapists we spoke to had trained in CBT, in addition to the core model they had initially qualified in, because 'it was needed if you want to get a job in counselling'.

Therapists described a shift from a time when the development of the therapeutic alliance sat at the core of clinical practice, together with a commitment to adapting practice to make it helpful and accessible to clients. Now they struggled with the new approach: 'We are told what to do – we are told "Identify the problem and then do this with it".' One participant observed that, in the current climate, 'anything that suggests a political element to people's experiences will probably not be funded in the first place'. Some of these interviewees worked in organisations that, historically, had often challenged statutory systems and whose work had been underpinned by the principle of social justice. Our interviewees reported a shift in this focus.

The manager of a community-based therapy service that worked in a culturally diverse area and with large numbers of refugees and people seeking asylum described the pain of losing their autonomy to manage:

> We had the freedom to work ethically and creatively. The luxury of open-ended work, where supervision was what helped you maintain your focus. The [service] was buzzy, with lots of energy and diverse groups. We worked with different communities and destitute clients,

people seeking asylum and we had bilingual staff and interpreters. It was incredible.

This same manager reflected on their own work as a bilingual therapist, and on the erosion of anti-oppressive practice within therapy:

It takes six to seven sessions to develop relationships. [Clients] have stories to tell and it takes time to build trust and learn what therapy is. In IAPT, you have the power; you are not reducing it but using it.

This was reported as eroding relationships with the communities with which these organisations sought to engage. Practitioners described being compelled to make uncomfortable decisions in the therapy room. A senior executive officer reflected:

What do you do if you reach six sessions and have not addressed the fundamental issues? What is the pressure on the counsellor to wind things up? The implications are huge.

There was a consensus that many services had become much more driven by technique. Interviewees described an expectation that 'interventions' had to be brief and focused on symptom reduction for 'people diagnosed with a mental health condition'. Some interviewees asked how inexperienced therapists could learn how to be genuinely present and engaged in a relationship when the work is so manualised and focused on symptoms. Although many practitioners could identify some positive impacts that IAPT had on their sector, they did not, in the main, speak positively about the model itself. Words such as 'mechanistic', 'prescriptive', 'conveyor belt' and 'superficial' were frequently used.

For some organisations, adapting to and adopting the IAPT model was necessary for survival. Indeed, some had already started down that route before IAPT was introduced, due to changes in the funding environment. As one manager said:

We had already started down that road when we were hit by the IAPT juggernaut, but we have translated it all to work for us. In the past we worked to a social model, we didn't diagnose, but now we just must translate it all, reassuring yourself that it means labelling, but within an anonymised data set... at least we get to stay open.

Practitioners reported finding subtle ways around the tight restrictions on services and practice, and in doing so demonstrated a rejection of the values and ethos of the IAPT ideology, while still trying to deliver services funded by it (Gillian Proctor and Maeta Brown's chapter that follows explores this ethical tension in more detail). This cognitive dissonance affected both morale and commitment, and was possibly contributing to a 'skills drain' from the third sector. Several interviewees had left posts due to the influence of IAPT. One clinical manager from a community-based service in a multi-cultural area told us:

> [IAPT compliancy] led to me leaving. We did try so hard, but I felt the manual got in the way. We ended up looking for evidence – not focusing on the relationship. It's the relationship where the healing comes from. We felt so pressured. Short-term was just not appropriate for so many of our clients.

Another clinical manager noted:

> We tried to deliver something we didn't believe in and that didn't fit with our clients. So many of our clients didn't understand what therapy was, let alone this fixed approach. Clients just didn't understand it. We thought that clients were often just too distressed to fill in the [sessional evaluation] forms.

The IAPT service practitioner identified something potentially more systematic at play:

> The counsellor in me thinks the powers-that-be are making it hard for me to be a counsellor. The medical model prevails, it doesn't like to see the world in other ways. A holistic view is just not popular.

One manager had left their previous organisation a year or so after it became IAPT compliant, to set up a small, not-for-profit therapy business. They were themselves from a marginalised community and described how it had affected their health to work as a therapist with the local south Asian community, using a model that they knew was not accessible to their clients.

Many participants reflected on the key performance indicators that have to be completed in the IAPT model. One practitioner, who was not currently working in an IAPT service, noted:

> IAPT clearly does not work for our clients; there is a clear recognition of this. However, I notice recent influences from the IAPT model within this organisation. I have noticed its influence on KPIs.

The same interviewee had recently been asked to pilot three different outcome measures, all standard within IAPT; it was, they said, due to a 'pressure to be evidence based'. One participant described how organisations were fudging completion of the key performance indicators (KPIs) on service delivery (a phenomenon also discussed by Elizabeth Cotton in Chapter 10):

> Assessment is now seen as the first treatment, as a way of delivering the KPI without actually delivering on it. Then [you] put people on a further waiting list for up to a year. This is what is actually happening in practice across the country. Now, the government knows this is happening; it's one way of dealing with it. So, there is a *second wait*, as it is called. There is also a difference between local and national targets, so services struggle to try and meet both or they won't get funding.

But, as they asked, 'where are the clients in all this?' It is a question we have often asked ourselves, as managers: what is the impact on clients? Some therapists described a corresponding shift in the power dynamics within the therapeutic encounter. One therapist spoke of the impact of the brief model:

> It's changed me, and I don't like it. I just keep checking myself; I feel this pressure to get results and so I'm driving the sessions now and not letting the client lead.

Could the pressure to deliver on KPIs be silencing clients? One issue to which practitioners kept returning was the pressure to secure positive outcomes in short time frames and the methods used to evidence these outcomes. One practitioner felt they could no longer offer the space and security of a true therapeutic alliance, and that this meant they steered away from 'the dangerous', to ensure targets were met – so the work remained focused but without depth. Others described how they felt they shut down dialogues in therapy because there was no time for them, and several therapists wondered whether they had become risk averse. Indeed, one therapist commented that they felt their whole service had also become risk averse, as the pressure to conform to a framework that was so prescriptive meant they steered away from the complex issues that were likely not to benefit from the IAPT model or to 'fail' within it. One counsellor said:

You are always mindful of how deep you can go. It's just not safe, you are always reining the work back in. The therapeutic relationship needs to be based upon an open dialogue, and honesty, but instead there are all these forms and a need for a diagnosis and this constant focus on the presenting issues. Where do you go from there?

Some practitioners admitted that they skimmed through the forms that needed to be completed, so the sessions were more user friendly, or simply because the client was not up to completing them:

Sometimes I know the forms need to be left because the client is not well, but I produce them as the pressure is there to get them done every time.

From these accounts, it could be said that the priority is now to feed the system, that KPIs are now the highest level of context within the therapeutic encounter and that our clients' sense of agency in driving the therapy to meet their needs is diminished. One interviewee reflected that 'IAPT is meeting the problem but not the human' – a view shared by the IAPT service practitioner:

IAPT is about targets, not values. Its approach to people is different and is driven by targets, mechanistic, and about labels; people are not *seen*.

Another practitioner said:

I see it happening all over, pressuring clients to report better scores for the data. The data is collected at every session. If you don't, you don't have overall data success.

Some participants wondered aloud whether they were now practising unethically at times. They certainly felt they were working against their value base:

I sometimes find myself wondering how my practice sits with how I was trained and what I believe in. I see person after person... whip through the forms and, by the end of each day, I'm not sure how helpful I've been or how real the relationship with them is. There's just too much to think about.

A therapist working with brain-injured clients said they now felt that if they didn't achieve the goals in the given time-frame, they had failed. They even wondered if 'we are losing the profession'. In the large town where they live, there are no services that aren't IAPT compliant – nowhere a therapist can work outside the IAPT model. The only option was to work privately if they wanted to practise in their preferred modality. However, they had instead chosen to work in a charity, as they wanted to work with communities who couldn't pay. They felt that, ironically, the IAPT model itself, introduced to improve access to psychological therapies, actively excluded marginalised communities:

> The voluntary sector is struggling to survive and to work with people where there are barriers to access. They have complex needs and their diagnosis excludes them. All groups have unique needs. Waiting lists are long, despite what they say, and they discharge so quickly. People's lives may be chaotic and messy. People have poor memory and are isolated, there is hardship in people's lives… there is a sense that it might alleviate pressure on GPs, but it does not, it seeks to service a narrow client group in terms of class, ethnicity and cognitive ability.

Others similarly questioned whether to continue in their profession as they were either not using their skills or not doing what they were trained to do. One asked:

> It's changed the reason why I went into this work; do I want to do this now? This is not how I want to work.

There were also signs that IAPT is driving a wedge between practitioners themselves, with practitioners in IAPT seen as an alien force driving out more experienced and qualified practitioners. The same counsellor noted:

> It's hard that these IAPT staff are taking jobs from experienced and qualified therapists, that's hard. Clients are not getting an informed choice.

This binary narrative could be viewed as a form of dysfunction or splitting. We noted that some therapists expressed alienation in response to the impact of IAPT on their profession and their organisation. It is outside the scope of this chapter but, with the cognitive dissonance expressed elsewhere, it raises interesting questions for further study about whether organisations and individual practitioners are at risk of vicarious traumatisation or compassion fatigue because of being compelled to work in ways that they don't believe in.

## 'I worry about the future'

Other fears for the future also emerged in the interviews. These were not solely about the survival of organisations but about the future of psychotherapy itself. One clinical lead reflected:

> I worry that the influence of IAPT will essentially extinguish the role of counselling completely.

Above all else, what came across was a fear that the counselling and psychotherapy world was damaged beyond repair by the prevalence of one model and its wholesale adoption, and, because of that, we were now failing marginalised communities. As one interviewee said:

> We all need different things at different times, and we have lost services that can respond in different ways to distress. We are producing technique-driven practitioners who are focused on results and outcomes.

Another counsellor told us:

> Newly qualified therapists are being trained to pathologise human experience. I worry about the future.

Interviewees were deeply concerned about the consequences of practitioners becoming deskilled or being unable to use the full range of their expertise. A clinical lead told us:

> [Therapy] could end up being defined by what can be achieved in six sessions. At the worst, we could end up training people solely for goal-directed therapy in six sessions. My worry is we will lose our knowledge and expertise.

Most talked about IAPT as merely a 'sticking plaster' and wondered how the structure of the model could ever enable an environment where marginalised people could reflect on the impact of oppression. Client's experiences of poverty and oppression were said to no longer be an area of concern or part of the therapeutic struggle; practitioners were not even creating opportunities for them to be acknowledged in the therapy room, let alone reflecting on their impact on identity: 'We are seeing the commodification of therapy... the big other is in the room.'

The 'big other' was not an understanding of systemic oppression or clients' experiences but data controllers, rigid service standards and a wider political agenda. One of us is now offering short-term therapy in a refugee agency and frequently notes there isn't time within sessions to be truly curious anymore, and that working to such short time-frames risks the practitioner relying on assumptions about shared understandings with the client.

The sadness in the interviews struck a chord with our own sadness about the organisations that have closed in the last decade and the distance we have travelled as a sector. A clinical lead noted that, in their geographical area: 'Funding to the refugee sector was cut by 60%. If this is reflected across the board, it is a struggle for counselling services to survive.'

One of the key themes that emerged early on in all the interviews related to funding and organisational survival. The relentless stress of ensuring the survival of third-sector organisations was evident in all our interviews. Many participants described a fear that their service could not continue. One organisation working long term with refugees doubted they would last beyond their current grant. The manager said they were determined that the organisation would not compromise their model to fit the IAPT template, but inevitably was worried this might be at the expense of their survival.

Everyone described the lack of funding available. Many said the only way most organisations could remain intact was to bid for an IAPT contract: 'IAPT put us on the map and we were taken seriously as a service.'

A clinical lead in a third-sector service with some IAPT provision told us they were:

> ... under pressure to show evidence-based practice across the agency, as well as to funders who have nothing to do with IAPT. This has impacted on our funding opportunities… funders are now looking at the IAPT model or NICE guidelines as the gold standard, and so trauma work is almost impossible to provide in a counselling context now... We work with survivors of sexual violence, people who may struggle to seek help or engage, who may struggle accessing organisations, and may have suffered organisational abuse in the past, might fear engagement with any kind of professional. IAPT provision may not pick up on

these issues, it may understand the anxiety but not understand sexual violence is at its root.

The traditional sources of funding have been drying up in recent years, as local authorities cut back on the services they commission and charities lose out in the tendering battle to continue a service they have provided to the NHS for many years, without question:

> In the past we may have got funding from local government in the form of a grant. Local authorities don't fund like this now. They are facing huge cuts, savaged by Westminster. That funding just doesn't exist anymore, lots of voluntary services have disappeared... the voluntary sector is struggling to find money. How will it survive?

A senior executive officer described the reality of survival in the third sector – that their organisation was more or less forced to become 'a resource-competitive organisation. The money that comes with [IAPT] is very attractive. Organisations can access greater financial resources if they sign up to IAPT.'

A young people's service manager talked about how IAPT funding had been helpful and given staff access to its training. However, having these extra, IAPT-trained staff did not help with the waiting list or workloads: 'There was so few young people that fitted the limitations of who could be seen [within the IAPT criteria].'

This manager did identify a positive for the IAPT trainees, in that they felt the third-sector service ethos influenced their attitudes and values. This was in contrast to the many other interviewees who did not believe they had the power to influence the IAPT machine.

Some participants whose service did not have an IAPT contract said that it 'increased traffic' to their service, as people for whom its model of therapy was not suited were then referred on to the third sector, in the hope that they could offer 'long-term work'. This seemed to frequently be the case with refugees and people seeking asylum. However, funding did not necessarily follow the referrals, meaning third-sector organisations were left with growing waiting lists and no money to pay for increased provision.

One participant noted that the outreach work their organisation did to attract more IAPT clients increased referrals, but then excluded many who proved unsuitable for the model on offer:

In the past, a lot of work was done to reach out to communities and services developed in response to this learning, but now communities are expected to fit into an industrialised approach, there is nowhere around it.

A senior executive officer noted bitterly:

If you released the resources IAPT has and developed a greater range of talking therapies and therapeutic support, you could do a lot more. What is the government saying – if you have more than mild to moderate mental health problems you can get stuffed?

## 'We have lost the flexibility'

As Mind's report on access to talking therapies, *We Still Need to Talk* (2013) showed, people from black and ethnic minority communities have historically been poorly served in primary care mental health services and are less likely to be referred for talking therapies. Only one in 10 people surveyed said that IAPT was meeting their cultural needs, and a third of local Mind organisations who responded disagreed with the statement that IAPT services met the needs of BME people in the community. Our participants still reported considerable doubt about the value of IAPT in dealing with issues of culture, class and systemic oppression.

Many therapists aim to practise self reflexively (Dallos & Stedmon, 2009), and, as previously noted, therapists we spoke to felt that the IAPT time-frame did not allow space for this. Nor did it allow existential dialogues to take place or for an examination of the impact of power and structural oppression in the therapeutic relationship.

Several participants described having no time to engage with clients from hard-to-reach communities. Some shared stories of clients from the past, when their organisation worked hard to encourage marginalised people to try therapy, and how this was no longer possible. The pressure to discharge clients when they missed appointments or cancelled was felt by everyone we spoke to:

We have lost the flexibility to gently bring someone in who might be ambivalent. People in trouble often can't be good attendees.

Another participant reflected: 'We need services in the community who know the community, we need creativity and flexibility in our models.' The NHS IAPT service practitioner noted:

I think a lot of people just get misunderstood. They are on the wrong medication, they have not had the language to express themselves. This speaks to me about oppression sometimes. There is a mismatch between what can be said and what can be heard. It's not just about doing these treatments, it takes meeting and understanding, expressing an interest in understanding a person's place and culture. IAPT is so intense, it's so hard to find space to be that person.

A significant block to clients whose first language is not English or who are unused to the protocols of counselling and therapy is the telephone assessment process. Most IAPT services use their least qualified staff, the psychological wellbeing practitioners (PWPs), to conduct the initial assessment, usually on the telephone, using a tick-box schedule of questions. Interviewees pointed out how inappropriate this could be: 'Why would you use the least experienced practitioner to screen or assess when it takes a highly skilled and experienced therapist to assess?' Many felt it alienated those unfamiliar with talking therapies who find it hard to talk about mental health. As one clinical lead put it:

What is problematic is that it is a short telephone conversation... but it's not uncommon for us to find that people have significant experiences such as violence and abuse that have not been disclosed on the telephone.

Many questioned the IAPT model's ability to work with complexity and truly respond to client needs or to engage in work that tackles systemic cultural oppression. As Bemak and colleagues note, in a racialised context:

Mental health professionals who presume that they are free of racism seriously underestimate the social impact of their own socialization and the inherited, in some instances unintentionally covert, racism. (Bemak, Chung & Pederson, 2003: 47)

One of us was reminded of a Congolese client, who, after a course of support within IAPT, described his difficulties in the words of the IAPT practitioner he had been seeing for his allotted six sessions. His adoption of the psychological jargon was unnerving; the words he used to describe his fear of being detained and returned to the DRC made evident his lack of understanding. Together, we unpacked what he had been told and explored what he actually wanted from the sessions. It certainly wasn't 'affect regulation'. Therapists quickly lose credibility with clients if they conceptualise their problems in a way that isn't congruent with the client's own belief systems (Elsass, 1997).

A psychotherapist and service manager working with complex trauma within the BME community noted that 'cultural contexts are not really considered in symptom-led approaches'. The senior executive officer described how they:

> ... had experience of working with people from Africa and a key concept that came up was one of the histories of slavery having a here-and-now impact. I doubt shorter sessions of CBT would be able to untangle this... if there is a wider oppression, cultural, historical it will not be addressed.

There was widespread frustration with the data collection and outcome measures that were irrelevant or even obstructive to IAPT's own imperatives to reach out to diverse communities. Some interviewees described the questionnaires as alienating many black and ethnic minority clients and taking up large chunks of sessions. As previously reported, some admitted that they skimmed through them to make the sessions more user friendly.

In our own work with refugees, we have questioned the ethics of using such questionnaires for non-English speakers. From our work with refugees and with other BME communities, we know it is often inappropriate to apply questionnaires developed in the West (whether translated or not) that are diagnosis or symptom-based. As one interviewee said, in relation to the diversity of cultural and educational backgrounds in the refugee population: 'I struggle with the tools we must use. I don't feel I can work with them. I try hard to be collaborative.'

Although some practitioners praised the reach of IAPT, reflecting that more people from marginalised communities could potentially access services, the BME and refugee practitioners from non-IAPT services told us that they often worked with people discharged or signposted on by IAPT and that there was a greater demand on their services as a result.

A senior executive shared their frustration that the professionalism of third-sector therapists was questioned by NHS managers, even though referrals were frequently made to the third sector to work with clients with more severe and enduring difficulties, including those with complex trauma. They described how many third-sector organisations were carrying elevated levels of risk and working with very vulnerable people, despite their apparent lowly status within the therapy field. They pointed out that often therapists working in the third sector have been practising for many years and have accumulated decades of continuing professional development to work with a range of difficulties, so could draw on a toolkit of techniques to meet the range of problems brought to them by the diverse communities they worked with.

It is our experience, and the experience of many of those we spoke to, that signposting is experienced by many black and ethnic minority clients as being sent away, especially refugee and asylum-seeking clients. They are then deterred from approaching another service and asking for help, especially if they are not comfortable anyway with asking for help for mental health distress. It can be especially hard for those for whom English is not their first language.

## Reflections and further study

We cannot draw conclusions from such a small, qualitative study, but we can reflect on key themes to make sense of what we heard. Most of our participants discussed the ethos of their organisations and expressed concern that the values of third-sector services are shifting. A key theme was the importance of congruence between what organisations say they are committed to in terms of client care and choice and what IAPT services genuinely offer communities.

Practitioners talked about the constraints they were having to work under as a consequence of IAPT's influence. They critiqued what one counsellor called its 'one-world view', which shut down the flexibility and curiosity needed when working across cultures. They also deplored the use of mechanistic measures that did not acknowledge cultural differences and the impact of the client's wider, holistic experience, and occupied scarce and valuable therapy time. They also reported the negative effects of the short time-frames for therapy and the pressure to put clients through the therapy process as quickly as possible.

It seemed clear to us that IAPT has shut down diversity within the therapy sector and closed off therapy from diverse communities and those whose needs are regarded as outside the perceived norm.

An unexpected outcome from talking with others in our sector was our shared sadness at the unforeseen impact of IAPT on the third sector, whether their service was IAPT-compliant or not. Some of the people we spoke with had left their roles or were actively considering doing so as a direct result of having to adjust to the IAPT model. Participants expressed fears about their work, practice and the future of therapy itself, as experienced practitioners are drained out of the profession.

Taken together, this certainly presents a worrying picture. Is the NHS creating a perfect storm in which the therapy profession may sink without trace?

Overall, our own experience and the experience of those we talked to indicates that we need to question the ability of IAPT to truly serve marginalised communities or address people's complex mental health issues.

We both describe ourselves as human rights practitioners: 'A human rights standpoint forces practitioners to look beyond survivors' individual needs and take action to support their rights as human beings' (Bashir, 2017: 206). We strove to adopt this in our management style:

> ... a democratic approach to management that values difference and participation, as well as ensuring that all staff have a voice in the direction of the organisation. It is our role to afford the same dignity and respect to the staff team as they are expected to afford their clients. (Boyles & Garland, 2016: 24)

At some point in the last decade, we have had cause to question whether we can still rightly claim this, or whether we had succumbed to being something very different. Our qualitative study reveals we are not alone in our observations and questions of ourselves.

The interviews impacted on us in different ways, and we realised that our concerns for the future of counselling and psychotherapy and third-sector clinical services were shared by others in the sector. The experiences of our colleagues tapped into our own different and complex experiences of managing third-sector services in the last two decades. It made us reflect on our struggles to retain a human rights ethos in service delivery, as well as in our therapeutic practice, and this same struggle is experienced by many.

Our interviewees reported fundamental shifts in the values and ethos of the organisations they worked for that reflects what Bashir (2017: 189) describes, referencing Lyotard (1979/1984):

> Adult psychotherapy in NHS primary care has increasingly become concerned with 'condition management', with experts who hold the power formulating linear CBT storylines and meting out standardised treatments that ignore the social and political 'conditions' of human experience.

Further study of this reported shift is needed. Are vulnerable clients now falling through exactly those gaps created by the rigidity in funding and service delivery that third-sector organisations emerged to address?

Despite the criticism of the manualised approach adopted by IAPT services, innovation and flexibility can still be found, because of the sheer tenacity and commitment of many therapists and some services and managers within the third sector. It is difficult to source many impact studies of the work that is being done in mental health in the third sector and it is an area for further study. It also raises questions about how passive the third sector might be in response to these funding-led changes and how effective it has been historically in evidencing its impact. The IAPT methodology has embedded data collection as the gold standard form of evidence gathering, but data are only one form of evidence and perhaps the third sector needs to be more robust when presenting how its own ethos can work effectively in response to the mental health needs of communities. The cognitive dissonance that was reported in relation to the disillusion described by practitioners and the tendency to try to get around things (which is also addressed in several of the chapters in this book) would also benefit from further investigation.

These conversations with practitioners revealed that some, at least, have found ways around the paperwork and are delivering services flexibly and responsibly, with the client at the heart of their work. Often these services have been able to source other funding to enable this flexibility and have retained their ethos, and in some cases can still offer some medium-to-long-term therapeutic work delivered by therapists from a range of different theoretical approaches.

We would like to thank all the interviewees for their time and candour.

We learn, when we respect the dignity of people, that they cannot be denied the elementary right to participate fully in the solutions to their own problems. Self-respect arises only out of people who play an active part in solving their own crisis. (Alinsky, 2010)

# References

Alinsky SD (2010). *Rules for Radicals* (reissue ed). London: Vintage.

Bashir C (2017). The application of Cognitive Behavioural Therapies with survivors of torture. In: Boyles J (ed). *Psychological Therapies for Survivors of Torture: a human rights approach with people seeking asylum*. Monmouth: PCCS Books (pp187–222).

Bemak F, Chi-Ying Chung R, Pederson PB (2003). *Counselling Refugees: a psychosocial approach to innovative multicultural interventions*. Westport, CT: Greenwood Press.

Boyles J, Garland R (2016). Leading from a human rights framework. *Healthcare Counselling and Psychotherapy Journal* 16(1): 23–26.

Dallos R, Stedmon J (2009). Flying over the swampy lowlands: reflective and reflexive practice. In: Stedmon J, Dallos R (eds). *Reflective Practice in Psychotherapy and Counselling*. Oxford: Oxford University Press (pp1–22).

Elsass P (1997). *Treating Victims of Torture and Violence: theoretical, cross-cultural and clinical implications*. New York, NY: New York University Press.

Fazel M, Wheeler J, Danesh J (2005). Prevalence of serious mental disorder in 7000 refugees. *The Lancet 365*(9467): 1309–1314.

Lavik NJ, Hauf E, Skrondal A, Solberg O (1996). Mental disorder among refugees and the impact of persecution and exile: some findings from an outpatient population. *British Journal of Psychiatry 169*: 726–732.

Lyotard J-F (1979/1984). *The Postmodern Condition: a report on knowledge* (Bennington G, Massumi B, trans). Manchester: University of Manchester Press.

Mind (2013). *We Still Need to Talk: a report on access to talking therapies*. London: Mind.

National Audit Office (2010). What are third sector organisations and their benefits for commissioners? In: *Successful Commissioning Toolkit*. [Online.] London: National Audit Office. www.nao.org.uk/successful-commissioning/introduction/what-are-civil-society -organisations-and-their-benefits-for-commissioners (accessed 14 February 2019).

NHS England (2014). *Five Year Forward View*. London: NHS England.

Turner S, Gorst-Unsworth C (1990). Psychological sequelae of torture: a descriptive model. *British Journal of Psychiatry 157*: 475–480.

Van der Veer G (1998). *Counselling and Therapy with Refugees and Victims of Torture: psychological problems of victims of war, torture and repression* (2nd ed). Chichester: John Wiley & Sons.

# Chapter 12

# Industrialising relational therapy: ethical conflicts and threats for counsellors in IAPT

## Gillian Proctor and Maeta Brown[1]

I (GP) am a survivor of IAPT, although I suspect I have not survived intact; I still carry the emotional scars and consequent mission to talk about the reality of life as a therapist in such a system and its implications for therapists and clients. I worked as a clinical psychologist in IAPT, but am more at home in counselling circles, as a person-centred therapist who eschews the expertise and technical focus of CBT (see Proctor, 2017a, 2017b, 2018; Loewenthal & Proctor, 2018). I worked in primary care mental health from 2003 to 2013, during which time IAPT arrived and the cultural landscape of primary care mental health was transformed. I then (2014–2016) worked in a university post, training counsellors in Counselling for Depression (now renamed Person-Centred Experiential Counselling for Depression (PCE-CfD)), an IAPT-accredited approach, joining forces with other person-centred and experiential counsellors and researchers who wanted to keep this type of therapy within the NHS, free at the point of access to clients who preferred it. I experienced many ethical conflicts, first when working within an IAPT service, then as a trainer for PCE-CfD counsellors (see Proctor & Hayes, 2017). However, when I wrote about these (in my experience)

---

1. We acknowledge the other members of our research team for their help in conducting this study – Shlomo Cohen and Sue McKelvie, who were unable to be involved in this chapter.

common and obvious conflicts, I was accused of being anecdotal and that I lacked evidence for my claims (in reviews of papers submitted to academic counselling journals). Hence, it seemed necessary and important to conduct some research to explore the experiences of counsellors in IAPT with respect to these potential ethical conflicts and to document these experiences.

I (MB) am a student on the University of Leeds MA in psychotherapy and counselling. I have worked for two years as a person-centred crisis support worker in a radical mental health charity providing non-medical, non-diagnostic support to people in acute mental health crisis. My trainee placement has been at a person-centred counselling service working with young people. Through both these roles, I have encountered the suffering of many people who have felt sidelined and injured by their experiences of statutory mental health care. As a distressed teenager I had a very negative experience of CBT (which was all my GP could offer me) and have since aspired to work in the NHS, with the (perhaps somewhat naïve) aim of offering clients something different. I was keen to get involved in research and therefore particularly interested in a project that set out to explore the experiences of counsellors doing just that. After conducting this research, I am left feeling sad and disheartened. As a newly qualified counsellor who had always hoped to work in the NHS, I no longer feel this pull. I hold hope for a ripple of change in how relational counselling is managed in the NHS that might allow for my dream to become a personally sustainable reality.

This chapter will explore the impact of the arrival of IAPT on primary care counselling and how it has forced many counsellors to straddle the contradictions between its organisational culture and the professional culture of counselling. We will describe the ethical conflicts inherent for relational counsellors working in IAPT, drawing on examples from our research (Proctor et al, 2019). We will report some of our research participants' perceptions of the impact of IAPT on clients, the costs to the counsellors of these conflicts, the threats to their ethical integrity, and what survival strategies they used. We will end by drawing conclusions about the future of counselling in IAPT.

## Professional culture of relational counselling

Counselling has clear relational roots, with an emphasis in most branches of the major schools (psychoanalytic and humanistic) on the relational, or the importance of the therapy relationship for the process of change.

The professional culture of relational counselling is well illustrated by the BACP *Ethical Framework for the Counselling Professions* (2018), which lists the counsellor's commitments to clients, beginning with 'put clients first' (Commitment 1, p6). Furthermore, it is clear that this cannot be interpreted to mean that all clients are offered the same 'evidence-based therapy', as this first commitment is closely followed by an emphasis on the uniqueness of each client's needs. Counsellors are expected to 'show respect by: a) valuing each client as a unique person' and 'c) agreeing with clients on how we will work together' (Commitment 3, p6).

The fundamental values listed in the framework include several goals that could fit with the IAPT framework, such as a commitment to both 'alleviating symptoms of personal distress and suffering' and 'enhancing people's wellbeing and capabilities' (Values 3, p8). However, other values are included that again emphasise the uniqueness of individual clients and the diversity of their situations and their values. These are a commitment to 'facilitating a sense of self that is meaningful to the person(s) concerned within their personal and cultural context' and 'appreciating the variety of human experience and culture' (Values 3, p8). At the same time, it is clear that counselling is a relational, not a technical endeavour, with another commitment to 'ensuring the integrity of practitioner-client relationships' (Values 3, p8). This relational focus is also enshrined in the principle of self-respect (Principles 5, p9) – 'fostering the practitioner's self-knowledge, integrity and care for the self' – thus acknowledging the emotional toll and personal investment involved for the counsellor in counselling relationships.

## The arrival of IAPT: changing the landscape for counselling

With the arrival of IAPT in 2008, the aims, operational structures and discourses surrounding the delivery of primary mental health care have undergone a major cultural shift. By cultural shift, we are referring to an organisational culture, defined as 'the values and behaviours that contribute to the unique social and psychological environment of an organisation'.[2] I (GP) have described elsewhere general trends in the changes in NHS culture over time (Proctor 2002, 2015), but it is also clear that how individual services interpret and implement such general political discourses varies widely and each service has its own organisational sub-culture. However, IAPT, as a national initiative, has requirements for behaviour and discourses that define values and goals and that comprise the IAPT culture as a whole. For example, the discourse of 'recovery rates' places symptom reduction, as measured

---

2. www.businessdictionary.com

by medically focused questionnaires, before the client's or counsellor's experience, as a measure of the quality or value for money of IAPT services.

The motivation behind IAPT is explicitly economic, springing from economist Professor Lord Richard Layard's original argument that investing money in talking therapies (predominantly CBT-based) would be recouped by the savings in benefits paid to people who were unemployed or unable to work due to anxiety and depression (see Scott Steen's Chapter 8 in this book). Thus, IAPT services are measured by 'recovery rates', changes in client-completed, symptom-based questionnaires, rates of return to work and improved functioning.

In IAPT, the emphasis is on a technical, manualised delivery of specific 'treatments', illustrating the medical and bureaucratic model on which it is based. The arrival of IAPT in primary care mental health services in 2008/2009 marked a clear culture shift, which continues to spread gradually throughout the NHS, from a patient-centred approach and individualised care to an industrial, privatised model of one-size-fits-all, where individual people (patients and staff) are irrelevant or expendable in the bigger focus on the efficiency of the system. This has happened via the discourses of 'efficiency', 'accountability', 'performance' and 'evidence-based practice' (see Proctor, 2015, 2002).

Within the IAPT system, clients are positioned as consumers with the power of choice; irrational thinkers who need to be educated to think more helpfully, and unfortunate or recalcitrant citizens needing guidance in how to manage their unruly emotions in order to return to the economic functioning required by our productive society. Counsellors and other IAPT workers are positioned as technicians with the knowledge to deliver this guidance who, at the same time, themselves need guidance and rules to keep their own functioning optimal in order to operate with maximum efficiency and productivity. The client-as-consumer is supposed to be able to choose between a number of options for therapy, yet, at the same time, IAPT's stepped-care model has a rigid structure and symptom-based criteria for where and how clients enter the system and what they are offered as they pass through it. The agency and individuality of both the client and the counsellor disappear into the well-oiled, smoothly working cogs of the system.

## Culture shift over time

When IAPT arrived, counsellors who were already employed in primary care trusts were usually gradually moved into the new IAPT teams. The consequent culture shift came as a shock to many of those who had been employed either directly by GP practices and/or by primary care trusts (PCTs). The first shock was the introduction of outcome measures, which the counsellor was required to get each client to complete every session. Many counsellors were already familiar with using CORE-OM[3] at the start and end of therapy and were well aware of its limitations as a measure of meaningful change for clients, despite its intended purpose to record progress in therapy. Measuring 'progress' every session was a significant shift away from the prioritisation of the therapy relationship and took away from the already limited time that counsellors had with their clients. The tools themselves (PHQ-9 and GAD-7) were designed to measure withdrawal from psychiatric drugs and focused solely on symptoms of ill health rather than any measures of change in mental wellbeing. The second major change was IAPT's strict limits on the number of sessions to be offered – a maximum of six at low-intensity level, rising to 12 (and at most 16 more recently) with clients stepped up to high-intensity interventions, thus removing from the counsellor the clinical autonomy to decide, with the client, how much therapy they would benefit from.

The third cultural change brought about by IAPT was the prioritisation of cognitive behavioural therapy (CBT) as the treatment of choice for the majority of clients, based on its supposed more robust evidence base of efficacy. From 2009, nearly all the government funding for IAPT was used to train and employ CBT therapists and psychological wellbeing practitioners (PWPs). The PWPs are seen as the bedrock of the IAPT workforce, comprising 36% of IAPT employees by 2016 (NHS England, 2016). They are mainly psychology graduates, who receive specialist training in basic CBT techniques and are expected to act as first point of contact, assess all referrals (usually by telephone) and provide the low-intensity, guided self-help offered to the vast majority of clients presenting with low-to-moderate anxiety and depression. Only a very few clients progress immediately to the next level of high-intensity, one-to-one therapy with a qualified counsellor/therapist. The therapies the PWPs offer are manualised, psycho-educational, technical interventions based on CBT, such as behavioural activation for depression ('Do more and you will feel better') or systematic desensitisation for anxiety ('Stop avoiding what you're worried about and you'll realise it's not so bad'). When more senior and experienced relational counsellors leave their posts, they are often replaced with CBT therapists or PWPs, and all therapy practitioners are called 'psychological therapists', eradicating any

3. www.coreims.co.uk

professional distinction or specialist model of practice: therapists are seen as interchangeable, but the clear preference is for those with a qualification in CBT.

The devaluing of counselling with the arrival of IAPT can also be seen in its focus on diagnosis for gatekeeping which clients receive a service from IAPT: those with low-to-moderate anxiety or depression, who are expected to respond well to manualised treatments with a 'proven evidence base'. Initially the NICE guidelines for treatment of low-to-moderate anxiety and depression (NICE, 2004) only recommended CBT for depression, although they were later amended to include a small number of other manualised therapies: interpersonal therapy, counselling for depression (CfD), couples counselling and brief psychodynamic therapy (NICE, 2009, 2017). Increasingly, counsellors in IAPT found themselves working with clients who did not fit the narrow diagnostic criteria for CBT and those with concurrent relational and social difficulties, for whom no therapy service was available elsewhere.

However, despite this difference in their client group, counsellors in IAPT are expected to follow the same protocols and guidelines that govern the whole IAPT programme with respect to the number of sessions offered, the rule to discharge clients who fail to attend sessions (irrespective of their reasons) and client throughput and recovery rates.

The discourse of 'evidence-based practice' is used repeatedly in NHS policy and IAPT literature to undermine the clinical autonomy of counsellors and other psychological therapists. Within this discourse of 'evidence-based practice', evidence is presented as scientific fact in a competition between competing technical solutions, with CBT always arriving in top place. It is used to present clinicians as unethical if they advocate using any other models. Yet, this approach to 'evidence' completely ignores the research findings that what makes a difference in therapy are the relational factors, which are common across all therapy modalities, with technique contributing only a very small part of the variance in outcomes (see, for example, Cooper, 2008; Wampold & Imel, 2015; see also Sami Timimi's Chapter 6 in this book). This focus on CBT in the provision of psychological therapies through IAPT services demonstrates the political influence behind the primacy of what counts as evidence (see Bohart & House, 2018; Loewenthal & Proctor, 2018).

## Ethical conflicts and culture clashes

These changed working conditions and culture for counsellors working in IAPT often conflict hugely with the values and principles of the profession, most of whom are guided by the BACP *Ethical Framework*. This, in its most recent iterations (BACP, 2010, 2018) has made a clear shift from an approach based on bio-medical principles to a relational approach (Proctor, 2014). In relational counselling (humanistic and relational psychoanalytic), the focus is on the therapy relationship as the causal factor for change, the very opposite of the technical, medical approach of CBT: the person of the counsellor and the quality of their relationship with the client are of crucial importance, and neither can be manualised (Wampold, 2001).

Relational counselling or therapy assumes the causes of distress are relational, social and political, and that the appropriate helping response needs to be relational. Thus, the unique, individual client and the unique, individual counsellor are of crucial importance, as the BACP *Ethical Framework* recognises (see above).

The ethical conflicts highlighted by this clash of cultures include: client vs data, relationship vs recovery, and management-dictated pathways vs counsellor clinical autonomy. In the BACP *Ethical Framework*, the commitment to the client is paramount; in IAPT, the data produced by the service are the primary focus and measure of success. For relational counselling, the counsellor's priority is the quality of the therapy relationship; in IAPT, what matters is that the client is 'recovering' steadily, as evidenced by their symptom measures. In relational counselling, the counsellor is responsible for their self- and relational-awareness to maintain integrity in the therapy relationship; in IAPT, the efficiency of pathways through its stepped-care model is the priority. It is clear that, at a service level, the aggregated, measurable experience of the many is what is under scrutiny, but this raises the question: at what point does this organisational focus over-ride the counsellor's primary commitment to the individual client?

There are often conflicts between the professional culture and the organisational culture within which the professionals work (see Bloor & Dawson, 1994; see also Penny Campling's Chapter 2 in this book), but we suggest there may be a tipping point beyond which it becomes impossible to straddle these two cultures, and where attempting to do so has serious costs to the professional. Our research illustrates how this was the case for many of our participant counsellors in IAPT: that there is a real risk that counsellors are unable to maintain their integrity and their commitment to ethical practice when working in many IAPT services.

These conflicts are not unique to counsellors within IAPT; they represent much broader cultural conflicts. O'Hara (2018:11) beautifully and accurately describes this as:

... two cultural paradigms that defined two civilizations – one grounded in the search for mastery, prediction and control, and another grounded in empathy, participation and love.

## Evidence of ethical conflicts from IAPT counsellors

In our research, we aimed to explore how relational counsellors in IAPT negotiate the two different value systems and deal with the potential ethical conflicts they face. What are the costs for clients and counsellors of attempting to do this? Is it even possible for counsellors to stay faithful to their relational training and beliefs within this culture and offer a genuine alternative?

The research methodology and findings are reported more fully in Proctor et al (2019), but the following is a brief summary of how we conducted the research.

*Methodology* – this was a qualitative study. Eleven semi-structured interviews were conducted by the research group, using Skype or telephone, and one focus group of four participants was conducted by the lead researcher with a counsellors' special interest group. This gave us a total of 15 participants (12 female and three male).

*Sample* – participants had to have been employed within the previous 12 months, or were currently employed, as a counsellor in an IAPT service. They were invited through three methods: 1) The lead researcher published an article in the BACP membership magazine *Therapy Today* about possible ethical conflicts for counsellors in IAPT, which informed readers about the research; 2) An email was sent to all counsellors working in IAPT who had accessed the PCE-CfD course at the University of Nottingham; 3) Counsellors' special interest groups in IAPT services were also contacted. The 15 participants had experience working for IAPT services for a varied number of years – the majority for more than five years and some since IAPT began.

*Analysis* – data were analysed using Brown and Gilligan's Voice Relational Method (1991), chosen for its particular focus on relations of power and the reflexivity of the researcher. Findings were collated into case studies that were cross-checked against recordings and transcripts and sent to the participants for feedback. Themes were then collated across participants.

The findings were collated into four main themes, as described in the table below.

**Table 1: Main themes**

Counsellors perceived a range of difficulties for the clients they worked with, as illustrated in Table 2.

**Table 2: Counsellors' perceptions of costs for clients**

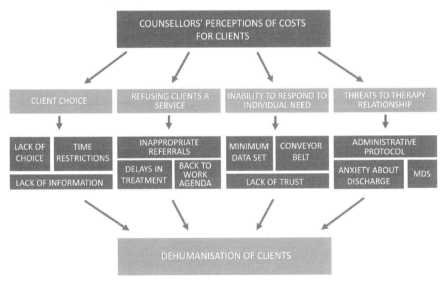

## 1. Client choice

Clients' lack of choice was a major theme in counsellors' concerns about the dehumanisation of clients in IAPT. This centred around the disempowering lack of choice in IAPT: clients cannot choose the counsellor to whom they are allocated – for example, to see a clinician with a particular speciality or someone with whom they feel they can connect. Clients also have no choice about the maximum number of sessions they receive – which, even though

PCE-CfD is taught as a 20-session model, is often delivered within six or eight. Six counsellors reported this as particularly restrictive:

> [Clients] don't get to choose at all... and we're not... in an office. We never see the team who deal with the referrals... they obviously don't really know who to allocate to because they don't know the counsellors; it's just random. (Hannah)

This clearly demonstrates the failure to translate into reality the rhetoric of the discourse of choice and client-as-consumer in IAPT.

### 2. Refusing clients a service

Another prevalent concern was about clients considered to have more serious and complex issues than the 'mild-to-moderate' depression and anxiety that IAPT was established to treat. On the one hand, counsellors were distressed that the service was exclusively selecting clients that would produce the right recovery rates, with more marginalised and distressed clients being refused and referred on to under-resourced secondary care or voluntary sector services with long waiting lists.

> It feels like we are cherry picking people to reach targets rather than a service that's there... to be a service to human beings that need us. There is such a focus on recovery that so many more people have been excluded from our service than were excluded from primary care, so we've had a huge gaping hole... That really doesn't feel moral or ethically right... It's been incredibly stressful. I find it difficult to face people, actually. 'There is no service for you,' or 'We'll have to send you to secondary care but I'm afraid there is a very long wait'... I've been told by management not to tell people that are on the waiting list but... it's up to two years. (Louise)

This illustrates clearly how the IAPT agenda leads counsellors to go against the main ethical mandate of their commitment to clients, to put them first.

On the other hand, counsellors felt pushed to work with clients beyond their ethical competence (again, conflicting with the BACP *Ethical Framework* requirement to work within their competence (Commitment to clients 2, p6)), due to a need 'to reach targets for numbers of people entering therapy' (Louise).

### *3. Inability to respond to individual need*

The strict pathways of IAPT also left participants feeling that clients were suffering from a reductive, 'one-size-fits-all' approach, where they were no more than items on a conveyor belt taking them back into work. These counsellors felt they did not have the flexibility to support the clients as individual human beings:

> I came into this work to be a therapist, to work with human beings,
> but it feels like more and more and more I'm being pulled to work with
> numbers and targets. (Louise)

This demonstrates how counsellors in IAPT struggle to follow the BACP *Ethical Framework* (2018) commitment to 'Show respect by: a) valuing each client as a unique person' (Our commitment to clients 3, p6).

Participants also felt that the risk-averse culture of the NHS and the organisational obsession with monitoring continual improvement speaks of a lack of trust in both the client and the therapy relationship, disempowering clients in the message it communicates. This clearly made it very difficult for counsellors to adhere to the BACP *Ethical Framework* (2018) commitment to 'ensuring the integrity of practitioner-client relationships' (Values 3, p8).

### *4. Threats to the therapy relationship*

Research participants felt that the strict limits on numbers of sessions, outside the therapist's control, undermined the therapist-client rapport – the therapy relationship is 'cut off by the middle person... the relationship is broken' (Afifa). This forces counsellors to use valuable time in sessions to soothe clients' anxiety around their approaching discharge when they may not feel ready to stop therapy, and find ways to surreptitiously bend the rules – resulting in further pressure on them:

> A lot of people come really worried about [not being able to make a
> particular appointment time]... it's a lot of energy... you know for the
> relationship... they really feel 'Any second I am going to be dumped'.
> (Sofia)

Counsellors shared with us their frustrations that the importance of the therapy relationship is completely ignored in IAPT, with clients 'blamed for being a human being... attempting to form a relationship, which is fundamental to how it works' (Pat). This is particularly evident in the focus on collecting the Minimum Data Set (MDS) symptom measures, which counsellors described as 'often superfluous and even intrusive' (Celia), and more to do with fulfilling statistical quotas than benefiting client wellbeing. They bear 'no correlation to what the patient is thinking and feeling' (Paul). These concerns demonstrate how this system of constant measurement threatens the counsellor's ethical commitment to put the client first.

The MDS were said not only to take up valuable counselling time (this was mentioned by more than half the participants), but also to be intrusive: they 'cut across the relationship' (Celia) and dominated client sessions:

> Sometimes I go in thinking, 'Fffff [sucking breath in through teeth] –
> gotta get the scores down for this one', but then when I'm actually with
> the client, there's another voice in my head which just says 'tough'. (Pat)

One participant, Phil, described receiving a lovely letter from a client thanking the service for saving her life. When he checked the outcome measures for that particular client over 16 sessions, he noted that her scores remained at rock bottom. He said:

> It's all wrong. I struggle with the values of that. It's the wrong type of
> measurement... IAPT isn't measuring the right thing. It's measuring
> something which is convenient for the funding provider, yeah – but
> it isn't measuring people's experience... Rather than recovery, it isn't
> measuring the experience of people within therapy.

Overall, participants felt that a need to present IAPT to clinical commissioning groups and budget holders as delivering 'successful' and 'cost-effective' therapy has replaced care for the individual needs and wellbeing of clients. They believed that relational therapy is not understood within IAPT and the measures it uses are not adequate to reflect its true efficacy. IAPT was seen by many of the counsellors we interviewed as the government paying 'lip service' to public demands for more counselling (Heather), and that its ultimate agenda is 'to get people back to work. It always has been' (Pam).

These counsellors felt they had to act as a buffer, to shield their clients from the dehumanisation of the IAPT system.

> I feel that there's the organisation, there's me in the middle and then
> there's the client, and I feel like I'm protecting the client from the
> organisation. (Emily)

# Particular ethical conflicts

## *1. Workload*

Participants reported ever-increasing expectations on them of the numbers of clients they had to see and percentages of those who demonstrated recovery. BACP guidance has traditionally suggested counsellors see no more than 20 clients in a full-time post, which has usually been followed by NHS employers. Since IAPT, this guidance has disappeared and not many IAPT counsellors are seeing fewer than six clients in a full working day.

In our research, counsellors regularly reported being frustrated by the pressures and constraints placed on their time, with inadequate allowance for paperwork, resulting in counsellors working unpaid, outside their office hours:

> I tend to sit in of an evening and do my clinical notes... to maintain the level of patients I have got to see. If all the patients turn up, in terms of admin, I'm screwed...You know what you don't want... is any child protection issues 'cause you haven't got the time. (Paul)

Counsellors acknowledged that the expectation to see so many clients in a day meant that clients were not getting the best quality of support, communicating a 'real lack of insight from management and the powers that be' (Emily) into the demands of the work. Those coming for sessions towards the end of the day were likely to get a lesser quality service, as Phil acknowledged: 'The sixth person just gets a conversation.'

> I'm not lazy... it's not that I begrudge having to work hard... but I do begrudge not having the headspace to focus on each client that I am working with. (Louise)

As a consequence, to maintain their integrity and their own health, some participants had reduced their working hours in IAPT:

> I now only do two days a week and I don't think I could do much more than that. (Jane)

## *2. Supervision*

IAPT workers all receive case management support, usually from line managers, where the progress of their clients through the system is monitored to try to increase recovery rates and the flow of clients through the system. Thus, counsellors in IAPT need to consider their practice not just in clinical supervision, with respect to ethical concerns, self-awareness and reflection on therapy relationships and blocks to progress, but also in case management, with respect to meeting targets for waiting lists and recovery.

Many participants in our research discussed how case management was used by managers to dictate how counsellors should be working with clients to achieve recovery, and that achieving targets was prioritised over relational and ethical concerns.

The BACP *Ethical Framework* (2018) is clear about the counsellor's ethical requirements for supervision:

> 61. Good supervision is much more than case management. It includes working in depth on the relationship between practitioner and client in order to work towards desired outcomes and positive effects. This requires adequate levels of privacy, safety and containment for the supervisee to undertake this work. Therefore, a substantial part or preferably all of supervision needs to be independent of line management. (Supervision 61, p22)

Furthermore:

> 72. Supervisees have a responsibility to be open and honest in supervision and to draw attention to any significant difficulties or challenges that they may be facing in their work with clients. Supervisors are responsible for providing opportunities for their supervisees to discuss any of their practice-related difficulties without blame or unjustified criticism and, when appropriate, to support their supervisees in taking positive actions to resolve difficulties. (Supervision 72, p24)

More than half our participants described the importance of external supervision to their ability to work ethically. To them, it not only offered a separate and confidential space to reflect honestly on client work; it was a lifeline when managing the conflicts and costs of surviving in IAPT:

> I quite often use a lot of my supervision about the impact of the work on myself... but the client work often seems really quite manageable... in comparison to managing the working environment! (Emily)

> I've had my own external supervision right through and that's been
> a place where I could just splurge whatever I wanted. It's been great.
> (Jane)

Despite this, participants reported an increasing shift away from and even discouragement of external supervision:

> We were told that we could no longer have external supervision. It was
> going to be internal, and what that's led to is duality... I maintain my
> external supervisor and my CEO is telling me that that might be cause
> for a disciplinary action. (Mark)

Participants feared that information disclosed to in-house supervisors might be used punitively – in Paul's words, to 'nail you to the wall'.

These findings suggest a collective organisational lack of regard within IAPT for independent supervision. Celia was appalled that, for six months, her team had been left without supervision at all, despite having to cope with growing numbers of complex cases:

> Getting more and more complex cases through... and not the
> supervision to help us with it. It's awful... really poor... I think it just
> speaks of the lack of understanding about the real nature of the work.

## Self-care in IAPT

The stress of trying to meet client needs while working tirelessly to protect them contributed significantly to the stress participants were already experiencing from organisational demands. So how do relational counsellors navigate these conflicts and continue to survive within IAPT?

The BACP *Ethical Framework* (2018) is clear about the obligation for counsellors to monitor and maintain their own health. It states, under 'Care of self as a practitioner' (s91, p27):

> We will take responsibility for our own wellbeing as essential to
> sustaining good practice with our clients by... b) monitoring and
> maintaining our own psychological and physical health, particularly
> that we are sufficiently resilient and resourceful to undertake our work
> in ways that satisfy professional standards.

These counsellors often struggled to maintain their own health. All spoke of the costs to their health from working relationally within the IAPT model – not just mental but also physical, due to 'agile working', where they had no permanent desk and had to carry their office, including their laptop, with them, and do administration work in non-ergonomic environments, often without internet connections, sometimes without even tables to work on:

> If we aren't having to carry our entire office with us from surgery to surgery every day... we'll save on neck injuries and back injuries... The technology... we've got to connect through phones... signals can be bad... there's no way you can use a laptop ergonomically. (Paul)

We collated emotional costs under five main themes (see Table 3).

**Table 3: Emotional costs of working in IAPT**

COUNSELLOR COSTS:

FRUSTRATION

EMOTIONAL RESPONSES

SADNESS/ HOPELESSNESS

ANGER

ANXIETY

EXHAUSTION

### 1. Frustration

Many counsellors felt a deep frustration that their energy was being taken with 'fighting the system' (Pat) rather than being focused on clients, and that the demands of the IAPT system were stopping them from being able to work ethically and effectively:

> Sometimes you can push it away and carry on and then something happens and... 'Oh, not again' – something else happens, you know, so you try to carry on, but then how long?... It's impacting me, it's affecting my health... what is more value for me?... Although I'm passionate about

my job... it's just... stuff comes in and disturbs it all, which frustrates me. (Afifa)

## 2. Anger

Frustration shifted into anger for some participants, who felt strong resentment about IAPT's treatment of both counsellors and clients. Pat acknowledged that the struggle to survive in IAPT was having an impact on her relationships outside work:

> I was aware of there being a rage underneath the surface all the time... somebody's only got to say the word 'IAPT' and I can go off on a rant!

## 3. Anxiety

Some participants reported feeling anxiety about their work, which was exacerbated by the public sharing of counsellors' recovery rates and reprimands if they failed to meet targets. Anxiety was particularly evident in participants who resisted IAPT measures surreptitiously and feared being caught:

> It's a lot of pressure... I think, 'I hope [the client] finish[es] before my next caseload management so nobody sees this'... but you know you have to carry these pressures every day with every client, breaking the rules. (Sofia)

## 4. Exhaustion

Unsurprisingly, given the costs and conflicts they faced when working in such a target-driven, manualised environment, many counsellors described feeling exhausted in their roles. Emily found it difficult and draining to try to maintain a person-centred framework and block out recovery-rate pressures when with clients:

> I feel exhausted by the end of the day... absolutely exhausted... It takes a lot of effort... and I'm really aware that it has an impact on me. (Emily)

## 5. Sadness/hopelessness

It was particularly difficult to hear the sadness, hopelessness and despair some participants felt about their work – the devaluing of their own role in the NHS, the sadness they felt for clients, and the hopelessness they expressed about the barriers that stood in the way of working ethically:

... that sense of being devalued and misunderstood was horrible. It really was... quite painful. (Celia)

Sadness with the clients, when they send client after client that really need support, you know you could offer something... this little bit could make a difference, but we can't and... it's really sad to have to go through that ending with clients. (Sofia)

These findings suggest counsellors are having to shoulder significant burdens in order to continue offering a relational alternative to what IAPT services mainly offer. They also show how hard these counsellors were working to find ways to negotiate the system.

## How counsellors deal with ethical conflicts and costs: survival in IAPT

I actually quite enjoy working in IAPT... but it's... because I've learnt how to cope with all the stuff that frustrates me. (Pam)

Participants had found various and often inspiring ways to navigate ethical conflicts and offset the costs of working in IAPT. Some made compromises and adopted IAPT practices, just to reduce stress:

I do only what I have to do, to keep them happy... I don't really get involved with anything else. (Pam)

I'm not precious, you can't be... in this work! (Natasha)

Others worked harder to protect clients from organisational dehumanisation and maintain integrity and job satisfaction in their client work, resisting in both overt and surreptitious ways:.

I have long felt that half my energy is spent fighting the system, and that that's the stressful bit, the clients is the straightforward bit in a sense. (Pat)

Surreptitious resistance included fudging the outcomes measures by, for example, putting in the previous week's scores if the client was too upset to rate how they were feeling, or suggesting an appropriate score to a client.

Other tactics included recording cancellations as telephone sessions so a client wouldn't be discharged for failing to attend and giving out personal contact information so clients could contact them directly, in order to side-step admin. This form of resistance resulted in anxiety for some participants, who feared being caught and reprimanded.

Such surreptitious resistance was always in the service of putting the client first, but also directly contradicts the BACP *Ethical Framework* (2018), which includes among key personal qualities required: 'Sincerity: a personal commitment to consistency between what is professed and what is done' (Personal moral qualities 12, p11).

Overt resistance included speaking out against what the counsellors perceived were dehumanising or misguided strategies (although no participants found this led to actual change) and resisting administrative and logistical measures more transparently:

> I don't take a lot of notice if somebody tells me to do something that doesn't meet governance. (Mark)

Celia felt she had enough clinical experience and confidence to stand her ground: 'I'm just a bit... resistant to authority if I think it's unhelpful.'
Others said that exhaustion and frustration had driven them to rebel:

> I'm a bit of a maverick now!... You know, if I'm working with someone that... the sessions are exhausting... if I have a free slot after, I just don't fill it. And I just think, you know, if they want to sack me then they can. (Emily)

Participants were well aware of their need to look after themselves and some described how self-care outside of work (prioritising down-time/sport/socialising) was an important factor in surviving in IAPT.

## A relational endeavour

Consistent with the professional ethos of counselling, our research findings indicated overwhelmingly that surviving in IAPT is a relational endeavour (Table 4).

An ability to reflect or focus on the client work ('I just love the one-to-ones!' (Pam)) and counsellors' ability to form relationships and facilitate meaningful change with clients, despite the IAPT culture, was felt by many

Table 4: Surviving in IAPT: a relational endeavour

## SURVIVING IN IAPT: A RELATIONAL ENDEAVOUR

| MEANINGFUL RELATIONSHIPS WITH CLIENTS | CLIENT RELATIONSHIP UNDERMINED BY BUREAUCRACY |
|---|---|
| SUPPORTIVE MANAGERS WITH AN UNDERSTANDING OF RELATIONAL COUNSELLING | CONTROLLING / PUNITIVE MANAGERS WITHOUT UNDERSTANDING OF PROFESSIONAL CULTURE OF COUNSELLING |
| INDEPENDENT AND CONFIDENTIAL SUPERVISION | CONFLICTING INTERNAL SUPERVISION / LACK OF SUPERVISION |
| CONTACT WITH TEAM OF PEER COUNSELLORS | LACK OF CONTACT WITH PEERS |

participants to be a powerful antidote to the organisational struggles. For some, it meant the job was sustainable.

Counsellors also felt far more able to manage the ethical conflicts when they were supported by managers who understood the relational approach and professional culture of counselling, had supervisors who facilitated the growth and relational needs of the counsellor, rather than the organisation, but understood the organisational context, and had peer support from other counsellors. Managers played a crucial role; those that understood the relational way of working facilitated the clinical autonomy many participants found essential to feeling valued in their work:

> I don't pay a lot of attention to [recovery rates], you know. I have a monthly meeting with my case manager... she's a breath of fresh air... I feel really valued... and I always seem to be ticking enough of the right boxes, so, that's fine... I'm always quite aghast really when I hear those colleagues who take those measures really, really seriously. (Celia)

Participants with controlling and punitive managers who had no time for counselling, those whose clinical supervisors were in managerial positions and those with little contact with sympathetic peers undoubtedly struggled the most. Some acknowledged the impossible position that IAPT managers are often in, trapped between counsellor frustrations below them and controlling clinical commissioning groups and budget-holders above. Many recognised that the important decisions were made further up the chain:

> I would have to go into politics I suppose... in order to address that... There's somebody a lot higher up who makes the decision of... what happens between the GP referral and me. (Emma)

Indeed, Phil's experience as a manager ultimately drove him to leave the NHS:

> When I got into management, that's when the struggle started. I couldn't change the way IAPT was interpreted because the trust were really tight... They wanted it done pretty much the IAPT way, they were quite fundamentalist in the way they approached it... That was a struggle for me… The people who I worked with who were counsellors – I entered into their struggle with them... I couldn't do anything about it. It just seemed really hard that, as a service manager, I couldn't tell the trust that we were gonna do things differently. (Phil)

He wasn't alone in finding IAPT unsustainable; more than half the participants (nine of the 15) were considering routes out of IAPT, most commonly retirement:

> I had never allowed the retirement word even to pass my lips. I can barely speak it, because it was so not in my thinking until only a few weeks ago... I'm now seriously [pause] thinking about it. (Pat)

I won't be able to carry on in this job until I retire. Sometimes I need to start looking for another... option. I don't think I can carry this... counting down the days until retirement and thinking, 'No way can I cope with this job'. (Sofia)

## Conclusion

What is the future for counselling in IAPT? With no recognition of the relational endeavour that is counselling and the crucial importance of the therapy relationship, it seems unlikely that it will ever sit comfortably and thrive within the IAPT culture. The current focus on technique and the industrialisation of therapy that IAPT embodies exacts a high cost from counsellors and clients. The constant battle to keep a place for the professional culture of relational counselling in IAPT is surely unsustainable for individual counsellors. However, there are pockets of hope: services where managers support counsellors to offer a relational approach and care about the client experience, not just recovery rates. These managers too are straddling the gap between the organisational culture of IAPT and the professional culture of counselling but can enable their staff to do the same, with benefits for staff wellbeing and client experience.

O'Hara (2018) tells us that we are at a point of cultural crisis where old orders are becoming unsustainable. She speaks of a conceptual emergency and the need for 'persons of tomorrow' to come forward and lead the way to survival. She describes several responses to the emergencies that face us, the most common being dictatorial – 'suppressing deviance and restoring an old sense of order through rigid regressive rule-making' (p12). This response perfectly describes the existence of IAPT and its dominant mode of operation.

However, she reminds us of an alternative response:

> ... to embrace the complexity and seize the opportunities present. If we engage with the turbulence, listen deeply to the cultural edges that are often to be found in transgressive and dissident voices, creative possibilities arise. When formal institutions and structures begin to lose their effectiveness, in the gap between the old certainties and human imagination, a space opens up for innovation. (p13)

The 'person of tomorrow' has flexibility, adaptability, authenticity, emotional intelligence and empathy, and also environmental support, she says. She identifies three core capacities that will enable people 'to both thrive and take effective action in an incoherent world' (p15). These are psychological literacy (understanding self and others), cultural literacy (understanding context) and epistemic literacy (ability to understand and shift between different systems of truth).

Relational counsellors in IAPT are already demonstrating these core capacities to survive in such a context. They are, in O'Hara's words (p17), both 'hospice workers' for the dying culture, 'treating the wounded and those left behind with empathy, care and love', and 'midwives' for the new world, supporting people through the inevitable anxiety of transition. She concludes by emphasising the importance of hope and solidarity as an alternative to despair. The question, perhaps, for counsellors is whether we can hold these possibilities of hope and transformation for counselling, for mental health services, for the NHS, for people in distress and for humanity.

## References

BACP (2018). *Ethical Framework for the Counselling Professions*. Lutterworth: BACP.

BACP (2010). *Ethical Framework for Good Practice in Counselling and Psychotherapy* (revised ed). Lutterworth: BACP.

Bloor G, Dawson P (1994). Understanding professional culture in organizational context. *Organization Studies 15*(2): 275–295

Bohart A, House R (2018). Empirically supported/validated treatments as modernist ideology, part I: the Dodo, manualisation and the paradigm question. In: Loewenthal D, Proctor G (eds). *Why not CBT? Against and for CBT revisited*. Monmouth: PCCS Books (pp286–303).

Brown LM, Gilligan C (1991). Listening for voice in narratives of relationship. *New Directions for Child Development 54*: 43–62.

Cooper M (2008). *Essential Research Findings in Counselling and Psychotherapy: the facts are friendly*. London: Sage.

Loewenthal, Proctor G (2018). Conclusion to the second edition: No single therapy should be the only game in town. In: Loewenthal D, Proctor G (eds). *Why not CBT? Against and for CBT revisited*. Monmouth: PCCS Books (pp397–400).

NHS England (2016) *2015 Adult IAPT Workforce Census Report*. London: NHS England. www.england.nhs.uk/mentalhealth/wp-content/uploads/sites/29/2016/09/adult-iapt-workforce-census-report-15.pdf (accessed 21 February 2019).

NICE (2017). *Depression in adults: treatment and management.* Draft for consultation. London: NICE.

NICE (2009). *Depression in adults: recognition and management.* Clinical guideline CG90. London: NICE.

NICE (2004). *Depression: management of depression in primary and secondary care.* Clinical guideline CG23. London: NICE.

O'Hara M (2018). Personhood at the edge of civilizational shift. *Self & Society* 46(2): 10–18.

Proctor G (2018). CBT: the obscuring of power in the name of science. In: Loewenthal D, Proctor G (eds). *Why not CBT? Against and for CBT revisited.* Monmouth: PCCS Books (pp33–51).

Proctor G (2017a). *The Dynamics of Power in Counselling and Psychotherapy: ethics, politics and practice* (2nd ed). Monmouth: PCCS Books.

Proctor G (2017b). Clinical psychology and the person-centred approach: an uncomfortable fit? In: Joseph S (ed). *The Handbook of Person-Centred Therapy and Mental Health: theory, research and practice* (2nd ed). Monmouth: PCCS Books (pp333–354).

Proctor G (2015). The NHS in 2015. *Therapy Today* 26(9): 18–25.

Proctor G (2014). *Values and Ethics in Counselling and Psychotherapy.* London: Sage.

Proctor G (2002). The NHS in 2015: science fiction or a scary possibility? *Healthcare Counselling and Psychotherapy Journal* 2(3): 2–6.

Proctor G, Brown M, Cohen S, McKelvie S (2019). Culture clash: the challenges of working as a counsellor in IAPT. *BACP Healthcare Counselling & Psychotherapy Journal* 19(2).

Proctor G, Hayes C (2017). Counselling for Depression: a response to counselling education in the twenty-first century. Ethical conflicts for a counselling approach operating within a medicalised bureaucratic health service. *British Journal of Guidance and Counselling* 45(4): 417–426.

Wampold BE (2001). *The Great Psychotherapy Debate: models, methods, and findings.* Hillsdale, NJ: Lawrence Erlbaum.

Wampold BE, Imel ZE (2015). *The Great Psychotherapy Debate: the evidence for what makes psychotherapy work* (2nd ed). London: Routledge.

# Contributors

**Catherine Jackson** is Commissioning Editor with PCCS Books. She has worked in mental health journalism and publishing since the early 1990s, after a brief career as a cartoonist. She is editor of *Therapy Today* and was previously founding editor of *Mental Health Today* magazine and managing editor of *Bereavement Care* journal. She also worked in mental health advocacy for several years.

**Rosemary Rizq** is a BPS chartered psychologist and a UKCP-accredited psychoanalytic psychotherapist. She is Professor of Psychoanalytic Psychotherapy at the University of Roehampton and worked for many years in the NHS, most recently for a secondary care psychoanalytic psychotherapy service in north-east London. She now has a part-time private practice in West London. Rosemary was submissions editor for *Psychodynamic Practice* from 2004–2010, is a reviewer for a number of academic journals and has published widely on issues related to organisational dynamics and psychotherapeutic training and practice.

**Jude Boyles** is a BACP senior accredited therapist and feminist activist, specialising in working with refugee survivors of torture/war and human rights abuses, including gender-based abuse. Jude is employed as VPRS Therapeutic Services Manager with the Refugee Council in South Yorkshire, working with Syrian refugees resettled from the conflict. In 2003, Jude established the first Freedom from Torture (FFT) rehabilitation centre for survivors of torture outside of FFT's London headquarters, which she managed for 14 years until April 2017. She has worked as a trainer in the field of therapy with refugee survivors of torture and conflict for 17 years, but has also trained extensively in the field of male violence against women for 23 years, having started her career within Rape Crisis and Women's Aid. She is editor of the book *Psychological Therapies for Survivors of Torture* (published by PCCS Books) and co-author of *Working with Interpreters in Psychological Therapy*.

**Maeta Brown** is a student on the MA in psychotherapy and counselling at the University of Leeds and has a background in radical, person-centred crisis work. She is currently the psychotherapist at Harrogate Homeless Project and involved in co-ordinating a new crisis service for young people in the Leeds area. Her MA research aims to explore the pernicious and often re-traumatising impact of receiving a borderline personality disorder diagnosis and the marginalisation, oppression and mistrust of the female voice.

**Penelope Campling** is a medical psychotherapist. She was consultant and clinical director of Francis Dixon Lodge, the personality disorder service in Leicester, for 20 years before retiring from the NHS in 2011. Her interest in groups and passion for therapeutic communities, where all involved have a significant say in what goes on, has led to an interest in healthcare institutions and how they could be organised in a way that brings out the best in all involved. For a while, she wrote a blog for the *British Medical Journal* on healthcare culture. She has co-edited two books: *Therapeutic Communities: past, present and future* and *From Toxic Institutions to Therapeutic Environments*. Her most recent book is *Intelligent Kindness: reforming the culture of healthcare*, which she wrote with her husband, John Ballatt. An expanded second edition of this book, entitled *Intelligent Kindness: rehabilitating the welfare state*, is to be published by Cambridge University Press in January 2020.

**Elizabeth Cotton** is a writer and educator working in the field of mental health at work. Her background is in workers' education and international development. She has worked in over 35 countries on diverse issues such as HIV/AIDS, organising and building grassroots networks, and negotiating as head of education for Industriall, one of the largest trade unions in the world, reflected in her book *Global Unions Global Business*. She teaches and writes academically at Middlesex University about employment relations and precarious work. She is Editor-in-Chief of an ABS4 journal, *Work, Employment & Society*, looking at the sociology of work. She blogs as www.survivingwork. org and set up www.survivingworkinhealth.org, a free resource, in partnership with the Tavistock and Portman NHS Foundation Trust. In 2017 she published the largest national survey about working conditions in mental health, www. thefutureoftherapy.org. She is a founding member of Action for Care-worker Wellbeing, a network established to campaign for better working conditions across health and social care. Her book, *Surviving Work in Healthcare: helpful stuff for people on the frontline*, was nominated for the Chartered Management Institute's practitioner book of the year.

**Marianna Fotaki** is Professor of Business Ethics at the University of Warwick Business School and holds a PhD from the London School of Economics and Political Science. Marianna was an Edmond J Safra Network Fellow (2014–2015) at Harvard University and co-directed an online think tank, the Centre for Health and the Public Interest (http://chpi.org.uk), *pro bono* (2014–2017). Before joining academia, she worked as EU resident adviser to the governments in transition, and as a medical doctor for Médecins Sans Frontières and Médecins Du Monde for 10 years in total. She has published more than 70 articles, book chapters and books on gender, inequalities and the marketisation of public services. Marianna currently works on whistleblowing (funded by the ESRC and British Academy/Leverhulme Trust), solidarity responses to crisis and refugee arrivals in Greece.

**Lynne Friedli** is a freelance researcher with a special interest in the relationship between mental health and social justice. From 2014–16 she conducted research on the (mis) use of psychology in workfare with Hubbub at the Wellcome Collection, which included reflections on the lived experience of unpaid labour and the welfare system, in partnership with Nina Garthwaite and residents of a hostel for homeless men. Lynne is also interested in the politics of strengths-based discourse (notably in Scotland), the use of positive psychology in the 'reification' of 'work' and how these developments have come to dominate (or perhaps colonise) ideas about recovery, as well as inspiring a resurgence of new forms of resistance to work. Her research at Hubbub (with Robert Stearn) features in a documentary, *Psycho-compulsion and Workfare,* by WellRedFilms.

**Michael Guilfoyle** was a clinical psychologist in Ireland and Extraordinary Professor in the Department of Educational Psychology at the University of the Western Cape, South Africa. His primary interest was in exploring therapeutic practices from a narrative and post-structural perspective. His book, *The Person in Narrative Therapy: a post-structural, Foucauldian account*, was published in 2014, and he contributed numerous journal articles and book chapters in international publications. He died in July 2017.

**Norma McKinnon Fathi** is a UKCP-registered counsellor and psychotherapist and a qualified community worker. Norma has 20 years' experience of working with vulnerable people who have experienced trauma, including survivors of childhood sexual abuse, childhood neglect, violence, conflict and torture. Norma is an experienced manager, trainer, facilitator and community development and engagement practitioner. For 11 years, her clinical work was with survivors of torture and she previously managed psychological services at a national charity. Norma works in private practice as a psychotherapist and supervisor and is a co-founder and Director of the social enterprise Mandala Consultants, whose mission is to nurture resilience and wellbeing within individuals, organisations and communities and to support social change. She is currently working with Mandala Consultants colleagues towards the development of a free counselling and psychotherapy service for people impacted by trauma from marginalised communities and for practitioners experiencing vicarious trauma.

**Gillian Proctor** is the programme leader of the MA in psychotherapy and counselling at the University of Leeds. She worked in the NHS for 22 years, for the last 10 years in primary care and then IAPT, and is now also an independent clinical psychologist and person-centred psychotherapist. She is an author and trainer and her particular interests are in values, ethics and power in therapy and research.

**Andy Rogers** trained at the University of East Anglia's Centre for Counselling Studies in the late 1990s, completing a postgraduate diploma in 1999, and has worked in and written about the therapy field ever since. For many years he managed counselling services in further and higher education, and now also runs a private counselling and supervision practice in Basingstoke, Hampshire (www.andyrogerscounselling.com). Andy has published several articles and book chapters on the politics of the psy-professions and the person-centred approach, is an active participant in the Alliance for Counselling & Psychotherapy campaign group and is a registered member of BACP. He is also a father, contemporary music obsessive, slow reader of dark novels, plucky but anxious DIYer, and keen home cook.

**Robert Stearn** is a PhD candidate in English and Humanities at Birkbeck, University of London, where he is writing a thesis on the rhetoric and depiction of skill in 17th and early 18th century England. He is also interested in the modern politics of skill, especially in how ideas about skill(s) are mobilised within contemporary labour market policy and psychological approaches to unemployment.

**Scott Steen** is Research Lead at Birmingham City University for the Service Improvement Learning Collaborative (SILC), which aims to establish and support learning communities dedicated to improving client outcomes and the delivery of talking therapy services. Scott has a background in implementation research across primary care psychotherapeutic services, involving understanding organisational dynamics and translating evidence into real-world clinical practice. Since 2016, he has worked with third-sector organisations to enhance their relationship with and use of data to improve service quality. He provides consultative support to CORE IMS and is currently responsible for the account management of the voluntary sector. He also provides independent research consultancy to the Centre for Psychological Therapies in Primary Care and the Elizabeth Bryan Foundation Trust. He continues to perform aggregate data analyses and develop resource materials for counselling and psychotherapy services across a range of sectors.

**Philip Thomas** worked as a consultant psychiatrist in the NHS for more than 20 years before leaving clinical practice in 2004 to write. He held a chair in philosophy, diversity and mental health at the University of Central Lancashire and has published on philosophy and its relevance to madness and society. He is well known for his work on post-psychiatry with Pat Bracken, and for working in alliance with survivors of psychiatry, service users and community groups. Until recently he was chair of Sharing Voices Bradford, a community development project working with black and minority ethnic communities. He was a founder member and, until 2011, co-chair of the Critical Psychiatry Network, and has authored or co-authored three books, most recently *Psychiatry in Context: experience meaning and communities* (published by PCCS Books). He is currently writing about the moral consequences of neoliberalism for mental health work. He is a grandfather and sings with Manchester's Hallé Choir.

**Sami Timimi** is a consultant child and adolescent psychiatrist and Director of Medical Education in the NHS in Lincolnshire and a visiting professor of child psychiatry and mental health improvement at the University of Lincoln. He writes from a critical psychiatry perspective on topics relating to mental health and childhood and has published more than 130 articles and tens of chapters on many subjects, including childhood, psychotherapy, behavioural disorders and cross-cultural psychiatry. He has authored four books, including *Naughty Boys: anti-social behaviour, ADHD and the role of culture*, co-edited four books, including, with Carl Cohen, *Liberatory Psychiatry: philosophy, politics and mental health*, and co-authored two others, including, with Neil Gardiner and Brian McCabe, *The Myth of Autism: medicalising men's and boys' social and emotional competence*.

# Name index

# Subject index

## A

age gap
  of mental health staff 215–216
antidepressant prescribing
  IAPT influence on, 134
anti-psychiatry 144
anxiety 56–57
  existential, 70
  (Lacan) 195, 193
  perversion and, 194–196
  social defences against (Menzies Lyth),
    68, 195
  survival-related, 75
'anxiety work' (Hinshelwood) 203
audit culture
  in IAPT 10
austerity 23, 24, 30–33, 44, 56
  global, 2, 204
  in HE/FE sector 147–148
  and inequality 24, 25, 34
  neoliberal, 40
  and performance management 219
  political, economic and health contexts
    of, 30–32
'austerity logic' (Pollitt) 218

## B

'Baby P' 191
*Beveridge Report* 45
Big Pharma 15
black and ethnic minority communities
  246–248
burnout
  within IAPT 146

## C

CABIN 228–229
care
  as relational act 73–74
CBT (cognitive behavioural therapy)
  benefits for children 135
  collaboration 108
  critiques of, 106–111

dominance in IAPT 144
  monoculture in IAPT 15, 145
  and political power 105
  as servant of the state 116–117
Children and Young People's Improving
  Access to Psychological Therapies
  (CYP-IAPT) 13, 123, 134–137,
  222
choice
  and illusion of control 75
  as value in public services 74
  in NHS market 64–66
choice policies
  failure of, 73
client choice
  in IAPT 261–262
clients as consumers 148, 256
codification of knowledge 48
cognitive dissonance
  between IAPT and third sector 239
'command-and-control' culture
  in IAPT 221
commodification of therapy
  in IAPT 244
competency framework
  university and college counselling, 149
conditionality 83–84
  psychological, 81
  welfare, 81
'consumer as sovereign' 6–9
consumerism 60, 62, 66
consumerist ethos
  in IAPT 17
CORE-OM 257
cost-benefit of IAPT services 168–173
costing mental health 160–161

## D

de-professionalisation
  of clinical roles 214–215
disavowal
  (Lacan) 190–193, 203, 205

# S

sadness
  defences against 70
  in third-sector services 244
  of counsellors in IAPT 236, 244, 249, 269–270
science
  discourse of, 111–112
science paradigm
  in therapy 110
self-care in IAPT 267–268
socio-economic conditions
  and mental distress 145
splitting
  as defence 68
  between therapists 242
staff retention
  in IAPT 173–175
staff training
  in IAPT 173–175
Stafford Hospital 52, 221
State Therapy 153
stepped-care model 164–165
stigma 143
  of medical model 131
subdivision of labour
  within IAPT 49
supervision
  as case management 266–267
  in IAPT 265–266
  relational, 272–273
survival in IAPT 270–271
survival surgeries 224–228
Surviving Work Survey 9, 210–212
  findings from 212–217

# T

technical focus
  of IAPT 125, 256
telephone assessment
  in IAPT 247
'technologies of self' (Foucault) 36, 41, 87
'The Nightingale and the Emperor of China' (Hans Anderson) 201
theoretical critiques
  of IAPT 158–160
therapeutic alliance
  importance of, 129
therapeutic hegemony 104, 115

therapists
  as government agents 117
therapy
  as 'treatment' 150
  as branch of healthcare 150
third sector
  as independent from the state 235
  IAPT influence on 236–237, 236
trades unions
  as source of support 223
transparency
  in IAPT 9–12
treatment choice 176
treatment equivalence 176
trust 53–54

# U

unemployment 161–163
  as social problem 124
undeserving 'others'
  under neoliberalism 75
unhappiness
  medical cure for, 12–15
university counselling 147

# V

validity
  of psychiatric diagnosis 127

# W

*We Still Need to Talk* 246
welfare benefits
  reductions/savings in, 219–220
welfare governance
  as virtual reality 205
wellbeing
  as emotional compliance 152
wellbeing teams 148
Winterbourne View Hospital 191
work
  cure 87
  as health goal 145
  intensification in IAPT 217
workfare 81, 83, 84–85
  campaigns against 88–89
  lived experience of, 90–95
  role in regulating labour 81
workforce strategy 209
workloads in IAPT 265